Accession

D1151882

...gman Companion to
...ropean Reformation, c.1500–1618

This
be

Longman Companions to History

General Editors: Chris Cook and John Stevenson

Now available

The Longman Companion to

The European
Reformation, c.1500–1618

Mark Greengrass

Longman
London and New York

Addison Wesley Longman Limited
Edinburgh Gate,
Harlow, Essex CM20 2JE,
United Kingdom
and Associated Companies throughout the world

*Published in the United States of America
by Addison Wesley Longman Inc., New York*

First published 1998

ISBN 0 582 061741 (PPR)
ISBN 0 582 06175X (CSD)

British Library Cataloguing in Publication Data

A catalogue record for this book is available from the British Library

Library of Congress Cataloging-in-Publication Data

Greengrass, Mark, 1949–
    The Longman companion to the European Reformation,
    c.1500–1618 / Mark Greengrass.
        p.   cm. — (Longman companions to history)
    Includes bibliographical references and index.
    ISBN 0–582–06175–X (cloth). — ISBN 0–582–06174–1 (pbk.)
    1. Reformation.   I. Title.   II. Series.
    BR305.2.G735   1997
    274′.06—dc21   97–14165
                                                                     CIP

Set by 35 in 9½/12 pt New Baskerville
Produced by Longman Singapore Publishers (Pte) Ltd.
Printed in Singapore

Contents

List of diagrams, genealogies and maps

Preface

The best (perhaps the only) justification for a book of this kind lies in its utility. Utility to whom? Throughout its preparation I have had most in mind the teachers and students of the sixteenth-century European reformation in departments of history, divinity and biblical studies. It does not seek to be comprehensive and those engaged in research in this area will doubtless not find it of great value. It is not so much a 'bluffers' guide'; more a 'friend in need' when coming to grips with the complex and interrelated chronologies of the reformation period and attempting to comprehend the sometimes unapproachable theological terrain which it occupies.

Compromises have been made at every turn to make the work of manageable length and at the right level of detail. These compromises will be evident in the course of the book and are justified on pragmatic grounds. One compromise leaves me uncomfortable. This is a history of the European reformation from which the events in the British Isles have been excluded. This is justified in part by the existence of Rosemary O'Day's excellent *Longman Companion to the Tudor Age* (1995) in this series which includes all that and more than would have been encompassed in these pages. Scotland and Ireland, however, are left betwixt and between and that is a matter for regret. The biographies in section eleven are not intended to be comprehensive; they provide only the most immediately relevant details with which to assess the significance of the individual concerned. The chronologies which are included at various points in the book are compilations from various well-known sources, not all of which have been specifically acknowledged in the text itself. They are mentioned, however, in the bibliography, which also contains a fuller list of background works which have been used in preparing this book.

Considerable attention has been given to providing comprehensive cross-references in four different ways. Firstly, individuals for whom a biographical entry is included in Section eleven are indicated with an asterisk (*) on their first mention in any paragraph. The asterisks are assumed rather than indicated for 'Luther', 'Zwingli' or 'Calvin' whose names appear so frequently that it would be irksome to keep repeating the cross-reference. Secondly, technical terms or institutions which may not be readily understood are indicated with a dagger (†) and are explained in the text. Bold page numbers in the index direct the reader to specific definitions. Thirdly, specific cross-references from one chapter to another are indicated by references to the pages in question. Finally, there is a comprehensive index which provides specific references to topics, persons and places by page number.

Various individuals have assisted in the preparation of this work in a variety of ways. Dr Andrew Chibi was responsible for undertaking some of the background research for parts of Sections eight, nine and eleven. At one stage, the book was going to become a joint publication between us. However his move away from Sheffield made it impossible to work on it conjointly. The eventual publication does not do credit to the amount of work which he put in to the sections on which he worked; but I am very grateful for what he did. Professor Joe Bergin acted loyally as a 'second pair of eyes' for various sections where it was particularly necessary. Nigel and Clive Griffen kindly lent materials or assisted with prompt replies to particular queries. Dr Vladimír Urbanek from the Czech Academy of Sciences kindly looked through the materials on eastern Europe and checked them for accuracy. Peter Derlien was invaluable in the last stages of proof-reading. To these, and other colleagues – companions in the European reformation one might say – who will recognize the points where I have been influenced by their particular specialisms, I am grateful.

Mark Greengrass
Sheffield

A note on dates

The age of the reformation witnessed important changes in the way Europe calculated its dates. It was one sign of the divisions introduced into Europe by the reformation that the changes were neither accepted nor introduced uniformly. The old Julian calendar (i.e. that introduced by Julius Caesar in 45 BC) had gradually fallen out of sequence with the solar year. To rectify this, the Gregorian calendar was introduced by a bull of Pope Gregory XIII* of 24 February 1582. This removed ten days out of the year 1582 (5–14 October inclusively). It also made a marginal correction to the leap years to minimize the error in the future. Henceforth, only the fourth of the final years of successive centuries would be a leap year. Known as the 'new style', the calendar was adopted immediately by catholic states in Europe (Italy, Portugal, Spain and France). The states of the German empire, protestant states and orthodox Christian Europe (Russia, the Balkan states and Greece), however, did not adopt it until after the end of this period.

At the same time, there was no general agreement about the date at which each year should start (the starting-point of each 'year of grace'). The Gregorian reform included an agreement to begin the year on 1 January and this gradually prevailed. But some protestant countries retained other dates; England continued officially to use the feast of the Annunciation (25 March) as the legal start of the New Year until 1752.

In this companion, dates are provided in the style locally applicable to the country in question at the relevant date. The starting-point of the year of grace, however, has been adjusted to 1 January where appropriate.

Acknowledgements

The publishers would like to thank the following for permission to reproduce tabular material: Figure 5.3.1 is adapted from Claus-Peter Clasen, *Anabaptism: A Social History, 1525–1618* (Ithaca and London, Cornell University Press, 1972), p. 21. Copyright © 1972 by Cornell University. Used by permission of the publisher, Cornell University Press. Figures 4.2.6, 4.2.7 and 4.4.1 draw upon material (on pp. 269, 216–19, and 271 respectively) in Euan Cameron, *The European Reformation* (Oxford, Oxford University Press, 1991), by permission of Oxford University Press. Figure 10.3.3 is a reproduction of Figure 1 from Miriam U. Chrisman, *Lay Culture, Learned Culture: Books and Social Change in Strasbourg, 1480–1599* (New Haven, Yale University Press, 1982), used by permission of Yale University Press.

The fabric of the church

1.1 Significant feast days (solemnities) in the church calendar and periods of the Christian year

1.1.1 Fixed dates

The catholic church designated various days as holy days. On such days the laity and clergy were forbidden to work and were obliged to attend mass. Such days included, of course, Sundays. The degree to which these days were retained as festival days in protestant Europe depended on the confessional stance of the particular region (see page 240).

1 January	Circumcision A relatively late addition to the Christian calendar, not established generally before the eleventh century. The protestant reformers were particularly hostile to it, partly because of its celebration being conjoined with New Year festivities.
6 January	Epiphany (lit: 'manifestation' of Christ to the Magi)
2 February	Candlemas The feast celebrating the purification of the Blessed Virgin Mary and the presentation of Christ in the Temple, 40 days after his birth. The blessing of candles was a distinctive rite of the festival by the time of the reformation and it was popularly seen as commemorating the end of winter. The reformers sought to abolish the festival because of its pagan connotations.
25 March	Annunciation (Lady Day) The feast commemorating the announcement of the Incarnation by the angel Gabriel to Mary and the conception of Christ in her womb. Attitudes of the reformers to it were ambiguous and, in the Book of Common Prayer it was retained as one of the appointed festival ('red letter') days.
24 June	John the Baptist (Feast of the Nativity of)
29 June	St Peter and St Paul
1 August	Lammas

The English word derives from 'loaf' and 'mass'. It was customary to consecrate bread made from the ripe corn of the harvest at mass. The festival often had much more than purely religious significance. Church dues for Rome were often collected at Lammas.

15 August   Assumption of the Blessed Virgin Mary
Feast marking the ascent of Mary, the mother of Christ, to Heaven. The significance of Marian devotions tended to increase during the century prior to the reformation.

29 September   St Michael the Archangel (Michaelmas)
Michaelmas day was connected with many popular customs. The date was widely used for the annual hiring of hands, the payment of debts and the settlement of accounts.

1 November   All Saints' Day (All Hallows)
The commemoration of all the Christian saints.

2 November   All Souls' Day
The commemoration of the souls of the faithful departed. Priests were permitted to celebrate three masses (only otherwise allowed on Christmas Day). Local lay customs warded off evil spirits and encouraged the spirits of the faithful to return.

25 December   Christmas Day.

1.1.2 Variable dates and festivals of the Christian year

Advent

The four Sundays (occasionally five) before Christmas, the first of which (Advent Sunday) is the Sunday next to St Andrew's Day (30 November). This is traditionally taken as the beginning of the church year. Advent was a season for self-examination and contemplation of the Second Coming of Christ, often stimulated by cycles of preaching in the pre-reformed church.

Ash Wednesday

The first day in Lent. Congregations were expected to assemble for general penance[†].

Lent

A forty-day period of fast which preceded Easter and began with the communal act of penance[†] on Ash Wednesday. Fasting consisted typically of one meal a day which might include fish and eggs ('white meats') but not meat. A light meal at night was also allowed. Lenten observance was regulated by both the secular and the ecclesiastical authorities.

Passion Week
The week before Easter, including Good Friday (the Friday before Easter).

Easter Day (*Pascha*)
A variable feast calculated to be the Sunday after the full moon on or next after 21 March. From the date of Easter in any particular year, the dates of the remaining variable festivals of that year followed.

Ascension Day
The fifth Thursday after Easter.

Corpus Christi
Latin for 'the body of Christ'. This was an important religious festival taking place on the Thursday after Trinity Sunday (generally June) in honour of the eucharist. It was a festival with an important part to play in civic pageantry and was often the occasion of fairs and mystery plays.

1.2 Sacraments of the traditional church

According to St Thomas Aquinas (d.1274) a sacrament was 'the sign of a sacred thing in so far as it sanctifies men'. In Christian theology, the scope of what constitutes a sacrament has varied widely. By the late middle ages, however, Peter Lombard's definition of the seven sacraments (accepted by St Thomas Aquinas) had become formally affirmed as an article of belief at the council of Florence in 1439. These were:

Baptism
The rite of initiation into the Christian community, of which there were many local variants. The ceremony involved a series of prayers and exorcisms performed over the child to be baptized, sometimes using salt to symbolize the candidate's savouring of the faith. Other ceremonies including the 'opening' of the child to spiritual regeneration. The priest would touch the eyes and nose of the child to make him or her open to spiritual regeneration. The water in the font was then blessed and sometimes mixed with holy oil. Godparents were invited to renounce Satan and his works on the child's behalf before the priest dipped the child three times in the water. The child was then dressed in a white robe, anointed with chrism, and presented with a candle. Traditionally, the church held that baptism was not only a *sign* of grace but actually *conferred* grace upon the baptized. This view was upheld and emphasized by the council of Trent+ (seventh Session).

Confirmation

Candidates for confirmation were anointed with unction in the sign of the cross by the confirming bishop to confirm their baptism. Children were not expected to receive the eucharist[†] before they were ten. The practice of anointing at confirmation was abandoned by the protestant churches.

Matrimony

Matrimony was conceived by medieval scholastic theologians as a sacrament conferring grace on human individuals. It was, however, a peculiar sacrament because the parties to be married themselves became the ministers of the sacrament, the priest being only an appointed witness. It was not until the central middle ages that the claim of the church to exclusive jurisdiction over matrimonial cases was widely accepted. This led to important parts of canon law laying down the degrees of 'affinity' (limiting the consanguinity of a marriage), outlawing bigamy, and stipulating the various other 'impediments' to marriage. It also prevented those in clerical orders from becoming married. The church absorbed the Roman law perception of marriage as the consent of two individual parties. It therefore required a prior degree of publicity to a marriage. This was ensured through the publication of 'banns' of marriage on three Sundays in the parishes of residence of both parties. However, marriages could also be celebrated by licence.

Extreme unction (*Unctio extrema*)

The sacrament, sometimes known as 'administering the last rites', of anointing the terminally ill. It was known as 'extreme' either because it was the last of the three sacramental unctions (after baptism and confirmation) or because it was normally only administered when the individual was dying (*in extremis*). The sacrament was nominally derived from *Ep. James* 4:14. Protestant reformers and churches abandoned the sacrament.

Penance (from *penitet* – i.e. 'repent for shame')

The sacrament of penance included the important separate elements of contrition, confession, satisfaction and absolution. These were all terms which had been much discussed by medieval theologians (see pages 31–2). They would also be the focus for Luther's initial critique of sacramentary belief and practice in the established church (see page 47).

Eucharist (from the Greek for 'Thanksgiving') – also known as the Lord's Supper and the Communion

This is the central rite of Christian worship based upon the Last Supper with his disciples when Jesus 'took bread, and gave thanks, and brake it, and gave unto them, saying, This is my body which is given for you: this do in remembrance of me. Likewise also the cup after supper, saying, This cup is the New Testament in my blood, which is shed for you' (*Luke* 22:19–20). This was when the bread and wine were 'consecrated' and transformed into the body and blood of Christ. A gesture of 'elevation' came to mark the moment along with the peal of a bell so that the faithful would know when adoration of the host was not idolatrous worship of mere bread and wine. The sacred power invested in the eucharistic elements was such that mere 'gazing' at them was regarded as contributing to grace. The frequency with which the eucharist should be received by the laity was much discussed. An annual communion was required by church council decree. Diocesan synods often stipulated three communions a year, of which one should be at Easter.

As the perceived power of the eucharist increased, so the risks of its defilement also grew. The possibilities of spillage of the wine host led to its being withdrawn from the laity in the central middle ages, leaving the clergy to receive 'in both kinds' and thus emphasizing the separation between clergy and laity.

Orders

Being 'in holy orders', or 'ordained' within the church was seen, rather like baptism, as imparting a sacramental grace which could not subsequently be completely removed, even if a cleric were 'degraded'[†]. The council of Trent (Session 23) clarified the established church's position, defining it as a sacrament instituted by Christ and as conveying the Holy Ghost.

1.3 The penitential and devotional framework

Breviary

The liturgical book containing the psalms, hymns and lessons for the Divine Office.

Canonical hours

The canonical hours were the times of daily prayer as laid down in the breviary[†]. There were seven daily canonical hours (mattins and lauds, prime, terce, sext, none (hence 'noon'), vespers and compline). 'Books of Hours' were (often lavishly illustrated) books of canonical prayers.

Commemorative masses

Anniversary masses[†], trental masses (30 days after the death of an individual) and other commemorative acts, often stipulated in wills.

Crucifix

A carved or sculpted representation of Jesus on the cross. It was a commonly venerated image.

Indulgences

A letter of indulgence was a remission of temporal penalties for sin, granted by the hierarchy of the Roman church, for individuals who had shown penitence. An indulgence was always granted on condition that defined penitential acts were carried out by the indulged (such as visiting the holy places of Jerusalem, or contributing money to the building of St Peter's in Rome). The sale of indulgences, especially 'plenary' indulgences at the time of a 'jubilee'[†] in the late middle ages, led to widespread criticism.

Mass (Latin: *Missa*)

The name given to the Latin service (the office or *actio*) of the eucharist[†] in the traditional church, the central part of which (the 'canon') began with the words *Te igitur* leading through to the consecration and distribution of the host. A 'high mass' was an elaborate, sung, form of the service. A 'low mass' was a simple form of mass, involving only one server, no deacon or choir, and no part of the service was sung. This was the usual form of mass except on Sundays or feast-days. Masses were often said on behalf of departed souls. The term 'mass' was rejected by the reformers because of its association with the doctrines of transubstantiation[†] and of salvation by good works[†] and also because of the theology of 'sacrifice' which underlay it.

Pax ('Peace')

The 'pax' (also *osculatorium*) was a board or ritual object, made of wood or precious metal, and carrying a representation of the crucifixion or of the Lamb of God. This was passed down from the clergy at the altar to be touched and kissed 'as a sign of peace' at the moment of the eucharist[†] when the majority of the congregation were not participating. Historians have stressed the way in which this ritual became a symbol of the central significance of the ritual of the mass[†] as a fosterer of communal unity. In practice, however, these rituals could also demonstrate and even reinforce existing feuds and local tensions.

Pilgrimage

A journey to a holy place, such as a shrine of a saint, as an act of thanksgiving or penance[†]. The chief places of pilgrimage during and after the Crusades were Bethlehem and Jerusalem. But there were also European places of pilgrimage, such as St James of Campostella (Spain), St Peter at Rome and St Thomas Becket at Canterbury (England). The Marian shrines (dedicated to Mary, the mother of Jesus) attracted the greatest popularity on the eve of the protestant reformation.

Purgatory

The foundation of the medieval doctrine of purgatory lay in the belief, found in St Augustine, that the fate of the individual soul is decided immediately after death, and in the certainty of purifying pains in the afterlife. Purgatory was gradually elaborated by medieval theologians as a place of waiting for the sinful who could not be admitted to Heaven until penance[†] had been done for their sins. According to St Thomas Aquinas, the guilt (*culpa*) of venial sin was expiated immediately after death and only the punishment remained to be served. That punishment, greater than the greatest pain on earth, might nevertheless be lessened by the faithful on earth, especially by the offering of masses for the souls of the departed. The official teaching of the church on purgatory was finally defined at the councils of Lyon (1274) and Florence[†] (1439). Purgatory gradually came to assume a central place in the penitential fabric of the church and the attack by Martin Luther upon the belief in purgatory was therefore of critical significance. The council of Trent[†] laid down that bishops should see that 'the sound doctrine touching Purgatory delivered by the holy Fathers and sacred councils should be believed, held and taught and everywhere proclaimed by the faithful of Christ' but without public discussion of its difficult and contested points.

Reliquary

A container, often elaborately jewelled and decorated, to hold the relics of a saint. The shape of the reliquary varied according to the nature of the relic – capsule, ampulla, vase, casket or case.

Rosary

Initially a set of devotions, consisting of 15 paternosters and glorias and 150 ave Marias, divided into three parts called 'chaplets'. Each chaplet contained five 'decades' of one paternoster, ten aves and one gloria. Rings of beads became an aid to the sequence of prayers. Rosaries were widespread in the pre-reformed church and ridiculed by the protestant reformers.

Saints, cult of

The decision to 'beatify' and then to 'canonize' (i.e. to declare a particular individual worthy of public cult) had become reserved to the Holy See in the central middle ages. Papal commissions were appointed to investigate the life and miracles of candidates for canonization. Unauthorized local cults, however, survived until the protestant reformation and it was not until the counter-reformation and the decrees of Pope Urban VIII

(1623–44) that a complete control of the cult of saints rested with the Roman hierarchy.

Shrine (from *scrinium*, meaning a 'chest')
The term 'shrine' was originally applied to the reliquary[†] for the relics of a saint. However it became used to refer to any holy place, especially one connected with pilgrimages. The faithful pilgrim might choose to leave a 'votive offering' (gift or commemorative plaque) at the shrine.

Transubstantiation
The doctrine that after the consecration, the bread and the wine of the eucharist[†] cease to be bread and wine except in appearance and become the real body and blood of Christ. This was confirmed by the council of Trent[†].

Worship
The layout of churches gave prominence to the administration of the sacraments[†] and the meaning attached to the rituals. Near the entrance of the church, symbolizing the ceremony of entry into the Christian communion and exorcism of baptism[†] stood the font, at which babies were baptized. Holy water was also often available for adult Christians to sprinkle over themselves in a ritual of purification. Around the church, on the walls, in stained glass and statuary were images of the saints, encouraging worshippers to pray to them and the Virgin Mary to intercede with Christ for salvation. The 'stations of the cross' (the images – usually 14 – of various scenes from Christ's crucifixion, used for meditation and prayer and displayed in churches) also served as part of the penitential fabric of churches. Other common scenes of late medieval church fabric included the entombment of Christ, pictures of members of Christ's family, hell and purgatory. The very wide range of religious iconography, and the changes in relative popularity of particular scenes provide historians with a way of measuring changes in religious sensibility. Side chapels (or 'chantries') were to be found off the nave (the main body of the church) where priests said masses[†] to intercede for the dead.

The altar for the eucharist[†] was centrally located close by the east-facing wall of the church. Upon it were arranged the cross and candles, the pyx (the plate for the bread) and the chalice (the cup for the wine) and the missal (the mass service book). The altar stood in the sanctuary (or 'sacred place'), and behind it stood the reredos or retable, an elaborately painted or carved altarpiece. This was the preserve of the clergy and was separated from the body of the congregation by the rood screen (itself often finely carved and bearing statues of Christ on the cross and of those closest to Christ: the Virgin Mary and St John). Once within the sanctuary, the priest mounted the steps to the altar to celebrate the mass, served by an acolyte (a minor order of the church, below that of sub-deacon and subject to a deacon).

1.4 The institutions of the church

1.4.1 Rome

The institutions of the papacy reflected the pope's dual role as both the titular and administrative head of the church of Latin Christendom and also the prince of the Papal States[†], which would be the largest and most coherent political entity in sixteenth-century Italy.

The pope (the 'Apostolic See')
The bishop of Rome claiming direct descent from St Peter and suprem-acy (the 'supreme Pontiff') within western Christendom. The claim, however, did not go uncontested. General councils of the church in the fifteenth century asserted that such supremacy lay within the body of the church in general, as represented by general councils ('conciliar-ism'[†]). There were also rival claims to the succession of St Peter in the early fifteenth century, one claimant residing at Avignon (the 'Avignon papacy') and the other at Rome. Although the papacy had survived these difficulties, it remained understandably nervous of any development likely to foster them once more. The election of popes took place in the 'conclave'[†] of the college of cardinals. (For the succession of individual popes, see page 201.)

The curia
The Roman court which encompassed the domestic and administrative offices within the papal 'palace'. It included the college of cardinals[†] and the pope's domestic prelates.

The papal household (It: *Famiglia palatina*)
The pope's domestic and administrative officials, including those in the Datary[†] and the Chamber[†]. The overall size of the papal *famiglia* grew during the period of the reformation, as did the royal courts of Europe in general. The numbers of retainers (and their servants) have been estimated as follows:

Pius II (1458–64)   230
Leo X (1513–21)   700
Pius V (1559–65)   over 1,000

The papal chapel (the Sistine Chapel)
Staffed by a sacristan, a Master of the Chapel, a Dean and Sub-Dean, two clerks, two writers and a librarian. The choir consisted of boy singers

and an adult choir. Castrati singers did not make their appearance in the choir until after 1550.

The Sacra Rota (the *Sacra Romana Rota*)

This was the supreme court for Christian ecclesiastical cases and (increasingly) the sovereign lawcourt for the Papal States[†] as well. It dealt with a huge range of legal cases referred to it by the papacy and from other episcopal tribunals. It was staffed by auditors who had to be doctors in canon law and theology. The influence of the papacy in the church at large was probably most considerably felt through the decisions of the Rota. The expense and delay of appealing cases to Rome was the cause of a substantial amount of criticism of the church in the later middle ages. Some states tried to limit the cases which went on appeal (e.g. England – statutes of Praemunire (1353, 1365, 1393); the French Gallican articles[†] also sought to limit appeals to Rome).

The Chamber (The *Reverenda Camera Apostolica*)

The financial chamber of the papal curia, originally in the hands of the chamberlain and financial secretary of the pope. The chamberlain was a major administrative figure and one of the few major papal officials whose powers were not suspended on a pope's death. He was also responsible for appointments of central and provincial officials in the Papal States[†]. Under his authority lay the vice-chamberlain and the apostolic treasurer. The latter was responsible for auditing and approving the accounts of the Chamber[†] for the revenues which it received. These receipts came from both 'spiritual' and 'temporal' incomes. The former were those derived from common services and annates[†] derived from the church at large – an appreciable and continuing revenue source. The latter came from a variety of sources. These included its taxes and patrimonial receipts from the Papal States (including taxes levied on the clergy there). It also had important revenues from Papal States monopolies. The latter included a monopoly on salt and (highly significant in the economic history of sixteenth-century Europe) on alum, essential in the manufacture of glass and cloth and for which the Papal States held the majority of Europe's easily available supplies (see page 212).

The Datary (The *Dataria*)

Originally formed from the chancery and camera, the Datary developed into an independent organism with its own fiscal and administrative practices under Pope Sixtus IV (1471–84). It received the revenues from venal offices within the papal bureaucracy, payments for the expedition of bulls[†] and special papal dispensations. During the sixteenth century the Datary provided a privy purse of revenues for unrestricted papal use which enabled the papacy to borrow substantial sums to fund its secular ambitions in and around the Papal States[†]. The Datary operated an arcane bureaucratic practice, designed (at least in part) to protect the pope from any charge that he was guilty of simony[†].

Venal offices

Colleges of offices in the papacy's legal and financial bureaucracy were made available for open sale from the second half of the fifteenth century onwards. 'Reversions' on the offices (transfers to another incumbent) were also purchasable. Payments were made in gold directly to the Datary, which borrowed money on the strength of the expected income. This revenue stream, and the borrowings which it permitted, enabled the papacy's finances to support its substantial temporal ambitions. The creation of new offices was particularly substantial on the eve of the reformation (under Pope Leo X*). Protestant reformers criticized this as one aspect of the papacy's corruption.

Total values of venal offices accounted at the Roman Datary[1] in selected years are given below:

1525   2,546,210 (gold florins)
1551   2,691,700 scudi d'oro
1561   3,208,000 scudi d'oro
1592   4,067,260 scudi d'oro
1599   3,790,980 scudi d'oro
1619   3,560,000 scudi d'oro

The papal chancery

Issued papal decrees known as 'bulls' (from the Latin *bulla* meaning seal). The chancery appended the papal signet to the wax seal on the bottom of decrees from the papacy. Such decrees (or 'decretals') were often known as *constitutiones* because they were issued on matters affecting the generality of the church and would join the other canons of the church. This distinguished them from 'rescripts' (*rescripta*) – particular decisions on matters of discipline sought by individuals in specific instances. The chancery also issued papal letters of provision to benefices throughout the Roman church.

Papal provisions

In theory, the papacy claimed, from the thirteenth century, the right to confer benefices directly, or to order conferment by others on apostolic authority. In practice, however, the papacy limited that right to particular classes of benefices which were 'reserved' to the disposition of the

---

[1] Figures from P. Partner, 'Papal financial policy in the Renaissance and Counter-Reformation', *Past and Present* No. 88 (1980), 24.

Holy See. These 'reservations' included all those benefices vacated by those resident in Rome (*Ad Sedem Apostolicam*). For those appointed to senior posts within the church, it was still vital to secure papal letters of provision to their benefice, even though they had secured letters of nomination from their collator. The power of provision was much criticized during the later middle ages. It was claimed to be a money-making apparatus and to lead to the preferment of benefices on foreigners and unsuitable individuals. It was also held to increase the incidence of pluralism, non-residence and the provision of individuals to non-existent (or non-vacant) benefices. Some states (e.g. England) introduced statutes to limit the powers of Rome (the Statutes of Provisors, 1351, 1353, 1365, 1389). However, despite the level of contemporary criticism, it was more often the case that, prior to the religious changes of the sixteenth century, the papacy attempted (rather ineffectually) to limit and restrain the unsuitable nominations made by lay patrons, for whom the church provided an indispensable means of sustaining aristocratic lineage and political authority.

The college of cardinals

The college of cardinals was perceived by contemporary Roman jurists as the 'senate' of the church of Latin Christendom, theoretically an inseparable and indistinguishable component of papal authority and sharing papal responsibilities. The meetings of the college of cardinals (in 'consistory', generally two or three times a week) were notionally to consider all matters relating to the church, including reports from its legates resident abroad, offering advice to the papacy and (at moments of papal succession) sitting in conclave to elect the new pontiff. In reality, however, from the middle of the fifteenth century, the authority of the college of cardinals was in decline. Cardinals were appointed uniquely by the papacy. The vote of cardinals for papal appointments became less important until it reached the stage where the pope merely communicated in consistory the names of those whom he had already chosen. Although there had been various internal proposals to reform the college in the fifteenth century, which involved choosing future cardinals from every region of Christendom on a proportional basis and in accordance with criteria of moral uprightness and doctrinal probity, they came to nothing. Cardinals continued to need substantial independent, private incomes to exercise their offices. The numbers of cardinals grew. The council of Konstanz[†] (1414–18) had fixed the number at 24. By the pontificate of Sixtus V it was established at 70 (1586). Some pontiffs secured their political position within the congregation of cardinals by making multiple new appointments to secure a loyal majority. Leo X*, when faced by a conspiracy of cardinals against him in 1517, created 31 new members of the college. Other means of pressure upon cardinals disloyal to the pontiff included lawsuits for corruption and embezzlement and, in 1517, execution for treason. The inevitable tendency for cardinals to be Italians was intensified in the sixteenth century, when the college was dominated by a relatively small number of powerful Italian families. There would be eight Carafa cardinals, seven Gonzaga, four Colonna, four Farnese, seven Medici and eight Della Rovere. With the growth of nepotism[†] also evident within the college, it gradually lost its effective autonomous authority and became an aristocracy dependent on the pope.

The Papal States
Also known as the 'lands of St Peter'; the principalities of the bishop of Rome in the Italian regions politically subject to his rule. They were administered by governors under the authority of the Apostolic Legate in accordance with the bull[†] of 1357 (*Constitutiones Aegidianae*) which conceded extensive liberties to its communes and nobility. The Papal States grew significantly during the period of the protestant reformation.

The conclave
The college of cardinals sitting during the vacancy of the see of Rome. It was accepted practice that the college could not exercise the power of jurisdiction and legislation during the vacancy of the Apostolic See. It did, however, exercise some papal authority in respect of the Papal States[†] during the interim, a power confirmed by a bull of Pius IV* of 1562 (*In eligendis*).

1.4.2 Church councils

Attempts to put an end to the Great Schism in the later medieval papacy caused by rival claims to papal authority led to the summoning of a sequence of church councils which were expected, so far as their proponents were concerned, to dispose of the validity of the contested claimant and promote a reform of the church in 'head and limbs'[†]. There were substantial debates over their precise role within the church (see pages 27–8).

1.4.3 The papacy and Europe's states

The complex relationship between the papacy and Europe's leading secular princes was the subject of modification in the period before, and during the protestant reformation as a result of the growing articulation of state power. The latter affected both the papacy (the 'papal monarchy' as it has been called) and monarchies such as France and the Empire.

One response to the need to define authority and prevent damaging political divisions over ecclesiastical power in particular regions was to negotiate 'concordats' with particular monarchs. The model for these was the concordat with the Empire in 1448.

The further response was to create a more permanent diplomatic representation for the papacy at important European courts. During the middle ages, the popes had often sent out cardinals with broad delegated powers to intervene in all aspects of church life. They were known as legates (*legati a latere*). In addition, popes had used a variety of semi-permanent *collectores* to receive revenues due to Rome from a variety of provincial locations and to act as bankers for its transfer. During the first half of the sixteenth century, the powers and responsibilities of legates and collectors were assumed by more permanent papal diplomats, known as nuncios (*nuncii cum potestate legati de latere* – though the representatives at the French court were never provided with legatine powers). Initially these permanent agents came from a variety of backgrounds in the church but, by the pontificate of Paul III*, they were almost all Italian bishops, responsible to the cardinal-nephew (later the secretary of state). They would play a major part in the diplomatic offensive against the protestant reformation in Europe (for the establishment of permanent nuncios, see page 208).

1.5 Primates, archbishops and bishops

For a map showing the bishoprics and archbishoprics of western Europe, see page 364.

Primate
Title used for the leading bishop in a province and, by the eve of the reformation, equated to the chief bishop of a particular state (or the pretension of a particular see to be so). The archbishop of Canterbury was the primate of all England as opposed to the archbishop of York, who was 'primate of England'. In Spain, the archbishop of the powerful and wealthy see of Toledo was the primate of Spain and was nearly always a cardinal. The see of Reims claimed the primacy in France, but it was vigorously contested. In Poland, the archbishop of Gniezno was primate and he acted as *de facto* monarch during an interregnum, summoning the diet to elect a new king.

Archbishop and bishop (in Latin, *archiepiscopus, episcopus*)
Bishops and archbishops differed from priests through their powers to ordain and to administer the rite of confirmation and confer orders†. Theoretically, the candidate for a bishopric had to be of mature age (30 years old by canon law), of legitimate birth, of attested character and

doctrine, and an ordained priest by the time of his consecration. In reality, the procedures for electing bishops did not apply the rules strictly and there were many examples of bishops who did not meet either the letter or spirit of these ordinances.

Rights to nominate to episcopal and archiepiscopal sees (i.e. 'seats') often rested in the hands of secular rulers or lay aristocrats, and these rights were sanctioned by local usage and law. In order to control and limit such practices, the papacy negotiated 'concordats'[†]. In France, the Pragmatic Sanction of Bourges (1438) was a document drawn up in a national council of the French church and ratified by the French king. It vested the rights of nomination to the bishoprics within France in the hands of cathedral chapters. In reality, they became prey to local and national lay interests. The agreement was renegotiated and accepted by the papacy in the Concordat of Bologna (1516). King Ferdinand of Aragon was granted a bull[†] by Innocent VIII giving him the patronage over all church appointments in the recently conquered kingdom of Grenada. In 1508, the monarchs of Spain (Ferdinand and Isabella) were granted rights of appointment to all benefices in the Americas. In Castile, the papacy merely ratified the royal nominees to bishoprics. Emperor Maximilian wanted to extend the Pragmatic Sanction throughout the imperial lands in the 1510s.

There were a variety of ways in which lay aristocrats and princes could legitimately sustain their patronage within the church through the established legal procedures of the church. One was the practice of exchanging one see for another. This was undertaken in order to secure a diocese closer to a family's local patrimony or to gain a wealthier see. Sometimes differences in income could be negotiated by means of issuing pensions to the previous incumbent from the revenues of the see. Thus, the majority of the income of a particular see could be held as a pension in 'confidence' by someone who was not the bishop of a see, and not even a churchman. The practice of resigning a see in favour of a relative, client or friend was very common (*resignatio in favorem*). The document on which a bishop submitted his resignation to the Holy See would include the name of the designated successor. By the rules of the papal chancery, however, the letters of resignation had to be approved in Rome at least 20 days before the death of the current incumbent in order to prevent bogus resignations. Such resignations became the object of negotiation and purchase and this was one of the principal ways by which simony[†] occurred in the senior appointments of the church.

Coadjutor
An assistant to a bishop, archbishop or abbot when ill, infirm or otherwise prevented (e.g. serving at Rome in an official capacity or holding other sees in plurality) from carrying out effectively his spiritual responsibilities.

1.6 Dioceses and parishes

1.6.1 Dioceses

Dioceses were, from the early middle ages, the main territorial unit of church administration and they were governed by bishops. Canon law required bishops to hold diocesan synods (i.e. 'councils of clergy') every year and archbishops to call provincial synods every three years. In fact, such synods were quite rare before the council of Trent[†]. Bishops were also required under canon law to undertake a regular visitation of their diocese (known as *Ad limina Apostolorum* visitations). In larger dioceses, these visitations required considerable energy and commitment. They occurred in a sporadic fashion and tended to be tasks devolved to a commissary of the bishop, especially the vicar-general, the deputy of the bishop in the diocese. The visitations tended to spend a substantial amount of time investigating parochial fabric and the condition of buildings and furnishings. Cases of abuse were generally referred to the ecclesiastical courts for further investigation. Some efforts were made to evaluate the educational standards of the clergy; the moral behaviour and religious education of the laity was rarely the subject of investigation in visitations prior to the council of Trent[†].

Other ecclesiastical figures attached to dioceses included the canons and prebendaries (i.e. someone who shares the endowment ('prebend') of a cathedral) of cathedral chapters, the dean (president of a cathedral chapter) and the chancellor or 'official' who kept the official seals of the diocese and presided over the ecclesiastical court of the diocese.

1.6.2 Parishes

The parochial structure of western Christendom was mostly of substantial antiquity by the time of the reformation. The size and density of the parish structure varied very widely from region to region. The parish was a largely self-governing entity in which the parishioners were responsible for maintaining the fabric of the local church and for providing the accessories for the services in terms of books and furniture (particularly fonts for baptism). In practice, such responsibilities were often carried out by churchwardens elected by the congregation or nominated by the patron.

Although each individual diocese knew something about the number and state of particular parishes within its limits through the visitations, its regulation of parochial life was often limited to the provision of parish clergy and the maintenance of a disciplinary framework through the church courts.

Parish priests were provided for from a variety of sources and, in the pre-reformation church, it was not always the case that the care of souls in a single parish devolved upon one individual alone. One common method was for a parish to have an endowment (typically consisting of rights to tithe[†] or other emoluments, and a house to live in – collectively known as the 'temporalities' of the 'living') to which a parish priest was appointed. This endowment was known as a 'benefice'. Sometimes it was also known as a 'cure' because the priest discharged a cure (care) of souls in exchange for which he received the small tithes from the parishioners. Confusingly for Anglicans (where the reverse is now the case), the vicar was generally the substitute for the curate (or, as in French, *curé*), *vicarius* being the Latin for 'substitute'. In parishes served by a vicar, the 'great tithes' of the parish were appropriated elsewhere (often to monasteries, cathedral chapters or even secular figures) leaving the vicar to survive on the remaining revenues.

The right to appoint someone in holy orders to an ecclesiastical benefice was known as the right of 'advowson' (*advocatio*) or *ius patronatus*. Many of the patrons to livings were within the church – bishops, cathedral chapters and monasteries (the right of 'collation'). But, although they were often unwilling to alienate the advowson completely, these ecclesiastical patrons were frequently willing to grant to a third party (in return for a sum of money) the right to present to an ecclesiastical benefice. These were known as 'hac vice presentations'. In eastern Europe (Poland, Bohemia, Moravia, Hungary) the rights of presentation to parish livings lay largely outside ecclesiastical hands and rested with the aristocracy. This, in large measure, helps to explain the speedy penetration of the reformation within the church in these areas, once the aristocracy had become influenced by protestantism.

The payment of tithe was required by canon law and supported by arguments from natural and divine law by pre-reformation theologians. Tithes were commonly divided into the 'great' tithes (those from the major crops) and the 'small' tithes (minor produce such as chickens, lambs, etc). The latter were harder to assess and collect. The method of payment had already, in parts of Europe, begun to be commuted to a fixed annual money payment in place of tithe – with long-term consequences for the revenues of churchmen in a period of inflation such as that which occurred during the sixteenth century. The commutation of tithe did little to prevent the considerable degree of controversy which its payment regularly generated, and which was the subject of disputes brought before the ecclesiastical courts.

1.6.3 Unbeneficed clergy

Clergy who wished to become priests ('major orders') had to be ordained. Candidates had to be of mature age, unmarried, and be able to recite the Divine Office[†]. The first stage of becoming a priest, however, was to become tonsured and gain the status of cleric. This was often gained at a very early age.

All clerics, whether beneficed or not, as well as those in regular orders (including nuns) enjoyed exemption from being tried in the secular courts. This was known as 'benefit of clergy'. It was typically extended to all those who were tonsured and could read a passage in Latin. The claim of 'benefit of clergy' attracted much criticism which was exploited by the protestant reformers.

1.6.4 Ecclesiastical discipline

Ecclesiastical courts
The diocesan ecclesiastical courts were amongst the most important elements of the pre-reformation church as far as the laity were concerned, although their significance varied widely in different regions of Europe, depending on whether there was an inquisition. They dealt with a wide range of business. They approved wills, admitted clergymen to benefices on behalf of the bishop, and issued a wide range of licences and dispensations from the requirements of the church. They also had a considerable degree of jurisdiction over disputes. They dealt with matrimonial problems and punished those found to have entered into extra-marital sexual relationships. They settled disputes relating to wills and prosecuted those who meddled with dead men's property without authority. They administered the laws of the church in respect of the observance of the Sabbath (Sunday) and Feast Days[†]. They exacted the payments of tithes[†] and dealt with disputes over the amounts to be paid and by whom. They carried out the canon laws of the church in respect of a whole range of defined moral offences from the most serious down to more trivial ones, e.g. disturbances in church and malicious gossip.

The church courts often had influential enemies. Wealthy urban families resented the fees which they charged for proving wills. Royal or princely courts (and their lawyers) viewed the rival jurisdiction with jealousy. In places with strong and effective secular jurisdiction (such as the city of Venice, or in the French monarchy) there were various ways by which the activities of the ecclesiastical courts were constrained or by which appeals of cases to secular courts could take place. These resentments were often reflected in anticlerical satire of the period immediately prior to the reformation.

The ecclesiastical court (sometimes known as a 'consistory' or, in French, *officialité*), sat in the episcopal palace or the cathedral. Proctors presented cases before the court and apparitors or summoners served the mandates of the court upon those required to attend it. Individuals might be required to undertake penance[†] (with the degree of publicity involved varying with the seriousness of the offence). Failure to attend the court or to comply with its decree was declared contumacious and the offender ordered to be either suspended or excommunicated. Excommunication was the automatic canonical penalty for more serious offences, including perjury, defamation, violence to clergy, simony[†], sacrilege and heresy. Although the court could offer its services to poor people for nothing, it generally charged for its services and these sums provided the revenues for its officials.

The inquisition

The inquisition (from the Latin *inquirere* – to look into) was a special ecclesiastical institution established in the thirteenth century to suppress the appearance of heresy. It was most significant in places where heresy had been prevalent. The medieval inquisition was not a distinct tribunal but a set of special but permanent judges who exercised their functions in the name of the papacy. These judges were generally drawn from amongst the Franciscans and (especially in the years prior to the reformation) the Dominicans. The procedures of the inquisition were well-established by the early sixteenth century. They began with the proclamation of a month's 'term of grace' by the inquisitor. The inhabitants were summoned to appear before him. Those who confessed of their own accord were treated lightly. Those who denied any wrongdoing, and against whom there was contrary evidence (which might well include the testimony of other condemned 'heretics' – since this was admissible evidence, despite the risks of perjury) were summoned before the inquisitor. Although the witnesses against them might be named to them, there was no confrontation or possibility of cross-examination of witnesses and witnesses for the defence were rarely admissible. As in Roman law, torture (the *quaestio* or 'putting to the question') was permitted in order to elicit the truth, although there were theoretically rules governing the way in which it was to be administered. Punishments included penance[†], imprisonment and excommunication[†]. Officially, however, it was not the inquisition that sentenced unrepentant or repeated heretics to death. That was the task of the civil and secular authorities – although, with representatives of the civil power attending the solemn ceremonials of the 'act of faith' (*auto-da-fé*) at which sentences were pronounced, the distinction was something of a technicality.

The Spanish kingdoms, along with many other parts of Europe, had a version of the medieval inquisition. However, the revived and reorganized 'Spanish inquisition' was a more recent and distinctive tribunal on the eve of the reformation. It was established during the reigns of Ferdinand and Isabella specifically to deal with the problems of pseudo-conversions of Jews (Marranos) and Moors (Moriscos) to Christianity. On 1 November 1478, Pope Sixtus IV empowered the Spanish sovereigns to establish the new inquisition which would become (unlike the medieval inquisition) a separate tribunal, set up by, and responsible to, the crown. (For further details on the Spanish inquisition, see pages 152–6.)

Canon law

The rules of the church concerning its organization, administration, government and discipline. Known as the *Corpus*, it grew up gradually and included a good deal of material borrowed from Roman law as well as decisions of the councils of the church. The most famous collection of these canons was that of Gratian, completed in 1140 and known as the *Decretum*. This formed the basis of the *Corpus Juris Canonici*, which also included various additional papal decrees. The *Corpus Juris Canonici* was not altered during the reformation by the established church and remained in force until 1917.

1.6.5 Various terms of ecclesiastical law and ecclesiastical abuses defined by canon law and the councils of the church

In commendam ('in trust')
When the revenues of a benefice were held temporarily by someone other than the incumbent, e.g. during a vacancy. The individual holding them might be a layman, who could not perform the spiritual duties attached to the benefice, and would need to appoint a vicar. Bishops often enjoyed benefices *in commendam* in addition to their dioceses and might do so for long periods.

Concubinage
The term used when a cleric was suspected of keeping a mistress ('concubine') and having thus broken his vow of celibacy.

Pluralism
The holding of two or more benefices at once by the same incumbent. Dispensations, however, could be obtained, and holding benefices *in commendam* (i.e. 'in trust') was an acceptable practice even where personal residence was required by statute or custom.

Nepotism
The bestowal of office or patronage upon close relatives (technically 'nephews' from the Latin *nepos*). The term is particularly used for the practice of promoting relatives which was widespread amongst the college of cardinals[†] and in the curia of fifteenth- and sixteenth-century popes.

Simony
A corrupt presentation to any benefice in return for money, gift or reward. The term is derived from the action of Simon Magus in the Bible (*Acts* 8).

Non-residence
Where the incumbent of a benefice was not resident and therefore unable to carry out the spiritual duties attached to it. There were numerous causes of non-residence, which was widespread in the pre-reformation church. Some non-residence was for legitimate reasons – for example, attending universities for study. Other cases of non-residence were the inevitable consequence of 'appropriation' (where the benefice was annexed to the perpetual ownership and use of some religious body such as a monastery). But there was also non-residence which occurred as a result of pluralism[†].

1.7 The monastic orders

The monastic orders were known as the 'regular' orders of the church because they were composed of men or women living in a community under a religious rule (*regula*) as monks or nuns, who had taken vows or 'made profession' to live according to the rule of their particular order. This was to distinguish them from 'seculars' – i.e. the clergy who were not 'professed' or enclosed. Some monastic orders (Franciscans, Dominicans, Carmelites) were known as the 'mendicant friars' by virtue of their commitment to corporate poverty. They were not liable to episcopal visitation and might not undertake parochial responsibilities.

1.7.1 Principal orders

Augustinians
The Augustinian Friars were formed from various Italian congregations of hermits who were placed under the Rule of St Augustine by the papacy in 1256. Their constitution was modelled on that of the Dominicans. By the late middle ages the order tended to concentrate its work in towns. There were also various 'reformed' congregations of Augustinians by the time of the reformation. It was to the German Reformed Congregation of Augustinians that Luther belonged.

Benedictines
St Benedict of Nursia (c.540) established a monastic rule for his monks at Monte Cassino which gradually became ubiquitous throughout Europe and established the model for the monastic orders. The monastic

rule of Benedict required obedience to a patriarchal abbot, commitment to live in one place (the monastery) and zeal to undertake the tasks
of the monastic community, the chief of which was the Divine Office[†]
(*opus Dei*) and accompanying private readings and prayers. All possessions were to be held in common. The way of life was modest but not
overly austere. Despite various papal efforts to bring the Benedictines
under one centralized institution, they remained independent of any
broader organizational framework beyond being loosely grouped into
'congregations'. In time, the Benedictine movement generated separate
orders, in which austerity and a greater degree of group organization
were more prominent. (See also Camaldolese, Carthusians, Cistercians.)

Carmelites (White Friars, after their white mantle)
Founded in Palestine (the 'Order of Our Lady of Mount Carmel') in
c.1154 by St Berthold. The initial rule of the Carmelites was one of
absolute poverty, solitude and abstinence. After the Crusades, the order
was reorganized along the lines of the other 'mendicant' orders and
an Order of Carmelite Sisters was founded in the Low Countries in
1452. The latter spread very rapidly in the years prior to the protestant
reformation.

Cistercians
Named after the mother house at Cîteaux, founded in 1098. The order
rose to prominence through the influence and reputation of St Bernard
of Clairvaux. By 1500, there were nearly 700 Cistercian foundations in
Europe.

Dominicans (*Ordo Praedicatorum* – 'Order of Preachers')
These were known as the 'Black Friars' in England from the black *cappa*
or mantle worn over their white habits and as *Jacobins* in France (after
the name of their first house in Paris, which was dedicated to St James
(i.e. 'St Jacques')).
The order took shape under the direction of St Dominic in the early
thirteenth century. Like that of St Francis, it initially practised corporate
poverty and enjoyed no possessions except its houses and churches;
members lived by begging. In the later middle ages, the order became
divided by various controversies. Some friars were granted exclusive rights
to preach and hear confessions in particular localities and allowed to keep
the proceeds. In 1475, the pope revoked the rule of corporate poverty
and allowed the order to hold property and enjoy permanent sources of
income. The Dominicans were particularly involved in teaching and study.
They established houses close to universities and provided many of the
scholastic theologians. The order was carefully organized and each convent sent representatives to annual provincial chapters, which (in turn)

sent representatives to the Chapter General, meeting in Rome. The order often provided the personnel for the inquisition, which led to their reputation as the 'watchdogs of orthodoxy' (*Domini canes*). The order thus inevitably attracted the particular criticism of protestant propagandists. They were much involved with missionary activity in the New World at the time of the reformation.

Franciscans (known in England as the 'Grey Friars' after the colour of their habit)
The mendicant order of friars founded by St Francis of Assisi in 1209. Their distinguishing mark was the insistence on complete poverty for individual friars and for the whole order. With the spread of the order during the thirteenth century, corporate poverty proved difficult to adhere to in practice and led to long-lasting internal divisions which eventually damaged the whole order. In the fifteenth century, an effort at reform, represented by a return to corporate poverty, was led by the so-called 'Observants' as against the 'Conventuals'. The former gained ecclesiastical recognition at the council of Konstanz† in 1415, which established them as a separate group within the order, with their own vicar-general and provincial organization. In 1517, they were finally separated from the Conventuals and declared the true Order of St Francis.

1.7.2 Lesser orders

Camaldolese
An order founded in c.1012 at Camaldoli, near Arezzo, in Italy. The order had no written rule and its various houses (principally in Italy) differed widely in their monastic practice by the time of the reformation.

Carthusians
A contemplative order founded by St Bruno in 1084 at the Grande Chartreuse (hence their name) monastery in the Dauphiné Alps. The monks were vowed to silence, mental prayer, and manual work in a rule which owed a good deal to that of Benedict. The order was not as affected by the decline of other monastic orders in the later middle ages and it prospered in the age of the reformation in Spain, France and Italy.

Minims
An order of friars established in 1435 by Francesco di Paola (1436?–1507). They regarded humility as their main virtue, seeing themselves as the 'least' (*minimi*) amongst the religious orders. Their first rule was based on that of St Francis of Assisi. Their particular characteristic was a vow of perpetual abstinence from meat, fish, eggs, cheese, butter and

milk. The order wore a black habit and was still expanding, especially in Italy, France, Spain and Germany by the early years of the protestant reformation.

1.8 Other orders

The Hospitallers (also 'Knights Hospitaller')
The order was also known as the Knights of Rhodes and (after 1530) the Knights of Malta. Although its origins are somewhat obscure, its early aims were to provide hospitality for pilgrims to Jerusalem. During the Crusades it established a regular army of mounted knights and this became the predominant element of the order after the suppression of the Knights Templar and the transfer of their wealth to the Hospitallers. The order had foundations throughout Italy, Germany, France and elsewhere. Rhodes provided the centre for its activities from 1309 until the island was captured by Suleiman the Magnificent in 1522. In due course, Emperor Charles V ceded the island of Malta to them in sovereignty in 1530. During the Turkish threat of the sixteenth century, the order retained some of its military significance.

1.9 Secular priests living in community

There were some groups in the church which bridged the formal division between the 'regular' (monastic) and 'secular' priests. These were priests who lived in communities and who had not taken monastic vows. In the areas where their convents were established, they often took on practical works of charity and education. They also accepted a degree of involvement in their work from lay authorities such as town magistrates which would have been rejected by a monastic house. They used to be regarded by reformation historians as 'precursors' of the protestant reformation. However, their influence was (at best) indirect and their houses were closed along with other monasteries in those regions which became reformed. There were also the clergy of collegiate churches and cathedral chapters who had an element of communal religious life.

Augustinian Canons (known in England as 'Austin' or 'Regular' canons)
'Secular' priests who accepted the rule of St Augustine.

Brethren (and Sisters) of the Common Life
A movement which originated in the late fourteenth century around Gerhard Groote, who established a group of 'devout' priests to run hospices in the Low Countries. By the reformation, there were about 100 houses of the Sisters and a further 40 of the Brethren in Rhineland

Germany and the Low Countries. They became practical exponents of the 'modern devotion'[†] (*devotio moderna*). Erasmus was educated by the Brethren of the Windsheim congregation (who accepted the rule of St Augustine).

Lateran canons

A congregation (of Augustinian canons) founded by Leone Gherardini from Padua, beginning at an abandoned monastery near Lucca. By 1500, there were about 40 houses, mainly in the cities of northern Italy.

Debate and dissension within the church on the eve of the protestant reformation

2.1 Senses of reformation

Unlike many conceptual frameworks adopted by historians for understanding the past, the term 'reformation' is not a neologism. Contemporaries used the term; but the ways in which they used it differed markedly from the meaning that it subsequently acquired. During the seventeenth century the term 'reformation' described the ecclesiastical changes brought about by Martin Luther. Only gradually did the notion of the 'reformation' as applied to a period of European history emerge in the eighteenth century to be precisely formulated by the German historian, Leopold von Ranke (1795–1886), as the 'Age of the Reformation'. This protestant-influenced conception of the reformation was not accepted by many catholic historians until comparatively recently. This acceptance came about especially when historians began to understand that there were underlying intellectual, social and institutional trends common to all religious change in the sixteenth century. Contemporaries of Martin Luther used the term in the following ways:

Reformation of statutes (*Reformatio iuris*)
This was a lay expression, used by lawyers and jurists, for the codification of common law or the revision of the charters and statutes of an incorporated body (such as a university or college). Luther's early use of the word 'reformation' referred to changes in the curriculum at the university of Wittenberg.

Reformation in head and limbs (*Reformatio in capite et in membris*)
This was the clerical expression (drawn from medical treatises) for the institutional reform of the church. It was to be found deployed at the general councils of the medieval church where the expression was intended to indicate that reform would begin at the top with the transfer of some papal jurisdictional powers to a regularly summoned council of the church.

Universal reformation ('reformatio')
This was the sense of dramatic reshaping of the world which would
occur in the days preceding the coming of the Apocalypse, and which
had been predicted in the prophetic books of the Bible (see page 38).

2.2 Conciliar reform

The calls for the institutional reform of the church were numerous, as
were the practical difficulties which it posed. Although there were many
attempted monastic reforms to the observance of their original rule
(see pages 21–3), and also dedicated individuals seeking to carry out
their responsibilities in new ways, institutional change proved obstinately
difficult to accomplish. The problems were illustrated by the history of
the conciliar reform movement in the century before the reformation.

The Great Schism in the late medieval papacy and the problem of
Hussite heresy led some contemporary exponents to advance the constitutional position of general church councils within the church at large
as a solution to these problems. Medieval historians have called them
'conciliar theorists'; but 'conciliarism' was far from the united and coherent ideology which the term suggests. The great councils of the early
church, as well as aspects of later canon law, gave a fundamental legitimacy to the suggestion that a general council of the church could embody
the universal church. So in these respects, conciliar thought was not
new. But one strand of 'conciliarism' called for an assembly of a council
to undertake ecclesiastical reform and this was a theme which re-emerged
regularly in each of the councils which were held in the century before
the reformation. A further, and more radical, strand wanted to make the
councils a more regular part of the institutional framework of the church.
This was embodied in the decree of 1417 at the council of Konstanz[†]
(*Frequens*). A still more contentious element of conciliar thinking was the
supposition that, in certain circumstances, a church council had supremacy in the church (even over the papacy). This was embodied in the
decree of 1415 at the council of Konstanz[†] (*Haec sancta synodus*). Strict
conciliar theorists did not question the spiritual authority of the papacy
embodied in its claim to the succession of St Peter. They did, however,
question its jurisdictional authority over the church at large.

Conciliarists were widely read and had considerable influence within
the late medieval church. It was on the basis of conciliar theory that theologians in France claimed that the French church had its own corporate
and inalienable privileges which not even the papacy could infringe
('Gallicanism'[†]). The fear that heretics would successfully appeal against
the authority of the papacy to a future general council led Pius II to condemn such views as 'erroneous and execrable' in a bull[†] of 1460 (*Exec-
rabilis*). The papacy avoided holding general councils of the church after

1449 on the grounds of the dangers they posed to papal authority and church unity. The revival of the papacy and the decrease of schism within the church led to a waning of conciliar theory. Those within the church still calling for a council to institute reform ceased to advocate the propositions of jurisdictional supremacy which strict conciliarists had once held.

However the continuing vitality of conciliar thinking and a degree of reforming concern led a group of cardinals to convene a council (known as the *conciliabulum*) at Pisa in 1511 which forced Pope Leo X to convene his own (the Fifth Lateran Council). It was at that council that the decree *Pastor aeternus* (1516) was agreed, which stated that popes had authority over all councils, including the right to convoke, transfer and dissolve them. This decree was of considerable importance when it came to the summoning of the council of Trent to undertake the reforming endeavours which had been unsuccessfully tackled by its predecessors. It is no surprise that Martin Luther should have twice publicly appealed from the authority of the papacy to a general council during the Luther affair (see Section Three).

2.2.1 Councils of the church

The legitimacy of some of these councils (or some of their sessions) was, or became, questioned by papal theologians, and this is indicated by italics.

Ecumenical Order	Sessions	Place
		Pisa (1409)
16th Gen	45	Konstanz (1414–18)
		Pavia–Siena (1423–24)
17th Gen	25	Basel (1431–49)
		– Ferrara (from 1438)
		– Florence (from 1439)
		– Rome (from 1443)
18th Gen	12	Rome (5th Lateran) (1512–17)
		Pisa (1511–12)

2.2.2 Some conciliar theorists

Jean (le Charlier de) Gerson* (1363–1429)
Pierre d'Ailly (Petrus Alliacus) (1350–1420)
Nicholas of Cusa (Nicolaus Cusanus) (1401–64)
Francesco Zabarella (1360–1417)

2.3 Academic debates

New universities joined the corpus of medieval university foundations in the era of the reformation (see pages 266–9). There were also lively debates within the faculties. Students studied grammar, dialectic and rhetoric (the *trivium*) as well as arithmetic, geometry, astronomy and the theory of music (the *quadrivium*) for a degree in the faculty of arts (*magister artium* or MA) before (possibly) more specialized work for a doctorate in the higher faculties (theology, canon or civil law, medicine). Methods of instruction remained remarkably similar in all institutions. The lecture – lasting sometimes two hours – was the central defining component. Disputations on a set topic also played a substantial role. The study of Aristotle continued to dominate a large part of the syllabuses in all universities, although the approach could differ markedly. The curriculum was generally established by university statute and, whilst we cannot be sure by how much university teachers diverged from the statutory curriculum, it is clear that some statutes allowed a much wider choice of interpretation than others. These interpretations were known as 'schools of thought' (or *Viae*). They were named after great exponents of the classic philosophical and theological problems of the day, or after a particular approach to the problem. Some universities (for example Louvain) allowed only one *Via* to predominate before the reformation according to their statutes. Other universities (for example, Heidelberg, Ingolstadt and Paris) were renowned for allowing several schools of thought to be taught within their arts and theology faculties. The result provided for rich debates about theological issues which had their contemporary relevance and which would continue to be of central significance during the reformation.

Summarizing these sophisticated debates in a work like this runs a serious risk of over-simplification. At the heart of later medieval universities, however, there were two central debates. One was about the degree to which, and how, we 'know' and 'understand' the world around us. In philosophy it is known as the problem of 'universals'. Most common nouns are 'universals' (e.g. hat, stone). Aristotle (and Plato to an even greater degree) had argued that, on the basis of our sense-impressions, we abstract the underlying common forms which exist in the objects to form what is understood as a 'stone' or a 'hat'. This is known as 'realism' because the form is not merely an abstraction in our minds but derived from the 'reality' of the form as represented to us. This analysis was broadly accepted by the greatest of the medieval philosophers, St Thomas Aquinas.

After Aquinas, however, medieval philosophers questioned this understanding. They have become known collectively as 'nominalists' although the term covers several different approaches to the problem of 'universals'. The most representative, and best-known, of them was William of Ockham* (c.1285–c.1349). For Ockham, the categories into which we place our sense-impressions are created within our minds only. 'Universals' only exist as a mental concept (or 'name' – hence 'nominalism') which we have either abstracted from reality or intuitively ascribed to it. So, if God chose to destroy all the hats in the world, we would still 'know' what a 'hat' was. In university curricula relating to the faculty of arts, this was sometimes known as the 'modern way of thought' (via moderna) to distinguish it from 'the ancient way' (via antiqua) of Aquinas and Duns Scotus.

The second great set of debates took place within the faculties of theology. It was about how man was 'saved' by God and it sought to square the circle between a God who was omnipotent and mankind who had free-will. Its various exponents drew upon the philosophical debates which have just been touched on, but in different ways and with different conclusions. They were all aware of, and sought to avoid, the 'heresy' of Pelagius†. Ockham himself had sought to resolve the problem on the basis of 'nominalist' philosophy and resorted to an analogy. People were not saved primarily because of any 'real' or 'intrinsic' merit of what they did during their lives. They were saved because God, who could do anything and everything (but chose to act in an ordered fashion), had made a covenant or pact with mankind. The fundamental consequence of God's covenant was to make what people did with their lives of greater value than it intrinsically possessed. Ockham illustrated this with reference to a small lead coin which was not worth much. If the coin had been made of gold it would have had considerable intrinsic value. Nevertheless a ruler (in whose name the coins had been issued) could choose to redeem the small lead coin for a much higher value than its inherent worth dictated. This enabled theologians of the via moderna to argue both that human actions were inherently of little (but not negligible) worth; and also that they had an ascribed (de congruo) value because of the covenant between man and God. Having acquired this 'merit', mankind could use it to acquire the 'habit of grace' in order to be 'justly' saved. This led to a picture of a God who rendered to each person his or her due and a picture of humans needing merely to do 'their best' in order to be saved.[1]

This was the balanced resolution of the problem that tended to prevail in those faculties where the via Ockhamii was argued. However, there were also nominalists (of whom Gregory of Rimini was the most distinguished), who developed a form of Augustinianism† which was extremely anti-Pelagian and which saw mankind as completely incapable of doing anything to contribute to its own salvation after the Fall. The human

[1] A. McGrath, The Intellectual Origins of the European Reformation (Blackwell, Oxford, 1987), ch. 3.

equivalent of the lead coin had no value whatsoever. People could not even acquire 'habits' of grace, let alone true contrition for sins on their own, but were solely dependent on 'divine acceptance' (*acceptatio divina*) of them. This was the view of the *via Gregorii* or the *schola Augustiniana moderna*. Although these schools of thought were apparently arguing about highly abstract issues, their influence filtered through to confessors' manuals and thereby had a wider impact than one might imagine.[2]

The degree to which nominalist thinking (and the 'modern Augustinian school' in particular) influenced the protestant reformers remains a matter of some debate amongst intellectual historians. Its significance should probably not be overestimated in comparison with the broader impact of Christian humanism.

2.3.1 Representative scholastic theologians of the late-medieval period

William of Ockham* (c.1285–1347)
Giles of Rome (Aegidius Romanus) (c.1245–1316)
Gregory of Rimini* (d.1358)
Gabriel Biel* (c.1420–95)

2.3.2 Some terms commonly used by scholastic theologians and in confessors' manuals

Accidents
According to medieval philosophy derived from Aristotle, an accident is an entity without any separate individual existence (no 'ens in se'). It exists only in another entity (as an 'ens in alio'). It was principally used to explain the mystery of the Real Presence in the eucharist. So, the colour, taste and quantity of the wine remained the same at the consecration because they were the 'accidents' of the wine whilst its 'substance' had fundamentally changed (transubstantiation†).

Absolution (*absolutio*)
Absolution was granted by the priest in confession. It 'showed' the sinner the grace which God had already given, but there were questions about the role of the priest in remitting the temporal punishment in respect of sin, and unresolved problems about what power the priest had to induce true contrition in a penitent, and to judge the penitent's degree of contrition.

---

[2] T. Tentler, *Sin and Confession on the Eve of the Reformation* (Princeton University Press, Princeton, 1977).

Attrition (*attritio*)
The 'unformed penitence' evoked in a sinner by the fear of the consequences of his sin. It was argued by some that such penitence was worthless since it was merely based on the constraint of fear. Others, however, argued that it was sufficiently 'meritorious' to begin to earn grace and forgiveness. In time, it could lead to a true contrition from which grace and forgiveness would flow.

Congruent merit (*meritum de congruo*)
The kind of merit which, it was argued, was acquired in the sacrament of penance† when, at absolution, mankind was restored to a 'state of grace'.

Contrition (*paenitentia*)
This was the sorrow which the penitent sinner was expected to show, or to develop, during the process of confession and which led to absolution. There was, however, a scholarly debate about whether 'perfect' contrition was possible for a human individual to achieve and, if so (in a more practical vein), what were the public marks of true contrition. It was argued by some that, on his own, the penitent was only capable of achieving 'attrition'†.

Covenant (*pactum*)
This was the term used by the theologians of the *via moderna* to describe God's ordained power of salvation. God had committed himself by a covenant ('pactum', 'foedus', 'testamentum') to bestow grace upon mankind, provided that they fulfilled certain preconditions.

'Doing one's best' (*Facere quod in se est*)
An injunction (which predated Ockham) which was seen as God's requirement of man. God's gift of grace was understood to be conditional upon man's 'doing what lies within his powers' in order to receive such grace. So, if an individual was sorry for his/her sins, that was what God required in order to give him/her the grace of absolution.

God's absolute power (*potentia Dei absoluta*)
The infinite and absolute power of God, by which he was potentially free to do anything which did not involve self-contradiction.

God's ordained power (*potentia Dei ordinata*)
The powers which God voluntarily chose to exercise in order to be faithful to the way in which he has ordered creation. The distinction made between God's absolute and his ordained power enabled scholastic

theologians, especially those of the *via moderna*, to discuss the questions
of salvation and free-will without limiting divine omnipotence.

Righteousness of God (*iustitia Dei*)
The embodiment of the arbitrary (to mankind) decisions of the divine
will.

Sins (*peccata*)
Scholastic theologians and confessors' manuals identified seven 'deadly'
sins (pride, avarice, extravagance, wrath, gluttony, envy and sloth). Latin
mnemonics and diagrams existed to help the penitent remember them
(e.g. SALIGIA = *Superbia, Avaritia, Luxuria, Ira, Gula, Invidia, Accidia*).
There was much scholarly and ecclesiastical debate as to the relative
seriousness of the deadly sins, which tended to become legalistic.

2.4 Christian humanism

The term '*Humanismus*' (in German) was first utilized in 1808 by a
German educationalist to describe the emphasis placed on the Greek
and Latin classics in education. The word has come to be used to refer
to the revival of classical studies in the Italian renaissance and the desire
to return 'to the original texts' (*ad fontes*). Part of the revival involved
the more technical aspects of critical textual scholarship known as
'philology', by which more reliable and precise editions of classical texts
could be established. Humanism was not, therefore, a precisely delineated philosophical system as the medieval scholastic philosophers would
have understood it but a general intellectual trend with some specific
educational objectives. It had its effects on the writing and teaching of
theology and biblical studies, as on every other area of learning on the
eve of the reformation. These are best characterized in theology and
biblical studies through the writings of the most characteristic 'Christian
humanists' of the period. The humanists corresponded and exchanged
manuscripts in a creative republic of letters, a commonwealth of learning in which they had considerable pride, and from which they drew great
strength. Although printing was one of the ways by which their impact
on the reformation was to become felt, it should not be overestimated.
Some of the Christian humanists eventually became protestants (such as
Huldrych Zwingli* and Philipp Melanchthon*). Many, however, remained
within the established church and there was no automatic connection
between Christian humanism and the protestant reformation. Humanism would become, however, one of the most significant developments for
the implementation of religious change in both the catholic and protestant reformations of the sixteenth century. It created the debates and
controversies upon which they would draw greatly for their inspiration.

2.4.1 Erasmus

The influence of Desiderius Erasmus* of Rotterdam (in Latin: *Erasmus Roterodamus*) (c.1467–1536) amongst Europe's intellectuals on the eve of the reformation is difficult to overestimate. He embodied for a generation the forces of Christian humanism. His enormous published output is impossible to summarize adequately here, but the following is a selection of Erasmus' works which had their greatest impact during the religious changes of the sixteenth century. The dates given are those of their first publication. Many went through numerous additions and changes in Erasmus' lifetime:

The Adages (*Adagia*) (1500)
A collection of Greek and Latin proverbs, much expanded in later editions (and some of which became moral essays in their own right), designed to be of use for educational purposes.

The Manual of a Christian Soldier (*Enchiridion Militis Christiani*) (1504)
This was ostensibly written as a manual of simple, but learned piety for the ordinary Christian layman. Erasmus stressed the importance of individuals studying the Scriptures for themselves rather than reading the commentaries of scholastic theologians. His underlying intention was to demonstrate that it was through this 'philosophia Christi' that the decay in the church would be rectified. Although it did not have a marked impact during the first decade of its publication (it was only reprinted once), it had an enormous impact after 1515, being reprinted 24 times and translated into various vernacular languages.

In Praise of Folly (*Moriae Encomium* (in Greek – a pun on the name of Sir Thomas More, to whom the treatise was dedicated); *seu Laus Stultitiae*) (1509)
A biting satire on monasticism and the corruptions of the church which went through seven editions within months of its initial publication. It was also an invitation to a debate with More about whether such abuses could be remedied by political and institutional measures.

Novum instrumentum omne (1516)
A full Greek text of the New Testament, with an accompanying new Latin translation which differed from the Vulgate at many points of fundamental significance. It included extensive notes to justify the alterations and make sarcastic remarks on contemporary ecclesiastical practices.

The Complaint of Peace (*Querela Pacis*) (1517)
A treatise about the limits of the 'just war' which provided Erasmus with the opportunity to advocate the significance of the establishment of peace for the good of Christendom.

Julius Excluded (*Julius Exclusus*) (1518 – though written earlier)
A satire on the 'warrior pope', Julius II, in the form of a dialogue between the pope, St Peter and a spirit at the gates of Heaven. The pope was unable to persuade St Peter to let him into Heaven.

Paraphrases (1520, 1522)
Summaries of the Pauline Epistles (and, in 1522, the Gospels) each dedicated to a particular prince or prelate whom Erasmus accounted a patron of the humanist commonwealth of learning. The Gospels were dedicated (in turn) to Charles V, François I, Henry VIII and Ferdinand I. The Bible narratives were treated in a historical fashion and some doubts were cast on the authenticity of some texts (e.g. the Epistle of St James; the Epistle to the Ephesians; the Epistle to the Hebrews).

On Free Will (*Diatribe de libero arbitrio*) (1524)
A lucid and serious attack upon Luther which drew from him the response *The Bondage of the Will* (*De servo arbitrio*, 1525).

Erasmus' writings generated many hostile responses amongst conservative theologians. They were especially challenged by his edition of the New Testament. The Dominicans were particularly virulent; but the Franciscans and Carmelites were also actively opposed to the 'philosophy of Christ', not least because of Erasmus' well-known jibe that 'monkery is not piety' (*monachatus est non pietas*). Their hostility became readily transferred to Luther and the protestant reformers in due course. Amongst those responsible for publishing the earliest invective against Erasmus, the most significant were Diego López Zúñiga (in Latin: Stunica), Noël Béda (c.1470–1537), Josse (van) Clichtove* (c.1472–1543), and Juan Ginés (de) Sepúlveda* (1490–1573). However, they often found themselves lampooned by Erasmus' supporters in turn.

2.4.2 French Christian humanists

French humanism registered its effects at the French court (under François I), within its universities (especially the law schools) and within the French church. It became associated with a renaissance of vernacular culture – a French school of thought in Roman law (*mos gallicus* as opposed to the *mos italicus*), Gallican† rights and privileges within its church, and the assertion of French language and literature. Within the church, it became particularly influential within the 'Meaux Circle'[†], a group of like-minded evangelical+ reformers around Guillaume Briçonnet* (c.1470–1534). Guillaume Budé* (1468–1540), Jacques Lefèvre d'Etaples* (1460?–1536) (Lat: *Faber Stapulensis*), Louis de Berquin* (c.1490–1529), and the king's sister Marguerite d'Angoulême* (also Marguerite of Navarre) (1492–1549) were amongst the key figures in French Christian humanism and during the very first stages of the impact of the Lutheran reformation in France (c.1530). The later impact of humanist-influenced individuals on the course of the French reformation is reflected in the careers of Jean Calvin, Théodore de Bèze* and Pierre Viret*.

2.4.3 Christian humanists in the Spanish peninsula

Christian humanists in the Spanish peninsula initially congregated around the powerful and significant prelate, Cardinal Francisco Jiménez de Cisneros*, archbishop of Toledo and primate[†] of Spain. Although not a humanist scholar himself, he founded the new university of Alcalá de Henares in 1508, not far from where he had been born. To it, he attracted humanist scholars from across Europe to work on the Complutensian Polyglot Bible[†]. These humanists were strengthened in their influence by the arrival of Charles of Ghent (Charles V) as king of Spain in 1517. He brought with him Burgundian courtiers amongst whom the influence of Erasmus*, coupled with that of the *devotio moderna*[†] and late medieval mysticism, was profound. They popularized the works of Erasmus and, in the 1520s and early 1530s, Erasmian influence at the Spanish or Portuguese court, in intellectual life, and amongst the urban elites, was significant. This can be seen in the careers of the most prominent Erasmians from the Spanish peninsula, especially Alfonso de Valdés* (c.1500–33), Alonso Ruiz de Virués* (c.1480–1545), Damaio de Góis* (1502–74), Juan de Vergara* (1492–1557) and Alonso de Fonseca (c.1475–1534). In due course, some of Erasmus' supporters became branded 'illuminists' or *alumbrados*[†] by the inquisition and they were generally regarded as the harbingers of Lutheran heresy. The inquisition kept a close watch on their activities and prosecuted them with increasing vigour from the 1530s onwards.

2.4.4 Christian humanism in German and Swiss lands

The influence of humanism in German lands was also strongly associated with the revival of vernacular culture, history and native traditions. Although the question of the influence of humanist traditions in the development of Luther's own thought remains problematic[3], there is no

---

[3] A. McGrath, *The Intellectual Origins of the European Reformation* (Blackwell, Oxford, 1987), ch. 2.

doubt about its impact on Zwingli*. In both Switzerland and Germany, there were strong humanist currents at work in certain quarters. These included the universities and teachers in the newly-founded grammar (or 'Latin') schools to be found in many German cities. The urban elites (both lay and clerical) found the humanist agenda to contain both ideals and a practical agenda which held its attractions for them. Both were discussed in literary clubs ('sodalities' (*sodalitates*)) which brought them together with the enterprising booksellers and printers whose output of humanist editions supplied both Germany and wider Europe. The Erasmian influence in these areas is well-illustrated in the careers of Jacob Wimpfeling* (1450–1528), Sebastian Brant* (1457–1520) and Jakob Sturm* (Lat: *Sturmius*) (1489–1553) in Strasbourg, Willibald Pirckheimer* (1470–1530) and Lazarus Spengler* (1479–1534) from Nuremberg, the scholar knight Ulrich von Hutten* (1488–1523), the great Hebraist scholars Johannes Reuchlin* (1455–1522) and Konrad Kürsner (Lat: *Conradus Pellicanus*)* (1478–1556), Erasmus' famous printer from Basel, Johann Froben* (c.1460–1527), and the private secretary to Elector Friedrich (the Wise)* of Saxony, Georg Burckhardt (always known by his Latin name: *Georgius Spalatinus*)* (1484–1545).

2.4.5 Christian humanists in the Low Countries

The impact of humanism in the Low Countries was equally strong and the influence of Erasmus inevitably profound. However, its vernacular affiliations were less clear-cut than in France or Germany because of the region's linguistic pluralism. In the Dutch-speaking Netherlands, the impact of the 'devout' of the 'modern devotion'† often overlapped with Christian humanism. Both were evident within the Chambers of Rhetoric (*rederijkerskamers*), which staged plays and acted as debating chambers for entertaining and educating the urban elites to new ideas. The careers of Johannes Sartorius* (1500?–57?) and Juan Luís Vives* (1492?–1540), in addition to that of Erasmus* himself, provide some of the flavour of Dutch humanism.

2.4.6 Eastern Europe

In eastern Europe, the influence of humanism was delayed. It generally occurred at the same time as, and often accompanied, the protestant reformation to the extent that the two movements were coterminous. Both appealed to strong vernacular aspirations which sharpened and focused the initial appeal of the reformation in those lands (see pages 156–7). In Poland, however, the influence of Erasmus was considerable from a relatively early date. Erasmus himself made a famous comment: 'Poland is devoted to me' (*Polonia mea est*). This is reflected in the careers of Jan

Dantyszek* (Lat: *Johannes Dantiscus*) (1485–1548) and Andrzej Krzycki* (Lat: *Andreas Critius*) (1482–1537).

2.5 Advocates of the Apocalypse

Apocalyptic (apocalypse = 'expectancy' of impending final disaster and transformation) thought, was based especially on passages in the biblical books of Daniel and Revelation. It stressed the coming of the end of the world and of time ('eschatology') in a divine drama in which each age was a crisis and the final act was imminent. It was a fundamental part of Christian thinking which had been somewhat overshadowed in the thinking of the medieval scholastic theologians. Although it was not always linked to revolutionary change, it often had those connotations and was regarded with suspicion by those in established authority. It had played a role in the social and political unrest of the fourteenth and fifteenth centuries (especially among the Taborites[†] of Bohemia) and the long memories of those links lasted through to the reformation. For some Christian humanists[†], however, it was a pattern of thought to rediscover and explore afresh in the era before the reformation. Since the millennium would only come when the Jews were finally converted to Christianity, some apocalyptic thought was associated with some Christian humanist philo-Judaism. The potential of apocalyptic thinking in an urban environment and in the right hands is reflected in the career of Girolamo Savonarola* (1452–98) in Florence. The impact of the following apocalyptic text in the course of the protestant reformation has also been stressed:

The '*Reformation of Emperor Sigismund*' (*Reformatio Sigismundi*)
An anonymous text, perhaps the work of a German priest in around 1438, was written around the formula of the coming of an apocalyptic 'Imperator' who would institute a reform of the world order leading to the coming of the millennium. Popes, cardinals and the institutions of the church would be purged. The clerical order would be disbanded. Priests would be allowed to marry and work like the laity. The text was printed and published several times in the years immediately before the reformation and evidently utilized by Luther in his treatises of 1520 (see pages 54–7).

2.6 Mysticism

The word 'mysticism' was not in use in the sixteenth century. It was not until the end of the seventeenth century that the 'mystics' were identified as having a distinct, individual and direct knowledge of God through the discipline of prayer and contemplation and without the mediation of the church. Christian mystical traditions had been largely confined within monasticism until the thirteenth century. Then, perhaps because of an increasingly hierarchical structure within the church, traditions of mysticism grew up outside the monastic orders and the church itself. There were accompanying changes in mystic practices as well. These included a greater emphasis on ecstatic union with God in contemplative trance and a correspondingly lesser emphasis on meditation on the biblical text. The 'freedom of the spirit' which it was supposed to release attracted papal condemnation as early as 1311, but this was far from preventing the tradition from continuing, especially in the Rhineland. Somewhat separate, but enjoying some common ancestries, were the 'modern devotion' traditions of the Brethren and Sisterhood of the Common Life (see pages 24–5). Nevertheless, mysticism remained somewhat on the margins of Christian experience, cultivated by the holy men and women (*beati, beatae*) who periodically became suspect to the institutionalized church for their apparent heterodoxy or for challenging social norms. But such margins existed to be tapped by both the magisterial protestant reformers and by the more radical lineages of the protestant reformation. Amongst the most influential of the medieval mystics whose works were printed by the time of Luther, were Maister Eckhart (c.1260–1327) and Johann Tauler (c.1300–61). The latter's sermons, printed at Leipzig in 1498, were much admired by Luther.

2.6.1 Followers of the 'modern devotion' (devotio moderna)

Jan van Ruysbroeck (1293–1381)
Author of various spiritual works, originally written in Flemish (such as *The Spiritual Espousals, The Kingdom of the Lovers of God* etc). Several were translated into Latin in the fourteenth century and circulated widely in manuscript; they were not printed, however, until 1552.

Thomas van Kempen (à Kempis) (c.1380–1471)
Probably responsible for the *Imitation of Christ* and numerous prayers, homilies and meditations (printed at Nuremberg in 1494).

2.7 Later medieval heresies and heretics

2.7.1 Heretic groups

Hussites
Followers of the reformer Jan Hus (c.1369–1415), the Bohemian reformer and heretic. Hus derived some of his doctrines from John Wyclif[†] and rejected the papacy, putting in its place the authority of the 'Law

of God' (the Holy Scriptures and the agreed doctrines of the universal church). In practice, the Hussites actively promoted the reading of the Bible in the vernacular and the distribution of the communion[†] to the laity 'in both kinds'.

After the condemnation and burning of Hus at the council of Konstanz[†], the Hussite revolution began with a successful uprising in Prague in 1419. However, the Hussites soon split into two groups, the moderate Utraquists (i.e. 'supporters of communion in both kinds') and the Taborites. The former sought to preserve the social order and remain loyal to the Bohemian crown whilst keeping the distinct religious practices of the Hussites. The latter drew on support from the rural populations of Czech-speaking lands and organized them into brotherhoods under lower clerics and nobles in order to await the millennium+ and reject the established order. Eventually the Taborites were defeated by the moderate Hussites in 1434 and, two years later, a peace was arrived at between the council at Basel[†], the Hussites, and Sigismund, the king of Bohemia and Holy Roman Emperor. The peace guaranteed the continued existence of the Hussite communities and their right to distribute the communion[†] in both kinds. It also theoretically guaranteed the rights of Hussites to hold public offices in the Bohemian kingdom. Church wealth which had been alienated during the war remained in secular hands. The settlement was not accepted by the papacy before the protestant reformation but the Hussites relied on the guarantees given them by the emperor and the recognition of Hussitism granted at the council of Basel[†].

The Hussite revolution has sometimes been called 'the first reformation'. It certainly created a separate and independent Utraquist church and an example which was not lost on the protestant reformers a century later. The more radical views of the Taborites survived in an attenuated form amongst the Bohemian Brethren ('Unitas Fratrum') and their millennial fervour was not perhaps entirely forgotten in the German towns where it resurfaced before and during the reformation where the conditions were appropriate.

Waldensians

Followers of the twelfth-century Peter Waldo of Lyon. They preached poverty and the renunciation of the world, appointed their own ministers (known as 'barbes' because of their beards) and became united with the Hussites. On the eve of the reformation, and despite persecution, the Waldenses survived in the rural upland communities of Alpine France and Italy. Their distinctive patterns of belief were retained in oral traditions and proverbial encapsulations of ancient Waldensian wisdom. These were far from being identical to the doctrines of the protestant reformation. However the remaining Waldensian communities, especially in Savoy and Piedmont, were subsumed into the more mainstream protestant movement in a longer process:

Waldensians and the protestant reformation

1523–26 Contacts between Waldensians and protestant preachers.

1530 Synod at Mérindol (Provence) at which disputed points of doctrine were drawn up by the Provençal Waldensians and submitted to Guillaume Farel*, Martin Bucer* and others.

1532 Synod of Chanforan (It: *Cianforan, Val d'Angrogna*). Historians dispute the significance of the synod; it was possibly a series of inconclusive meetings between Waldensian leaders and protestant reformers, one of which may have taken place at Chanfaron.

1532 Waldensians in contact with Bohemian Brethren (Autumn).

1543 Provençal Vaudois fortified themselves at the village of Cabrières in the Luberon against legal efforts to enforce heresy edicts.

1545 Cabrières, Mérindol, Tourves and other Provençal Vaudois strongholds razed by French royal troops (April); inhabitants massacred.

1555 Arrival in Piedmont of first Calvinist ministers from Geneva; establishment of Calvinist-style congregations in the protestant 'Alpine churches'.

Lollards

The name possibly means 'mumblers of prayers'. Initially restricted to the followers of John Wyclif (c.1329–84), the English reformer and philosopher, the term became more generally applied in England to all those who criticized the church. The original Lollards had distinctive teachings on personal faith, the importance of divine election, and, above all, the significance of the Bible. The Scriptures were the sole authority in religion and every man had the right to read and interpret them for himself. The Lollards attacked clerical celibacy, transubstantiation[†], indulgences[†] and pilgrimages in ways which led the protestant martyrologists to claim the Lollards as their spiritual forebears. By the eve of the reformation, Lollardy was not extinct, but it had apparently become restricted, partly due to prosecution, to particular regions, especially those with a component of rural craftsmen or urban artisans.

Bohemian Brethren (*Unitas Fratrum: Brüdergemeinden*)

The communities of the Brethren grew out of the Hussite communities that had adhered to the Taborites. They rejected all connections with the established church and recognized only the Scriptures and the way of Christ and his apostles as the patterns for their faith and practice.

They had their own worshipping congregations which were led by four chosen elders (*seniores*). The elders came together in a council of twelve, with the sovereign authority for the corporate decisions of the Brethren being vested in a synod. The most important of their congregations in Bohemia were at Jungbunzlau (Cz: *Mladá Boleslav*) and Leitomischl (Cz: *Litomyšl*); in Moravia they were at Prerau (Cz: *Přerov*), Eibenschitz (*Ivančice*) near Brno, and Fulnek. They were regarded by the Utraquists as well as the established church as heretics and a Bohemian royal decree of 1508 permitted their persecution; but, despite being illegal, they were protected by the lesser gentry of Bohemia and Moravia and they survived into the era of the protestant reformation.

The Luther affair

3.1 Luther and the reformation

There is a long-standing and natural tendency to simplify the discussion of the immediate causation of the protestant reformation in terms of Luther's own life. This was a tendency which began in his own lifetime and was not restricted to hostile propagandists, keen to present Luther as the embodiment of the evil forces tearing Christendom apart. When, later in life, he came to consider and reflect upon what had happened in the early years of the reformation, Luther's views of his own role were themselves somewhat ambiguous. Some of this ambiguity, however, may be the effect of the *Table Talk*, in which some of his later opinions are recorded. This work was not written by Luther but compiled by his friends and colleagues from Luther's conversations and it should only be used as supporting evidence and in conjunction with other sources. On the one hand, Luther insisted that he had achieved relatively little through his own efforts. The word of God had strangely worked to create the reformation and he had done little. On the other hand, however, he was occasionally tempted to see himself as the vehicle for that strange work. The latter perspective tended to make him interpret his own life within the patterns of momentary divine intervention which inevitably heightened and dramatized the role of Luther within the early reformation in Germany. This was subsequently preserved and enhanced in German Lutheran pietist circles in the seventeenth and eighteenth centuries to become the substance of the heroic biographies in the nineteenth century. So, although the outline of Luther's life is well-known and not in doubt, some of its apparently significant personal moments of dramatic development are unlikely to have been exactly as they have been traditionally presented.

Examples of this tendency towards hagiography in the interpretation of Luther's life are as follows:

The thunderstorm

Luther himself is the source for the story that, a fortnight before Luther entered the monastery at Erfurt in July 1505, he was caught up in a storm. In fright, he made a vow to St Anne that he would become a monk if he was saved from the storm. He told it to friends in July 1539, 34 years later. He glossed the event in the context of the later development of his theology – 'Anna' meaning in Hebrew 'under grace, not by the law'. Whether the events took place in precisely the way that Luther described and with the significance he ascribed to them is impossible to verify.

The 'Tower Experience'

In a fragment of the *Table Talk* dating from 1532, Luther referred to the moment of his theological breakthrough concerning the true meaning of the 'righteousness of God' as having taken place 'in this tower and heated chamber'. This has become known to Luther scholars as the 'Tower Experience' (*Das Turmerlebnis*), and much effort has been expended in trying to find a precise date as to when it occurred. Some Luther scholars have argued that it took place relatively early during Luther's initial years in Wittenberg (in the winter of 1512–13), whilst others have argued for the much later date of 1518–19 on the basis of some autobiographical remarks made by Luther in the preface to the first volume of a collected edition of his works, published in 1545. In both cases, the 'Tower' is assumed to be a room in the castle at Wittenberg. Many scholars now accept, however, that whatever Luther was held by his reporters to have referred to in the *Table Talk* (and one printed version of the conversation in question omits any reference to such a 'Tower'), it is highly unlikely that the complexities of Luther's theological development were resolved in a moment of dramatic illumination. In the autobiographical fragment from 1545, coming directly from Luther, he does, however, recall a period when an emerging clarity over the issue of the righteousness of God began to assert itself in his mind: 'At last ... as I meditated day and night on the connection between the words "the righteousness of God is revealed" ... and "the righteous shall live by faith", I began to understand that [this phrase] "the righteousness of God" refers to that by which the righteous lives by the gift of God, namely by faith; and [I also then understood that] this sentence, "the righteousness of God is revealed" refers to a passive righteousness, by which the merciful God justifies us by faith; as it is written, "the righteous lives by faith". This immediately made me feel as though I had been born again [*renatum*] and as though I had entered through open gates into paradise itself'.[1] This fruitful period of emerging clarity is now generally taken to have occurred in the year 1515.

Nailing the 95 Theses to the door of the cathedral of Wittenberg (31 October 1517)

According to the revised statutes of the theology faculty at Wittenberg (1508), theological disputations were a regular part of university edu-

---

[1] Cited from A. McGrath, *Luther's Theology of the Cross* (Oxford, Blackwell, 1985), p. 97.

cation. They included regular disputations in university term-time and 'occasional disputations' (*disputationes quodlibeticae*) on subjects of the choosing of senior members of the faculty or the church. By posting his theses at the church door (and there has been some scholarly doubt as to whether this was in fact ever carried out), Luther was simply following well-established procedures for the equivalent of posting a lecture timetable on a board. That Luther intended them to be controversial is indicated by the date. The following day (the Feast of All Saints) was important in the calendar of Wittenberg cathedral. It had a significant collection of relics and they were placed on public display on All Saints' Day. The relics had last been displayed on 27 April 1517 and, the day before, the dean of the theology faculty in Wittenberg, Andreas Bodenstein von Karlstadt*, had also posted 151 theses for disputation, also concerned with the question of justification. In some respects, Karlstadt's theses were more radical than Luther's. In both instances, however, there was no resulting public disputation and this is apparently not because of any attempt to suppress the debate proposed. Although both Karlstadt and Luther were doubtless aware of the controversial nature of the propositions they contained, the issues were theologically technical. Luther should certainly not be seen as a lone individual knocking nails into the coffin of the medieval church by posting his theses on 31 October 1517.

It is important, therefore, to distinguish the relatively narrow issues of Luther's own theological development from the broader issues of the theology taught at Wittenberg and the dimensions of the 'Luther affair' which began over the question of indulgences in 1517.

3.2 The faculty of theology at Wittenberg

1502 Foundation of the university of Wittenberg by Friedrich (the Wise)*, Elector of Saxony (to rival the university of Leipzig in neighbouring ducal Saxony). Johannes von Staupitz* became the first dean of the faculty of theology and professor.

1506 Appointment of Christoph Scheurl to the law chair at Wittenberg – he became rector of the university in 1507 and published the *Rotulus doctorum Wittenberge profitentum* (*Register of the Wittenberg professors*) in which he itemized those teaching in Wittenberg, their subjects and hours of lecturing. This characterized the Wittenberg curriculum at that date as teaching in accordance with the *via antiqua* in its Arts Faculty.

1508 Revision of the university statutes undertaken by Scheurl upon instruction from Elector Friedrich. These statutes incorporated the *via moderna* within the curriculum of the Arts Faculty at Wittenberg.

1513   Conferment of a doctorate on Andreas Bodenstein von Karlstadt*
and his appointment to a chair in theology at the university
(Nov). He was initially (1515) opposed to Luther's evolving
Augustinian interpretations but eventually became convinced
(1517 onwards) and a firm defender of Luther within the faculty.

1518   Philipp Melanchthon* delivered his inaugural lecture in the
university (Aug).

Student attendance at the universities of Leipzig and Wittenberg
(1500–60)

Years	Leipzig	Wittenberg
1501–10	1,529	835
1511–20	1,524	964
1521–30	506	629
1531–40	557	957
1541–50	957	1,519
1551–60	868	1,860

Source: From figures in Franz Eulenburg, 'Die Frequenz der
deutschen Universitäten von ihrer Gründung bis zur Gegenwart',
*Abhandlungen der philologisch-historischen-Klasse der königlichen sächsischen
Gesellschaft der Wissenschaften*, 24 (Leipzig, 1904), pp. 55, 102–3.

3.3 Summary of the dates for Luther's career and evidence for his theological development

1501   Matriculated as a student at the university of Erfurt (Summer).

1502   Gained bachelor of arts degree at Erfurt (Sep).

1505   Gained master of arts degree at Erfurt (Jan).

1505   Joined the reformed Augustinian order (Sep).

1507   Ordained to the priesthood (3 April) and took his first mass
(2 May).

1508   Appointed to the Augustinian chair of moral philosophy in
the Faculty of Arts and began to lecture on Aristotle's *Ethics*
(text lost).

1509   Returned to Erfurt and lectured on the *Sentences* of Peter
Lombard (Oct).

1510   Travelled to Rome on Augustinian order business (Nov).

1511   Returned to Erfurt (April).

1511   Transferred to the Augustinian monastery at Wittenberg
(Summer/Autumn).

1512 Doctor of theology degree conferred (19 Oct). Began teaching theology at the university of Wittenberg (22 Oct) – 'When I became a doctor, I did not yet know that we cannot expiate our sins'.

1513 First lecture course on the Psalms (Aug). Evidence for his earlier thinking can be extracted with difficulty from his 'Lectures on the Psalms' (*Dictata super Psalterium*). 'God has made himself a debtor to us through the promise of him who is merciful, not through the dignity of the human nature of him who merits. He required nothing except preparation, in order that we might be capable of receiving this gift, just as if a prince or king of the earth would promise a robber or a murderer one hundred florins, providing that he awaited him at a specified time and place. Thus it is clear that the king would be a debtor through his gratuitous promise and mercy without that man's merit; nor would the king deny what he had promised on account of that man's demerit'.[2] 'Even grace and faith, through which we are justified today, would not justify us of themselves, without God's covenant. It is precisely for this reason, that we are saved: God has made a testament (*testamentum*) and covenant (*pactum*) with us, so that whoever believes and is baptized shall be saved. In this covenant God is truthful and faithful, and is bound by what he has promised'.[3]

1515 Lecture course on St Paul's Letter to the Romans began (Nov). Texts in Luther's hand of these lectures survive. They provide strong evidence for the fact that Luther had developed a sustained objection to fundamental aspects of *via moderna* theology, particularly the notion of the 'justice of God' and the idea that man can save himself by 'doing his best'. 'They know that man cannot do anything from himself (*ex se*). Hence it is totally absurd (and also strongly Pelagian!) to hold the view summed up in the well-known statement: "God infallibly infuses grace in the one who does his best" (*quod in se est*). . . . Hence it is not a matter for surprise that practically the whole church is subverted on account of the confidence that this statement expresses'.[4] In its place, Luther began to develop a distinctive notion of how God clothes the sinner with the alien righteousness of Christ – using images of Boaz covering

[2] D.M. *Luthers Werke. Kritische Gesamtausgabe* (Weimar, 1883), 4, 261 (32–9) – henceforth 'WA'.
[3] WA, 3, 289 (1–5).
[4] WA, 56, 502–3 (32/–5).

Ruth with his cloak, or a mother hen covering her chicks with her wing.

1516   Lecture course on St Paul's Letter to the Galatians began (Oct). Evidence for these lectures survives only in the form of two students' notes. Luther later published his commentary on Galatians in 1519 but, although it is based on his lectures, they were apparently substantially revised before publication.

1517   Lecture course on St Paul's Letter to the Hebrews began (Easter). The 95 Theses (31 Oct) see page 49.

1518   Presided over the opening disputation at the chapter of the Augustinian order in Heidelberg. Luther had drawn up a series of disputations for discussion there at the invitation of Johannes von Staupitz*. These theses (which have survived) reveal the beginnings of a mature Lutheran 'theology of the cross', in which God reveals himself to man through the passion and cross of Christ. This revelation destroys any illusion of the capacity of human reason to discern God in any other way but through faith.

1518–21   Second lecture course on the Psalms, the text for which survives in the Operationes in Psalmos. 'CRUX sola est nostra theologia!' he declared in the course of this work, composed in the shadow of the growing atmosphere of tension after the Leipzig disputation. Luther refers to the sense of helplessness and despair experienced as one follows the way of the cross. In comparison with the earlier lecture course, it is evident that Luther had a much better knowledge of Hebrew and a very different theological approach.

3.4 The indulgences dispute (1514–18)

1514   Albrecht von Brandenburg* elected cardinal-archbishop of Mainz (9 March).

1515   Pope Leo X* issued Albrecht with a bull (31 March) giving him authority to offer the indulgence (the proceeds of which would rebuild the basilica of St Peter's in Rome).

1517
22 Jan   The Dominican Johann Tetzel* entered the service of Albrecht as the agent for the indulgence in the province of Magdeburg.

24 Feb   Luther criticized indulgences in a sermon.

April   Tetzel in Jüterbog on the borders with electoral Saxony.

4 Sep   Luther published his Disputation against Scholastic Theology.

31 Oct   Luther invited a debate over indulgences in his 95 Theses
and wrote to Cardinal-Archbishop Albrecht about the false
notions which were being spread abroad about the benefits
to be gained from purchasing an indulgence. He enclosed
a copy of his theses. In these, Luther challenged the claims
of indulgence preachers, asserted his views about true penance, and implicitly questioned the authority of the pope.

He queried the claims of indulgence preachers to be
able to remit sins (Theses 5–6). He questioned the application of indulgences to remit individuals from purgatory
(Theses 8, 20). God alone had the power to release souls
from the burden of sin (Theses 27–8). Those who steered
clear of the licence and extravagant claims of indulgence
preachers were blessed (Theses 72, 75, 77, 79). Those who
permitted such foolishness should be answerable for it
(Thesis 80).

Inner repentance was a continuous and unremitting process (Theses 1–4). True contrition sought further punishment; indulgences tried to encourage individuals to avoid
it (Theses 39–40). Every Christian could gain repentance
without letters of indulgence (Theses 36–7). The gospel
and grace of God were the true treasure-house of the church
(Theses 53–5, 62). Christians should be taught to follow
Christ and his suffering (Theses 94–5).

The pope could only grant indulgences for those penalties imposed according to the laws of the church (Theses
5, 20). The pope should be prepared to see St Peter's sold
rather than build a temple on the flesh and bones of his
flock (Theses 50, 57). He should criticize those who, under
the pretext of indulgences devalued holy love and truth
(Theses 73–4). By failing to criticize them, the pope was
making it difficult for learned men to defend him from the
slander of the laity (Thesis 81). The pope should pay for
the rebuilding of St Peter's himself, rather than expose the
church to the ridicule of its enemies (Theses 86, 90).

Nov   Publication of the 95 Theses without Luther's involvement
or consent; the publication was a success and generated
widespread popular comment.

13 Dec   Albrecht reported that he had forwarded a copy of the 95
Theses to Rome with an accompanying denunciation of
Luther.

1518

Jan   Tetzel* replied by defending 106 theses (prepared by
Conrad Wimpina, professor of theology at the university of

	Frankfurt an der Oder) at a meeting of the Dominican order of Saxony.
Feb	Luther announced that he would publish a further explanation of his theses.
Mid-March	Wittenberg students burned copies of the Tetzel/Wimpina theses. Luther preached and published his *Sermon on Indulgence and Grace.*
24 March	Luther reported seeing a copy of Johann Eck's attack on him in the treatise *Obelisci* ('Obelisks') in which Luther's theses were described as 'false', 'impudent' and 'Bohemian poison' (i.e. full of the heresy of Jan Hus†). Luther responded shortly afterwards with his own *Asterisci* ('Asterisks').
April	Tetzel published his extensive *Rebuttal of a Presumptuous Sermon Containing Twenty Erroneous Articles on Papal Indulgences.* . . .
9 April– 15 May	Luther attended a chapter meeting of the Augustinian order in Heidelberg and defended his theological stance; Tetzel issued a further set of 50 theses praising (and defending) papal authority.
May	Karlstadt* issued 380 theses against Tetzel* and Eck* without Luther's prior knowledge. These defended the position that the judgment of an individual Christian in matters of faith (when based on Scripture) should, if necessary, take precedence over all other forms of authority – a more extreme position than Luther himself was yet prepared to assume.
30 May	Luther dedicated his *Explanations of the Ninety-Five Theses* to Pope Leo X* (published in August). He amplified his views of papal authority, distinguishing between the person of pope and the office of the papacy. Individual popes were men who could err in matters of faith and morals. Only a universal council of the church could declare a new article of faith. Accepted articles of faith were to be established on the basis of a consensus of authority established between Holy Scripture, the church fathers, and the canons and decrees of the papacy. He hoped for a just verdict from Pope Leo, whom (unlike some of his advisors and flatterers) he admired and respected. Luther also wrote a letter to Johannes von Staupitz*, vicar-general of the reformed Augustinian order of Germany, asking him to present the case favourably and continue his support for him.
June	Luther published his *A Defence of the Sermon Concerning Indulgence and Grace.*

3.5 Broadening conflict (1518–19)

1518

26 April
: The Dominican Thomas de Vio (Cardinal Cajetan)* nominated papal legate to the imperial diet[†] at Augsburg.

c.May
: At the order of Pope Leo*, the summons of Luther to Rome was prepared by the legal officer of the papal curia, Jerome Ghinucci; a theological response to Luther was commissioned from the official papal theologian, Sylvester Prierias (Sylvester Mazzolini), entitled *Dialogue Concerning Papal Power against the presumptuous positions of Martin Luther.* The response concentrated on four premises relating to church power and infallibility as the basis on which to reject substantial elements of Luther's 95 Theses.

c.June
: Luther preached his sermon *On the Power of Excommunication* (published at the end of August).

July
: The summons to Rome and Prierias' *Dialogue* were forwarded to Cajetan in Augsburg to be sent on to Luther in Wittenberg. Luther responded by asking for advice from Georgius Spalatinus*, the private secretary of Friedrich the Wise*.

5 Aug
: Emperor Maximilian denounced Luther as a heretic in a letter composed by Cajetan. He offered to enforce ecclesiastical sanctions against Luther.

8 Aug
: Luther petitioned Elector Friedrich (attending the diet of Augsburg) to see that his case was heard in Germany, rather than in Rome.

23 Aug
: Pope Leo directed Cajetan (in the papal letter *Postquam ad aures*) to demand a recantation from Luther and to arrange for his arrest and deliverance to Rome if he refused.

End Aug
: Luther issued a *Response* to Prierias' *Dialogue* which reinforced his position on authority in the church.

Sep
: Elector Friedrich persuaded Cajetan to treat Luther in a gentle fashion and not to arrest him. Friedrich departed Augsburg on 22 September and Luther left Wittenberg for his meeting with Cajetan on 26 September.

12–20 Oct
: Luther in Augsburg. According to Luther's brief account, Cajetan received him 'with kindness'. Although specifically enjoined not to enter into debate with Luther, Cajetan responded to Luther's request to be shown specifically where he was in error. He cited Thesis 58 (and presented it as in contradiction to a papal decree) and Thesis 7 (where Luther had asserted that the person about to receive the sacrament of penance should trust with certainty in the

words of absolution), arguing that anyone about to receive the sacrament remained uncertain of obtaining grace. Luther replied to the former by saying that the papal decree was against 'the unanimous opinion of the whole church' – i.e. the consensus of authorities in the church. On the latter point, Luther replied with a summary of his understanding of how faith alone works to justify human kind: 'No disposition [on any individual's behalf] can make them worthy, no work can make them fit for the sacrament, but only faith. For only faith in the word of Christ justifies, makes alive, makes one worthy and prepares one. Anything else is an exercise in presumption or despair'.[5] Cajetan accepted a written statement from Luther, who placed a legally-registered document on the cathedral door in Augsburg before he left, resubmitting his case to Pope Leo, 'a badly-informed pope who needs to be better informed'.

23 Oct   Returning through Nuremberg, Luther was shown a copy of the papal brief to Cajetan (*Postquam ad aures*) which, along with the effect of the encounter at Augsburg, made him more pessimistic about papal intentions. By the end of December, Luther began to voice his fears that the Antichrist[†] might be at work amidst the Roman hierarchy.

25 Oct   Cajetan issued a demand to Elector Friedrich the Wise to hand Luther over to Rome or to banish him from his territories.

9 Nov   Pope Leo issued the bull[†] *Cum postquam*, drafted by Cajetan, which reinforced catholic teaching on indulgences[†].

Nov   Friedrich the Wise forwarded the ultimatum of Cajetan to Luther for comments; Luther prepared an account of the meeting with Cajetan for publication (the *Acta Augustana*) and appealed to a legitimately convened universal council of the church.

Early Dec   Although Luther expected the worst, Friedrich the Wise refused Cajetan's ultimatum and declined to banish Luther from Saxony.

1519

Dec–Jan   Attempted mediation between the papacy and Elector Friedrich the Wise by Karl von Miltitz (c.1490–1529), a Saxon nobleman and papal chamberlain.

Jan   Emperor Maximilian I died; the papacy suspended further attempts to enforce the summons against Luther.

[5] WA, 2, 14 (5–8).

March	Johann Eck* issued a set of 13 Theses, revising those which he had issued against Karlstadt* six months previously and challenging Luther to a disputation at Leipzig.
May	Luther responded with a set of 13 counter-propositions, the last of which (Prop.13) was expounded in published form before the Leipzig disputation. In it Luther maintained the view that only 'the most intemperate decrees of the Roman pontiffs issued these last 400 years prove that the Roman church is superior to all other; against these stand the accepted history of the last 1,500 years, the text of divine scripture and the decree of the council of Nicea, the holiest of all councils'.[6] He stopped short of rejecting all papal authority but drew on his intensive recent study of canon law to reject the claim that the bishop of Rome was head of the church by divine right. Luther displayed a remarkable resilience, despite the continuing tension; '. . . I fear neither the pope nor the name of the pope, much less those little popes and puppets'.
24 June	Karlstadt, Luther and the Wittenberg delegates arrived in Leipzig for the disputation.
27 June	Debate between Luther and Karlstadt began.
28 June	Charles V elected Holy Roman Emperor in Frankfurt. The papacy continued to suspend further efforts to enforce the summons against Luther until the end of the year.
4–14 July	Debate between Eck and Luther. Eck revived the familiar accusation that Luther was a new Hus (and Wyclif). Luther replied by affirming that some of the articles of belief of Hus and the Bohemians were 'most Christian and evangelical' and could not be condemned. This enabled Eck to challenge Luther to say whether a council of the church (such as the council of Konstanz[†] (1414–18) which had condemned them both) could also err. Luther was forced to admit that he regarded Scripture as the norm by which other authorities within the church should be judged.
July/Aug	Accounts of the debate were published both by Melanchthon* (on behalf of Luther and Karlstadt) and by Eck himself. Eck declared Luther a heretic and invited the universities of Paris and Erfurt to judge the matter in his favour. Eck wrote 17 treatises against Luther over the next few months to publicize the dangers Luther represented.
30 Aug	Luther condemned by the university of Cologne.

[6] WA, 2, 161 (35–8).

Early Oct   Luther received a copy of Jan Hus' treatise on *The Church* from Prague. He declared that he found himself in agreement with Hus over a wider area than he had declared at Leipzig. 'Up to now I have unwittingly taught and held all the beliefs of Jan Hus. Johann Staupitz has equally taught them without being aware of it. In short, we are all Hussites without knowing it. Even Paul and Augustine are in reality Hussites'.[7]

Oct   Luther's sermon *On the Sacrament of Penance*[†] – the first of three important statements of the impact of his thinking for the sacraments of the church.

7 Nov   Luther condemned by the university of Louvain.

9 Nov   Luther's sermon *On the Sacrament of Baptism.*

Dec   Luther's sermon *On the Blessed Sacrament of the Holy and True Body of Christ* – banned in ducal Saxony when it was published. The effects of the widening controversy were felt by Luther to be at once alarming and energizing; in January of the following year he wrote 'This tribulation does not frighten me at all, but it fills the sails of my heart with an incredible wind … We are completely unaccustomed to the Christian life. Therefore, let it be. The more powerfully they rise up, the more securely I laugh at them. I am resolved to fear nothing …'.[8]

3.6 Luther's excommunication (1520–21)

1520

9 Jan   The case against Luther reopened at Rome.
Expanded German version of Luther's sermon *On the Power of Excommunication*[†] published early 1520 – including warnings about the 'tyrants' who 'today' unjustly make use of the power of excommunication – Luther's willingness to write in German and reach a different lay audience became noticeable in 1520.

1 Feb   Pope Leo* appointed the first commission to investigate Luther's writings and prepare the case against him.

11 Feb   Appointment of second commission to investigate Luther's writings.

Feb   Luther read an edition of Lorenzo Valla's *Donation of Constantine*, which demonstrated that a key document in

---

[7] Letter to Spalatin, c.14 Feb 1520 (*D.M. Luthers Werke. Kritische Gesamtausgabe: Briefwechsel* – henceforth WABr), 2, 42 (22–6).

[8] WABr, 1, 611 (57–61) (14 January 1520).

the papal claims to temporal power was a forgery. Valla was a noted Italian fifteenth-century humanist whose philology (i.e. his textual criticism) had much impressed Erasmus. 'I am so tormented, I can hardly doubt that the pope is properly that Antichrist which by common consent the world anticipates . . .'.[9]

March   Eck* arrived in Rome and played a prominent part in the drafting of the papal bull[†] of excommunication[†].

26 March   Luther responded to the condemnations of errors in his works issued by the universities of Louvain and Cologne.

April   Appointment of a third commission (including Eck) in Rome to prepare the text of a bull against Luther.

May–June   Luther published his *Treatise on Good Works* in German. As against all the worthless good works of satisfaction and ceremonies, Luther argued that the genuine good works were the commandments of God which can only be observed when the greatest travail of all (faith) is at work. The text was intended for ordinary laymen and was dedicated to the brother of Elector Friedrich*, Duke John of Saxony: 'Would to God that . . . I had brought about the conversion of one lay person'.

May   Luther published his short manuals of evangelical faith for the laity in German: *A Short Form of the Ten Commandments, A Short Form of the Creed,* and *A Short Form of the Lord's Prayer.* The first provided a succinct evocation of our human sinfulness. The second showed where the remedy was to be found. The third showed how to obtain it. The works went through numerous editions in 1520 alone and formed the basis for Lutheran liturgical developments later on.

20 May   Roman curia[†] sent an ultimatum to Elector Friedrich the Wise.

June   Luther published a treatise in German, entitled *The Papacy at Rome.* It further publicized his attack on the claim of the papacy to be the head of the church by divine right.

15 June   The papal bull against Luther (*Exsurge Domine*) was promulgated. It threatened him with excommunication[†] if he did not recant and seek pardon within 60 days of its publication in Saxony. The church must 'rise up' to protect the vineyard of the Lord from the 'wild boar' which had invaded it. Two days later, Eck (promoted to papal nuncio[†]) and Aleandro Girolamo were appointed to see to its distribution in Germany.

[9] WABr, 2, 48–9 (20/–2).

18 Aug   Luther's *Address to the Christian Nobility* appeared. Luther's most popular treatise in 1520. He wrote it at the behest of the legal officers of the Elector and dedicated it to one of them, a close colleague and supporter Nikolaus von Amsdorf. The citadel of ecclesiastical reformation was protected by three walls behind which the 'Romanists' and 'papists' had protected themselves. When they were attacked with force, they claimed that spiritual power had precedence over the secular arm. When scripture was used against them, they said that only the pope could interpret scripture. When they were threatened with a council, they claimed that only the pope could summon a council. If the 'papists' did not surrender these outer defences, they were the agents of Antichrist. A radical reformation was necessary, beginning with the worldly pretensions of the pope. The pope should not be the representative of the glorified Christ but of the crucified Christ, weeping and praying daily for the toils of Christendom. The practice of indulgences[†], which deceived and exploited poor, simple people, proved that the pope was the Antichrist. 'Hear this, pope, not most holy, but most sinful: God will destroy your see straight from heaven and plunge it into the depths of hell'.[10]

Sep   The papal bull published by Eck in Meissen and Brandenburg; Aleander published it in Cologne and Antwerp. The 60-day 'period of grace' given to Luther in the bull began. Luther's supporters published it in Saxony as a way of gaining support for Luther.

Aug–Sep   Luther wrote his treatise *A Prelude on the Babylonian Captivity of the Church*. The church was subjected to the tyranny of the 'papists' and needed to be liberated. The papacy was the equivalent of the kingdom of Babylon. The entire sacramental fabric of the church was the instrument of its tyranny and its tyrants insisted that they were above criticism. 'Although they are wolves, they wish to be regarded as shepherds; although they are Antichrists, they wish to be honoured as Christ. For this liberty and awareness alone I cry out'.[11] The treatise ended with a defiant ultimatum; 'Because few know this glory of baptism and joy of Christian liberty (nor can they know it owing to the tyranny of the pope), I hear and now liberate myself and

---

[10] WA, 6, 453 (12–14).
[11] WA, 6, 537 (5–12).

redeem my conscience, and I charge the pope and all papists that, unless they lift their own laws and traditions and restore to the churches of Christ the liberty which is theirs and see that this liberty is taught, they are guilty of all the souls which perish in this miserable captivity and the papacy is indeed nothing but the kingdom of Babylon and the true Antichrist'.[12]

Oct	Bull received in Wittenberg; Elector Friedrich the Wise and Emperor Charles V conferred in Cologne cathedral.
Nov	Friedrich met the papal nuncios at Cologne and refused to surrender Luther.
	Luther's treatise on *The Freedom of a Christian* appeared in German and Luther appealed for the summoning of a general council of the church.
10 Dec	Luther burnt the bull *Exsurge Domine* and other works in Wittenberg.
27 Dec	Luther published his treatise on *Why the Books of the Pope and His Disciples Were Burned* – in effect a 'counter-bull' in which Luther selected 30 texts from canon law[†] ('the pope's own books') as damnable.

1521

23 Jan	Luther's excommunication[†] formally pronounced in Rome in the bull[†] *Decet Romanum Pontificem*.
27 Jan	Opening session of the imperial diet at Worms.
Feb	Artist Lucas Cranach* prepared the woodcuts for his *Passional of Christ and the Antichrist*, a sequence of 13 twin images, illustrating the contrast between Christ and the pope and based on Luther's *Why the Books of the Pope and His Disciples Were Burned*.
6 March	Luther was summoned to appear at Worms by Emperor Charles V.
15 April	The theological faculty of the university of Paris (the Sorbonne) condemned the writings of Luther.
16 April	Luther arrived in Worms.
17–18 April	Luther appeared before the diet and presented a speech.
24–25 April	Negotiations between Luther and representatives of the diet.
26 April	Luther left Worms.
4 May	Luther was 'kidnapped' by agents of Elector Friedrich the Wise and taken to the Wartburg Castle (near Eisenach), where he remained until 1 March 1522.

[12] WA, 6, 537 (22–7).

8 May	Emperor Charles V placed Luther under the ban of the Empire.
26 May	Emperor Charles V published the edict of Worms against Luther.
29 Sep	Luther's supporters in the Augustinian cloister at Wittenberg decided to discontinue the traditional celebration of the mass and Luther reinforced their decision with a treatise on *The Misuse of the Mass* which he dedicated to them (published in November). '. . . how difficult it is to call back a conscience dulled by long acquaintance with impiety to the wholesome knowledge of piety'.[13]
Nov	Luther's treatise *On Monastic Vows* dedicated to his father.
1 Dec	Pope Leo died in Rome.
25 Dec	Karlstadt celebrated an 'evangelical'† eucharist† in place of the mass in Wittenberg cathedral against the express wish of Elector Friedrich* the Wise.

[13] WA, 8. 411-12 (27/-10).

The implantation of the reformation in Germany, Scandinavian lands and the Swiss cantons

4.1 The Holy Roman Empire

4.1.1 Rulers

Habsburg dynasty	Regnal dates
Maximilian I (1459–1519)	1493–1519
Charles V (1500–58)	1519–58
Ferdinand I (1503–64)	1558–64
Maximilian II (1527–76)	1564–76
Rudolf II (1552–1612)	1576–1612
Matthias (1557–1619)	1612–19

4.1.2 Constitution

The constitution of the Holy Roman Empire was very complex. In essence an elective monarchy, candidates to the imperial throne were elected by the seven electors to the Empire. In the early sixteenth century, these were the margrave of Brandenburg, the count palatine, the archbishops of Cologne, Mainz and Trier and the king of Bohemia (of the Romans). The electors were in a position to extract a 'capitulation' from candidates for election – promises which the emperor was obliged to fulfil. Capitulations extracted from emperors from Charles V onwards tended to ensure the survival of protestantism within the Empire.

The diets (*Reichstage*) or meetings of the German estates were called by the emperor (with the electors' permission) every three years. They consisted of three colleges (*curiae*) known as the imperial estates (*Reichsstände*). The first college consisted of the electors. The second was composed of the princes, although this also included the prelates and smaller counts. The third (only recognized as coequal with the other two in 1489) consisted of representatives of the free imperial cities (*Frei- und Reichsstädte*) who sat in two 'blocs' as the Rhenish and the Swabian cities.

Following the opening of a diet, the imperial proposition was read out and this constituted the agenda for the estates. The estates met separately and, if they agreed on a recommendation, it was transmitted to the emperor by the chancellor. When the diet was completed, its conclusions (and the emperor's consent to them) were published as a 'recess' (*Abschied*). Each recess applied to the Empire as a whole and constituted an act of imperial legislation. The degree to which the conclusions of a diet were binding upon absentees, or even upon those who had expressed minority opinions on particular subjects was, however, a subject for debate. This provided a framework for legitimate opposition to the emperor by protestant princes and cities.

Although the causes and chronology of the development are unclear, Roman law gradually became more predominant in the affairs of the Empire in the course of the sixteenth century. It received considerable impetus in the legislation which created the Imperial Cameral Court (the *Reichskammergericht*) in 1495. This was one of the few permanent administrative instruments of the Empire.

4.1.3 Imperial chronology

1521   Diet of Worms (Jan–May).

1522–23   Diet of Nuremberg (Nov 1522–Feb 1523). The estates were dominated by proposed legislation to regulate the Empire's economic life and institutions. Negotiations with the nuncio Francesco Chieregato, who sought the enforcement of the decision against Luther at the diet[†] of Worms, were met by counter-demands from the estates for a 'free Christian Council'. The recess[†] of 9 Feb confirmed this demand.

1522–23   The 'Knights' War'. The free imperial knights, part of the independent estates of the Empire, had already proved a disruptive (even bandit) element to the peace of the Empire in the 1510s. Led by Franz von Sickingen (1481–1523), an able mercenary captain, they formed a 'fraternal association' in Franconia and the Rhineland, and mobilized forces against the bishops of Bamberg and Würzburg. They were particularly provoked by a law, part of the recess of the diet of Worms, which made it criminal for a nobleman to enter into a feud with another member of the Empire. The revolt certainly exploited elements of the instability caused by the religious crisis and von Sickingen was supported by the humanist noble Ulrich von Hutten*. It did not take much effort, however, for the princely armies of the Swabian League to repress the revolt, razing the castles of those who had taken part.

1524–25   Great Peasants' War (see pages 75–81).

1526   Diet of Speyer (June–Aug). It took place in the shadow of the creation of the defensive league at Torgau and the recent defeat of the Peasants' War. The emperor proposed to eradicate heresy and rebellion and enforce the edict of Worms against Luther. The princes feared for their privileges and, by the recess of 27 Aug, the diet declared that each estate was to deal with religious problems on a territorial basis until the meeting of a general council or national assembly.

1529   (Second) diet of Speyer (March–April). Catholics predominated amongst the estates. The imperial proposition demanded the revocation of the previous Speyer recess and the enforcement of the edict of Worms wherever possible. A majority of the estates agreed and banned any further religious novelties. The recess of 22 April banned the introduction of Zwinglianism[†] in the Empire and condemned to death anyone convicted of adult baptism[†]. In territories where Luther's teaching had made inroads, the celebration of the mass[†] was to continue. This was declared unacceptable by a minority of estates who produced a minority decision.

1529   The publication (19 July) of the minority decision or protest (hence the term 'protestants'), signed by a small number of princes and 14 cities of the Empire. It declared that a decision of a majority could not annul a unanimous decision (the recess of Speyer of 1526) and that decisions of conscience in religious matters were between an individual and God. The 'evangelical'[†] estates of southern German cities, where Zwinglianism had gained adherents, found it impossible to join the protest (see Colloquy of Marburg, on page 232).

1530   Diet of Augsburg (April–Sep). The diet was held in the presence of Emperor Charles whose propositions announced his intention to abolish religious diversity in the Empire whilst guaranteeing everyone a fair hearing. His chancellor asked for written statements on the religious question. The protestants responded with the Articles of Torgau, which dealt mainly with questions of ecclesiastical organization. Philipp Melanchthon*, however, who attended the diet, decided to include a statement of doctrine amongst the documentation. On 11 May, he sent it to Luther for his endorsement. It was presented under the signature of seven princes and two cities to the estates on 25 June and became known as the 'Confession of Augsburg' (see page 247). A further confession, known as the 'Tetrapolitana', and composed by Wolfgang Capito* and Martin Bucer* was also submitted (see page 248). Both statements were rejected by the assembled catholic theologians (in the *Confutatio*, or 'Refutation' of the Augsburg Confession). The recess of the diet of Augsburg (22 Sep) required the enforcement of the edict of Worms throughout the Empire, the suppression of all heretical innovations and the compliance of protestants to these terms by 15 April 1531. Failure to comply would result in the use of force and prosecution before the Imperial Cameral Court[†].

1531   Emergence of the Schmalkaldic League of protestant estates of the Empire (Feb). In response to the recess of the diet of Augsburg, Landgrave Philipp of Hesse and Elector Johann of Saxony, the leaders of the protestant princes in the Empire, convened a meeting at the town of Schmalkalden (Thuringia) in December 1530. The original members of the League included seven north German princes and the cities of Bremen and Magdeburg. The League later saw many new adherents and, in the end, only the city of Nuremberg and the principality of Brandenburg-Ansbach amongst the protestant territorial entities of the Empire stood aloof from it. By its charter, any attack on one member was an attack on all and should be resisted by the full force of the League. Each member was assessed in order to provide a substantial military force of 10,000 infantry and 2,000 cavalry. The League adopted the Augsburg Confession as its religious statement and attempted to frustrate efforts to use the Imperial Cameral Court against it. It remained the major protestant confessional bloc in the Empire until the outbreak of the Schmalkaldic War in 1546.

1532   'Peace' of Nuremberg offered by Emperor Charles to the princes of the Schmalkaldic League. Cases due to be heard by the Imperial Cameral Court were rescinded. No action would be taken against protestant princes by the Emperor until a meeting of a general church council.

1540–41   Colloquy of Hagenau (1540); Worms (1540–41); Regensburg (1541) (see pages 245–6).

1546–47   The Schmalkaldic War, in which Emperor Charles secured the alliance of the duke of Bavaria and the protestant Duke Mauritz of Saxony, promising him the electoral title. Although the protestant League had superior numbers of troops, they had difficulties in coordinating and paying them. When Duke Mauritz invaded Electoral Saxony, the Elector retreated to defend his territories, splitting the protestant forces.

1547   Elector Johann Friedrich of Saxony captured and defeated (24 April). His title and much of his territory passed to Mauritz of Saxony by the Wittenberg capitulation of the following month. Philipp of Hesse also surrendered, leaving only Magdeburg and some other northern cities prepared to continue resistance.

1547–48   The so-called 'armed diet' of Augsburg. Emperor Charles' reform of the Empire resisted as an infringement of its constitution.

1548   The 'Augsburg Interim' decreed by the emperor at the close of the diet of Augsburg (15 May). It was designed as an interim compromise settlement of religious questions, imposed by the emperor, which would stand until the conclusions of the church council convened at Trent[†]. The compromise concentrated on practical matters of religious worship and ritual, rather than on doctrine. Concessions were made to protestants over married priests and communion[†] in both kinds to the laity. Images[†] were to be retained but not venerated. Feast days[†] in the church calendar were retained. A clause on confession[†] suggested some acceptance of justification[†] theology. The Interim made no mention of ecclesiastical properties.

1548–51   Various protestant elements, led by the city of Magdeburg, rejected the Interim. Some protestant pastors chose to resign their posts rather than operate under the compromise which it required of them. The pastors of the city of Magdeburg began a propaganda campaign against the Interim and refused to accept it within the walls of the city. This resulted in a prolonged siege and the Magdeburg Confession (see page 239).

1552   Second Schmalkaldic War in which the protestant princes, led by Duke Mauritz of Saxony and enjoying the support of Henri II of France, resisted the emperor. Invasion of the three bishoprics of Metz, Toul and Verdun by French forces led to military stalemate.

1555   Peace of Augsburg.

The terms of the religious peace of Augsburg recognized both catholicism and Lutheranism as legitimate religions in the Empire, extending legal recognition to those who accepted the Augsburg Confession of 1530 and guaranteeing them the right to exercise their religion. The peace incorporated the decisions in the recess of the diet of Augsburg, meeting from February to September 1555. It was largely the achievement of Ferdinand, Charles V's brother, who had supervised the diet, and the princes. The electors and many of the imperial cities had refused to attend the diet.

The peace of Augsburg also provided that, in the secular territories of princes and imperial knights, the ruler had the right to determine the religion of his subjects. This was subsequently known as the principle of *cuius regio, eius religio*. The princes insisted, however, that the imperial cities which had adopted Lutheransim had to allow minority catholics the rights to worship in the catholic institutions reopened by the 1548 Interim[†]. Other protestant confessions, by implication, were officially banned from the Empire. Special clauses applied to the ecclesiastical estates of the Empire. Those 'secularized'[†] before the peace of Passau of August 1552 were to remain Lutheran. Spiritual princes who became protestant in future would automatically forfeit their lands, titles and privileges. This was known as the 'ecclesiastical reservation' (*reservatio ecclesiastica*). Its effects were partially offset by a secret declaration of Ferdinand (*declaratio Ferdinandea*) to protestant estates in ecclesiastical principalities that they would, in practice, not be molested during any future changes. The peace of Augsburg made a virtue of limited religious pluralism and provided some stability in the Empire for the rest of the century.

1576   Invasion of the principality of Fulda by the bishop of Würzburg to prevent its Lutheran secularization (June).

1583   Deposition of the archbishop of Cologne by the papacy to enforce the reservation and prevent its possible secularization (March).

1585   Problems with potential secularization of the bishoprics of Paderborn and Osnabrück.

1592–1609   Contested regency and succession in the Rhine duchy of Jülich-Cleves between protestant and catholic claimants on the death of Duke Wilhelm (in 1592). His only surviving son (Johann Wilhelm) was mentally unstable. His (catholic) wife (and her successor) acted as regent with support from catholic princes in Germany. When he too died (1609) there was a serious international incident over the possible succession of the duchy to either of his protestant sisters (who belonged to the houses of Brandenburg and Neuburg respectively).

1598   Disputed recatholicization of the imperial city of Aachen.

1607   Recatholicization (with military intervention from Bavaria) of the imperial city of Donauwörth.

4.2 Reformation and reaction in selected German principalities

4.2.1 Saxony

Institutional background

It was inevitable that the reformation in Saxony would have its own particular dynamic and provide both a pattern for others to follow and a lesson in the paths to avoid. Saxony had been divided in 1485 for dynastic reasons into two separate entities, Ernestine (or 'Electoral') Saxony and Albertine (or 'Ducal') Saxony (see map on page 366). Ernestine Saxony did not have a regular meeting of estates and its prince took decisions on the basis of the advice he received from his personal council and advisors. The cautious Friedrich allowed considerable latitude for evangelism. It was left to his successor to establish a framework for reformation throughout the electoral domains. Following a military invasion, Albertine Saxony assumed the electoral dignity and confined the Ernestine line to ruling a small part of Thuringia.

Rulers
(the Wettin dynasty)

Ernestine Saxony	Regnal dates
Friedrich ('the Wise')	1486–1525
Johann ('the Constant')	1525–32
Johann Friedrich	1532–54

Albertine Saxony	
Georg ('the Bearded')	1500–39
Heinrich	1539–41
Mauritz (later elector)	1541–53
....	
Augustus (elector)	1553–86
Christian	1586–91
Christian II	1591–1611
Johann-Georg I	1611–56

Chronology for the Lutheran reformation in Saxony

1521	Karlstadt* and Gabriel Zwilling* celebrated an 'evangelical'[†] communion[†] service (i.e. a revised and simplified mass[†] with communion in both kinds to the laity) in Wittenberg (25 Dec).
1522	
19 Jan	Karlstadt married.
Jan–Feb	Reform at the Augustinian monastery in Wittenberg turned to riot and iconoclasm[†]. This was encouraged by the arrival in Wittenberg of the 'Zwickau Prophets'[†].
25 Jan	The Wittenberg town council adopted a new order for the church. This established a common chest for the poor, banned begging and prostitution, and laid down rules for church worship. The ordinances were based on proposals from Karlstadt.
6 March	Luther returned to Wittenberg.

9 March	Luther preached eight sermons on consecutive days in the first week of Lent against the 'loveless liberty' which had led Wittenberg to impose a new order without allowing God to undertake his strange work of love upon individuals. The new order had sought to impose changes in areas (such as the destruction of images†) where there was no need for coercion or immediate and hasty change. Individuals should not be forced to handle the bread and the wine, or forced to abandon fasting or do away with private confession†. The latter, indeed, had great potential value if used rightly. Reformation should not be undertaken until the gospel was thoroughly preached and followed in the city. The time was not yet ripe for wholesale reformation.
April	Luther met the 'Zwickau Prophets' and dismissed their prophetic powers as the work of the devil.
April/May	Luther published his treatise *Receiving Both Kinds in the Sacrament*, containing advice on how to approach religious reform via this specific example. 'Formerly the devil made us too papistic, and now he wants to make us too evangelical'. Luther undertook a preaching mission to the towns of Altenburg and Zwickau.
20 Sep	Luther completed his German translation of the New Testament (see page 259).
1523	
April	After a week spent in the Autumn in the small town of Leisnig, its congregation decided to elect an evangelical pastor. The town council asked Luther for advice on the disposition of church property and other ecclesiastical foundations in the new order as well as for guidelines on worship. Luther responded with the *Ordinance of a Common Chest*, Luther's first advice on the establishment of an evangelical church organization. Those in monasteries should be given freedom to remain or take up another occupation. The buildings should be turned into schools or put to communal use. Bishops and abbots should also be prepared to surrender their temporalities for the common good. Luther was particularly concerned to see that ecclesiastical goods were not appropriated into private hands. Luther assigned the right to elect a pastor to the congregation itself which had responsibility for the common chest out of which the minister would be paid. Luther's *Ordinance* did not, however, receive the approval of Friedrich and would only be adopted in 1529; it was one of a series of changes for which the communities of Electoral Saxony became the testing-ground. These may be summarized as follows:

Town	Preacher	New dispositions	Dates
Allstedt	T. Müntzer*	Orders of service	1523–24
Alltenburg	W. Linck	Common chest	1522
Coburg	—	Orders of service	1524
Colditz	W. Fues	—	
Eilenburg	G. Zwilling*	Cup to laity	1523
Eisenach	J. Strauss	—	
Gotha	F. Myconius*	—	
Leisnig	—	Common chest & appointments of pastor	1523
Schweinitz	—	German mass	1524
Torgau	—	Church ordinances	pre-1529
Zwickau	N. Hausmann	German liturgy	1524–25

Source: The details in this table are taken from E. Cameron, *The European Reformation* (Oxford, Clarendon Press, 1991), p. 215.

	Appointment of Johann Bugenhagen as pastor to the Town Church of Wittenberg.
	Luther published his *Formula of the Mass* (*Formula missae et communionis*) in Latin as the new order of service.
24 Dec	The Castle Church, Wittenberg accepted the new order of service.
1524	Luther published his treatise *To the Councilmen of All Cities in Germany that they establish and maintain Christian Schools* (early 1524). Education was a vital component to the evangelical reformation. Now was the time to encourage the study of languages and build a sound public educational framework for that reformation in schools and libraries.
	Publication of the first of Luther's hymns in *The Eight Hymn Book* (*Acht Liederbuch*).
1524–25	Great Peasants' War (see pages 75–81).
	Luther published his treatise *Against the Heavenly Prophets in the Matter of Images and Sacraments* aimed at Karlstadt.
1525	Initial visitations[†] of selected regions (Eisenach and Zwickau) attempted by agents of Elector Johann. Luther aware of substantial deficiencies in many areas – 'everywhere the congregations are in poor shape. No one contributes anything, no one pays for anything . . .'[1].

[1] WABr 3, 595 (36–56) – Luther to Elector Johann, 31 October 1525.

1526	Luther published his *German Mass* to provide a German order of service, along with a purified Latin rite.
22 Nov	Luther's proposal for an expanded visitation.
6 Dec	Appointment of visitation commission.
1527	First visitations and the Instructions and *Briefing* (*Unterricht*) for visiting commissioners (Aug).
1528	Appearance in print of revised Articles of Visitation (Spring).

The organization of the Saxon church

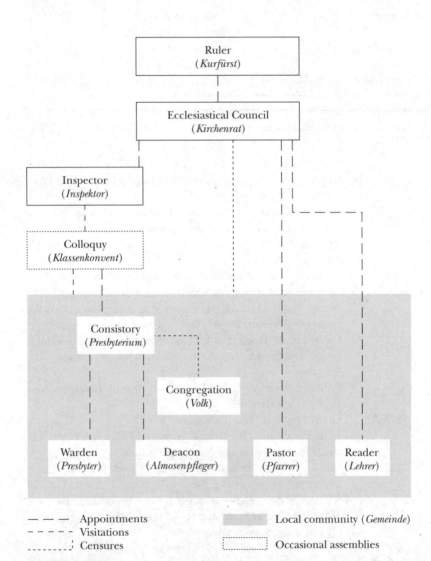

— — — Appointments	Local community (*Gemeinde*)
- - - - - Visitations	
·········· Censures	·········· Occasional assemblies

4.2.2 Hesse

Institutional background

Hesse was a principality of scattered territories ruled by a landgrave (*Landgraf*), bordering on Saxony to the east, Braunschweig-Lüneburg to the north, the duchy of Württemberg to the south and the Rhine Palatinate to the west. The leading towns of the area (Frankfurt and Wetzlar) were imperial cities and so the capital of the principality was at Cassel. Its Saxon neighbours exercised a good deal of influence on its politics in the first half of the sixteenth century, although this was not directly the reason for its early support for the Lutheran reformation. Its representative assemblies declined in significance in the early sixteenth century.

Rulers

	Regnal dates
Philipp*	1509–67
Wilhelm IV	1567–92
Mauritz	1592–1627

Chronology of the Lutheran reformation in Hesse

1518	Philipp* declared by the emperor to be of age.
1518–19	Defeat of the noble factions which had emerged during his minority.
1525	Landgrave actively suppressed peasants' uprising.
1526	Synod of Homburg (Oct) at which the landgrave Philipp submitted a plan for ecclesiastical reformation in the principality (*Reformatio Ecclesiarum Hassiae*) with autonomy for local congregations who would elect bishops and synods. Luther opposed it and the Hesse reformation proceeded along Saxon lines.
1527	Monastic revenues expropriated to a nominated committee – in practice to the landgrave's council.
1532	Ecclesiastical regulations.
1534	Philipp intervened militarily in Württemberg, reinstated the exiled duke, and introduced the Lutheran reformation there.
1537	Ecclesiastical orders.
1547	Landgrave Philipp surrendered to imperial forces and kept captive for five years.

4.2.3 Electoral Brandenburg

Institutional background

Brandenburg was a large territorial principality ruled by a margrave (*Margraf*) who was also an imperial elector. It was bounded to the north by Mecklenburg and Pomerania and to the south by Magdeburg, Anhalt, Saxony and Lusatia, to the east by Poland, and to the west by Brunswick (Braunschweig-Lüneburg and Braunschweig-Wolfenbüttel). The control of the bishoprics of the Mark (Brandenburg, Lebus and Havelberg) and neighbouring Magdeburg and Halberstadt were important objectives in the Brandenburg princely reformation. The territories' various enclaves had different capitals. That of the Middle Mark was at Berlin–Cölln. The margravate had regular meetings of representative institutions through which taxation was negotiated.

Rulers

House of Hohenzollern	Regnal dates
Joachim I	1499–1535
Joachim II	1535–71 (partible inheritance of the margravate with his brother Johann)
Johann-Georg	1571–98
Georg-Friedrich	1598–1603
Joachim-Friedrich	1603–8
Johann-Sigismund	1608–19

Chronology of the Lutheran reformation in Brandenburg

1539   Joachim II received communion in both kinds and accepted Lutherans at his court and dominions (1 Nov).

1540   Highly conservative ecclesiastical ordinances (retained all the old ritual and ceremonial elements including exorcism and chrism in baptism, private confession and absolution and the traditional church calendar).

1543   Establishment of the Brandenburg consistorial court to act as an ecclesiastical tribunal for his territories. The superintendant-general and the chief court preacher became significant figures in the Brandenburg reformation.

1572   Revised ecclesiastical ordinances prepared by the superintendant-general Andreas Musculus along orthodox Lutheran confessional lines.

4.2.4 The Rhine Palatinate

Institutional background
The Palatinate (*Kurpfalz*) owed its curious name to the title of its rulers, the counts palatine. It was composed of two separate territories, the lower (or Rhine) Palatinate (*Unterpfalz*) which lay along the middle Rhine and Neckar and the upper Palatinate (*Oberpfalz*) which lay close by Bavaria. The lower Palatinate had no representative institutions (largely because

the local nobility were mainly free imperial knights). The upper Palatinate, however, which was generally ruled by the elector's heir apparent, had regular meetings of its estates. The capital of the Rhine Palatinate and the site for the supreme palatine court (*Hofgericht*) was at Heidelberg.

Rulers

House of Wittelsbach to 1559, thereafter Pfalz-Simmern	Regnal dates
Ludwig V	1508–44
Friedrich II	1544–56
Ottheinrich	1556–59
Friedrich III ('the Pious')	1559–76
Ludwig VI	1576–83
(regent: Johann-Casimir	1583–92)
Friedrich IV	1583–1610
Friedrich V	1610–23

Chronology

1546   Ecclesiastical ordinances introduced moderate Lutheranism to the Palatinate.

1548   The Palatinate accepted the interim imperial settlement and protestant ecclesiastical ordinances were withdrawn.

1556   New protestant ecclesiastical ordinances introduced Lutheran church government.

1557   Removal of images from Palatine churches caused iconoclasm[†].

1563   Calvinist church discipline[†] and catechism[†] introduced into the Palatinate provoking controversy about church–state relations (see page 230).

1576   Re-establishment of Lutheranism in the lower Palatinate; the upper Palatinate retained the Calvinist Reformed traditions under Johann Casimir.

1583   Lutheranism abandoned and the Reformed confession reintroduced into the lower Palatinate.

4.2.5 Bavaria

Institutional background

Bavaria was a large and politically significant duchy in southern Germany which had been reunified by Duke Albert IV after dynastic divisions in the fifteenth century. The capital was at Munich and, in 1506, he completed the process by establishing the principle of primogeniture in the principality. After his death, however, his younger son (Ludwig X

(1516–45)) forced his elder brother (Wilhelm IV (1508–50)) to give him a part of the duchy and, during this period, the estates of the duchy enjoyed an Indian summer of influence. The duchy was reunified when Ludwig died; but the dangers to the state and to social cohesion perceived by Wilhelm and his influential advisor Leonhard von Eck from the estates and the reformation during this period influenced the shape of events thereafter. Wilhelm set the duchy against the reformation and towards political centralization, assisted by important ecclesiastical rights conceded to him for his loyalty by the catholic church. This was further developed in the second half of the sixteenth century when the duchy became a showcase for the catholic reformation in southern Germany.

Rulers

House of Wittelsbach	Regnal dates
Albert IV	1467–1508
Wilhelm IV	1508–50
Albert V	1550–79
Wilhelm V	1579–97
Maximilian I	1597–1651

Chronology

1520s   Lutheran influence growing in Munich and in the university at Ingolstadt.

1522–24   Edicts excommunicating Luther, forbidding discussion of his teaching and authorizing the arrest of all his supporters. All Lutheran literature was strictly forbidden within the duchy.

1531   Duke Wilhelm IV briefly allied with Lutheran princes. Pressure for religious change felt at the duchy's estates in the 1530s and 1540s.

1546   Duke Wilhelm IV firmly supported the emperor in the Schmalkaldic War, but against the opposition of his estates.

1556   Pressure from the estates of the duchy to suspend fines on those receiving communion 'in both kinds'[†] led to concessions from Duke Albert V.

1564   Discovery of an aristocratic conspiracy in the duchy with links to Lutheran causes led to show trials of leading Lutheran nobles, the collapse of opposition in the estates, and new penalties for attending Lutheran services.

1567–68   Regular visitations of parishes begun in Bavarian dioceses leading to the establishment of a new 'consistory' (*Geistliche Rat*) to supervise orthodoxy. It became responsible for the shaping of the catholic reformation in the duchy's schools, universities and public life in the later sixteenth century.

4.2.6 Summary of the spread of the Lutheran reformation to other German principalities (to 1555)

It would be impossible to chart the progress of the reformation in detail through every German principality in a book of this compass. The following list of the dates at which other territories accepted the Lutheran reformation obscures the variety of ways by which the process occurred. Princes were well aware of the possible advantages to be gained from annexing neighbouring secularized ecclesiastical bishoprics and lands. But they were also concerned about the possibilities of imperial reaction to their conversion and of retaliation from their neighbours. Two changes (that of Württemberg and Braunschweig-Wolfenbüttel) were the result of military intervention. Dynastic rivalries as well as conscientious decision played their part in a complex process; for each change had a destabilizing effect in the Empire (and especially so where an electorate was concerned, since this had potential implications for the imperial succession).

Dates of the Lutheran reformation in the German principalities

Territory	Dates of key changes	Prince
East Prussia	1523–24	Albrecht of Hohenzollern
Brandenburg-Ansbach	1524–28	Kasimir (d.1527)
		Georg (d.1543)
Braunschweig-Lüneburg	1526–27	Ernst (d.1546)
		Otto (d.1549)
		Franz (d.1549)
Mecklenburg-Schwerin	1526(i)	Heinrich (reversed 1528)
	1533–35(ii)	Magnus (1516–50)
Anhalt-Köthen	1526–on	Wolfgang
Mansfeld	1525–26	Gebhard (d.1558)
		Albrecht (d.1560)
Liegnitz	1527	Friedrich II
Holstein	1528	Christian
Anhalt-Dessau	1532–24	Johann (d.1551)
		Georg (d.1553)
		Joachim (d.1561)
Pomerania	1534–35	Philipp (1531–60)
		Barnim (1532–73)
Württemberg	1534	Ulrich (d.1550)

(with military assistance from the Schmalkaldic League)

Territory	Dates of key changes	Prince
Brandenburg-Neumark	1536–38	Johann von Küstrin (1513–71)
Braunschweig-Grubenhagen	1538	Philipp (1494–1551)
Braunschweig-Kalenberg	1540–on	Erik II (1540–84)
Braunschweig-Wolfenbüttel	1542–43	Heinrich (1514–68)
(achieved through the Saxon/Hesse military intervention)		
Neuburg	1543	Ottheinrich
Henneberg	1545	Wilhelm; Georg-Ernst

Source: Details in this table come largely from E. Cameron, *The European Reformation* (Oxford, Clarendon Press, 1991), p. 269.

4.2.7 Summary of the spread of Calvinism in German principalities and cities (post-1555)

The spread of Calvinism amongst a minority of German principalities and cities in the second half of the sixteenth century is sometimes termed the 'second reformation' (*Zweite Reformation*) by German historians to distinguish it from the earlier Lutheran reformation. Although there were continuing Lutheran reformations post-1555 (in the episcopal cities of Bamberg, Trier and Würzburg, for example; or in the cities of Aachen, Dortmund and Essen), the main changes were the Calvinist reformations imposed by princely fiat or city injunction. These princes were influenced by international events and tended to be supportive of, or become engaged in, the civil wars to the west of the Empire in France and the Netherlands. They were also impressed with a sense of disillusionment with the Lutheran reformation's failure to enact a fundamental change in religious life and perception amongst the people at large. Below is a list of the states where Calvinism was officially introduced. There was a further set of (larger) principalities (Brandenburg and electoral Saxony) where attempts were made to introduce Calvinism in the early years of the seventeenth century, but where the rulers did not succeed in overcoming Lutheran opposition.

Principality (cities in brackets)	Date of official introduction of Calvinism[2]
The Palatinate	1561
(Wesel)	1564

[2] Information from Henry J. Cohn, 'The territorial princes in Germany's second reformation, 1559–1622' in Menna Prestwich (ed.), *International Calvinism, 1541–1715* (Oxford, Clarendon Press, 1985), ch. v, pp. 136–7.

Sayn	1565
Wittgenstein	1567
Mörs	1574
Nassau-Dillenburg	1577
Solms	1580
(Bremen)	1581
Isenburg	1583
Tecklenburg	1586
Zweibrücken	1588
(Colmar)	1589
(Emden)	1589
Steinfurt	1591
Hanau-Münzenberg	1591
Bentheim	1592
Anhalt	1596
Hesse Cassel	1601
Lippe	1601
Wöhlau	1609
Ohls	?
Leignitz	1609
Brieg	1609
Beuthen	1616
Jägerndorf	1616

4.3 The Great Peasants' War (1524–26)

Although the Peasants' War drew on a tradition of rural armed unrest and uprising in Germany, it was on a different scale and of greater complexity. The surviving records are complex. They include published contemporary accounts, extant correspondence, lists of grievances and interrogation records. Historians are not in entire agreement about its causes and nature, let alone about the part played by religious turbulence provoked by the decade of protestant evangelism. However, the difficulties are in part because the revolt had different (but interlinked) manifestations in varying parts of Germany. A regional analysis is essential, but even this only identifies in a somewhat arbitrary fashion the local events which acted as a focus for the war. The following chronologies[3] are designed to be read alongside the map on page 368.

[3] Based on Janos Bak (ed.), *The German Peasant War of 1525* (London, Cass, 1976); P. Blickle, *The revolution of 1525: the German Peasants' War from a new pespective* (Baltimore and London, Johns Hopkins U.P., c.1981); T. Scott and Bob Scribner (eds), *The German peasants' war: a history in documents* (New Jersey, Humanities Press International, 1991).

4.3.1 The Black Forest and Upper Swabia

1524

30 April   The subjects of the abbey of St Blasien in the Black Forest rebelled and declared they would pay no more feudal dues or tithes. Tithe[†] disputes had occurred in the region since 1523.

24 June   Peasants of the county of Lupfen and Stühlingen rose under the Austrian banner against their count; mutual oath-taking and appointment of a former mercenary captain as a spokesman of the peasant bands.

Aug   Contingents of peasants marched on the town of Waldshut; the count of Lupfen refused to meet them. Negotiations were arranged for 10 Sep at Schaffhausen, which resulted in a proposed compromise settlement in 39 articles; other peasant contingents joined the uprising.

Sep   Peasants in the Klettgau around Waldshut refused to compromise; preaching and support within the town were assisted by a voluntary contingent from Zürich. Peasants marched through the Black Forest to raise more support and protest.

Oct–Nov   Further rebel armies raised; attempts were made by their lords to broker compromises; St Blasien abbey was occupied and other convents sacked.

1525

Jan   The Klettgau peasants called on the Zürich magistrates to help them broker a settlement with their lords on the basis of Scripture and godly law; the banners of Zürich appeared in the protests.

Jan–Feb   The revolt was extended to the region around the imperial cities of Ulm and Biberach; large armies were raised and another peasant leader (Ulrich Schmid) called on evangelical[†] preachers at Memmingen to broker a settlement. Over 300 charters of peasant grievances were turned into the famous '12 Articles of Memmingen'.

Jan–March   Additional peasant bands formed around Lindau and the Bodensee (Lake Constance) and congregated as the 'Christian Assembly'.

Jan–March   Additional peasant bands formed in upper Swabia; the prince-abbot of Kempten was a target because of aggressive serfdom; some negotiations but 8,000 peasants raised a common banner (24 Feb) and (27 Feb) declared the 'Christian Union'.

5 March   Peasant bands congregated at Memmingen for a 'peasant assembly'; they created a common 'Christian Union', but disbanded it a month later.

April   New peasant bands formed in the Black Forest.

April–May   Peasant bands were levied in the duchy of Württemberg by Duke Ulrich, who had been exiled from his duchy in 1519. He exploited the peasant revolt to regain his duchy; he was defeated on 12 May.

May Freiburg was besieged and taken (17–23 May); Breisach forced to surrender (26 May); but military success was undermined by failure elsewhere in Franconia and Thuringia.

4.3.2 Franconia

Tauber valley

1525
21–22 March Peasant unrest in and around the imperial city of Rothenburg ob der Tauber. They issued the 'Rothenburg Articles'.

April Peasant bands from Rothenburg marched up the Tauber valley, intimidating local nobles (many castles were destroyed), to unite with the peasantry from the bishopric of Würzburg and with subjects of the monastery at Mergentheim.

May The bishop of Würzburg fled during negotiations and the town was seized (8 May).

2 June Failure to take the fortress at Marienburg and news of defeats elsewhere led to rapid dispersal.

Odenwald-Neckar

1525
March–early April Peasants from the Odenwald and Neckar valleys rallied and assembled at the convent of Schöntal. Anticlerical and anti-noble violence was much in evidence.

19 April The town of Heilbronn negotiated and admitted the rebels.

early May Peasant assembly of Heilbronn; they issued the Amorbach Articles.

May Peasant bands threatened the archbishopric of Mainz; the cardinal-archbishop's regent failed to defend the territory and was besieged in the castle of Aschaffenburg; he was forced to accept the peasant articles (7 May) in a capitulation.

June Collapse of the rebellion with news of defeat elsewhere.

Bildhausen

1525
12 April Peasant band at Münnerstadt attacked monasteries and occupied the convent at Bildhausen. They established a 'peasant council' dominated by territorial towns and issued (19 April) moderate demands for the redress of grievances and Christian love.

early May Indecision and unwillingness to act in cooperation with other peasant rebels in Franconia were evident. They turned north to confront Philip of Hesse in Thuringia.

3–5 June   Peasant band seized Meiningen where they were besieged and eventually surrendered.

4.3.3 Thuringia

1524
Mid-Sep   11 Mühlhausen Articles advocated government according to the word of God and divine justice.

19 Oct   Urban revolt began in Mühlhausen, assisted by the evangelical[†] preaching of Heinrich Pfeiffer and sustained by the leadership of Thomas Müntzer*.

1525
17 March   Radical evangelical changes proclaimed at Mühlhausen; Müntzer announced the 'Eternal League of God'.

April   Peasant bands formed in the lands of the abbey of Fulda, following a bungled attempt to dismiss the evangelical preacher in the town of Fulda (Feb); the abbey's coadjutor was forced to leave and revolt spread to other ecclesiastical lands; there were appeals to the Word of God and the 12 Articles of Memmingen.

3 May   Fulda revolt was suppressed by force by Landgrave Philipp* of Hesse.

April–May   Separate peasant bands formed in the Werra valley around Völkershausen; they attacked nobles and captured various towns including Eisenach.

April–May   Separate peasant movements in various parts of Thuringia, often in association with the towns.

May   Mühlhausen band planned to attack Count Ernst von Mansfeld's fortress at Heldrungen but delayed to attack castles and convents on the way. Duke Georg of Saxony, Landgrave Philipp of Hesse and the count of Mansfeld coordinated forces and inflicted a massive defeat on the peasant army at Frankenhausen (15 May). Müntzer was captured, tortured and executed outside the walls of Mühlhausen (27 May).

4.3.4 Alsace

1525
Jan–Feb   Anticlerical revolt at the town of Saverne (residence of bishops of Strasbourg); there were rural demands for evangelical[†] preachers.

2 April   Peasant bands amassed to release a radical preacher (Clemens Ziegler) who had been imprisoned at Strasbourg for preaching illegally.

17 April   Evangelical preachers of Strasbourg (Bucer*, Zell* and Capito*) were invited to address the peasant bands around Saverne; the peasantry were told to disband in order that their grievances might be considered. Saverne was taken by the rebels.

Late April Revolt spread with other peasant bands being established in the Sundgau, Montbéliard and also to the north of Strasbourg; the band at Atorf became the leading and coordinating force with a recruiting committee, military organization and supreme military commander (Erasmus Gerber). The 12 Articles of Memmingen were adopted.

16 May Saverne was besieged by Antoine, duke of Lorraine. A negotiated surrender of the town was agreed but 18,000 peasants were killed as they left the town; Gerber was seized and hanged.

5 June There was a negotiated truce between the Sundgau rebels and the authorities; the revolt was eventually broken by force in November.

4.3.5 The lower Palatinate

1525

9 April Peasant bands formed around Durlach and (19 April) in the bishopric of Speyer; the peasant declaration of Bruhrain stated grievances.

29 April The rebels took the bishop of Speyer prisoner and forced him to negotiate; the bishop agreed to the free preaching of the Word and the election of pastors. The peasant bands dispersed.

May More radical peasant bands formed. They tried to take various towns and Elector Palatine Ludwig V met peasant captains (10 May) and agreed to hold an assembly to consider demands.

26 June The elector returned from Franconia to crush the revolt in his own territory; a force of 8,000 peasants was defeated at Pfeddersheim, near Worms.

4.3.6 The Austrian Tyrol

1525

Jan–Feb Attempts began to foment revolt amongst miners in Schwaz; Archduke Ferdinand of Austria arranged for some concessions in the Tyrol diet at Innsbruck (6 March).

May Major revolts led to a peasant assembly at Merano, meeting on 30 May. They elected Michael Gaismair as their leader and issued the Merano articles of grievance. Ferdinand called a further diet on 12 June which was attended by 200 peasant delegates. Some demands were conceded (freedom for fishing and remission of a feudal due to landlords); a proposal for a new Tyrol constitution to be drafted later was accepted.

1526

March The new Tyrol constitution was published; it contained some concessions (guilds abolished; Roman law suspended; peasant dues moderated; small tithes abolished etc).

Oct Gaismair fled to the Grisons with supporters under threat of reprisals.

1532
– The new constitution was suspended and concessions abandoned.

4.3.7 Inner Austria

1525
8 May Revolt began in the archbishopric of Salzburg; it was joined by the miners of Gastein and spread rapidly to the Austrian Alps (Styria and Carinthia) and upper Austria.
4 June Salzburg seized by the rebels; the Gastein articles of grievance were issued.
3 July Negotiated agreement at Schladming granted the peasantry many of their demands.
July The archbishop of Salzburg was rescued from the siege by the peasantry; the treaty with the peasants promised a diet to consider grievances.

1526
– The diet finally met (Jan) but it produced no agreement and was adjourned *sine die*. Peasants tried to summon their own assembly (March) but this, and the accompanying further revolt was resisted by force (2 July).

4.3.8 Peasant demands and leaders

Some main articles of grievance and demands of the peasants are given below:

Articles of Schaffhausen (10 Sep 1524)
Eleven Articles of Mühlhausen (mid-Sep 1524)
Twelve Articles of Memmingen (Jan–Feb 1525)
The Merano Articles (June 1525)
The Gastein Articles (June 1525)

Some leaders of peasant bands are listed below, together with details of their social origins (where known) and the regions where they were active:

Hans Müller (mercenary captain)	Lupfen
Balthasar Hubmaier* (preacher)	Waldshut
Thomas Müntzer* (preacher)	The Klettgau;
	Mühlhausen; Thuringia
Ulrich Schmid	Baltringen

Sebastian Lotzer (preacher)	Memmingen
Matern Feuerbacher	(duchy of Württemberg)
Hans Wunderer	(duchy of Württemberg)
Stephan von Menzingen (lesser noble)	Rothenburg
Johann Teuschlein (preacher)	Rothenburg
Georg Metzler (innkeeper)	Ballenburg
Wendel Hipler (minor legal clerk)	The Odenwald
Margaret Rennerin	Heilbronn
Heinrich Pfeiffer (former Franciscan)	Mühlhausen
Hans Sippel	Vacha
Clemens Ziegler (gardener and preacher)	Strasbourg
Erasmus Gerber (peasant)	Molsheim
Eisenhut (former priest)	Bretten
Michael Gaismair (secretary and clerk)	Tyrol

4.4 The German reformation in its urban setting

The rapidity of the spread of Lutheran evangelism† through the cities of Germany in the decade of the 1520s is difficult to encapsulate, but it left an indelible mark on the protestant reformation. This was where the protestant reformation found its greatest dynamism and variety. Although the process was begun by the events in Saxony, it was by no means dictated by them. Each town had its own internal evolution and, although there was a loose affiliation to the basic thrust of Luther's message, individual preachers in particular cities felt free to take up particular issues and follow the direction of reformation in their own fashion. Determining the precise date of the reformation in any one city is not always easy since it was often a movement which magistrates chose to undertake gradually and piecemeal. Often the process began with the urban magistrates issuing revised church ordinances which laid down different patterns of worship in the city, or closing its monasteries. In others, especially in the central Rhineland, the significant changes were marked by ordinances which permitted evangelical preaching in the city alongside the traditional patterns of worship before pressure from within the city's polities (especially the trade guilds) forced the town council to complete the reformation. Many of the initial changes in the cities took place in the 1520s but the process had not been completed by 1530. It was most precocious in the central Rhineland and Franconia. It was more tentative in the southern German cities and more leisurely still in the cities of the Baltic littoral and the north. Whilst the princely reformation consolidated itself in the territories where protestantism was adopted as the main religion, the urban reformation, especially in the Rhineland, went on to become the basis for the continuing reformation.

4.4.1 Dates of the protestant reformation in selected towns in Germany

Towns have been arranged in accordance with the following regions:

Franconia and central Germany in the 1520s

Town	Preacher	New orders	Dates
Crailsheim	Adam Weiss	Church ordinances	1526
Heilbronn	—	Reformation	1525–32
Kitzingen	—	Poor-law ordinance	1523
		Preaching ordinance	1524
		Baptismal ordinance	1526
Nuremberg	—	[see pages 84–5]	1523–33
Reutlingen	M. Alber	German liturgy	1523–24
Schwäbisch-Hall	Johann Brenz*	Church ordinances	1526
Weissenburg	—	New order of service	1528
Windsheim	—	Common chest	1524
Rothenburg	—	Church ordinances	1559
Schweinfurt	—	Church ordinances	1543

North Germany and the Baltic coast

Town	Preacher	Dates of major changes
Bremen	—	–1528
Braunschweig	—	1528
Celle	—	1526
Göttingen	—	1529–32
Goslar	—	1528
Hamburg	—	1528
Hanover	—	1533–34
Lübeck	—	1531
Münster	[see pages 109–12]	1531

Central Rhineland and Swiss margins

Town	Preacher	New orders	Dates
Strasbourg	[see pages 85–6]		1523–34
Konstanz	A. Blarer	Preaching ordinance	1524
	J. Zwick	Mass abolished	1528
		Church ordinance	1531–34
Memmingen	C. Schappeler	Preaching ordinance	1523–24
	S. Schenk	Mass abolished	1528
		Church ordinance	1528
Lindau	T. Gassner	Church ordinance	1525
Basel	Johannes Oecolampadius*	Secularization of monasteries	1525
		Abolition of church festivals	1527
		Mass abolished	1529
Mühlhausen [Mulhouse]	—	Mass abolished	1528–29
		Church ordinances	1523; 1528–29

Southern Germany

Town	Preacher	New orders	Dates
Augsburg	W. Musculus	Mass abolished	1537
		Church ordinances	1534/7
Ulm	K. Sam	School ordinance	1528
	M. Frecht	New hymnbook and psalter	1529
		Mass abolished	1531
Biberach	B. Millius	Mass abolished	1531
		Church ordinance	1531

Source: Details for tables in section 4.4.1 have been taken (with adaptation) from E. Cameron, *The European Reformation* (Oxford, Clarendon Press, 1991), pp. 216–19.

4.4.2 Examples of the urban reformation in Germany

Nuremberg

Nuremberg was an imperial city of considerable eminence in the Empire. It had a wealthy merchant ruling-class and enjoyed great commercial success on the eve of the protestant reformation. By imperial standards it was a large city with a population of around 50,000 inside its walls and a further 50,000 living within its jurisdiction outside. It was a centre for international trade and a flourishing centre for engraving and printing. It became the home of leading intellectual figures and artists of the reformation period including Albrecht Dürer and Lazarus Spengler*. This elite was an eager recipient of Luther's ideas. Lazarus Spengler, the city fathers' first secretary, was Luther's friend, and Christoph Scheurl was the council's clerk. Johann von Staupitz* was also a preacher in the city who spread Lutheran ideas. Yet the Nuremberg patriciate had to tread delicately. The diet of Worms had voted to locate the Imperial Cameral Court in Nuremberg and it was also the city of important imperial diets in 1522–24. So, whilst professing undying attachment to the emperor, Nuremberg's council nevertheless invited Lutheran preachers to its pulpits. It joined the Speyer protest of 1529 and signed the Augsburg Confession of 1530 but did not join the Schmalkaldic League. Nuremberg managed, albeit with difficulty, to retain both its very moderate brand of Lutheranism and its reputation for loyalty to the Empire.

Chronology of the reformation in Nuremberg

1517   Johann von Staupitz* attacked indulgences in his Advent sermons.

1519   Lazarus Spengler* published a defence of Luther in Nuremberg which pictured Luther's teachings as liberating and based upon Christ and the Bible. Eck* was ridiculed in another pamphlet whose author was believed to be the Nuremberg humanist, Willibald Pirckheimer*.

1520   A new city cathedral provost (a supporter of Luther from Wittenberg) was appointed.

1521–22   Ordinances invited protestant preachers to the city but left the ecclesiastical order untouched: new ordinances (1522) restricted alms-giving.

1523   The papal nuncio's demand for the arrest of the city's preachers was ignored; a former monk propagated Lutheran evangelical ideas in the city.

1524–25   Ordinances on baptism[†] were announced: the reformed mass was introduced on 1 June. Peasant unrest was close to the city and refusal to pay tithe, was widespread around it; the city magistrates punished those who took part in the peasants' revolt and expelled radicals like Hans Denck*.

1525   An important disputation on the scriptural authenticity of Lutheran changes took place before the city council (3–14 March) in order to prevent further religious disruption. Catholic preachers lost the argument and, on 17 March, they were barred from preaching and taking confession. The city's monasteries were sequestered and new ordinances for the mass[†] were introduced.

1528–33 The bishop of Bamberg sought to re-establish his rights in the city (backed by the Swabian League). A commission of theologians and councillors visited the parishes in and around the city and prepared new ecclesiastical ordinances. These were put into practice in 1533.

1529 The city joined the Speyer protest.

1530 Nuremberg signed the Augsburg Confession[†].

1546–47 Nuremberg stayed neutral during the Schmalkaldic War[†], although it paid money to the Emperor Charles and (secretly) to the protestants.

1552 Nuremberg was forced briefly to join the Schmalkaldic League, having accepted the Augsburg Interim[†] (June).

1555 Nuremberg became a moderate Lutheran city with a minority catholic population under the peace of Augsburg.

Strasbourg (also spelt Strassburg)

Strasbourg was a Rhineland imperial city whose autonomy was so considerable that it made almost no financial contributions to the Empire and had the right to conduct its own foreign policy. Its patrician oligarchy had been challenged in the fourteenth century by the guilds, with the result that the city's constitution allowed non-patricians a say in its government (*Magistrat*) through representatives of its 20 guilds on the city senate (*Rat*). It had a history of opposition to the Burgundian princes (of whom the Emperor Charles V was a descendant) and was prepared to seek alliances with nearby France to protect its autonomy. With a population of about 25,000 at the time of the reformation, it also had a reputation for being relatively willing to accept residents from outside its walls. In due course, it would play host to Erasmian humanists, Lutherans, Zwinglians, anabaptists, refugees from France (including Calvin himself), English émigrés, and millenarian enthusiasts (see page 106). The city's willingness to play this role declined, however, in the 1550s and, by not long after the peace of Augsburg, it became not merely officially, but also in reality, an orthodox Lutheran stronghold.

1500/1510 Influence of the humanist and clerical reformer Jacob Wimpfeling* was felt in the city. He was joined by the influential preacher Johann Geiler von Kaysersberg (1445–1510) who became one of the outstanding preachers of the

Empire on the eve of the reformation, advocating the need for reform of the clergy and the laity.

1521   Arrival of Matthias Zell* as an episcopal official and preacher in the cathedral. His sermons on Paul's letter to the Romans in 1522 drew huge crowds.

1523   Arrival in Strasbourg of Wolfgang Capito*, Martin Bucer* and Caspar Hedio, who had already become associated through their connections with Erasmus* at Basel.

1524   Communion[†] in both kinds was offered to the laity; the first German mass and baptism[†] was celebrated. Martin Bucer published his manifesto of reform (*Grund und Ursache aus göttlicher Schrift*) in early 1525.

1524/5 Celebrations of the mass[†] gradually forbidden in the city.

1527   Capito's *Catechism* was published.

1529   Mass was completely forbidden in the city; the monasteries were closed; the city joined the Speyer protest.

1530   Following the controversy between Lutherans and the sacramentarians[†] at Zürich the city submitted its own confession to the diet of Augsburg (known from the sponsoring cities which signed it as the 'tetrapolitan' confession) (see page 248).

1531   Establishment of a church commission under Bucer's direction; eventually a reformed welfare structure and a new marriage and moral tribunal for the city were established.

1536   City adopted the Augsburg Confession and subscribed formally to Luther's views.

1538   Establishment of a new college (*Gymnasium*) under Jakob Sturm* to replace the parochial school.

1547/8 Expulsion of some of the city's eminent politicians during the Schmalkaldic War; Martin Bucer retired to England.

1551   Strasbourg accepted the Interim[†] and reintroduced the mass into the cathedral and other city churches.

1552   Appointment of the strict Lutheran Johannes Marbach as the city's chief pastor, who established a Lutheran stability in the city.

4.5 Imperial leagues

The princes of Germany were already organized into loose confederations (known as 'Circles') to assure a degree of mutual protection and common defence. This was reinforced during the reformation by the formation of defensive leagues along confessional lines. They tended to form and reform in response to one another and in response to the politico-religious tensions of the moment.

Imperial leagues

League	Date	Members (towns in brackets)	Confessional affiliation
League of Regensburg	June 1524	Archduke Ferdinand; duke of Bavaria; various southern German ecclesiastical princes.	catholic
League of Dessau	July 1525	Duke Georg of Saxony; Archbishop Albrecht of Mainz; elector of Brandenburg; duke of Braunschweig-Kalenberg; duke of Braunschweig-Wolfenbüttel	catholic
League of Torgau	1526	Elector of Saxony; Landgrave Philipp of Hesse; duke of Braunschweig-Lüneburg; duke of Braunschweig-Grubenhagen; count of Mecklenburg-Schwerin; count of Mansfeld; count of Anhalt (Magdeburg)	protestant
League of Speyer ('protesters')	1529	Elector of Saxony; landgrave of Hesse; count of Brandenburg-Ansbach; duke of Braunschweig-Lüneburg; count of Anhalt-Köthen (Nuremberg; Nördlingen; Heilbronn; Reutlingen; Weissenburg; Windsheim; Strasbourg; Ulm; Konstanz; Lindau; Memmingen; Kempten Isny; St Gallen)	protestant
League of Schmalkalden	1530–31	Elector of Saxony; landgrave of Hesse; duke of Braunschweig-Lüneburg; count of Anhalt; count of Mansfeld (Strasbourg; Ulm;	protestant

League	Date	Members (towns in brackets)	Confessional affiliation
Additions	1532	Konstanz; Reutlingen; Memmingen; Lindau; Biberach; Isny; Lübeck; Magdeburg; Bremen) Count of Brandenburg-Ansbach (Esslingen; Heilbronn; Schwäbisch-Hall; Kempten; Weissenburg; Windsheim; Braunschweig; Goslar; Einbeck; Göttingen; Nordhausen; Hamburg)	
Additions	1535	Duke of Pomerania; duke of Württemberg; count of Anhalt-Dessau (Augsburg; Frankfurt; Hanover)	
Imperial League	Autumn 1547	King Ferdinand Emperor, duke of Bavaria; Mauritz of Saxony	catholic
League of Saxony	1552–53	Elector of Saxony; landgrave of Hesse and others in collaboration with King Henri II of France	protestant
League of Landsberg	1564	Duke of Bavaria; various bishops	catholic
'Evangelical Union' at Anhausen (near Nördlingen)	May 1608	Elector Palatine; count of Neuburg; duke of Württemberg; rulers of Ansbach, Kulmbach and Baden-Durlach	protestant
Catholic League	July 1609	Archduke Leopold; bishops of Würzburg, Augsburg, Regensburg and Konstanz; (later) Speyer, Worms, Bamberg, Cologne, Trier and Mainz	catholic

Source: This table is adapted from material presented in E. Cameron, The European Reformation (Oxford, Clarendon Press, 1991), p. 271.

4.6 The reformation in Baltic lands

The protestant reformation in Scandinavia was a 'princely reformation', heavily influenced by the intellectual contacts which already existed with north Germany across the Baltic. But, especially in Denmark and Sweden, it had elements of urban and popular participation within it at various stages. This is because it took place within a context of political change and social instability in the Baltic lands. The Union of the three Scandinavian kingdoms (Denmark, Sweden and Norway) which had been created in 1397 collapsed in 1521 with the rebellion of the Swedish noble, Gustav Vasa. The Danish King Christian II was subsequently deposed by his council in early 1523. In his place, the council elected Christian's uncle, Duke Frederik of Schleswig and Holstein. Baltic events were then dominated by the activities of the exiled Christian II who established himself in Wittenberg, befriended Luther and Melanchthon*, and converted to protestantism. His efforts at military intervention to restore himself to the throne of Denmark ended in fiasco in 1532. Denmark dissolved into civil war on the death of Frederik in 1533. Thereafter, events in the Baltic were overshadowed by Danish–Swedish rivalries.

4.6.1 Kingdom of Denmark and Norway

Rulers	Regnal dates
Christian II	1513–23
Frederik I	1523–33
(Interregnum and civil war)	
Christian III	1534–59
Frederik II	1559–88
Christian IV	1588–1647

Constitution

Denmark's elective monarchy was reinforced by the deposition of Christian II. Having been elected by the council (Dan: *Rigskrådet*) where aristocracy and bishops dominated, he had to accept a coronation charter. Meetings of the Danish Parliament (Dan: *Herredag*) were constitutionally important.

Chronology

1526   Evangelical[†] preachers active in Jutland, encouraged by contacts with Schleswig and Holstein and given royal letters of protection. *Herredag* at Odense abandoned nomination to senior ecclesiastical posts in Rome and required all fees formerly paid to Rome to be paid to the crown (Dec).

1527   Evangelical reform established at Viborg; monasteries secularized and a training school for ministers established with a printing press.

1528–29   Reformation at Malmø enforced despite clerical opposition by the city magistrates.

1530   *Herredag* at Copenhagen (July). Disputation between evangelical preachers and bishops. Royal charter granted towns rights to introduce evangelical services if they wished.

1533–34   Civil War (Dan: *Grevens Fejde*) won by protestant Duke Christian; catholic bishops and aristocrats exiled or imprisoned.

1536   *Herredag* at Copenhagen (July) decided for a full Lutheran state reformation completed by church ordinances of 1537, decreed by the king. 7 Lutheran superintendants appointed.

4.6.2 Schleswig and Holstein

Rulers   see Denmark, above.

Constitution

The duchy was part of the patrimony of Frederik I and governed as a 'state with estates' (*Ständestaat*) by the duke in conjunction with a Parliament (*Diet*). Christian II (king of Denmark) administered two fiefs in it (Haderslev and Tø) on behalf of his father and this enabled him to promote an evangelical† reformation there.

Chronology

1521–22   Evangelical† influence in the duchy through contacts with Saxony and through the influence of Christian.

1524   Arrest and execution of Henrichs van Zutphen, an evangelical preacher at Heide.

1525   Diet at Rendsburg; evangelical reformation proclaimed (May).

1526   Christian appointed two experienced evangelical preachers to be superintendant and chief preacher in the duchies.

1527   Diet at Kiel; ecclesiastical exemption from taxation abandoned. A synod (April) of the clergy from Christian's patrimonial fiefs agreed new evangelical articles of faith, including decrees of fasting, faith versus works, the right of the clergy to marry etc.

1528   Reformation in duchy's towns complete; signs of sacramentarian† and radical (anabaptist†) leanings suppressed.
Ordinances of Haderslev established a state Lutheran church.
All ministers were required to swear loyalty to the duke and to preach (in German or Danish, as appropriate). Rural deans were given powers to inspect local parishes and to assess

teaching in schools as well as preaching and the morality of the laity.

4.6.3 Kingdom of Sweden

Rulers

Vasa dynasty	Regnal dates
Gustav I	1523–60
Erik XIV	1560–68 (deposed)
Johann III	1568–92
Sigismund III	1592–99 (deposed)
Karl IX	1600–11
Gustav II (Gustav Adolf)	1611–32

Chronology

1523 Appointment of Laurentius Andreae* as Chancellor to the kingdom.

1524 Olaus Peterssen (Petri)* promoted to be clerk and minister of Stockholm.

1526 Disputation between catholic clergy (presented in writing) and evangelical[†] preachers (presented verbally by Olaus Petri to the king).

1527 Popular revolt amongst Swedish peasantry (the *Daljunkern* revolt) in part in reaction to religious changes. The Swedish *Riksdag* met in Västeras (June 1526) and secularized all the episcopal fiefs and monastic lands. Bishops exiled.

1529 National Synod at Örebro under Laurentius Andreae* (Jan). Feast days abolished; modified Latin mass retained with sermons in vernacular. Further popular rural revolt in south-west Sweden, in part against religious changes (Apr). Parliament at Strängnäs distanced the king from religious changes.

1530–36 Protestant reform given no further political backing; conspiracy (1536) amongst German protestant Hansa merchants to blow up the king foiled; but Laurentius Peterssen* and Olaus Peterssen* were disgraced for failing to teach obedience to secular authority.

1539 *Riksdag* at Örebro where full royal supremacy was established over the Swedish church (Dec). New church ordinances (8 Dec) influenced by Wittenberg. Episcopal incumbents would be allowed to die in post but a new structure was established with a superintendant, an assistant (*adjunkt*) and religious council as well as a layman (*konservator*) and two clergy (*seniores*) in each diocese.

4.7 The reformation in Switzerland

4.7.1 The Confederation

The term 'Schwitzerland' (in use in the sixteenth century) came from the region of Schwyz, one of the original allies grouped around Lake Luzern (Lucerne) which made up the 'Swiss Confederation' (the 'forest cantons' of Schwyz; Uri, Unterwalden). Subsequently, the other cantons and communities attached themselves to this original core (Luzern (1332); Glarus (1351); Zürich (1351); Zug (1352); Bern (1353); Solothurn (1481) and Freiburg (1481)) as well as numerous smaller communes. The proximity of the confederation to Austria, however, created enmities, and especially when the Habsburgs acquired the imperial title. When the latter tried to take over parts of Switzerland, the inhabitants in the disputed regions formed three separate leagues, two of which joined the confederation in 1497 and 1498. The most effectively organized of these was known as the Grey Leagues (*Graubünden* or *Grisons*). The threat from the Habsburg empire, and Emperor Maximilian's attempt to apply to the Swiss Confederation the constitutional reform measures agreed at the diet[†] of Worms in 1495 (including the newly created Imperial Cameral Court[†]) led to an unusual degree of unity which secured the Swiss their final independence from the Holy Roman Empire. The reformation coincided with the independence of Switzerland, and also the moment when it reached its greatest territorial extent.

The communities within the confederation were themselves often loose conjoinings of self-governing communities, alike only in their relative independence from other princes or rulers. The confederation between the cantons and communities worked rather similarly to the internal politics of the cantons themselves. There were complex agreements touching on mutual access to the Alpine passes, to mountain pasture, and the related transhumance husbandry. Matters of common significance were discussed in meetings of the confederation diet (the *Tagsatzung*). Otherwise, they governed themselves. The structure was able to cope with a wide variety of linguistic divergence. Northern and eastern Switzerland (the majority of the population) spoke a Swiss-German dialect. The French-speaking part was confined to the west in the cantons of Fribourg and Bern. A curious Romance language was spoken in the Grisons and some Italian in the southern cantons.

The great threats to the survival of the confederation in the sixteenth century came from the business of mercenary army service and the protestant reformation. Both endangered the confederation's capacity to absorb fundamental differences. Mercenary service led individuals in large numbers (in comparison to the overall Swiss population) to become pensionaries (*Pensionherr*) to the emperor, the king of France or the papacy, especially during the Italian wars of the sixteenth century. The risks of rival pensionaries from different cantons dividing the confederation were real, especially when exacerbated by religious conflict. The dangers were increased by the size and expansionist endeavours of the two major protestant-influenced 'outer' cantons of Zürich and Bern. The Swiss cantons were able, however, to reach a *modus vivendi* after an interlude of fighting. This enabled the 'inner' Swiss cantons (the forest cantons plus Luzern) to reject the reformation and the outer cantons to pursue a protestant reformation in a way which turned out to be distinctively different from that which was emerging in Germany. (See map on page 369.)

4.7.2 Overall chronology

1516 Treaty of Fribourg (29 Nov) settled outstanding subsidy payments owed by the French monarchy and agreed a 'perpetual' treaty to provide mercenary forces in future.

1519 Geneva (not part of the Swiss Confederation) signed an alliance with Fribourg.

1521 Treaty (7 May) regulating the detailed terms for the mercenary forces to be provided to the French monarchy (not less than 6,000, not more than 16,000 infantry).

1522–24 First reforming impulses in Zürich and Bern; opposition to change in Luzern. Claus Hottinger (from Zürich) executed (8 March 1524) in Luzern for his opposition to images in churches and Zwingli* burnt in effigy.

1524 Federal diet at Luzern (April) heard proposals to exclude 'heretics' from participation in the confederation (i.e. Zürich).

1524–25 Effects of German Peasants' War felt in German-speaking Switzerland.

1526 The federal diet called for a disputation, to resolve differences (20 Mar). Representatives were summoned to Baden to meet the bishops of Konstanz, Basel, Sion and Chur. The debate was orchestrated by Johann Eck*; the evangelical[†] case was presented by Oecolampadius* from Basel and Berthold Haller* from Bern. Zwingli absented himself on the grounds that the Bible was not the final arbiter to the disputation and that the place was not 'free'. The conclusions to the disputation were hostile to the protestant reformers in Switzerland who ignored its findings.

1526–29 Geneva signed an alliance with both Bern and Freiburg. Progress towards protestant reformation in Zürich and Bern.

1529 Formation of the League of protestant cantons (the 'Christian Civic Union' (*Christliche Burgrecht*)) which included (after

February), Zürich, Bern, Basel, St Gallen, Bielen Strasbourg, Mühlhausen and Schaffhausen. The alliance guaranteed mutual protection, and encouraged the suppression of monasteries. Formation of a counter League amongst the catholic inner cantons (Luzern, Uri, Schwyz, Unterwalden and Zug) (23 April). This 'Christian Alliance' (*Christliche Vereinigung*) secured the protection of Duke Ferdinand of Austria and sought to uphold the 'old true Christian faith and sacraments'.
'First Kappel War' ended without bloodshed with a negotiated truce at Landfrieden on 24 June. The 'Christian Alliance' was dissolved; the 'Christian Civic Union' was recognized and accepted; cantons were exhorted to renounce foreign pensions and gifts for mercenaries.

1531 'Second Kappel War' (June–Oct) led to skirmishes and defeat of the forces of the Zürich canton at Kappel (11 Oct) and those of Bern at Gubel (24 Oct) which brought it to a negotiated end.
Second Peace of Kappel (20 Nov); those regions which had chosen to accept protestantism were not to be compelled to change religion. Catholic parishes, however, could not henceforth alter their religious allegiance. The religious map of the Swiss cantons was thus determined. The 'Christian Civic Union' collapsed, Konstanz remained outside the Swiss Confederation and the inner cantons remained catholic.

1536 Bern, allied with Fribourg, conquered the Vaud and the regions of Gex and Chablais from the duke of Savoy, thus making Lake Geneva a Bernese lake and Geneva a 'protected' city.

1564 Bern compelled to return the regions south of Lake Geneva to the duke of Savoy; the city of Geneva lost its degree of 'protection' from its Savoyard neighbour.

4.7.3 Zwingli and the reformation in Zürich

None of the cities of Switzerland was large. That of Zürich, which (partly because of its proximity to southern Germany) acted as a leading diplomatic and political instrument of the confederation, was probably no larger than about 7,000 inhabitants at the time of the reformation. The town constitution (1498) laid down a delicate equilibrium between the town and the rural hinterland of the canton and between the representatives of the notability and the guilds. The former dominated the Small Council (of 50), the latter the Great Council (of 212). The Great Council made the major decisions about the canton's external affairs and about the future direction of the city; but they were advised by a 'privy council' (*der heimliche Rat*). The city was in the bishopric of Konstanz.

The weakness of episcopal authority in the city (where the city fathers already took responsibility for the maintenance of true religion within the canton), and the opposition amongst the clergy of the city to its bishop, contributed to the early progress of the reformation in Zürich. But the pace of the reformation in Zürich was dictated by the need to convince the city fathers of the advantages of a particular change at each stage. This gave the Swiss reform a rhythm punctuated by public debate and a particularly 'civic' tone and outcome.

Chronology

1519 Zwingli elected stipendiary priest (*Leutpriester*) by the Great Minster (*Grossmünster*) chapter at Zürich (1 Jan).

Mid-1520 Zwingli purchased numerous treatises by Luther; growing clarity of his evangelical[†] convictions.

1522

23 March Zwingli preached on the second Sunday in Lent about fasting – arguing that it was not obligatory for Christians. The sermon was printed as *Of freedom of choice in the selection of food* (*Von Erkiesen und Freiheit der Speisen*). The city authorities enforced Lenten abstinence.

2 July Zwingli and colleagues drafted a petition to the bishop calling for the abandonment of celibacy. Priests began to marry in Zürich in 1523 with the connivance of the city authorities. The argument appeared in print in *A friendly request and warning to the Swiss* (*Eine freundliche Bitte und Ermahnung an die Eidgenossen*).

6 Sep Publication of Zwingli's *Of the clarity and certainty of the word of God* (*Von Klarheit und Gewissheit des Wortes Gottes*) – a short introduction to Bible study prepared for some Zürich nuns. God's word was irresistible and always lucid to those who sought its meaning in the right way.

10 Oct Zwingli publicly resigned his post as stipendiary priest and was appointed 'preacher' by the city council.

1523

23 Jan First public debate about the reformation. The bishop of Konstanz refused to take part in person. The text of the Bible was to be the deciding authority in this and subsequent debates. The debate took place in the town hall. Zwingli prepared 67 theses (*Schlussreden*) to defend. The main issues were:
  – reverence to images[†] in churches
  – efficacy of prayers to saints
  – meaning of the word 'church'
  – authority of the pope

- the mass[†] as a 'sacrifice'
- purgatory[†].

The outcome saw the confirmation of Zwingli as the city's preacher and the publication of Zwingli's theses.

29 Aug   Publication of Zwingli's first extended discussion of the mass[†] – an elaboration of one section of the previous theses. In *An essay on the canon of the mass* (*De canone missae epicheresis*) Zwingli attempted a scholarly and textual analysis of the mass liturgy which attempted to show that the prayers were of varying antiquity and authenticity, and that the notion of the mass as a sacrifice was unwarranted.

26–28 Oct   The second public debate concentrated on the question of images[†]; as a result images were removed from all Zürich churches by council decree (15 June 1524).

1524   Impact of German Peasants' War in the canton; problems over payments of tithes[†].

1525   Disputes with anabaptists[†] (see pages 102–3).

15 Jan   Institutional changes: Secularization[†] of the monasteries begun; creation of a common chest for poor relief.

Spring   The sketch of an alternative service to the mass in German (published as *The form or manner of the last Supper* (*Aktion oder Brauch des Nachtmals*); replacement of the mass by an evangelical[†] communion service at Eastertide (13 April).

Zwingli published his most substantial treatise on *Religion, true and false* (*De vera et falsa religione commentarius*). Designed as a personal confession of faith and dedicated to the French king, François I, it used the distinction between false religion (superstitious Rome) and true religion (the true faith derived from the Bible) to provide a picture of the world as a continuing struggle between the two since Creation and a running commentary on current Christian doctrine and practice. The church was the assembly of the faithful, wherever that occurred, and should not be identified with a particular hierarchy or group. There were only two sacraments[†] (baptism[†] and the eucharist[†]). Child baptism could not be directly proved from scripture but could be derived by implication. The eucharist was not a sacrifice. When Christ said 'This is my body' he meant 'signifies', a symbolical explanation which was both scriptural and intelligible by faith. Purgatory[†] was a money-making invention. The pope was Antichrist[†]. The worship of images[†] detracted from true religion and they should be removed. The Gospel did not necessarily promote civil disorder. A ruler who supported the 'true' religion would command the obedience of his subjects; but a ruler who maintained a 'false' religion was necessarily a tyrant.

10 May Institution of the marriage tribunal in Zürich under the authority of the town council (*Ehegerichtsordnung*).

19 June Beginning of daily language (Latin, Hebrew and Greek) and Bible study at the Great Minster (*Prophezei*).

1526

Feb Zwingli published his *A Clear Exposition of Christ's Last Supper* (*Eine klare Unterrichtung vom Nachtmahl Christi*). This was one of seven expositions in the years from 1525–27 of his distinctive view of the sacraments which led to Zwingli and his adherents being described as 'sacramentarians'[†].

1527 Final disputes and expulsion of anabaptists[†] from Zürich (see pages 103–4).

1528

Jan Public debate at Bern.

21 April First reformed synod of Zürich.

1529

1 April Introduction of the reformation (with Zürich influence) at Basel.

1–3 Oct Colloquy of Marburg (between Luther and Zwingli) (see page 232).

1530

3 July Zwingli presented the Zürich confession (*Fidei ratio*) to the diet of Augsburg.

1531

July Zwingli renewed his appeal to François I in his *Confession of Faith* (*Fidei ratio*). Reformed Christianity was no danger to the established order. Careful doctrinal statements were presented on the fundamental and unchallenged components of belief (the sovereignty of God, salvation through Christ alone, his ascension and resurrection, the Trinity, the sacred witness of the Bible, etc). The eucharist, however, was a symbolical memorial. The established order of society and authority was not affected. The prophets were there to warn kings of spiritual dangers. He warned François I of the dangers of false religion and appealed to him to allow the Gospel to be preached freely within his dominions.

11 Oct Zwingli's death at the battle of Kappel.

4.7.4 Bern and its satellites

Bern (also Berne) was, like Zürich, a small town with a substantial responsibility for a rural canton. But it was constitutionally rather different.

In comparison with Zürich's mildly participative constitution, Bern was an oligarchy which took its decisions prudently and deliberately, and with one eye on its immediate neighbours and allies. It had traditionally enjoyed the protection of the French monarchy, and had strongly backed the agreement to provide the French with mercenaries at the treaty of Freiburg. Its patricians hoped to realize the benefits of the French alliance by securing the protective overlordship of its western neighbours. Small territories at Orbe, Grandson and Morat were already jointly administered with Fribourg. The *pays* de Vaid, and the satellites of Gex, Thonon and Ternier outside the Swiss Confederation would finally be 'liberated' by Bern in 1536, taking advantage of the French invasion of the duchy of Savoy. This left the episcopal city of Geneva, also not a member of the Swiss Confederation, as a city which was poised between its overlord, the duke of Savoy and its 'protector', the canton of Bern for the decade from 1526 to 1536.

Bern's patricians, like those of Zürich, were concerned to regulate what was said from the pulpit, to decide whether the clergy should be taxed, and whether excommunication of Bernese citizens by its bishop (Basel) was legitimate. Bern's decision to support the reformation was neither easy nor lightly made. It strained its traditional alliances with the catholic French and with Freiburg. On the other hand, it brought it stronger links in the confederation (with Zürich) and the possibilities of exploiting the unrest in Geneva. Bern's decisions of 1527–28 were to prove critical to the survival of the evangelical religion in the Swiss Confederation.

Chronology

1509   'Jetzer affair'. Hans Jetzer, a tailor from Bern who joined the Dominican order, claimed to see visions and work miracles. An investigation by the city authorities revealed fraud and deception.

1522–23 Circulation of Lutheran literature in Bern; some humanist-influenced teachers and clergy acted as catalysts.

1523   City ordinances (15 June) requiring preachers to teach only what could be found in scripture (official Minister preacher: Berthold Haller*). These were reinforced in 1524 and 1525.

1525   Council abolished indulgences, clerical dues, and the fiscal and legal privileges of the clergy; priests to reside in their parishes; no pilgrimages, processions or confessions. Magistrates had the exclusive right to appoint and dismiss clergy. No 'evangelical'† reformation.

1526   Rural parts of the canton rejected further changes pressed for by some in the city of Bern. A small uprising in support of the city preacher, Berthold Haller, which politicized the city for change (Jan–Feb).

1527 Elections to the Great Council of the city (Easter) tipped the city fathers in favour of 'evangelical' change. Priests were allowed to marry openly; masses for the souls of the dead sponsored by the guilds were abandoned; the need for a public disputation about the religious future of the city was accepted (15 November).

1528 Public disputation (6 Jan). Agenda devised by Berthold Haller. Topics included tradition, chastity, marriage of priests, purgatory[†], images[†], intercession of the saints, the mass[†] as a sacrifice, the eucharist[†], the definition of the church and its powers. Zwingli attended with observers and delegates from St Gall, Graubünden, Strasbourg, Konstanz, Ulm, Nuremberg, Augsburg, Mühlhausen and elsewhere. The outcome determined the Bernese reformation along Zürich lines.

The city banned the mass, provided for the removal of altars and images, confiscated monastic property and allowed priests to marry (26 Jan).

1532 Synod of Bern (9–14 Jan) established its church organization, including a court of morals (*Chorgericht*) in each parish and a superior ecclesiastical court with rights of excommunication (*Oberchorgericht*).

1536 Bern 'liberated' the pays de Vaud and Gex, Thonon and Ternier.

4.7.5 Geneva (to 1536)

Geneva was an independent French-speaking, episcopal city, ruled by a bishop, which had gradually been turned into a family possession of the duchy of Savoy. The *bourgeois* (the old-established Genevan notable families) steadily increased their influence over their own affairs so that, by 1519, they had gained a substantial measure of self-government. This was exercised through four syndics as chief officials acting on the authority of the small council of 24 (exclusively reserved for the *bourgeois*). Other councils such as the council of 60, the council of 200 and the general council of the city occasionally met to debate and decide important issues and elections. Independence from Savoyard influence and confederation with the neighbouring Swiss cantons became the divisive issue in Genevan politics from 1519 onwards. The Genevan reformation rode on the back of it. (For further developments in Geneva post-1536, see pages 178–82.)

Chronology

1519 Faction of *Eidgenossen* led by Philibert Berthelier to 'deliver' Geneva from Savoyard overlordship against the *Mamelukes*, supporters of the duke of Savoy and the bishop of Geneva. Berthelier was executed.

1526 *Eidgenossen* faction once again seized control in the city councils and signed an alliance of confederation (*combourgeoisie*) with Bern and Freiburg (12 March).

1528–29 Bishop and duke of Savoy attempted to recover the city by military force and formed in the city a confraternity loyal to them (the 'Gentlemen of the Spoon'); the ducal siege of 1530 was thwarted and the *Eidgenossen* weakened.

1532 Geneva, fearful of its fragile political position, tried to prevent the French evangelical preacher Guillaume Farel* from visiting the city (Oct).

1533 Anthoine Froment preached reform in the city; Bern tried to offer him protection against the Genevan council (Jan). There were riots in the city but the bishop of Geneva failed to regain his position.

1534 First disputation to decide Geneva's religious direction (27 Jan–3 Feb). The reformers, supported by the *Eidgenossen* and the canton of Bern, were given the right to use one church in the city.

1535 Guillaume Farel* and Pierre Viret* settled in the city (April). Second disputation (June). The council provisionally abolished the mass and alienated the monastic wealth of the city.

1536 A general assembly of the city took an oath to live by 'the holy law of the Gospel' (21 May).

SECTION FIVE

Sectarian lineages

5.1 Radical typologies

The protestant reformation has been much 'sub-divided' by modern historians. Some historians have designated a 'people's reformation' (*Volksreformation*) to describe the evangelical[†] first decade of the German reformation.[1] This is to distinguish it from the 'princely reformation' (*Fürstenreformation*) which eventually subsumed it and became dominant. Most of the sub-categories have created difficulties of one sort or another and have not been universally accepted. The category of 'radical reformation' is equally of relatively recent vintage. If not invented by, it was given its emphatic delineation by G.H. Williams.[2] The term suggests that, among anabaptists and other related groups, there were movements which were more fundamental in their theology as well as politically and socially more radical. In reality, those who are often classified as 'radical reformers' had little in common beyond the fact that they in some way or another failed to comply with the pattern of reformation established by the 'magisterial reformation'[†] – the religious changes proposed by the theologically-trained masters (*magistri*) such as Luther, Zwingli and Calvin and the secular authorities whose religious changes they orchestrated.

There were *some* features amongst the 'radicals', however, which (although they were far from universally shared) helped to explain their exclusion from the mainstream of ecclesiastical and religious change in the sixteenth century. Many of them broke with the established lineage of Christendom through repudiating baptism in infancy. The insistence on a believer being rebaptized into the true faith created a sectarian separatism which was reinforced by their reordination of ministers, their engaging in missionary campaigns and (in some instances) their inviting of their own martyrdom. They were sometimes referred to as 'enthusiasts' (*Schwärmer*). In some cases they conspicuously turned their back on established learning and social values, espousing the simplicity of peasant

---

[1] L.J. Abray, *The People's Reformation. Magistrates, Clergy and Commons in Strasbourg 1500–1598* (Oxford, Blackwell, 1985).

[2] G.H. Williams, *The Radical Reformation*, 3rd edition (St Louis Center for Reformation Research, 1992).

dress and lifestyle, preferring vernacular Bibles to theologically-inspired treatises. Although they initially shared many objectives in common with the reformation at large (the recovery of Scripture, the desire to reform society and the church), their separatism created sectarian 'lineages' which mushroomed in the early phases of the reformation. Despite sustained persecution and hostility, some of which was intensified as the direct and indirect result of the uprising at Münster, they managed to survive within disparate and dispersed communities which are difficult to document completely and characterize precisely.

5.2 Early enthusiasts and lay preachers

5.2.1 Saxony

Definition implies exclusion. The changes at Wittenberg in the years from 1521 to 1529, during which the Saxon reformation took shape, were only achieved through the exclusion of those who had been Luther's collaborators, or those who had been initially attracted to the movement for change. The identifiable group was known as the 'Zwickau Prophets'.

The 'Zwickau Prophets'
The group inspired by Thomas Müntzer* whilst he was preacher in the small weaving town of Zwickau from August 1520 to April 1521. Nikolaus Storch, a weaver, claimed to have prophetic visions from the Holy Spirit and joined with Marcus Thomae (known as Stübner because his father ran a bathhouse) and Thomas Drechsel, a blacksmith, to form a conventicle in Zwickau in which women were reported to be preaching and where 'prophets' claimed to have conversations with God and to prophesy. Luther was unimpressed with their testimony and the activities of the conventicle were suppressed. There is no apparent connection between it and later anabaptism† in Saxony.

5.2.2 Zürich

Although the scriptural basis for infant baptism† had already been challenged by Karlstadt* and others in Wittenberg, the question only came to the fore in the process of the Zürich reformation. It was Zwingli who coined the term 'catabaptists' (or 'antibaptists'). Zwingli's successor at Zürich, Heinrich Bullinger*, first used the term 'anabaptist' (meaning re-baptist), which the anabaptists themselves rejected because, for them, there was only one baptism and that was for adults only. The issue was hotly debated at a critical juncture in the Zürich reformation. This resulted in the first anabaptist martyrs.

Chronology of radicalism at Zürich

1523
October Signs of dissatisfaction with the pace of change amongst a group of enthusiasts in Zürich. They met in a discussion-group centring around Konrad Grebel*.

1524
August Some rural parishioners around Zürich persuaded by members of this group not to present their babies for baptism[†].
11 August Zürich city council insisted on observance of infant baptismal rites.

1525
17 Jan Public disputation between Grebel (and associates) and Zwingli before representatives of the city; they renewed their order on baptism.
21 Jan Several enthusiasts expelled from the city. The same day, Grebel rebaptized Georg Blaurock (Cajakob)* and 15 others in defiance of the city's ruling and left Zürich for the rural parish of Zollikon.
End Jan Further arrests and temporary expulsions of rebaptizers.
6–8 Nov Further public disputation between Zwingli (and others) and Grebel, Blaurock (and associates) in the Great Minster of Zürich. Rebaptizers were imprisoned, forced to recant, or expelled.

1526
7 March Mantz, Grebel and Blaurock sentenced to imprisonment in Zürich on bread and water 'until they wither and decay' with the stipulation that rebaptizing activity would be punishable by drowning. Grebel died (after release).

1527
5 Jan Felix Mantz tried and drowned by the public executioners; Blaurock expelled.
Feb Schleitheim Confession (see pages 250–1).

Early enthusiasts and pioneer anabaptists
Andreas Bodenstein von Karlstadt* (1486–1541)
Georg Cajakob ('Blaurock')* (c.1492–1529)

Konrad Grebel* (c.1497–1526)
Ludwig Hätzer* (c.1500–29)
Balthasar Hubmaier* (c.1485–1528)
Felix Mantz* (c.1500–27)
Thomas Müntzer* (c.1490–1525)
Wilhelm Röubli* (Reublin) (c.1484–1559)

5.3 Anabaptist persecution and diaspora

Anabaptist ideas spread quickly from the south German cities outwards down the valleys into the rural world, exploiting the embers of discontent left by the collapse of the Great Peasants' War. The early enthusiasts often acted either directly or indirectly as a 'lightning conductor' for radical ideas. Of critical importance in the 'lineage' of radicalism were Hans Denck* and Hans Hut*; but they were two individuals amongst more numerous groups of *Schwärmer*[†] whose conventicles and activities we can begin to detect through the prosecution of the authorities, especially after 1530.

The anabaptists inevitably faced the hostility of the orthodox churches for their views. However, a good many of the anabaptists in the Empire began to develop a more 'disengaged' view of secular authority. They saw it as inherently evil and worthy of, at best, passive obedience[†]. Others incorporated such a picture within a more apocalyptic[†] vision, predicting an imminent Day of Judgment when the true children of God would arise and defeat the non-believers, thus preparing the way for the return of Christ. To all such views, princes and city governments reacted with predictable hostility. Leaders and groups were arrested, imprisoned and executed. Such actions were confirmed by the imperial diets of Speyer (1529) and Augsburg (1530), where the estates restated the Justinian Code's condemnation of rebaptism as worthy of the death penalty.

Despite the persecution, however, anabaptist groups survived, partly through apparently conforming to established religious obligations whilst unobtrusively continuing to hold conventicle meetings of their own. They were doubtless assisted by local degrees of tolerant acceptance of quietist adherence. They also had the assistance of missions from their Hutterite brethren in Moravia. Although they did not establish much of a presence in the reformed Lutheran states of northern Germany, they were able to survive in rural central Germany and in the urban centres of the Rhineland. Although never likely to become a majority faith anywhere in the Empire, their survival is one of the more fascinating features of the European reformation.

5.3.1 The expansion of anabaptism in southern Germany and Switzerland, 1525–1618

Anabaptist converts, 1525–1618

Area	1525–29	1530–49	1550–1618	Total
Switzerland	588	478	481	1,547
Rhine Valley	549	336	1,054	1,939
Swabia	654	703	1,575	2,932
Tyrol	455	1,178	379	2,012
Austria	422	99	16	537
S-E Germany	323	83	98	504
Franconia	466	157	31	654
Thuringia	112	202	21	335
Hesse	48	451	216	715
Total	3,617	3,687	3,871	11,175

Communities with an anabaptist presence

Area	1525–29	1530–49	1550–1618	Total (1525–1618)
Switzerland	116	182	128	363
Rhine Valley	29	72	246	294
Swabia	39	178	252	379
Tyrol	74	150	97	212
Austria	35	24	7	55
S-E Germany	57	20	29	96
Franconia	107	46	14	151
Thuringia	35	65	8	94
Hesse	15	96	95	177
Total	507	833	876	1,281

Source: Statistics for the above tables are taken from C-P. Clasen, Anabaptism: A Social History, 1525–1618 (Ithaca and London, Cornell University Press, 1972), p. 21.
(See map on page 370 for locations.)

5.3.2 Leading anabaptist figures

Hans Denck* (c.1500–27)
Oswald Glait (var: Glaidt)* (1490–1546)

Hans Hut* (c.1490–1528)
Melchior Hofmann* (1495?–1543)
David Joris* (c.1500–56)
Pilgram Marpeck* (c.1495–1556)
Dirk (Dietrich) Philips* (1504–68)
Obbe Philips* (c.1500–68)
Menno Simons* (c.1496–1561)

5.3.3 Anabaptist foyers

Strasbourg
Strasbourg (the 'strategic crossroads of the Radical Reformation'[3]) was known as the 'city of hope' or 'refuge of righteousness' to the anabaptists. In addition to its own radical lay preachers such as Clement Ziegler and Katharina Zell*, the city became the temporary host to refugee radicals from elsewhere in Germany in the late 1520s and 1530s, the period when the internal divisions of its own governing authority (*Magistrat*) provided a degree of latitude. Martin Bucer* found himself in a succession of disputes with them over the widening range of issues which the Lutheran reformation had raised, but hardly solved. These radicals included Michael Sattler* (1526), Hans Denck* (1526), Pilgram Marpeck* (1528–32), Caspar Schwenckfeld (1529–34), Melchior Hofmann* (1529–30; 1531–32; 1533), Sebastian Franck (1529–32) and Michael Servetus* (1529). The issues which were raised, and which were discussed amongst the radicals themselves during these years, included adult baptism†, antitrinitarianism†, the eucharist†, the nature of the church and the godly community†, excommunication†, usury†, spiritual birth and rebirth, and Christ's coming and second coming.

The Netherlands
Dutch anabaptism† took root amidst the evangelical† and sacramentarian† supporters to be found in the lower Rhineland cities and politically disparate provinces of the Netherlands. From the province of Flanders comes some information about the social background of those prosecuted for heresy, a significant minority of whom were anabaptists. However, the statistics fail to reflect the significance of anabaptism in the 1530s and 1540s, which was the period when it 'absorbed the sacramentarian movement . . . and dominated the Dutch Reformation'.[4]

[3] G.H. Williams, *The Radical Reformation*, 3rd edition (Philadelphia, Westminister Press, 1962), p. 159.
[4] C. Krahn, *Dutch Anabaptism: origin, spread, life and thought, 1450–1600* (The Hague, Nijhoff, 1968), p. 118.

Persons accused of protestant opinions in the province of Flanders, 1521–65

	1521–44		1545–65		
Social class	Lutheran	Anabaptist	Reformed	Anabaptist	Total
Clergy	20	1	39	0	60
Nobility	2	0	5	0	7
Middle classes	67	1/4	456	83	607
Lower classes	71	24/20	489	260	844
Totals	160	26	989	343	1,518

Source: Figures taken from Geoffrey Parker, *The Dutch Revolt* (London, Penguin, 1977), p. 60; in turn based on J. Decavele, *De dageraad van de Reformatie in Vlanderen*, 2 vols (Brussels, Academie voor Wetenschappen, Letteren, en Schone Kunsten van België, 1975), i, p. 549 (table).

Significant centres for anabaptist influence included Amsterdam and Leeuwarden, where the first Dutch anabaptist 'martyr' was beheaded (20 March 1531). The support for Melchior Hofmann* grew rapidly in the early 1530s. One of the consequences of increasing alarm amongst the authorities at the development was the exile of Dutch anabaptists to Münster (see pages 109–10). Supporting apocalyptic[†] movements to that occurring in Münster arose in the Netherlands in 1534–35. On 10 Feb 1534, seven men and women burned their clothes and ran naked through the streets of Amsterdam proclaiming the coming of the kingdom. The subsequent débâcle at Münster increased the prosecution of anabaptist suspects in the Netherlands and encouraged the emergence of more quiescent, outwardly conformist anabaptist communities with a greater stress upon internal discipline. God's church (*gemeente Godts*) was to be protected by appointed elders who undertook the adult baptisms[†] and supervised the ban[†] against association with unbelievers. The churches had two bishops, one of whom (Gillis von Aken) was executed in 1557 whilst the other (Lenaert Bouwens) lived on to 1582. The registers he kept of baptisms into the faith provide invaluable evidence on the strength of Dutch anabaptism.

One effect of the use of the ban, however, was to encourage the fissiparous tendencies of Dutch anabaptism, which became evident in the second half of the century. In 1555–56, the 'Waterlanders' (in the region to the north of Amsterdam) separated from the Mennonites[†] and held their own gatherings, calling themselves 'Baptist supporters' (*Doopsgezinde*) to distinguish themselves from their highly orthodox brethren. Another division occurred on linguistic lines between the Flemish anabaptists (from the Flemish-speaking southern Netherlands) and the Dutch-speaking anabaptists. These splits weakened Dutch anabaptism and affected anabaptism more generally in Europe.

Moravia

The margravate of Moravia was a separate but interlinked political entity with the Czech kingdom. The majority of its population was Czech but there was a significant German minority, especially in the towns. The majority of the Moravian nobility were Utraquist (see page 40) and their dissenting traditions and the constitution of the margravate provided the anabaptists with sufficient religious latitude to establish substantial communities in rural Moravia. Balthasar Hubmaier* was here, as elsewhere, a focus for the initial anabaptist implantation. He arrived at Mikulov (Nikolsburg) in 1526 and, with the support of a local noble (Leonhart of Liechtenstein) established an anabaptist community that became the model for many others. Although it is difficult to know how many anabaptists there eventually were in Moravia, it is possible that there were over 20,000, the majority of whom had come from outside the margravate. As was the case with other refugee reformations, they brought with them a variety of technical skills as masons, weavers, beekeepers and mechanics which were put to good use. At the same time, ethnic and religious disagreements over such issues as pacifism led the Moravian anabaptists to fragment. The problems surrounding the establishment of their farms and communities led to the sharing of possessions. It was particularly encouraged by the Tyrolean anabaptist Jakob Hutter. The 'community of goods' which was a noted feature of some of the Moravian anabaptists in the sixteenth century grew out of practical necessity as well as theological imperative.

Poland

Polish anabaptism was initially an outgrowth of exile and refuge from its persecution in the Empire. In 1535, the first significant communities of baptized brethren ('initiated' – *eingeweiht*) moved to Torún (Thorn). In the same year, a similar community of Slovac anabaptists arrived from Hungary and settled near Poznań. Meanwhile, taking advantage of Dutch trading contacts with the Hansa ports, Dutch Mennonites[†] sought refuge from prosecution at home in and around Gdańsk (Danzig). Polish anabaptist communities, especially in rural locations, would survive the sixteenth century. They had their greatest significance, however, in their influence on the Polish Brethren[†]. After the general synod of Pińzców[†] (1563) the separate Unitarian Minor Reformed church of the Polish commonwealth accepted adult rebaptism and, in time, absorbed many of the former anabaptist communities.

(For the Polish political and religious background, see pages 166–8.)

Italy

The impact of anabaptism in the northern Italian cities and principalities should not be underestimated. It made its first appearance in the later 1520s and was sustained by Hutterite missions. The first prosecution for anabaptism was a Tyrolean master-carpenter in Venice (1535). Il Tiziano, an anabaptist elder, was actively setting up conventicles as late as 1549–53. He rebaptized Pietro Manelfi, a priest from Ancona, in Ferrara in c.1549. His evidence to the inquisition[†] in 1551 compromised many anabaptists and crippled the movement thereafter. (For the Italian political and religious background, see page 145.)

5.3.4 Hutterite missions

Location	Date	
	1530–49	1550–1618
Switzerland	1	18
Rhineland	1	17
Swabia	7	20
Austrian Tyrol	16	25
Austria	8	2
Bavaria and South-East Germany	4	16
Franconia	1	1
Thuringia	0	2
Hesse	8	13

Source: C-P. Clasen, Anabaptism: A Social History, 1525–1618 (Ithaca and London, Cornell University Press, 1972), p. 21.

5.4 The anabaptist rising at Münster

5.4.1 Chronology

1531 Lutheran preaching begun by Berndt Rothmann*, supported by Berndt Knipperdollinck*.

Resignation of bishop of Münster; death of successor (late 1531).

1532 New preaching ordinances issued by city fathers, allowing Lutheran preaching in six city parishes (May).

1533 Temporary exile to the city of Lutheran protestants from the duchy of Jülich-Cleves; also refuge of a group of Melchiorites[†] from the Netherlands.

1534

Feb   Arrival of two Melchiorite apostles in Münster, despatched by Jan Matthys* from Haarlem. The apostles were rebaptized in the city; Rothmann and others took the lead. Two apostles replaced by two further anabaptist enthusiasts, one of whom was Jan Bockelson*.

8 Feb   Call for mass repentance; apocalyptic visions reported; processions; seizure of the town hall and market-place. Anabaptists granted liberty of conscience and freedom of worship in the city.

23 Feb   Annual elections to the city council; anabaptists gained a predominance there and Knipperdollinck was elected as one of the two council leaders (*Burgomeister*); Matthys effectively leader of the city.

end Feb   Looting of monasteries and churches, some iconoclasm[†].

27 Feb   Matthys preached a sermon advocating a 'new Jerusalem purified of all uncleanness'. He advocated the immediate execution of all catholics and Lutherans. The city voted for the expulsion of all opponents to the new regime; street gangs enforced the ordinance on those who refused to comply. About 2,000 left the city and about 2,500 anabaptists arrived.

28 Feb   Exiled bishop of Münster, having organized a mercenary army, began to lay siege to the city by laying earthworks.

1–3 March   Mass rebaptism of all remaining inhabitants in the market-place. Everyone was enjoined to call one another 'brother' and 'sister' and live in community, bound together by love and without sin.

Easter   Confiscation of exiles' property which was placed in warehouses in the city. After praying for three days, Matthys declared the names of seven deacons to administer the warehouses on behalf of the poor. One account claimed that a blacksmith questioned the legitimacy of these proceedings. Matthys summoned the populace to a prayermeeting in the market-place where Matthys preached that the Lord was outraged by the slandering of his Prophet and that the slanderer had to be cut off from the Chosen People; Matthys was said to have stabbed the blacksmith in front of those assembled.

4 April   Easter Sunday; the date when Jan Matthys had predicted the end of the world would begin. Jan Matthys was killed leading a sortie against the besieging forces.

April–May   Population held loyal by regular sermons from Bockelson, Rothmann and others. Suspected doubters locked in a church and threatened with death unless they showed signs of repentance. According to one account, Bockelson ran naked through the city and fell into silent ecstasy lasting three days. When his speech returned, he called the population together to announce that God had revealed to him that the old constitution of the town must be replaced by a more godly one consisting of 'the 12 Elders of Israel'. In practice, the new constitution was designed to accommodate the immigrant anabaptists with the old Münster notables.

June   New ordinances stipulated a strict direction of labour for public purposes; capital offences for crimes of murder, theft, lying, slander, avarice and quarrelling. Knipperdollinck was appointed executioner and given the 'Sword of Justice' and an armed bodyguard. Money was abolished. New coins were issued for public purposes involving dealings with the outside world. Communal ownership of main commodities was declared. At each town-gate there were dining rooms established for those requiring meals. Sleeping accommodation was also to be made available in former monasteries and churches.

July   Bockelson proposed the introduction of polygamy on the grounds that God had revealed to him that the Biblical injunction of *Genesis* 1:28 ('Go forth and multiply') was a divine commandment. The proposal was not immediately accepted and only after dissenters had been threatened with the wrath of God did the Elders accept it. A brief rising against the ordinance for the sharing of women was put down by force and 50 were executed. The ordinance required that all women should be married; marriage was declared a civil ceremony and divorce was permitted. Domestic discord was punishable by death.

late Aug   An attack by the besiegers was routed.

Sep   One of the immigrant anabaptists proclaimed that God had revealed to him that Bockelson was to be king of the whole world, holding dominion over all kings, princes and great ones on earth. He took the sword of justice and presented it to Bockelson, anointed him and proclaimed him the Prophet-King of the New Jerusalem. Bockelson accepted the kingship and proclaimed that Münster would be delivered by the following Easter.

Autumn   All streets and gates in the town renamed to celebrate the New Jerusalem and its King. Sundays and feast-days were abolished and the days of the week renumbered on an alphabetic system. Gold and silver commemorative coins were minted, an emblem and badge for the new kingdom issued, and the new king's court established. Divara, the widow of Jan Matthys was made chief spouse and queen.

Oct   Rothmann's pamphlets, the *Restitution* and *The Announcement of Vengeance*, were published. These proclaimed the three Ages of the world and announced the imminent Third Age (blowing of the Final Trumpet and Feast of the Lord). Copies were smuggled out to encourage supportive risings in Gelderland, West Frisia and Minden in January 1535.

1535

Jan   Total blockade of the city by the forces of the Upper and Lower Rhine Circle.

Easter   Failure of the city to be liberated in accordance with Bockelson's prophecy led to disillusionment.

24 June   Surprise attack led to collapse of the rising. Anabaptists were promised safe quarter but large numbers were put to death.

5.4.2 Leaders of the Münster rising

Jan Bockelson (Jan van Leyden)* (1509–36)
Berndt Knipperdollinck* (1490?–1536)
Jan Matthys (var: Matthijsz)* (?–1534)
Berndt Rothmann* (1495?–1535)

5.5 Spiritualists

Schwenckfeldians
Followers of the German radical spiritual nobleman, Kaspar von Schwenckfeld (1489–1561). He responded enthusiastically to Luther's message, had a series of prophetic dreams in 1519 and put himself at the head of an evangelical movement in Silesia, where he had his estates. By the climax of the Peasants' War, he had his doubts about the effects of the Lutheran movement and these were reinforced by a further dream sequence as a result of which he criticized Luther's eucharistic views and began to elaborate his own. He left Silesia before he was banished and retired to Strasbourg in 1529. By then his distinctive theological views were publicized through conflicts with magisterial reformers and also with other anabaptists. Schwenckfeld believed that Christ had become 'heavenly flesh'. When particles of this heavenly flesh are eaten at the eucharist[†], we become reborn and, in effect, two human beings, an old (outward) corporal being and a new (inner), spiritual

one. What happened to this 'inner' being was more important than what happened to the outer one. The Lord's Supper was a symbolic representation of an 'inner supper' where heavenly flesh had really been consumed. 'Inner baptism' was more important than any formal representation (whether for infants or adults). No persecution was effective since the inner soul could not be coerced. Schwenkfeld's influence extended to the establishment of congregations in his name in Silesia (about 17 communities) with further adherents in southern Germany (over 30 communities), the Rhineland and the Netherlands which survived through to the Thirty Years' War and beyond.

Franckists
Supporters of Sebastian Franck (1499–1542), a printer and spiritualist who had admirers rather than followers and who established no formal sect. Like other spiritualists, his views evolved from initial evangelical[†] enthusiasm generated by Luther. From 1530 to 1532, he was resident in Strasbourg. Expelled in 1533, he retired to Ulm whence, once more compelled to move, he went to Basel. His considerable writings, and commentaries on the works of others, concentrated on the comparison between an outer corrupt world of the flesh and an inner world of God's word which could not be constrained by any institution, church, movement, sect or organized body of thought.

Familists (Family of love)
Sect founded by the visionary and spiritualist from the Netherlands, Hendrik Niclaes (1502–80) in the wake of the collapse of the millenarian Melchiorite[†] enthusiasms of the 1530s. He claimed to have had a prophetic vision in which God had told him to go to a land of piety and proclaim the kingdom of love. He left Amsterdam for Emden, where he made his living as a merchant, wrote his first books and organized his brethren into a community. At Familist meetings, the works of Niclaes were read out. They contained his vision of the true community of believers, inspired by love for one's neighbour and mutual charity, a model of the world after the final coming of the Messiah. His adherents established Familist groups in the Netherlands and England in the sixteenth century. The Familists enjoyed (thanks to Niclaes' mercantile contacts and wealth) support amongst the mercantile elite. The printer at Antwerp, Christoper Plantin, was a Familist and he published Niclaes' work. The sect died out in the early seventeenth century.

5.6 Refugee radicals

The categorization 'refugee radicals' is far from watertight. However, the existence of various strands of libertine thinking in Mediterranean lands is evident in the rational natural philosophic speculation which was produced there. When those strands met the currents of the reformation, they produced the most heterodox and challenging radical individuals of the sixteenth century. They were often denounced as unbelievers[†], and not merely in catholic Europe. They also found no favour in the mainstream protestant centres where they sought refuge.

Sebastianus Castellio* (1515–63)
Michael Servetus* (c.1509–53)
Lelio Sozzini (Socinus)* (1525–62)
Fausto Sozzini (Socinus)* (1539–1604)

5.7 Unitarian churches

The Polish Brethren

The Polish Brethren, like the Czech Brethren, were an independent ecclesiastical entity whose roots lay in radical religious division and whose survival rested on gentry support. They became one of the two significant movements formed from the antitrinitarianism[†] of the radical reformation. They were also known as the 'Minor' reformed church of Poland, to distinguish them from the 'Major' reformed church of the Calvinists (see pages 167–8). They split from the other Calvinist protestant reformed groups after a sequence of synods (culminating in the synod of Pińczów (1563)) failed to find a compromise on the issue of belief in the Trinity. The unitarian separatists held their first synod at Brezeziny (Lithuania) in 1565 and described themselves as 'the Brethren from Poland and Lithuania who have rejected the Trinity'. They saw themselves as called to finish the reformation which Luther, Zwingli and Calvin had begun. The focus for the Minor church was at Raków where it had the steady protection of the Polish landed magnate Michał Sieniecki (1521–81). By 1566, however, there were more than 60 worshipping congregations in Lithuania, Poland and Ruthenia with significant figures amongst the Polish nobility (*szlachta*) offering support (e.g. Prince Mikolaj Radziwiłł).

Transylvanian unitarians

The unitarian church of Transylvania was perhaps the only radical movement which emerged from the reformation to receive a measure of official recognition and support. At the court of Prince János Zsigmond Zápolya (1540–71), his Italian physician (Giorgio Biandrata (1516–88)) and his Hungarian-German preacher (Francis Dávid (G: *Franz Hertel*) (c.1520–79)) provided the influence behind the prince's open conversion to antitrinitarianism at the religious colloquy of Oradea Mare

(G: *Grosswardein*; Hung: *Nagyvárad*) (1569). Although the large latitude given to religious expression in sixteenth-century Transylvania allowed the unitarian church to flourish, in the later sixteenth century it was somewhat weakened by internal divisions and the later prosecution of Dávid (1578–79) (for Transylvania, see pages 162–6).

SECTION SIX

Reactions to the reformation

6.1 France

Rulers	Regnal dates
Valois dynasty	
Charles VIII	1483–98
Louis XII	1498–1515
François I	1515–47
Henri II	1547–59
François II	1559–60
Charles IX	1560–74
Henri III	1574–89 (assassinated)
Bourbon dynasty	
Henri IV	1589–1610 (assassinated)
Louis XIII	1610–43

6.1.1 Constitutional and political background

The kingdom of France was theoretically an absolute monarchy. At the coronation, the kings were consecrated and anointed from an ampulla of sacred ointment to demonstrate that their powers came from (and their responsibilities lay to) God. Yet, like all old and complex governing systems, France had a variety of established legal and representative mechanisms which had a significant place within the state. These included its sovereign courts (*parlements*) in Paris and the provinces, which registered and enforced royal decrees and had various important administrative responsibilities. The judges in the *parlements* held their offices (to an increasing degree in the sixteenth century) from the crown through purchase and inheritance and they had an exalted view of their task to maintain justice and the state. Laws were not made through any representative institutions; the various provincial assemblies (*états*) had, at best, powers to present grievances and negotiate over taxes. The national assembly (*états généraux*) only met occasionally when required by the king, and generally in times of national crisis.

The French kingdom had grown substantially since the *débâcles* of the Hundred Years' War. Its expansion fostered (and made still more

irksome) the Habsburg dynastic coalition which made the Habsburg–
Valois rivalry the dominant feature of Europe's international politics
for the first half of the sixteenth century. The official reactions to the
appearance and growth of heresy within the kingdom were dictated, at
least to some extent, by the prevailing demands of international tension
at any particular moment.

6.1.2 National chronology relating to the protestant reformation and the French civil wars

(For royal edicts and the protestant movement in France, see pages 121–
3).

1521	Lutheranism condemned by the Sorbonne.
1525	Defeat and capture of François I at Pavia; Louise de Savoie (the queen mother) became regent in France; first active repression of heterodox religious elements in France led by the *parlement* of Paris. Lefèvre d'Etaples* and Farel* left France.
1529	Sporadic persecution of evangelicals[†]; the execution of Louis de Berquin*.
1532	François I associated with the Schmalkaldic League of German princes.
1533	Lutheran sermon delivered by Nicolas Cop (c.1501–40), rector of the university of Paris (1 Nov–All Saints' Day). King François exiled and disgraced some of the doctors at the Sorbonne.
1534	The Sorbonne began prosecution of the royal professors of the *Collège royale* (The *Collège de France* – a new royal academy) before the *parlement* of Paris; king forced to intervene. The affair of the placards (billboards stuck up in public places in various cities including Paris, challenging the orthodox conception of the mass[†]) (18 Oct).
1545	Massacre of the Waldenses[†] (Vaudois) in Provence.
1546	Meaux reformers amd Etienne Dolet executed.
1547	Creation of the *Chambre Ardente* at the *parlement* of Paris to try heresy (sat as a separate chamber until 1551).
1551	Alliance between Henri II and Mauritz of Saxony who, having supported the emperor in the Schmalkaldic War, joined the other protestant princes of Germany.
1559	
3/4 April	Treaty of Cateau-Cambrésis.
May	First national synod of the French reformed churches in Paris.

Political instability 1559–62

July   Death of Henri II; accession of François II, an adolescent king 'in tutelage'; his council governed by François de Guise and Charles, cardinal of Lorraine; intensified persecution of protestants.

23 Dec   Execution of Anne du Bourg, a judge at the *parlement* of Paris who expressed his protestant sympathies openly.

1560

March   Tumult of Amboise (an organized *coup d'état* involving various members of the lesser French nobility and implicating others).

Summer   Religious disturbances became more widespread throughout France. Louis de Condé*, leader of the Huguenots, was arrested and sentenced to death for complicity in the conspiracy at Amboise.

Dec   Death of François II; accession of Charles IX, a boy king, with the regency secured by his mother, Catherine de Médicis. Antoine de Bourbon, king of Navarre (Condé's elder brother) was appointed lieutenant-general of the kingdom. His wife, Jeanne d'Albret openly professed Calvinism. Condé was released and the estates-general summoned.

1561

Jan   Estates-general at Orléans dismissed.

Aug   Estates-general reassembled at Pontoise with demands to secularize church wealth. Catholic clergy agreed to repay some royal debts.

Sep   Colloquy of Poissy (see page 246); theological resolution within a national context failed.

Autumn   Huguenot support rapidly increasing, especially in the provincial cities and amongst the rural nobility in certain provinces; signs of Huguenot military organization.

1562

March   Massacre at Vassy (Champagne) by François de Guise acted as prelude to massacres and riots around Eastertide throughout France.

April   Condé set up his military headquarters at Orléans.

First three civil wars (1562–70)

July   Military hostilities of the **first civil war** began.

Autumn   Huguenot military leaders (Condé and Coligny*) allied with Queen Elizabeth I; siege of Rouen (Navarre died).

Dec   Battle of Dreux; capture of the Constable Anne de Montmorency by the Huguenots and Condé by the royalist forces.

1563	Siege of Orléans (Jan–Feb); assassination of catholic military leader, François, duke of Guise.
	Pacification of Amboise (March).
1567	Huguenot attempts to seize the court at Meaux. **Second civil war** began (Sep).
	Battle of St-Denis (Constable Anne de Montmorency killed (Nov).
1568	Pacification of Longjumeau (March).
	Attempted arrest of Condé and Coligny; Huguenot leaders withdrew to La Rochelle. **Third civil war** began (Angust).
1569	Battle of Jarnac (March) (Condé killed). Coligny assumed military leadership of the Huguenots. Protestant reinforcements despatched from Germany.
1570	Pacification of St-Germain (Aug).

Massacre of St Bartholomew and its aftermath (1572–76)
1572

18 Aug	Marriage (cross-confessional) between Henri de Navarre and Marguerite de Valois (king's sister).
22 Aug	Failed attempt to assassinate Coligny.
24 Aug	Massacre of protestants began at Paris (massacre of St Bartholomew).
Sep–Oct	Massacres in provincial centres. Henri de Navarre and Henri de Condé kept in close confinement at court. **Fourth civil war** began.
1573	Siege of La Rochelle, followed by temporary peace (June); but war continued (**fifth civil war**) in southern France, where protestants began to strengthen their political and military organization within a federal and separatist framework.
1574	Death of Charles IX (May). War continued with protestants joined by malcontent catholics ('Politiques').
1575	Protestant reinforcements despatched from Germany.
1576	Henri de Navarre escaped from court and proclaimed his Calvinism (Feb).
	Peace of Beaulieu (Monsieur) (May).
1577	Estates-general of Blois; attempted forcible recatholicization of the kingdom (Dec 1576–March 1577).
	Sixth civil war (April–Sept) ended by the peace of Bergerac.

Wars of the League and Bourbon succession
1585	Treaty of Joinville between the Guise and Spain (Jan).
	Treaty of Nemours (negotiated royal submission to the League) (July).

Pope Sixtus V* excommunicated Henri de Navarre and Henri de Condé (Sep).

1586 War of the League began.

1587 German protestant military reinforcements entered France. League plots in Paris, organized by the 'Sixteen' (*Seize*). Battle of Coutras (Oct); Navarre defeated royal army and killed its commander (Joyeuse). Surprise of Vimory; Guise defeated the German mercenaries.

1588

March   Death of Henri de Condé.

12 May 'Day of Barricades'; insurrection in Paris followed by escape of the king from the capital.

July   Edict of Union; royalist capitulation to the League.

Oct   Estates-general summoned to Blois.

23 Dec Henri, duke of Guise and Louis, cardinal de Guise, assassinated on the king's orders at Blois; other League members of the estates arrested.

1589

Jan   Open rebellion in Paris and many major towns. The League 'council of 40' elected the duke of Guise's brother, Charles duke of Mayenne, lieutenant-general of the kingdom.

July   Assassination of King Henri III, who eventually died 2 Aug. Navarre's uncle, the cardinal de Bourbon, declared King Charles X by the League.

Sep   Battle of Arques (Normandy).

1590 Battle of Ivry (March); first siege of Paris (relieved in September).

1592 Siege of Rouen (relieved March).

1593 League estates-general at Paris to choose League king. League *parlement* of Paris declared for the Salic Law (and the Navarre succession to the throne) (June). Henri IV abjured protestantism at St-Denis (July); many League centres began to acknowledge his kingship.

1595 Declaration of war against Spain by Henri IV. Final submission of Charles, duke of Mayenne in the edict of Folembray (Dec); pockets of League resistance still outstanding.

1598 Final League resistance to succession ended with submission of the duke of Mercoeur in Brittany (March). Pacification at Nantes (April). Peace of Vervins ended war with Spain (May).

6.1.3 French edicts against heresy, 1525–60

Date	Place	Summary
10 June 1525	—	Implemented papal bull[†] against Lutherans; members of the *parlement* of Paris were nominated to assist the inquisitor in searching for heresy within the jurisdiction of that *parlement*.
29 Dec 1529	St-Germain	Required the royal courts to assist the cardinal legate and inquisitors in the search for heresy throughout the kingdom.
29 Jan 1535	Paris	Edict against harbouring and concealing protestant suspects.
16 July 1535	Coucy	A limited amnesty for all heretics who were not repeat offenders and 'sacramentarians'[†] (*sacramentaires*). In future, however, the death penalty was prescribed for all those who read, translated or printed any doctrine contrary to the Christian faith.
24 June 1539	Paris	Previous measures to eradicate heresy were admitted to have failed; those spreading heresy were known to be protected by grandees. The sovereign courts (*parlements*) and the lesser courts were required to assist in the prosecution of offences.
1 June 1540	Fontainebleau	This clarified the previous edict by making heresy a criminal offence and giving the sovereign courts a leading authority in heresy trials.
23 July 1543	Paris	Defined heresy in 25 articles prepared by the Sorbonne[†].
11 Dec 1547	Fontainebleau	Stricter control on printed books. The Sorbonne was to censure all works on the Scriptures, including those from abroad. It was forbidden to sell or possess any book proscribed by the Sorbonne Index[†].

Date	Place	Summary
19 Nov 1549	Paris	Attempt to resolve conflicts of jurisdiction between various courts dealing with heresy cases.
27 June 1551	Châteaubriant	The first comprehensive statute to deal with heresy. Previous measures were admitted to have failed. Only the *parlements* and the lay courts were to proceed against disorders arising from seditious heresy. Strict censorship was proposed. All appointments to royal office, teachers in schools and universities had to provide a certificate of catholicity. Individuals had a duty to inform on suspected heretics who could be prosecuted for religious observances in their own homes. Church attendance was made compulsory and the clergy were required to read out the Sorbonne articles every Sunday.
24 July 1557	Compiègne	Tougher penalties on convicted heretics. The death penalty was made automatic and without appeal for all those convicted of preaching in public or private without licence, on all who defaced or damaged images, on all who took part in illegal or seditious assemblies, and on all who possessed illegal books.
4 Sep 1559	Villers-Cotterêtz	Made the penalties stricter for illegal meetings, assemblies and conventicles by night. Houses where such meetings took place were to be razed to the ground. A further edict in November included rewards for informers.
7 July 1585	Nemours	In response to pressure from the Catholic League this revoked all edicts of pacification and all rights to exercise the protestant religion. Pastors were to be banished within a

Date	Place	Summary
		month and protestants were to abjure within six months or be exiled. Protestants were declared ineligible for public office and benches of judges to deal with cases involving protestants were disbanded. Garrison towns were to be dismantled.

Source: Based on N.M. Sutherland, *The Huguenot Struggle for Recognition* (New Haven and London, Yale University Press, 1980), appendix.

6.1.4 French edicts of toleration and pacification

Date	Place	Summary
March 1560	Amboise	Amnesty for those suspected of heresy offences (except for protestant ministers and those guilty of sedition).
May 1560	Romorantin	All jurisdiction in heresy cases was removed from the secular courts, including the sovereign courts. Bishops were commanded to reside in their dioceses and attend to heresy. But laws against illegal and seditious assemblies were retained; so, too, were those against illegal preaching, printing and distribution of forbidden books.
19 April 1561	Fontainebleau	Outlawed all forms of mutual name-calling, including the use of terms such as 'Papist' and 'Huguenot'. Nobody was to be prosecuted for religious observance in their own homes. Those who had taken up exile for religious reasons could return and reclaim their property.
17 Jan 1562	St-Germain	Known as the 'edict of toleration'. It granted limited rights of assembly

Date	Place	Summary
		for religious purposes outside towns; but all seditious meetings were to be prevented. Synods and consistories were to require official permission. All charitable giving was to be voluntary and not to be used for military purposes. Established feast-days were to be observed. Ministers were to swear to obey the edict and not to engage in seditious preaching. Distributors of seditious literature would face the death penalty on a second offence.
(First civil war) 19 March 1563	Amboise	First edict 'of pacification'. The nobility were allowed to hold religious services on their domains for their household and servants (the *culte privé de concession*). Elsewhere permission was given for protestant worship in one location in each local jurisdiction (*bailliage*) (the *culte de permission*). All church property was to be restored. An amnesty for all acts of war and the release of prisoners was declared. Leagues and associations inside and outside the kingdom were forbidden.
(Second civil war) 23 March 1568	Longjumeau	Second edict 'of pacification'; restored the preceding edict of Amboise.
(Third civil war) 8 Aug 1570	St-Germain	Third edict 'of pacification'. Rights of worship for nobility (*culte privé*) restored. Rights to worship granted in two locations in each local jurisdiction (*culte de permission*) each of which was specified in the edict. Religious discrimination in schools, universities, hospitals and royal

Date	Place	Summary
		offices was outlawed. All lawsuits relating to heresy were to be suspended and the records erased. Four garrison towns (*places de sûreté*) granted for two years (La Rochelle, Montauban, Cognac and La Charité) as a guarantee of its enforcement.
(Fourth and fifth civil wars)		
6 May 1576	Beaulieu	Fourth edict 'of pacification' and known as the 'edict of Monsieur'. Free, general and public protestant worship permitted by consent of the local inhabitants except in Paris. Legal possession of churches (*temples*) granted and burial grounds permitted. King undertook to appoint protestant judges and officials and create separate benches of judges of mixed faith to hear protestant cases (*chambres mi-parties*). All those involved in the massacre of St Bartholomew were exonerated and amnestied. Leagues and associations were forbidden. Eight garrison towns (two in each of the southern provinces) were permitted.
(Sixth civil war)		
17 Sep 1577	Poitiers	Fifth edict of pacification (known as the peace of Bergerac). Worship was granted to the nobility on their estates (*culte privé*). It was also permitted in every location where it had existed on the date of the edict (*culte de concession*). In addition, it would be permitted in one location in each local jurisdiction (*culte de permission*) to be determined by commissioners of the edict. Benches of judges of mixed faith (*chambres mi-parties*) were to continue to judge cases involving protestants. Separate

Date	Place	Summary
		('secret') articles granted the protestants eight garrison towns for six years in the southern provinces and provided funds to pay for the garrisons.
28 Feb 1579	Nérac	Clarified the terms of the preceding edict and provided the protestants with ways to raise money to pay pastors.

(Further limited military engagements)

| 26 Nov 1580 | Fleix | Restored the peace of Bergerac. |

(Wars of the League and Bourbon succession)

| 4 July 1591 | Mantes | Restored the peace of Bergerac. |
| c.13 April 1598 | Nantes | Comprehensive pacification of the wars of religion. Full amnesty, restoration of catholic property and worship throughout France. The rights of protestant nobles to worship on their estates was confirmed (*culte privé*). Worship was also conceded in every location where it had existed in 1577 (*culte de concession*) to be determined by commissioners for the edict. In addition, one further location in each local jurisdiction was permitted (*culte de permission*). Churches were allowed to be built in these locations and burial grounds permitted. No religious exclusion allowed in schools, universities, hospitals or royal offices. Benches of mixed-faith judges reinstated to judge cases involving protestants. No synods or political assemblies were permitted without royal authorization. Further separate ('secret') articles allowed for the payment of pastors and the garrisoning for eight years of those |

Date	Place	Summary
		strongholds which the protestants held in August 1597 (estimated to be c.100), with the king contributing to the garrison costs.

6.1.5 French protestant organization

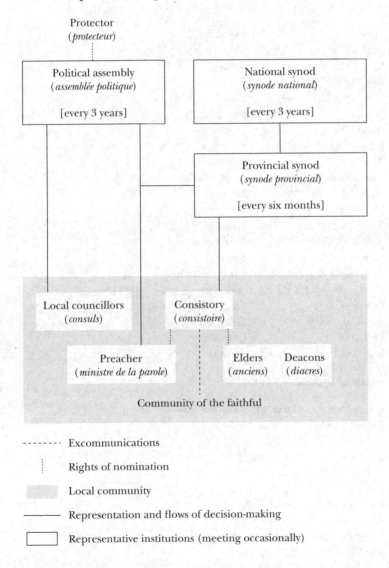

Protector
(*protecteur*)

Political assembly
(*assemblée politique*)

[every 3 years]

National synod
(*synode national*)

[every 3 years]

Provincial synod
(*synode provincial*)

[every six months]

Local councillors
(*consuls*)

Consistory
(*consistoire*)

Preacher
(*ministre de la parole*)

Elders
(*anciens*)

Deacons
(*diacres*)

Community of the faithful

- - - - - - - Excommunications

⋮ Rights of nomination

  Local community

——— Representation and flows of decision-making

  Representative institutions (meeting occasionally)

6.1.6 French protestant political assemblies, national synods and protectors

Political assemblies (to 1612)

Protestant political assemblies gradually evolved from disparate regional bodies in the south of France to become a component constitutionally empowered to represent the political and military unity of the protestant movement in France. The following lists those assemblies which, following the massacre of St Bartholomew, assumed the greatest significance within the Huguenot movement at large and were 'national' in terms of the delegates who attended them:

Date	Location
Aug 1573	Montauban
Dec 1573	Millau
July/Aug 1574	Millau
May–July 1577	Nîmes
July 1579	Montauban
April 1581	Montauban
June 1582	St-Jean d'Angély
Aug 1584	Montauban
Nov 1588	La Rochelle
Oct 1593–Jan 1594	Mantes
May 1594	Ste Foy
April–Sep 1596	Loudun
Nov–Feb 1597	Vendôme
March 1597	Saumur
June 1597–June 1598	Châtellerault
Nov 1599–May 1601	Saumur
Oct 1601	Sainte-Foy
July–Aug 1605	Châtellerault
Oct 1608	Jargeau
May 1611	Saumur

National Synods (to 1618)

Location	Date of commencement
Paris	25 May 1559
Poitiers	10 March 1560
Orléans	25 April 1560
Lyon	10 Aug 1563
Paris	25 Dec 1565
Verteuil	1 Sep 1567
La Rochelle	2 April 1571
Nîmes	6 May 1572
Ste Foy	21 Feb 1578

Figeac	2 Aug 1579
La Rochelle	10 July 1581
Vitré	15 May 1583
Montauban	15 June 1594
Saumur	15 June 1596
Montpellier	26 May 1598
Jargeau	9 May 1601
Gap	1 Oct 1603
La Rochelle	1 March 1607
St Maixant	25 May 1609
Privas	14 May 1612
Tonneins	2 May 1614
Vitré	18 May 1617

'Protectors'

Louis, prince de Condé	1562–69
Gaspard de Coligny, Admiral of France	1569–72
(Henri de Montmorency-Damville; governor of	
Languedoc and *de facto* protector 'in the absence of'	
Henri II, prince de Condé	1574–76)
Henri de Bourbon, King of Navarre	1576–1610

6.2 The Netherlands

6.2.1 The 'Seventeen Provinces' of the Netherlands

The Netherlands was composed of a congeries of largely self-governing and, before the sixteenth century, independent counties and duchies which were part of the Holy Roman Empire. They had their own institutional arrangements and separate assemblies (Fr: *Etats*; D:*Staten*). Only gradually during the fifteenth century had they evolved a separate assembly for delegates from each province or 'states-general' (Fr: *états généraux*; D: *Staten Generaal*). The deputies to the states-general were required to refer back to the local States on any important issue. Since the states-general only met every three years, decisions were only reached very slowly. They became known as the 'Seventeen Provinces' although some of them were not provinces in any other sense than that they were titles to rule in particular localities. The Emperor Charles V thus was 'Duke of Brabant, Limburg, Luxemburg and Gelderland, Count of Flanders . . .'. Some parts of the Netherlands (notably the provinces of Liège and Ravenstein, and parts of Gelderland) remained independent of Habsburg control. On 26 June 1548, in the wake of his victory in the Schmalkaldic War, Charles V persuaded the Diet of the Holy Roman Empire to allow him to form his Netherlands dominions into a governing entity separate from the Empire (the 'Augsburg transaction'). This was the moment when the consolidation of the Netherlands into a conglomerate state began to become a reality. It was a reality which only lasted a generation, however, for the Dutch Revolt split the conglomerate in such a way that a federation of northern provinces came together in January 1579 at Utrecht to agree an act of alliance and union (the Union of Utrecht) by which they decided to act in perpetuity in future 'as if they were a single province' in questions of war and peace. The signatories to the Union became known as the 'United Provinces' and, in the seventeenth century, as 'the Dutch Republic'.

Province	Date of acquisition
Artois	pre-1400
Brabant	pre-1400
Drenthe and Overijssel	1528/36
Flanders	1384
Friesland	1523–24
Groningen and Ommelanden	1536
Gelderland	1543
Hainaut	1428
Holland	1428
Limburg	1430
Luxemburg	1451
Mechelen	1384
Namur	1421
Tournai	1521
Utrecht	1528
Walloon Flanders	1384
Zeeland	1428

(Cambrai and the Cambraisis, although a separate governing entity which had been acquired by conquest in 1543, was not a province in its own right, and remained part of the Holy Roman Empire until 1678.)

6.2.2 Division of the provinces in the Dutch Revolt

The signatories to the Union of Utrecht (29 January 1579)
Friesland
Gelderland
Holland
Ommelanden (part of Groningen)
Utrecht
Zeeland

(Overijssel and Drenthe and various towns of Flanders and Brabant did not accede until later (e.g. Ghent signed the union on 4 Feb 1579). Some of the latter were subsequently captured by the Spanish. Additional areas later annexed by the Dutch from Brabant, Limburg and along the border with Germany were allowed no separate provincial representation in the Dutch Republic because they had not been signatories to the Union.)

6.2.3 Sovereign rulers

Habsburg overlordship

Philip I	1482–1506
Charles V	1506–55 (abdicated)
Philip II	1555–98
Isabella and Albert, archduchess and archduke of Austria	1598–1621

Governors and captains general of the Netherlands (representing Habsburgs)

Mary, queen of Hungary	1530–55
Margaret, duchess of Parma	1559–67
Fernando Alvarez de Toledo, duke of Alba (Dutch: 'Alva')	1567–73
Luís de Requesens	1573–76
Don John of Austria	1576–77
Matthias, archduke of Austria	1577–78 (nominally until 15 March 1581)
(François, duke of Alençon (later duke of Anjou))	1578 (by invitation of the estates-general)
Alessandro Farnese, prince of Parma (duke after 1586)	1578–92
Albert, archduke of Austria	1595–98

Protectors and governors of the northern provinces

1578–79   Johann Casimir (1543–92), count palatine of the Rhine.

29 Sep 1581   François, duke of Anjou (see genealogical table, page 331) contracted overlordship of the Netherlands in return for military assistance and guarantee of the privileges of the provinces (to 1583).

10 Jan 1586   Robert Dudley, earl of Leicester elected governor-general by the states-general (to 1588).

6.2.4 Political chronology and the reformation in the Netherlands

The complexities of the chronology of the Dutch Revolt are indispensable to an understanding of the politics of western Europe in the second half of the sixteenth century. The Low Countries became the focus of international military and diplomatic involvement, which was heightened by confessional loyalties that transcended national boundaries. This political chronology concentrates on the domestic events within the Netherlands and does not attempt to present the wider international picture.

1520	First translations of Luther's works into Dutch at Antwerp; papal bull (*Exsurge domini*) against Luther published at Antwerp (Sep).
1521	War with France began. Public burning of suspect books in cities of Flanders and Brabant.
1521–23	Public support for Luther from the Augustinians at Antwerp: their prior forced to abjure errors in Brussels (Feb 1522) and two Augustinians burnt in Brussels (July 1523) for Lutheran heresy.
1523–	Appearance of evangelical[†] conventicles and private religious gatherings.
1529	Peace with France (The 'Ladies' Peace' (*La 'Paix des Dames'*)) (3 Aug).
1530–	Growth of anabaptist congregations in the Netherlands (see pages 106–8).
1534–35	Anabaptist missions from Münster to muster support from the Netherlands for the siege (see pages 110–12).
1535–36	Renewed repression of heresy in the wake of the Münster uprising.
1536–37	Further hostilities with France (ended truce of Bomy, 30 July 1537).
1542	Renewed war with France.
1544	Peace of Crépy (18 Sep).
1544–45	Renewed repression following the arrest of Pierre Brully at Tournai (an early apostle from Geneva and Strasbourg).

From the 'Augsburg Transaction' to the First Revolt

1551	Renewed war with France.
1555	Abdication of Charles V in favour of Philip II (25 Oct).
1556	Truce of Vaucelles (Feb–July) in war with France.
1559	Peace of Cateau-Cambrésis (3/4 April).
	Papal agreement (May) to the proposal to create 14 new bishoprics in the Netherlands to combat heresy; also the creation of a 'primate' of the Netherlands in the archbishopric of Mechelen. Two canons of each bishopric were to be diocesan inquisitors.
	Philip II departed Brussels for Spain (5 July).

1561–63	Opposition to wartime levels of taxation and the new bishoprics became focused on the Spanish minister in the Netherlands, Antoine Perrenot, Cardinal Granvelle (1517–86).
1562–63	Temporary refuge from civil war of French Calvinists in the southern Netherlands. Formation of 'churches under the cross' (i.e. in secret).
1563	The princes (Orange*, Egmont and Hornes) present ultimatum to dismiss Granvelle (11 March). Granvelle dismissed (Dec) and went into exile (13 March 1564).
1564	
30 July	Council of state in Brussels offered to withdraw contested features of the new bishoprics scheme in return for cooperation from higher nobility on the Council of state and consent to taxation.
Dec	Egmont's embassy to Madrid to gain Spanish consent for extensive concessions. He remained in Madrid until April 1565 and returned convinced that he had secured the king's consent to relax the heresy laws and to recognize the Council of state's concessions of July. The Council of state proposed to establish a theological commission to investigate the heresy laws and their application.
1565	
July/Aug	Riots and disturbances in cloth-towns (including Ghent).
17/20 Oct	Philip II signed the 'Segovia Woods' letters which rejected any concessions, including the proposed theological commission, and asserted the right of the Spanish Council to overrule the Council of state in Brussels.
Dec	'Compromise' (i.e. 'confederation') of about 400 nobles under Jan Marnix to resist the introduction of the inquisition+ into Dutch lands.
1566	
April	'First Request' (petition) against the inquisition presented to Regent Margaret of Parma by an armed posse of confederates sent to her court; one of her advisors described them as a band of 'beggars' (Fr: *Gueux*; D: *Geuzen*) and this became the name which the rebels consciously adopted.
Spring	Calvinist preaching took place outside city walls in Lent to avoid compromising the city magistrates ('hedge preachers').
30 July	'Second Request' from the confederates presented to the Regent requesting freedom of protestant worship where it was already *de facto* being allowed. Philip II's reply to the 'First Request' arrived the following day with minor concessions.

August	Outbreak of systematic image-breaking in and outside churches, spreading from Flanders to the northern provinces (see map on page 372).
23 Aug	Regent Margaret agreed to the 'Second Request' and the confederates signed an 'Accord' with Orange*, Egmont and Hornes to prevent further iconoclasm.
25 Aug	Confederation dissolved and image-breaking continued. Local compromises with iconoclastic† contingents agreed in local accords. Regent warned Philip II of the possibility of complete loss of authority in the Netherlands. Philip II decided to send an army to quell the troubles.
3 Oct	Leading nobles met (at Dendermonde), aware of the possibility of an army of repression. Some left to arm their local strongholds. Others took up refuge in Germany.
Nov	Details of the Flanders army decided and duke of Alba appointed commander (29 Nov).
1567	
April	William of Orange resigned his stadholderships and withdrew from the Netherlands to Nassau (Germany).

From the Alba repression to the Pacification of Ghent (the Second Revolt) (1567–76)

August	Arrival of duke of Alba with Spanish army of 10,000 to crush the rebellion (reached Brussels, 22 Aug).
5 Sep	Formation of the 'Council of Troubles' by Alba. Regent Margaret resigned and Alba succeeded as governor-general, organizing the council along Spanish lines.
1568	
April/May	Aborted invasion of the Netherlands by William of Orange and associated contingents. Formation of the privateering Sea Beggars (Fr: *Gueux de Mer;* D: *Watergeuzen*) around the Ems estuary.
5 June	Execution of Hornes and Egmont at Brussels for treason.
1568–69	Imprisonments, investigations, trials and executions of the Council of Troubles (see page 141 for estimates of the numbers of those investigated).
1569	Proposed new taxes placed before the estates-general (March). These were a one per cent tax on current capital values ('Hundredth Penny'), a five per cent tax on property transfers ('Twentieth Penny') and a ten per cent sales tax ('Tenth Penny'). Vocal and considerable resistance to the latter.
1571	Second aborted invasion of the Netherlands by William of Orange and other nobles in exile.

Duke of Alba proposed to collect the 'Tenth Penny' without consent of the estates-general (31 July).

1572

March   Tax strike in various provinces, especially Hainaut, Artois, Flanders and Brabant. Further landed invasion of the Netherlands by William of Orange and other nobles in exile planned with French Huguenot assistance.

1 April   Landing of Sea Beggars at Den Briel (The Brill); revolt fostered amongst smaller towns of Holland.

7 July   William of Orange entered the Netherlands with an army of 20,000; French supporting invasion thwarted.

19 July   States of Holland at Dordrecht; declared William of Orange 'the general governor and lieutenant of the king over Holland, Zealand, Friesland and the bishopric of Utrecht as he had been previously' on the grounds that he had never been formally dismissed by the States in accordance with its privileges. On 20 July they promised freedom of religious worship to all the 'Reformed and Roman catholics, in public or in private, in church or in chapel'.

12 Sep   Orange withdrew from siege at Mons and retired with remnants of army northwards, and then to Holland (Nov).

Dec   Beginning of the siege of Haarlem by Spanish forces.

1573   Fall of Haarlem (12 July) threatened the revolt of Holland by splitting the area under Orangist control.

Arrival of Luís de Requesens (appointed 30 Jan) as replacement to the duke of Alba (17 Nov).

1574   Siege of Leiden begun (March) (later lifted, then reimposed).

Land around Leiden flooded and Spanish siege broken (3 Oct). Spanish troops mutinied (Dec).

1575   Acceptance by the two provinces of Holland and Zealand of William of Orange as 'sovereign and supreme head' (*souverein ende overhooft*) during the war and establishment of the 'provincial council' (*landraad*) to advise him (11 July).

1576

5 March   Death of Spanish governor Requesens.

April   The 'Closer Union' of Holland and Zealand agreed at Delft, giving William of Orange powers to administer justice (including the right of pardon) with the Court of Holland, to appoint magistrates in the cities (whilst respecting urban privileges) and to maintain the Reformed[†] religion to the exclusion of the exercise of all other religion (whilst accepting freedom of conscience for individuals). All municipal officials were required to take an oath of loyalty to him.

July/August   'Spanish Fury'; sack of Aalst (west of Brussels); mutiny spread and Council of state put under house arrest by elements (probably) in sympathy with Orange (4 Sep).

Sep   States-general summoned to Brussels by the Council of state (without Philip II's permission). Forces were recruited to protect the provinces against Spanish mutineers; negotiations with deputies from the rebel provinces of Holland and Zealand begun.

Oct/Nov   'Pacification' of Ghent between the rebel provinces and the states-general of the Netherlands begun (10 Oct) and completed (30 Oct) with ratification in November. The states would nominate a new governor-general to Philip II, providing that he accepted the Pacification, dismissed all foreign troops and governed only through 'natives'. The states-general would decide matters of religion in due course, but in the meantime, all measures against heretics would be withdrawn. William of Orange to be accepted as stadholder in Holland and Zeeland.

From the Pacification of Ghent to the Act of Abjuration (The Third Revolt) (1576–81)

1577   William of Orange entered Brussels in triumph (Sep).
Arrival of Don John of Austria (Philip II's half-brother) as governor-general.

July   Don John seized citadel of Namur; seen as remilitarization of the Netherlands and resisted by the states-general.

Dec   States-general dismissed Don John as governor-general and invited Archduke Matthias to be the new governor-general in his place. Philip II refused to accept the nomination and supported Don John with the despatch of Alessandro Farnese, duke of Parma (1542–92) with an army.

1578
Feb/March   Calvinist outrages in southern Netherlands towns (Oudenarde, Kortrijk, Bruges, Ieper).

Oct   Death of Don John and succession of duke of Parma as governor.

Autumn   Refusal of southern provinces (Flanders, Brabant, Hainaut and Artois) to contribute funds to the common cause agreed at the Pacification of Ghent. Spanish troops restive and mutinying.

1579
6 Jan   Union of Arras concluded between the provincial States of the catholic provinces in the southern Netherlands. The aim was to be reconciled with Philip II and to collaborate

with the duke of Parma and re-establish the traditional shared authority between king and States.

Jan	Union of Utrecht (signed 23 Jan), an 'undying agreement' of military alliance between the northern States.
29 June	Maastricht capitulated to Parma's army.
27 July	Mechelen fell to Parma.
1580	Groningen reconciled to Parma and Spain (3 March). Ban outlawing William of Orange issued by Parma (15 March). William of Orange replied with the *Apology*, published by the states-general.
1581	Act of Abjuration of the northern States (26 July).

From the Act of Abjuration to the Twelve-Year Truce (1581–1609)

1582	François, duke of Anjou returned to the Netherlands (10 Feb).
1583	
Jan	'French Fury' at Antwerp when Anjou's troops tried in vain to seize the city.
June	Duke of Anjou left the Netherlands.
July/Aug	Surrender of Dunkirk, Nieuwport, Diksmunde and Bergues to the Spanish.
Oct	Further Spanish successes in the Scheldt estuary, confirmed in the Spring of 1584.
1584	Assassination of William of Orange (10 July). Surrender of Ghent to the Spanish (17 Sep) – most of Brabant fell with it.
1585	Fall of Brussels to the Spanish (10 March). Mechelen surrendered to the Spanish (19 July). Antwerp capitulated to Parma's forces (17 Aug). English forces relieved siege of Flushing (Sep). Seizure of all English and Dutch shipping in Spanish ports (Dec).
1586–87	Further Spanish gains at Deventer and Sluis (a deep-water port for the planned Armada fleet).
1588	Defeat of Spanish Armada; failure of Spanish siege at Bergen-op-Zoom (relieved Nov).
1589	Peace plan proposed by Parma: rejected by Philip II (Oct).
1590	Parma invaded France to support the Catholic League (July).
1591	Beginnings of Dutch reconquest (Nijmegen, Zutphen and Deventer recaptured).
1592	Parma died (6 Dec).
1593–1607	Further slow Dutch gains assisted by periodic Spanish troop mutinies and desertions. Informal 'talks about talks' in 1598 and 1600 to try to break stalemate with diplomatic truce.
1607	Negotiations began formally between Brussels and the Dutch states-general (Feb) leading to a ceasefire (29 March).

1609   Formal truce for 12 years agreed between Spain, the states-general and the archducal government in Brussels (9 April). *De facto* diplomatic recognition of the United Provinces followed shortly afterwards from other European powers.

6.2.5 *Official measures against heresy in the Netherlands*

The institutional and political context for the repression of heresy within the Low Countries was highly complex. The dioceses (Utrecht, Liège, Cambrai, Tournai, Arras and Thérouanne) were large and part of two archdioceses which were not within the Netherlands (Cologne and Reims). In addition, each province had its own 'liberties' and 'privileges' which were protected by the estates and promoted by the urban elites, whose town governments were enshrined in their charters. These charters often gave a measure of protection, or at the least the opportunity for legal delay and controversy, against heresy legislation edicted by the sovereign ruler. The initiative for repressing heresy initially lay with the diocesan inquisitors. As their efforts appeared to lack cohesion and effectiveness, they were reorganized on an 'apostolic' rather than 'diocesan' basis. Their authority was also supplemented by the ordinances of the sovereign ruler which gradually made heresy a crime of treason (*crimen lesae majestatis divinae*). These ordinances were often published (Fr: *placards*: Dutch: *placarten*) and the word became synonymous for the legal penalties attached to heresy trials. Treason cases could be 'evoked' to be tried in whatever courts were appropriate, and this infringed the rights of many towns and the majority of the provinces to try criminal cases within their own boundaries. Those convicted of treason also had their goods confiscated to the crown. These elements of the emerging civil jurisdiction were particularly resisted at local level. So Philip II proposed to reform the diocesan structure of the Netherlands in 1559 to provide a still more effective ecclesiastical inquisition to counter the growing menace of separatist and sacramentarian[†] heresy. This is important background to the interpretation of statistics relating to the repression of heresy in the Netherlands provided below (see pages 139–41). Only a small selection of the most general edicts relating to heresy is presented:

Date	Edict
May 1521	Dutch version of the edict of Worms published for Emperor Charles V's Dutch lands.
1522	Creation of an apostolic inquisition[†] in the Netherlands to assist in the removal of heresy.

Date	Edict
1540	Edict preventing the sale of (c.20 specified) forbidden books and allowing bookshops to be inspected by theologians to check for suspect literature.
30 June 1546	Edict against the sale and publishing of forbidden literature specified in the Index[†] of forbidden books produced by the university of Louvain. All booksellers required to advertise their wares and also display the printed Index. Rules for censorship of printed literature were laid down and booksellers and schoolteachers were required to be licensed. Fines were stipulated for a first offence.
1546	Reorganization and strengthening of the apostolic inquisition, giving inquisitors the rights to question magistrates and to arrest anyone and to commit them for trial wherever appropriate in the Netherlands.
16 Dec 1557	Edict requiring the theologians of the Faculty at Louvain to produce an up-dated Index of forbidden books and to require all relevant civil authorities to enforce the ban on such books circulating from abroad.
1566	New bishoprics at St Omer, Bruges, Middelburg and Ieper established and bishops installed.
(The First Revolt: 1565–68)	
1570	Remaining new bishoprics established and bishops installed.
July	Legislation to unify criminal law and procedure in the Netherlands' provinces. The Index of the council of Trent[†] republished.

6.2.6 Statistics relating to the repression of heresy in the Low Countries

Executions for heresy, 1524–66

Date	Flanders	Holland	Walloon towns (Mons, Tournai, Valenciennes, Lille)
1524	1		
1525		1	
1526	1		
1527	1	1	
1528			1
1529		3	

Date	Flanders	Holland	Walloon towns (Mons, Tournai, Valenciennes, Lille)
1530	2	1	
1531	3	11	4
1532	2	2	
1533	3	1	6
1534	1	57	2
1535	3	125	
1536	4	24	
1537		3	
1538	10	3	
1539	2	51	
1540	3	15	1
1541	2	5	1
1542	4	4	4
1543	2		
1544	3	23	
1545	10	3	13
1546	1	4	2
1547	4	2	5
1548			1
1549	4	10	6
1550		6	1
1551	15		
1552	2	17	4
1553	12	6	1
1554	4	1	4
1555	3	2	12
1556	6		2
1557	13	3	1
1558	12	11	1
1559	20	2	1
1560	17	1	2
1561	23		16
1562	40	1	11
1563	16	1	32
1564	9	1	6
1565	3		3
1566	5		
Total	265	403 (incl. 2 undated executions)	141

Source: Figures taken from Alastair Duke, *Reformation and Revolt in the Low Countries* (London and Ronceverte, Hambledon Press, 1990), p. 99.

Cases before the Council of Troubles (1567–73)[1]
Numbers of cases tried: c.12,000
Individuals found guilty and punished: c. 8,900 (of whom c.1,150
                                         were executed)

6.2.7 The governing structures of the United Provinces

Stadholders (*Stadhouders*)

The stadholders were the governors of the provinces in the Netherlands. Chosen by the Habsburgs from amongst the leading aristocratic families of the Netherlands (Egmont, Hornes, Orange-Nassau), they had ill-defined military powers and acted as part of the informal power structures of the Netherlands. They had rights to appoint or to influence the appointment of municipal offices within the provinces during the annual elections (the *wetsverzetting*). During the Dutch Revolt, however, William of Orange, stadholder in the counties of Holland, Zealand and Utrecht from 1559, used these powers to establish his military influence and political credibility in the northern provinces and become *de facto* military leader of the revolt and the emerging republic.

William I, Prince of Orange and Count of Nassau (known as 'le
  taciturne'/*de Zwijger*/'the Silent') (1559–66 and 1572 ('declared'
  stadholder by the rebel States)–1584)
Maurice, Count of Nassau (1584–1625)

States' officials

The instruments of government of the emerging Dutch Republic were highly complex. They were an outgrowth of the revolt itself and the 'regents' who were the magistrates in the main towns of the northern provinces. Each town had officials who were appointed from the city councillors (*vroedschappen*) who were themselves chosen from amongst the local patricians. Guilds and local civic militias (*schutters*) generally had only an informal influence upon decision-making. The States of Holland, which paid over half the federal budget, gained an unchallenged predominance at the states-general and, after 1593, the states-general regularly met in The Hague (the governing capital of Holland). Administrative 'colleges' of the states-general handled Dutch federal finances and foreign affairs. The leading spokesman of the States of Holland came to be its leading syndic or 'advocate'. Between March 1586 and May 1619, the advocate of Holland was Jan van Oldenbarnevelt* (1547–1619).

---

[1] Taken from A.L.E. Verheyden, *Le conseil des troubles. Liste des condamnés, 1567–1573* (Brussels, Palais des académies, 1961).

6.2.8 The Dutch Reformed church

The Dutch Calvinist (Reformed[†]) church was, in its organization and fundamental experience, a product of the renewed repression in the wake of the first revolt. There had been a scattering of Calvinist communities, especially in the southern Netherlands, prior to 1559 and this was expanded by the temporary refuge of French Calvinists in the southern Netherlands in 1562–63. But it was the experience of covert congregating, repression and substantial exile which created the exclusive synodical discipline of the Dutch Reformed churches. During the second and third revolt, however, the establishment of that organization in the northern provinces took place in the context of military threat and political instability. Its chronology was different in the various provinces. Nowhere, however, did the Dutch Reformed church become a 'state church' in the sense that this was commonly understood in the sixteenth century. Although catholic worship was forbidden in public, private worship was permitted (as for anabaptists and other sects). Ecclesiastical property and rights were transferred to the Reformed churches but many important aspects of local church fabric (e.g. churchyards, or appointments to sextons, etc) remained in the hands of the local town councillors. There were numerous areas (e.g. schools and the appointment of schoolmasters) where there was room for disagreement between the church and the local laity, especially if the latter were not confessing members of the Reformed church. Representative statistics of church membership from the province of Holland suggest that only a small minority were prepared to swear to the Reformed church confession and discipline. The remainder (known as 'fellow-travellers' (liefhebbers) might well attend the sermons on Sundays but leave before the communion, from which they were formally excluded. The debate about the dangers from unbelievers[†] was therefore particularly acute, especially amongst the pastors. The latter were inadequate (in numbers) and very overstretched.

6.2.9 The gradual consolidation of the Dutch Reformed church

1566–67   Establishment of Calvinist church government (consistories) at Amsterdam, Delft, Den Briel, Gorcum, Leiden, Alkmaar, The Hague and Naalwijk.

1567   Collapse of Calvinist church government in the Netherlands and exile of most of its ministers (post-March).

1571   General Assembly (Konvent) of Wesel – attended by representatives from various exiles from the Netherlands and from refugee churches in Germany and England.

Provincial synod (July) brought together delegates from the refugee communities in Germany.

Synod of Emden (4 Oct); the articles of Emden stipulated the organization, discipline and confession of the Dutch Reformed church to which all members were required to subscribe.

1572–75 Calvinist church gradually gained control of part of the church buildings and ecclesiastical property in the states of Holland. But they did so against the background of official protection for the freedom of both catholic and Reformed faiths (Dutch: *religievrede*) and local hostility to radical changes.

1573 Catholic worship forbidden in public in Holland (Feb). Arrangements put in hand for the payment of ministers from the revenues of the catholic church.

Remaining schools in ecclesiastical hands in Holland handed over to Calvinist church (March).

1574 Provincial synod of Holland at Dordrecht (June). Signs of disarray in Calvinist church structure.

1575 Foundation of the university of Leiden (see page 268).

1579–1609 Gradual consolidation of Calvinist church organization in the other provinces which had signed up to the Union of Utrecht, assisted by migrants from the provinces of the southern Netherlands (possibly as many as 100,000 in the period 1572–1609), who provided a transfer of wealth and skills to the northern provinces and a significant contribution to the consolidation of the Calvinist church.

1603 Jacobus Arminius* (D: *Jacob Harmensen*) appointed professor of theology at the university of Leiden.

1604 Arminius presented his theses on predestination at an inaugural lecture and was attacked by his colleague Franciscus Gomarus (1563–1641). This was the beginning of the 'Arminian' affair (see page 221).

1610 The *Remonstrance and Representation* (D: *Remonstrantie ende Vertooch*) presented (14 Jan) by the Dutch Reformed clergy of the province of Holland who supported the views of Arminius, asking the states to uphold their rights to maintain and uphold his doctrine. The latter was summarized in the Remonstrance, which 44 ministers signed, probably at Gouda. The document was probably drawn up by Johannes Wtenbogaert (1577–1644), court chaplain at The Hague. The states of Holland replied with an ambiguous resolution granting tolerance to the Arminians but refusing to make their statement an additional confessional requirement for the ministry.

1611   Conference at The Hague (11 March) where the *Counter-Remonstrance* of the orthodox Calvinist ministers, who opposed the *Remonstrance*, was drawn up. It summarized the orthodox Calvinist position on predestination and grace.

1611–18   Pamphlets and intense controversy over the issues raised by the *Remonstrance* which became enmeshed in the internal politics of the Dutch republic.

1618–19   The Synod of Dordrecht (Dort) (Nov 1618–May 1619). It brought together about 100 Reformed ministers, including important foreign delegations from Geneva, England and France. It included 13 prominent Remonstrant theologians who argued that it was not a body which could decisively determine doctrine and were eventually dismissed. The synod eventually issued the 'Canons of Dordrecht' (see page 250).

6.2.10 Dutch national synods

1571

Summer   The so-called 'Convent' of Wesel. The date, location, and significance of the documents of this gathering have long remained an enigma. They have been variously attributed to a meeting at Antwerp (late 1566 or early 1567), Wesel (3 Nov 1568) and, most recently, to the summer of 1571.

4–13 Oct   Synod of Emden. Deputies from Frankenthal, Heidelberg, Emden, Wesel, Emmerich, Cologne, Aachen, Antwerp, Ghent, 'Flanders', Amsterdam, Schagen, Den Briel, Hoorn, Castricum and Twisk signed the minutes.

(1574)   Provincial Synod at Dordrecht (15–28 June). Attended by representatives from the classes at Delft, Dordrecht, Den Briel, Schouwen and Walcheren.

1578   Synod at Dordrecht (3–18 June). Attended by representatives from the classes of Alkmaar, Hoorn, Enkhuizen, Edam, Haarlem, Leiden, Delft-Rotterdam, The Hague, Gouda(?), Zaltbommel (Gelderland), Walcheren, Brabant, East and West Flanders, the Walloon churches, three congregations in England, the Palatinate, Cleves and Cologne.

1581   Synod at Middelburg (30 May–21 June). Attended by representatives from Brabant, Flanders, Zeeland, Holland, Friesland, Overijssel, Gelderland, Utrecht, the Walloon churches in the Low Countries, the Walloon churches in England, the Dutch churches in England, and Cologne.

1586   Synod at The Hague (20 June–1 Aug). Attended by representatives from synods of Gelderland, South and North

Holland, Zeeland, Friesland, Utrecht, Overijssel, Flanders and the Walloon churches.

1618–19   Synod at Dordrecht (13 Nov–9 May).

6.3 The Italian peninsula

6.3.1 The Italian polities

Like Germany, Italy was a baffling mixture of political entities, the largest of which was the Papal States[†]. Contemporary Italian political commentators were liable to be most impressed by its republics – Venice, Florence, Genoa and Siena. In reality, however, the majority of Italy was in the hands of princes and the term 'prince' was widely used for a government without relating to the particular constitution of the state in question. Many of the Italian states had new or revised constitutions in the first half of the sixteenth century which allowed both for an official (sometimes symbolic) head of political authority (a 'duke' or 'doge') and for councils of supposedly elected magistrates (the elections were often the subject of influence and intrigue). Both kinds of rulers provided an additional degree of legitimacy and stability to governments which were increasingly in the hands of their chancellors and secretaries of state.

Overshadowing Italian politics in the first half of the sixteenth century was the Habsburg dynastic coalition, whose wars with Valois France from 1494 to 1529 had concentrated on Italian soil. The reality of the Habsburg sphere of influence had already been acknowledged in southern Italy in the Spanish overlordship of Sicily and Naples. It was asserted in northern Italy by the devolution of the dukedom of Milan (upon the death of the last Sforza duke) to the Emperor Charles V in 1535. Ferrara, Mantua and Savoy became client states to the Habsburgs. The hegemony was sealed by diplomatic influence and symbolized by contingents of Spanish troops stationed in Lombardy, Siena, Naples and Sicily, the guarantee against future French invasion. Only the Papal States and Venice remained less than dependable allies of the Habsburgs during the period from 1529 to 1559 when the Italian peninsula felt the impact of protestant reformation ideas.

6.3.2 Significant heads of political authority in the Italian peninsula

Ferrara (dukes from 1471)

Este dynasty

Ercole I	1471–1505
Alfonso I	1505–34
Ercole II	1534–59

Alfonso II   1559–97
Cesare   1597–98

Florence (dukes of Tuscany from 1532; grand dukes from 1569)

Medici dynasty
Alessandro   1531–37
Cosimo I   1537–74
Francesco I   1574–87
Ferdinando I 1587–1609
Cosimo II   1609–1621

Genoa (doges – changed every two years from 1531 onwards; office often in the hands of the Spinola, Leucara, Grimaldi and Cebà clans.)

Mantua (marquises until 1530: thereafter dukes)

Gonzaga dynasty
Francesco II   1484–1519
Federico II   1519–40
Francesco III 1540–50
Guglielmo   1550–87
Vincezo I   1587–1612

Naples (kings; represented when absent by viceroys)
The Aragonese dynasty to 1516: then the Habsburgs.
(See Spanish kings on page 152.)

Parma (dukes)

Farnese dynasty
Pier Luigi   1545–47
Ottavio   1547–49 (papal rule, 1549–50) 1550–86
Alessandro   1586–92
Ranuccio   1592–1622

Savoy (dukes of Piedmont-Savoy)

House of Savoy
Filiberto II   1497–1504
Carlo III   1504–33
Emanuele Filiberto   1533–80
Carlo Emanuele I   1580–1630

Urbino (dukes)

Rovere dynasty after 1521
Guidobaldo I di Montefaltro   1482–1508
Cesare Borgia   1502–3

Francesco Maria I Della Rovere	1508–16
Lorenzo de'Medici	1516–19
(Papal rule: 1519–20)	
Francesco Maria I (Della Rovere)	1521–28
Guidobaldo II (Della Rovere)	1528–74
Francesco Maria II (Della Rovere)	1574–1621

Venice (doges)

Leonardo Loredano	1501–21
Antonio Grimani	1521–23
Andrea Gritti	1523–38
Pietro Lando	1539–45
Francesco Donà	1545–53
Mercantonio Trevisan	1553–54
Francesco Venier	1554–56
Lorenzo Priuli	1556–59
Girolamo Priuli	1559–67
Pietro Loredano	1567–70
Alvise Mocenigo I	1570–77
Sebastiano Venier	1577–78
Nicolò da Ponte	1578–85
Pasquale Cicogna	1585–95
Marino Grimani	1595–1605
Leonardo Donà	1605–12
Marcantonio Memmo	1612–15
Giovanni Bembo	1615–18
Nicolò Donà	1618

6.3.3 Valois incursions and Habsburg influence in the Italian peninsula (1494–1559)

1494 First French invasion of the Italian peninsula in order to advance Angevin claims to the kingdom of Naples (King Charles VIII entered Rome; withdrew 1495; French garrison at Naples surrendered 1496).

1495 Invasion of Naples by King Ferdinand of Aragon in support of his cousin Ferrante, dethroned king of Naples.

1497 Agreed partition of Naples between King Louis XII of France and King Ferdinand of Aragon.

1499 Second French Italian invasion (King Louis XII occupied Milan).

1500 Ferdinand stationed an army close to Naples.

1501–2   Louis XII and Ferdinand invaded Naples and divided the kingdom. French subsequently defeated and forced to withdraw in 1503.

1504   French recognized Ferdinand's claim to the kingdom of Naples.

1509   Louis XII at war (League of Cambrai) with Venice.

1512   French withdrew from northern Italy following military defeat at Ravenna.

1513   Third French Italian invasion (attempted recovery of Milan frustrated at battle of Novara).

1515   Fourth French Italian invasion (King François I defeated Swiss at the battle of Marignano and occupied Milan).

1522   French defeat in Italy at Bicocca.

1524   French defeat in Milan; François I headed the army of recovery.

1525   French defeat (and capture of François I) at Pavia.

1526   Release of François I, who organized the League of Cognac with Pope Clement VII against Charles V.

1527   Fifth French invasion. French troops defeated and Rome sacked by imperial army. French army of recovery sent to besiege Naples.

1528   French defeat at Aversa.

1529   French defeat at Landriano; François I abandoned claims in Italy.

1529–30   Charles V in Italy; summoned delegates of Italian states to a meeting at Bologna to resolve differences and win their accedance to Habsburg hegemony (Nov 1529–Feb 1530).

1533–34   Charles V in Italy; summoned delegates of Italian states to a second meeting at Bologna.

1535   Death of Francesco Sforza in Milan caused a succession dispute between Charles V and François I. Charles V in Italy (1535–36).

1536   Sixth French invasion (French troops occupied Turin and overran part of the duchy of Savoy).

1552   Siena expelled its Spanish garrison and invited the French into the city; seventh French invasion force.

1553   French invaded Corsica.

1559   Final French withdrawal by treaty of Cateau-Cambrésis.

6.3.4 Reformation ideas in the Italian peninsula and their repression

There is no general scholarly agreement about the nature and extent of the Italian reformation. Research has, at least until recently, tended to concentrate on the perspective of ideas for religious change spreading from the heterodox currents which had existed within the peninsula on the eve of the protestant reform. Italian 'evangelism'[†2] contained elements of the Erasmian critique of the established church, coupled with a practical intention to reform elements of the church fabric by local initiatives, and reforming endeavours based on internal persuasion and argument. This distinctive and indigenous movement was compromised by its gradual association with protestantism. The influence of Italian evangelism is epitomized in the careers of the Italian reformist prelates who served on the committee established by Pope Paul III* in 1536 to produce proposals for church reform (the *Consilium de Emendanda Ecclesia*) (see page 199). These were moderate reformers who, without intending to, formed what passed for the leadership of the Italian reformation. It is now, however, clearer that the movements for religious change in the Italian peninsula were quite broadly based, and that they were manifested in different ways throughout the peninsula. It has also become more evident how skilful and adept Italian reformers often were at masking the extent to which they drew on the works of Luther, Zwingli and Calvin for their inspiration. Translated Lutheran works were published in a sanitized form and in several editions. Preachers, especially Augustinian hermits and Franciscans, were very active, especially in the northern Italian states in the 1520s and 30s. The growing influence of Calvinist protestantism over the Waldensians in the Italian Alps has already been detailed (see pages 40–1) as has the significance of Italian anabaptism (see page 190). But the existence of the papacy as the largest Italian state (and one which exercised an inevitable leadership in matters of religious orthodoxy) could not be ignored by Italian reformers; and nor could the military campaigns being fought out on Italian soil. Italian reformers became adept at masking their real opinions, at being 'nicodemite'[†] and waiting upon events to unfold north of the Alps. In the late 1530s, Italian protestantism began to coalesce into the establishment of conventicles, especially within the cities. Discreet support was forthcoming from the court of Ferrara where the French princess Renée, duchess of Ferrara*, protected and advanced protestant heresy. The discovery of these conventicles prompted moves to establish better instruments for the repression of heresy both at Rome and in other Italian states. Those instruments, especially the inquisition[†], provide historians with the potential to know more about the existence of heresy in the Italian peninsula, but the evidence has yet to be fully analysed. The specimen data now available from the early years of the Roman inquisition suggests that protestantism had gained a stronger grip amongst the Italian mercantile and artisan classes in northern Italy than had

---

[2] E-M. Jung, 'On the nature of evangelism in sixteenth-century Italy', *Journal of the History of Ideas*, vol. xiv (1953), 511–27; D. Cantimori, *Italian Heretics of the Sixteenth Century* (Cambridge, Cambridge University Press, 1979).

previously been imagined. By contrast, protestant heresy was only a very minor affair at the tribunals of the inquisition in Naples. But there was an underlying diffuseness to Italian heresy which may have contributed to its decline after 1555 as repression began to have its impact.

Chronology

1487   Introduction of a Spanish-style inquisition into the kingdom of Sicily.

1510   Attempt by Ferdinand of Aragon to introduce a Spanish-style inquisition into the kingdom of Naples rejected by the Neapolitan nobility.

1528   Renée* de France married Hercule d'Este, duke of Ferrara; her court became a haven for French evangelical reform in Italy.

1529/30 Banishment of Antonio Brucioli by the state of Florence for referring to Luther and Bucer in his Bible commentary. Other trials and investigations began in other Italian states.

1531   Lutheran ideas prominent amongst students at the university of Padua.

1537   The commission on ecclesiastical reform (*Consilium de Emendanda Ecclesia*) presented to Pope Paul III*. The report was prepared by nine members, the majority of whom were known advocates of moderate reform from within (inc. Gasparo Contarini*, Jacopo Sadoleto*, Girolamo Aleandro*, Gian Matteo Giberti*).

1537–41 Protestant activity more apparent to the authorities in Milan, Mantua, Ferrara, Siena and Venice.

1540   Publication in Venice of the *Most Useful Treatise of the Beneficence of Christ Crucified* (*Trattato utilissimo del Beneficio di Jesu Christo crocifisso*) – the best-known protestant tract in Italian.

1541   Siena issued decrees against expression of 'Lutheran' opinions in print or from the pulpit.

1542   Establishment of the central Congregation of the Inquisition in Rome by papal bull (*Licet ab initio*) (4 July). All appointments of inquisitors as well as the overall direction of the inquisition were to be supervised from Rome. The initial tribunal in Rome was staffed by a standing committee of six cardinals meeting once a week under the presidency of the pope. It was empowered to proceed, independent of existing authorities, against anyone, regardless of title or rank. Although it could proceed without difficulty throughout the Papal States, it had to negotiate its rights (especially those of extradition) with the other states in the Italian peninsula. In time, important offices of the revived inquisition were also established at Naples, Milan and Florence.

1545   First show-trial of the Roman inquisition at Lucca, following
the anti-Spanish Burlamacchi conspiracy. Senate of Lucca
compelled citizens to attend mass.

1546   Publication of the *Tragedy of Free Will* (*Tragedia del Libero
Arbitrio*), a popular vernacular crypto-protestant text by
Francesco Negri.

1547   Venetian Senate established three 'Deputies on Heresy' (*Tre
Savii sopra Eresia*) (22 April) with the task of suppressing heretical opinions in public in the diocese of Venice, in cooperation
with the papal legate and the ecclesiastical inquisitor – the
origins of the Venetian inquisition (a variant in which lay participation was a distinctive feature).

1547   Emperor Charles V attempted to introduce a Spanish-style
inquisition into the kingdom of Naples; withdrawn after insurrection against Spanish rule.

1548   Publication of the Siena Index of forbidden books. The Italian translator of Calvin's treatise *Against Nicodemites* imprisoned at Florence.

1549   Establishment of the Venetian Index of forbidden books.

1551   Venetian inquisition extended beyond the diocese of Venice
and throughout its dominions; branches in Aquieia and Concordia (now Friuli). Papacy and Venice reached a compromise over the role of laymen in the inquisition. First Italian
auto-da-fé held at Florence.

1555   Election of Gian Pietro Carafa as Pope Paul IV*. Beginning of
the 'Carafa War' against heresy, pro-Spanish influences and
those hostile to his pontificate.
Renée*, duchess of Ferrara forced publicly to abjure heresy.

1564   Publication of the Roman Index (see page 273).

6.4 The Spanish peninsula

6.4.1 The kingdoms of the Spanish peninsula

There had been five major Christian kingdoms in the Spanish peninsula
in the middle ages: Castile and Leon, Aragon, Catalonia and Valencia,
Navarre, and Portugal. Aragon had acquired a significant empire in
the Mediterranean (Majorca and the Balearic Islands, Sicily, Sardinia
and Naples). Castile had absorbed the majority of the Pyrenean kingdom
of Navarre by the end of the fifteenth century. The marriage of King
Ferdinand of Aragon with Queen Isabella of Castile in 1469 created a
union of the kingdoms which became the conjoined inheritance of their
Habsburg descendant, Charles of Burgundy (Carlos I of Spain, Charles
V of the Holy Roman Empire) in 1516 (see pages 358–9). Despite the

uniting of the kingdoms to create what is now known as the Spanish monarchy, the different institutions were retained in the distinctive kingdoms. Catalonia, Aragon and Valencia were governed independently from Castile and each had their own laws and their own representative assemblies (*Cortes*). Portugal was annexed by Philip II of Spain in 1580.

6.4.2 Spain

Rulers

Habsburg dynasty post-1516

Isabella of Castile (1451–1504) ⎫	
Ferdinand of Aragon (1452–1516) ⎭	1469–1516
Charles I	1516–55 (abdicated)
Philip II	1555–98
Philip III	1598–1621

6.4.3 Portugal

Rulers

Aviz dynasty to 1580

Manoel (Manuel) I ('the Great' or 'the Fortunate')	1495–1521
João (John) III	1521–57
Sebastian I	1557–78
Henry	1578–80 (deposed)
(Annexed to Spain, 1580–1640)	

6.4.4 Elements of political chronology in the Spanish peninsula

The inquisition and the repression of heresy in the Spanish peninsula

1478   Bull[†] of Pope Sixtus IV (1 Nov) permitted the appointment of several priests as inquisitors throughout the kingdoms of Castile and Aragon with powers of appointment and dismissal granted to the Spanish crown.

1480   Royal commissions issued at Medina del Campo (27 Sep) to the Dominicans Juan de San Martín and Miguel de Morillo (with Juan Ruiz de Medina as assessor).
First inquisitorial activity around Seville, Córdoba and other towns in Andalucia (Oct); mass exodus of *conversos*[†].

1481   First *auto-da-fé*[†] at Seville (6 burnt at the stake) (6 Feb) after *conversos* suspected of plotting to overthrow the state.

REACTIONS TO THE REFORMATION

1482

Feb   Beginning of the war of reconquest of Granada from the
           Muslim emirate (Moors).

11 Feb   Seven additional inquisitors appointed, including Tomás de
           Torquemada*. Beginnings of wave of punishments against
           conversos which lasted a decade.

1482–83 Further offices of the inquisition established at Córdoba,
           Ciudad Real (transferred to Toledo in 1485) and Jaén.

1483   The *Consejo de la Suprema y General Inquisición* (the *Suprema*)
           created as a branch of the royal council of Castile. Its pres-
           ident became the Inquisitor General. Papal bull (17 Oct)
           accepted the powers of the Inquisitor General (Torquemada)
           over Aragon, Valencia and Catalonia as well as Castile.

1484   The first set of inquisitorial procedural regulations agreed
           (the *Instrucciones Antiguas*) (29 Nov); modified in 1485, 1488
           and 1498.

1484–90 Further offices of the inquisition established despite opposi-
           tion from the regional *Cortes*.

1492   Fall of the city of Granada (2 Jan) ended the war of recon-
           quest; mass exodus of Moorish population (200,000?) to North
           Africa. Royal edict (31 March) requiring all Jews in Spain
           to accept baptism or leave the country within four months.
           Mass exodus from Castile (150,000?) and Aragon (30,000?) to
           Portugal, North Africa, Italy and the Turkish sultanate.

1497   Expulsion of Jews from Portugal. Mass exodus to the Nether-
           lands, other Mediterranean lands and the Portuguese New
           World.

1499   Beginning of compulsory conversion of Moorish population
           (*Mudejars*) of Granada led to widespread revolt in the pro-
           vince (Dec 1499–March 1500). Completion of forcible con-
           version (or exile) of the Moorish population – Christianized
           Moors became known as *Moriscos*.

1502   All *Mudejars* of Castile forcibly converted or forced to leave
           (12 Feb).

1519–21 Revolt of towns of Castile (*Comuneros*) and Aragon (*Germania*).

1521   First ban on Lutheran books circulating in Spain issued by
           the Inquisitor General (7 April).

1524   'Edict concerning the *alumbrados*' issued (23 Sep) by the
           Inquisitor General, itemizing 48 heretical propositions to be
           found in the works of the *alumbrados*†.

1529–32 Show-case trials of suspected Erasmians, Lutherans and
           alumbrados in Castile.

1529   House arrest and disgrace of the Inquisitor General (Aug),
           suspected of Erasmian leanings.

1531	First papal bull to institute the Portuguese inquisition (17 Dec).
1536	Second papal bull (*Cum ad nil magis*) to enforce the creation of the Portuguese inquisition (23 May).
1547	Third papal bull (*Meditatio cordis*) to enforce the creation of the Portuguese inquisition (19 July).
1551	First published Spanish inquisitional Index of prohibited books printed (Sep) (see page 273).
1557–62	Second wave of show-trials of suspected Erasmians, protestants and *alumbrados*.
1558	Decree by the Spanish Regent (Doña Juana) banning the import of all foreign books in Spanish translation as well as requiring strict licensing of all printed works (7 Sep).
1559	Arrest of Archbishop Carranza of Toledo, primate of Spain on charges relating to heretical associations (Aug).
	Second published Spanish inquisitional Index of prohibited books (Aug) (see page 273).
	All Spanish students studying at foreign universities ordered to return (22 Nov).
1561	Modified inquisitorial procedures issued (*Instrucciones nuevas*).
1564	Third published Spanish inquisitional Index of prohibited books (see page 273).
1571	Fourth published Spanish inquisitional Index of prohibited books (see page 273).
1572	Arrest of three professors at the university of Salamanca (Luis de León, Gaspar de Grajal and Martin Martínez de Cantalapiedra) by the inquisition on grounds of suspected heresy (March).
1583	Fifth published Spanish inquisitional Index of prohibited books (with an additional Index of expurgated books of 1584).
1600	Seizure and sequestration of the papers of Francisco Sánchez, professor of grammar at the university of Salamanca, by the inquisition on grounds of suspected heresy.
1609	Decree of expulsion of the *Moriscos* (4 Jan). Mass exodus (300,000?), principally from Valencia and Aragon.
1612	Sixth published Spanish inquisitional Index of prohibited books (with an appendix in 1614).

Establishment of the inquisition in different regions

Place of tribunal (region in brackets if different from the place)

Seville (Andalucia)	1482
Córdoba (Jaén initially) (Andalucia)	1482
Zaragoza (Saragossa) (Aragon)	1482

Valencia	1482
Barcelona (Catalonia)	1484
Llerena (Extremadura)	1485
Palermo (Sicily)	1487
Valladolid (Leon and Old Castile)	1488
Murcia	1488
Palma (Mallorca and Balearic Islands)	1488
Sassari (Sardinia)	1492
Las Palmas (the Canary Islands)	1505
Logroño (Navarre and the Basque lands)	1512
Granada	1526
Lisbon (central Portugal)	1547
Evora (eastern and central Portugal)	1547
Coimbra (northern Portugal)	(1547–8)
Mexico (Central America and the Philippines)	1565–70
Lima (Peru, Chile and Argentina)	1570
Santiago (Galicia)	1574
Cartagena (Columbia, Venezuela and the Spanish Caribbean)	1610

Inquisitors General of Spain

Tomás de Torquemada	1483–98
Diego de Deza, archbishop of Seville	1498–1507

(From 1507 to 1518, Aragon and Castile had separate Inquisitors General)

Francisco Jiménez de Cisneros, cardinal archbishop of Toledo	
– Inquisitor General for Castile	1507–18
Juan Enguera	
– Inquisitor General for Aragon	1507–17
Adrian Dedel, cardinal (later Pope Adrian VI*)	
– Inquisitor General for Aragon	1517–22
– Inquisitor General for Castile	1518–22
Antonio Manrique de Lara	1523–38
Juan Pardo de Tavera	1539–45
Juan García de Loaysa	1546
Fernando de Valdés	1547–61
D. Francisco de Pecheco y Toledo	1561–66
D. Diego de Espinosa	1566–72
D. Pedro Ponce de León	1572–73
D. Gaspard de Quiroga	1573–95
D. Geronimo Manrique de Lara	1595

D. Pedro Portecarrero   1596–99
D. Fernando Niño de Guevara   1599–1602
Juan de Zúñiga   1602
Juan Baptista Acevedo   1603–8
D. Bernardo de Sandoval y Rojas   1608–18

6.5 The Danubian lands

The reformation in the Danubian lands was periodically overshadowed by the military threat from the Turks, whose incursions into the Balkans had become a regular feature of the politics of east-central Europe from the 1480s. The financial demands which this placed upon the Habsburg-dominated polities around the Danube led to compromises with the local nobilities, including granting them rights of private worship in whatever religion they chose. The main periods of Turkish incursion into the Danubian lands were as follows:

1521–33

1521   First Hungarian campaign by Turkish Sultan Sulaimān (the Magnificent).

1526   Second Hungarian campaign led by Sulaimān succeeded (at the battle of Mohács, 29 Aug 1526) in overrunning the majority of central Hungary. Turkish forces reached Buda (10 Sep) and crossed to Pest and western Hungary.

1529   Third Hungarian campaign led by Sulaimān arrived before Vienna (29 Sep) and retreated (14 Oct) after a brief siege.

1532   Fourth campaign led by Sulaimān to Inner Austria.

1533   Truce between Sulaimān and King Ferdinand (Archduke of Austria) (June) which determined the new borders between 'royal' (western) Hungary and Turkish (central and eastern) Hungary.

1541–47

1541   Campaign to Buda, led by Sulaimān, to establish Turkish overlordship over Transylvania.

1543   Campaign to Buda, led by Sulaimān, to attack Gran (taken 10 Aug).

1544   Further Turkish attacks in western Hungary led by Turkish provincial governors (Mehemmed Pasha, commander at Buda).

1547   Five-year truce between Sulaimān and King Ferdinand.

1549–62

1551–61   Renewed military conflict in Transylvania, begun by efforts of the Austrian Habsburgs to destabilize the Transylvanian

Turkish vassal state. Several fortresses with Habsburg troops held out against lengthy sieges but without changing the military balance of force which lay with the Turks.

1562 Truce of 1547 renewed; the Austrian archduke (King Ferdinand) paid tribute to the Turkish sultan and Transylvania remained a Turkish vassal state.

1566–68
1566 Final campaign, led by Sulaimān, to Belgrade and thence to despatch forces to Transylvania. Gyula and Szigetvár (western Transylvania) captured.
1568 Truce renewed.

1587–93
Border incursions with Inner Austria and Hungary.

1593–1606 ('The Great Hungarian War')
The complexities of this arduous series of military campaigns are not followed in detail. The main features of the campaign were determined by the revolt in the Turkish-dominated Balkan provinces of Wallachia, Moldavia and Transylvania. The former encouraged Polish intervention in the war whilst Transylvania was fomented by the Austrian Habsburgs. The war descended into a debilitating series of sieges around the lines of communication into Transylvania for the Habsburgs and around the Danube routeway. Peace was reached in Nov 1606. The emperor agreed to a single and final 'gift' to the sultan and, in return, would pay no further tribute. Both sides would retain territories subject to their control. The Ottomans gained two frontier fortresses and the frontier dividing Hungary was reinforced.

6.5.1 Austria

Institutional context
The Austrian lands were part of the Habsburg dynastic inheritance. With some reference to historic divisions and administrative convenience they were organized into Upper Austria (*Oberösterreich*) which corresponded to the Tyrol, and Inner Austria (*Innerösterreich*) which comprised the eastern parts of present-day Austria and Slovenia (Carinthia, Styria and Carniola (the *Kraina*)). Its capital lay at Graz. Beyond these two regions lay Lower Austria (*Niederösterreich*) which was itself divided into two components. These were the part 'over the Enns' (with its capital at Linz) and that 'under the Enns' (with its capital at Vienna). Each region had its own diet (parliament) and was often governed by the younger scions

of the Habsburg dynasty ruling as appointed archdukes. The necessity of raising taxation to fight the Turkish menace meant that the Habsburgs were confronted, despite their inherent opposition to protestantism, with the need to reach an accommodation with local ruling elites which embraced a measure of pragmatic toleration of heresy. This degree of accommodation gradually evaporated as the catholic reformation developed its political energies.

Rulers
(See Holy Roman Empire, page 59.)

Archdukes of Austria

Ferdinand (later Emperor Ferdinand I); appointed ruler of the hereditary Austrian possessions (1521–64).

In 1564, Ferdinand divided the governing responsibilities for his Austrian lands amongst his three sons:

Maximilian (later Emperor Maximilian II) was granted Lower and Upper Austria (1564–76).
Archduke Charles was granted Inner Austria (1564–90).
Archduke Ferdinand was granted the Tyrol (1564–95).

Their successors were:

Archduke Ernst for Lower and Upper Austria from 1576; Inner Austria (1590–93).
Archduke Matthias (later Emperor) for Lower and Upper Austria (1593–) below the Enns.
Archduke Ferdinand (later Emperor Ferdinand II) for Inner Austria (1596–).
Leopold (d.1632) Bishop of Passau, for the Tyrol (1576–1602).
Archduke Maximilian (d.1618), for the Tyrol (1602–18).

Chronology

1519–22	Numerous pamphlets by Luther republished at Vienna.
1523	Ruler Ferdinand condemned Luther's ideas.
1527	Edict demanding the confiscation of all the property, exile and (in the event of contumacy) death of all those who refused to abjure Lutheran teachings.
1529	Turkish forces reached Vienna and besieged the city.
1532	Further Turkish incursions reached close to Vienna.
1550s	Large numbers of Lutheran preachers active in Lower Austria. Many nobles educated at protestant universities in Germany; a majority of the nobility of Austria may well have been protestant by c.1580.

1568	Emperor Maximilian agreed with the estates of Lower Austria to the free exercise of Lutheranism in the private houses of nobles (but not in royal towns) in return for assistance with imperial debts. They were not allowed to build separate churches or chapels.
1578	Similar concessions were agreed by Archduke Charles with the estates of Inner Austria.
1580	Archduke Charles excluded protestant worship from the cities of Inner Austria.
1585	Opening of the Jesuit college (later university) at Graz.
1599	More vigorous efforts begun by ruler Ferdinand II to recatholicize Inner Austria.
1609	Matthias agreed concessions to religious freedom with the diet of Lower Austria above the Enns. This area would join the Bohemian revolt in 1618. Other areas in Austria were more open to continued recatholicization efforts which led to the protestants being eventually classified as 'un-Catholics' (*Akatholiker*).

6.5.2 Bohemia

Institutional context

The lands of the kingdom of Bohemia included those of Bohemia itself, with its capital at Prague, as well as the margravate of Moravia to the east, upper and lower Lusatia to the north, and the various duchies of Silesia beyond that. It was an elective monarchy and its diet (or parliament) (G: *Landtag*; Cz: *sněm*) had to approve all taxes and laws. Laws could only be passed with the agreement of all three estates (*curiae*) – the higher aristocracy, the lower nobility or knights, and the royal free cities. The supreme court of Bohemia (G: *Landrecht*) and its provincial governing structures were largely composed of the nobility. The other areas (Moravia and Silesia) had their own provincial estates. The effect of the Hussite wars of the fifteenth century (see page 40) had been to strengthen the dominance of the Bohemian nobility. The latter had acquired much of the patrimony of the church (which had, in consequence, little part to play in the formal political structures of the kingdom) as well as a substantial amount of the crown lands. The kings of Bohemia were customarily the candidates for election as king of the Romans and heirs apparent for election as the next head of the Holy Roman Empire. The desire of the Habsburgs to secure their successors' election to the crown of Saint Václav led to their making regular concessions to the Bohemian nobles. Utraquist[†] loyalties were already well entrenched amongst the latter before the protestant reformation made its appearance. The Bohemian Brethren, too, had their protectors amongst the magnates of Moravia and the lesser nobles of Bohemia. The gradual appearance of Lutheranism in Czech lands owed a good deal to the developing protestant inclinations of the Bohemian Brethren as well as an increasing amount of support for it amongst the German-speaking populations of north and north-west Bohemia. The latter included the silver- and tin-mining communities where skilled labour was often recruited from Germany. The local nobility also had a good deal of German ancestry. Both groups used their regional influence to spread Lutheranism through the appointment of local preachers and school-teachers. Such developments were shielded from any negative reactions by the powerful Bohemian diet, even after the latter led a failed revolt against royal attempts to raise taxation for the Schmalkaldic War in 1546–47. The Bohemian reformation proceeded locally and by stealth. Its chronology has relatively few defining moments of national crisis.

Rulers

Ferdinand I	1526–63
Maximilian II	1563–75
Rudolf II	1575–1611
Matthias	1611–17
Ferdinand	1617–19 (deposed)
Friedrick (Elector Frederick V of the Rhine Palatinate)	1619–20 (militarily defeated and deposed)

Chronology

1524   Utraquist[†] synod (Feb) reached decisions which brought the Utraquist church close to Lutheranism: the primacy of Holy Scripture, baptism[†] and communion[†] as the two sacraments, and rejection of the sacrificial theology of the mass[†].

late 1520s   The beginning of Lutheran protestant influences amongst the Bohemian Brethren was indicated in the election of the *seniores* of the church.

1530s   Attempt by King Ferdinand to keep the Utraquist church in conservative and loyal hands ('old Utraquists') – but growth of Lutheran tendencies in Prague and amongst the royal towns of east Bohemia ('neo-Utraquists').

Publication of the *Apology* of the Bohemian Brethren – a manifesto of the Brethren's teaching, presented with a protestant gloss.

1535   Publication of the *Confession* of the Bohemian Brethren (1538 in Latin).

1539   Memorandum laid before Ferdinand by the powerful magnate Jan of Pernstein, requesting complete freedom for the Utraquist church from political interference. The spread of Lutheranism became of increasing concern to the 'old Utraquists'.

1543   The Utraquist synod sought a rapprochement with the Bohemian Brethren on the grounds of common (protestant-influenced) theology and the proposal to create a common church with a bishop, subject to the Bohemian diet. The insistence of some 'old Utraquists' that the bishop had to be confirmed by both the king and the pope led to the scheme's failure.

1540s   Early contacts between the Brethren and Martin Bucer* at Strasbourg and Jean Calvin at Geneva.

1546–47   Anti-Habsburg uprising led by the noble estates of the Bohemian diet against royal taxation (without consent) for the Schmalkaldic War. Attempts to ally Bohemia with Lutheran Saxony failed and the revolt was suppressed by royal forces.

1549   King Ferdinand demanded that the Utraquists submit to the authority of Rome, but he met stubborn resistance. The Bohemian Brethren, however, were increasingly persecuted in Bohemia and many withdrew to Moravia (which took no part in the tax rebellion).

1562   Failure of King Ferdinand's efforts to establish a joint Catholic-Utraquist archbishopric in Bohemia and the reconciliation of 'old Utraquists' to Rome. 'Neo-Utraquists' issued their confession.

1566   Appearance of Jesuits in Prague.

1567   Bohemian Brethren's confession issued – attempted to mediate between Lutheran and Calvinist theological tendencies (published in Latin in 1573).

1570s–80s   Increasing influence of Calvinism amongst Czech magnates and lesser nobility through study at the increasing range of German and Swiss Calvinist academies and universities.

1575   A commission of the Czech diet (six members each from the three estates) drafted the Czech Confession and accompanying Ecclesiastical Ordinances. The Confession (*Confessio Bohemica*) was based on the Augsburg Confession of 1530 with Czech additions and modified to accommodate the views of the Bohemian Brethren (see page 250). The Ordinances provided for the election of 15 'defenders' (five from each estate) who were to be the council at the head of the diet-directed Czech church. The Unity of Brethren retained its own organization. 'Old Utraquists' refused to accept it. 'Neo-Utraquists' constituted its primary supporters. The clergy were placed under the control of regional superintendants and the 'defenders' were to meet every year to resolve major issues.

1579   Foundation of the Jesuit-based Moravian university at Olomouc.

1593   Publication of a new Czech translation of the Bible (the 'Kralice Bible' – see page 258).

1600s   King Rudolf's chancellor, the catholic Count Lobkowitz, attempted to renew the persecution of the Brethren[†] in Bohemia and curb the protestant tendencies of the Czech church. These attempts were vigorously resisted by the Czech diet.

1609   Moravian diet secured a substantial guarantee of freedom for religion (embracing the Bohemian Brethren and the Moravian anabaptists) from Emperor Rudolf. The Czech diet, joined by that for Silesia, remained loyal to King Rudolf but only on the basis that he gave written recognition to the Czech Confession and Ecclesiastical Ordinances. This (the *Letter of Majesty*) was forthcoming on 9 July. Members of the Bohemian diet were invited to adhere to the *Letter* where it gained widespread adherence. It recognized the liberty of worship for the Bohemian church, guaranteed the church properties in the hands of protestant and catholic magnates and permitted the Bohemian church to build churches on both former royal domains and in royal towns. The existence and role of the 'defenders' appointed by the diet was also accepted.

1617   King Matthias appointed 10 deputy governors to rule Bohemia during his absence in Vienna. The majority of them were catholics and a minority of them had refused to swear adhesion to the *Letter of Majesty*. Problems over the siting of protestant churches and the imprisonment of protestants grew more numerous, despite the terms of the *Letter*.

1618   Meeting of the 'defenders' appointed by the diet in Prague (21 May). Two of the 10 deputy governors and a secretary thrown out of a window of the Hradschin palace (the 'Defenestration of Prague') (23 May) and the beginnings of the Bohemian revolt.

6.5.3 Hungary and Transylvania

Institutional background

The determining event in the history of sixteenth-century Hungary was the battle of Mohács (29 Aug 1526). The young king of Hungary (Louis Jagiello) was killed. The essential two dozen or so magnates who ruled

Hungary with him were also either wounded or killed, along with over three-quarters of the Hungarian army which had been the main bulwark of Christendom against Turkish incursions since the 1480s. The destabilization of east-central Europe which followed 1526 would last a century and provide a series of opportunities for the Turks to assert their hegemony in the region.

Following the death of Louis, the Hungarian crown of St Stephen was claimed by Archduke Ferdinand of Austria following his marriage to Anna, Louis' sister, on the grounds of inheritance and fraternal alliance. However, many of the Hungarian lesser nobility maintained their rights to elect a king in the place of Louis. They asserted this right at a meeting of a diet at Székesfehérvár (G: *Stuhlweissenberg*; Lat: *Alba Regalis*) in November 1526. This put on the throne János Zápolya, count of Spiš. A minority of the nobility, including the remnants of the magnates, met a month later and elected Ferdinand as their monarch at Bratislava. The two claimants bitterly contested what remained after the Turks had claimed hegemony in central and south Hungary before agreeing in 1538 to a partition at the treaty of (in Latin) Oradea Mare (G: *Grosswardein*; Hung: *Nagyvárad*). János Zápolya was recognized by Ferdinand as voyvode (*vojvod, vojevod*: Slav for 'Palatine ruler') in the eastern part of Hungary, east of the river Theiss. This was known (in Latin) as Transylvania (G: *Siebenbürgen*; Hung: *Erdély*). In return, Zápolya recognized Ferdinand as king in what remained of western (or 'royal') Hungary and accepted Ferdinand as his successor to the region. However the pact did not have the support of the Turkish sultan and it was as a result of Turkish intervention that Transylvania retained its separate existence, first in 1541, and then successively throughout most of the first century of the protestant reformation, generally as a Christian vassal state of the Turks and more occasionally in revolt against that overlordship.

Rulers

'Royal' Hungary

House of Habsburg

Ferdinand	1526–62
Maximilian	1562–72
Rudolf	1572–1608
Matthias	1608–18

Transylvania

House of Zápolya, 1526–71; House of Báthory, 1571–1605

János Zápolya (Hung: *Szapolyai*) (elected king of Hungary)	1526–40

János Zsigmond Zápolya	
(elected king of Hungary 1559–71)	1540–71
István (Stephen) Báthory	1571–76
Zsigmond (Sigismund) Báthory (abdicated the overlordship of Transylvania to Rudolf in 1588 and replaced by a prince regent; Zsigmond later resumed the overlordship)	1576–1605
István (Stephen) Bocksay	1605–6
Gábor (Gabriel) Bethlen (elected king of Hungary in 1620)	1613–26

Chronological elements of the reformation in Hungary and Transylvania

Military conflict, destabilization and population displacement all contributed to the background in which the Hungarian reformation took root. With a multi-ethnic and linguistic population composed of Magyars, Slovenes, Slovaks, Croats, Serbs and Germans, it was the latter who, although a minority, tended to be of initial significance in importing to Hungary, and in producing the first positive reactions towards, the protestant reformation. As in Bohemia, however, there was also the considerable influence resulting from the education of Magyar nobles at universities in Germany. A considerable number studied at Wittenberg and, later, in the Calvinist academies of Germany and Switzerland (see page 268). It was especially the latter who returned with a humanist culture which intertwined with their religious convictions; it was not difficult for both to become associated with the enunciation of a distinctive Magyar linguistic and historical identity. This was reinforced by the translations of protestant Bibles and other associated texts into Magyar. By the early seventeenth century, Magyar Calvinism, with its 'Geneva' at Debrecen, became one of the most flourishing Calvinist reformations in Europe.

1523	The Hungarian diet accepted a royal decree that all Lutherans should have their property confiscated and be punished with death (April).
1524–25	Efforts by the archbishop of Esztergom to seek out and destroy Lutheran pamphlets in circulation.
1525	Renewed demands from the Hungarian diet to imprison and burn heretics (May); all foreigners to be expelled from the court for importing Lutheran ideas into the country.
1529	Excommunication of János Zápolya.
1530s and **1540s**	Gradual penetration of protestant ideas into Transylvania and northern Hungary through the appointment of preachers

	and city pastors and the unwillingness of Zápolya to undertake any active repression. The main centres were at Spiš, Šariš, Prešov and Zemplin (in north-eastern Hungary) and at Soibiu, Brassó and Sighişoara (in Transylvania).
1531	Return to Buda from studying at Wittenberg of Mátyás Bíro Dévay* (also Dévai), the 'Hungarian Luther'. When not under arrest by the Habsburgs or travelling abroad in protestant lands he preached in Hungarian cities, taught in schools and acted as chaplain to protestant-minded Hungarian magnates.
1541	Publication of the Hungarian translation of the New Testament at Sárvár by János Sylvester.
1544–64	Missions of protestant reformer Michael Sztárai* to Turkish-occupied Hungary to establish protestant congregations there.
1544–46	Protestant synods at Oradea Mare (G: *Grosswardein*; Hung: *Nagyvárad*) (in Transylvania, 1544), Erdöd [Rom: *Ardud*] (1545) and Prešov (G: *Eperies*; Hung: *Eperjes*) (in north-eastern Hungary, 1546) accepted the Augsburg Confession with disagreements over some of its formulations.
1547	Publication of Lutheran church ordinances for the minority of German-speaking protestant churches in Transylvania.
1548	'Royal' Hungarian diet at Bratislava issued decrees against anabaptists and 'sacramentarians'† in Hungary and created a commission of enquiry to conduct visitations to root out radical heresy.
1549	Representatives of the 'royal' cities of north-east ('Upper') Hungary presented their confession (the *Confessio Pentapolitana*) to the visiting commission.
1552–58	Synods at Beregszáz (1552), Ovár (1554) and Erdöd (Rom: *Ardud*) (1555) and Czenger (1558) reflected growing Reformed† influence amongst the protestant preachers in Hungary culminating in the signed confession of 1558 (*Confessio Czengerina*) (see page 249).
1563	Adoption by János Zsigmond Zápolya in Transylvania of protestantism and subsequent drift towards unitarianism (see page 114).
1570s	Jesuit schools established in Transylvania (with the encouragement of István Báthory) at Kolozsvár (Rom: *Cluj Napoca*) Oradea Mare (G: *Grosswardein*; Hung: *Nagyvárad*) and Alba Iulia (G: *Weissenburg*; Hung: *Gyulafehérvár*).
1572	Accession of Rudolf gradually led to less toleration for Lutheran views in 'royal' Hungary. His attacks on Hungarian political and religious liberties alienated him (esp. post-1600) from many of the magnates of Hungary.

1581   Colloquy at Csepreg failed to produce an accommodation
               between the views of Hungarian Lutherans and Calvinists.

1604–6   The insurrection of István Bocskay in Transylvania, exploit-
               ing the pressures of the 'Great Hungarian War', led to his
               being proclaimed the first Calvinist prince of Transylvania.
               Although he only ruled briefly he established a pattern of
               rule which was taken up by successors, especially Gábor
               Bethlen.

6.6 Poland-Lithuania

6.6.1 Institutional background

The Polish kingdom was in the process of growth and transformation during the sixteenth century. The heartlands of the old Polish
state centred around the Warta and Vistula rivers. The former comprised the region traditionally known as 'Great Poland' (*Polonia maìor*;
P: *Wielkopolska*), whilst the latter was known as 'Minor Poland' (*Polonia
minor*; P: *Malopolska*). During the fifteenth century, the region around
Gdańsk was conquered from the Teutonic Knights and became known
as 'Royal' (or 'Polish') Prussia. The remaining lands of the Teutonic
Knights were held by the Grand Master of the Order as a fief of the
Polish crown and was known after 1525 as 'Ducal' Prussia. Its capital lay
where it had been for centuries at Kraków.

The Polish monarchy in the sixteenth century was in the latter stages
of becoming elective. In 1505, the Polish constitutional document known
as *Nil novi* ('Nothing new') had enunciated the doctrine that nothing in
the Polish commonwealth (known in the later sixteenth century as the
Respublica Poloniae et Lithuaniae (P: *Rzeczpospolita Obojga Narodów*)) could
be decided without the consent of the council and delegates of the
Polish nobility (the *szlachta*). It was at meetings of the lower house of the
Polish diet (the *sejm*) that such decisions were enforced and elections
to the Polish crown took place. In the course of the first half of the
sixteenth century, the nobility entrenched their political and social
hegemony within the Polish commonwealth. Locally, the nobility already
had the right to be consulted about the raising of troops and taxation
(in the provincial assemblies (*sejmiki*)). In the first half of the sixteenth
century, the national diet codified the laws which articulated their privileges, including (from 1562–63) their exemption from the jurisdiction
of the church courts. The crown was forced to repurchase its alienated
lands and live off the proceeds. The nobility appointed local clergy and
teachers. To the extent that travel and study in western Europe introduced

a substantial fraction of the Polish nobility to protestant ideas, the Polish reformation was therefore a movement which the Polish monarchy had little authority to restrain.

In 1569, the crowns and diets of the kingdom of Poland and the grand duchy of Lithuania were united by the Union of Lublin. By this date, the grand duchy comprised, in addition to Lithuania proper, the regions of White Ruthenia (now Belarus), Courland (G: *Kurland*) and Livonia to the north and Volhynia and Ukraine to the south. The union thus brought together a state of huge size and potential. The monarchy moved the capital to Warsaw to be conveniently located for the new condominium but in most other administrative respects, the two areas remained separate. The Lithuanian nobility were granted the rights of the Polish *szlachta* and within a generation were indistinguishable from their neighbours. They rapidly absorbed the same concerns to limit the central authority of the new conjoined commonwealth still further. At the election of the Valois Henri d'Anjou (the younger brother of the French king Charles IX – see genealogy on page 360) to the Polish crown in 1573, the nobility required the monarch's assent to three documents during the negotiations leading up to his election. Together, the *Pacta Conventa*, the *Warsaw Confederation* and the *Henrician Articles* (*Articuli Henriciani*) required the monarchy to guarantee the privileges of the nobility. Amongst other requirements, the Polish king was required to summon the diet every two years and not to wage war or levy taxes without its consent. It was the *Confederation* which enshrined the Polish nobility's entire freedom to practise any religion they chose.

As in most multi-ethnic polities, religion tended to develop an ethnic specificity. By the end of the sixteenth century, the Poles (who made up less than half the country's population) tended to retain their links with catholicism. The Ruthenians (P: *ruski*) (Ukrainians and Belorussians) naturally adhered to the orthodox church, the substantially Jewish minority to Judaism and the Tartars on the south-west marches of settled Europe gravitated towards Islam. This left the German minority in Poland, who were particularly numerous in Polish Prussia. There were also substantial German populations down the Warta in Great Poland and in Silesia. It was in these areas that Lutheranism rapidly gained a foothold in the early 1520s, though it was a somewhat clandestine movement because, at this date, the Polish monarchy was still capable of reinforcing the ecclesiastical authorities to some effect and repressing heresy.

By the 1550s, however, this was beginning to change. Under pressure from the Polish nobility, a minority of which began to protect the protestant religion, Zygmunt August II granted concessions which allowed Lutheran churches to be established in certain places and opened the door to a significant Calvinist (or 'Reformed'†) presence in Poland. The supporters of the latter included the important Radziwiłł family. Their estates became the heartland of the reformation, especially in the Grand Duchy where they played an important role on the council of the duchy too. After the *Warsaw Confederation*, the Polish state became a haven for religious dissent of all kinds across Europe. Anabaptists found they could survive there. Antitrinitarians were more of a threat to established Christian churches of all kinds (orthodox and western) and it was the emergence of 'unitarianism' within the emerging Calvinist congregations which split the Polish 'Reformed' church at precisely the moment when it might have been expected to play its largest part in Polish public life. In general, however, the blanket toleration of noble religious freedoms masked the real tensions at a more local level between (and, in the case of the Calvinists, within) the coexisting religious and ethnic communities, especially in the towns. These tensions were heightened by the way that the laws relating to religious freedom were applied differently to those who were of Polish descent and those who were 'strangers' to the Polish commonwealth.

Although there were times when the supporters of Reformed protestantism came close to claiming a majority in the diet, it is difficult to imagine the Polish kingdom losing its strong attachments to the established catholic church in the sixteenth century. In the interregnum of 1572–74, it was decided for the first time that elections of a new king would be held *viritim* – i.e. with all nobles of whatever rank in the commonwealth eligible to participate in person. This secured the continuing presence of catholics on the Polish throne since the majority of the *szlachta* remained loyal to Rome. At a time when the monarchy was struggling to retain some areas of its traditional secular authority, its adherence to the catholic church seemed to become all the more important. This was as true under Zygmunt August II (whose religious convictions have been much debated by historians) as under any of the other rulers of sixteenth-century Poland. It did not require the Habsburgs, whose military intervention in 1588 to advance the claim of the Habsburg Archduke Maximilian to the Polish throne ended in complete defeat, to protect the catholic religion in Poland. It was secured (and the catholic reformation eventually promoted) from within.

6.6.2 *Rulers*

Zygmunt (Sigismund) I Jagiełłon	1506–48
Zygmunt II August Jagiełłon	1548–72
Henri d'Anjou (later King Henri III of France)	1573–75
István (Stephen) Báthory	1575–87
Zygmunt (Sigismund) III Vasa	1587–1632

6.6.3 Chronology of the Polish reformation

1523   King Zygmunt I issued decrees forbidding the import of Luther's teaching into Poland.

1525   Gdańsk city council abolished the institutions of the catholic church in the city in a municipal insurrection which was repressed by the Polish crown with force.

The Grand Master of the Knights of the Teutonic Order converted to Lutheranism and did homage to the Polish crown for the secularized lands of the order in the duchy of Prussia.

1539   Calvin dedicated his commentary on the mass[†] to Zygmunt August in the hopes of winning him over to the reformation.

1554   Beginnings of a Calvinist church organization in the regions around Kraków and Lublin (i.e. 'Little') Poland. First Calvinist synod at Słomnicki.

1555   Sustained demands in the *sejm* for religious liberty. The authority of the ecclesiastical courts over royal courts was suspended by royal decree.

Agreement between the Calvinists and exiled Bohemian Brethren in Poland over common points of doctrinal unity.

1556   Return of Jan Łaski* to Poland and the beginning of his efforts to unite the different components of Polish protestantism into one confession.

1557   Łaski met Zygmunt II August at Vilnius and tried to persuade him to establish a 'national' reformed church in Poland along the lines of the English reformed church. His proposal was rejected although it remained on the agenda for some Polish catholics.

1562–63   Further decrees disbanded much of the authority of the church courts.

Diet of Pietrków – further efforts to unite the Lutheran and Calvinist churches in Poland.

1569   Unitarians established at Raków; bitter divisions within their movement in the following years before the publication of the unitarian catechism at Raków in 1575.

1570   Union of Sandomierz (*Consensus Sandomiriensis*) united Calvinists, Bohemian Brethren[†] and Lutherans in Poland against the unitarians[†]. The union created a mutual consensus in which each confession retained its own organization and order of services. It was agreed, however, to hold regular synods in common and to prepare a common catechism.

1573   The 'Confederation' of Warsaw (Jan). There was an agreement that there should be a mutual peace between the various religions (*pax inter dissidentes de religione*). The agreement was signed by protestant, orthodox and catholic lay representatives as well as one token bishop. It was confirmed by Henri de Valois on his election to the Polish crown to allay Polish fears that there would be a repetition in Poland of what had occurred in France at the massacre of St Bartholomew (in which there were fears that their new king had had a hand). Special courts were proposed for dealing with interconfessional problems (*processus confederationis*) but this was never enacted by the diet.

1574	Destruction of the Calvinist church at Kraków by hostile crowds.
1587	Second destruction of the Calvinist church at Kraków by hostile mobs.
	Archduke Maximilian of Austria invaded Silesia with an army (Oct) intending to claim the Polish throne against the newly-elected Zygmunt III.
1588	Archduke Maximilian's army crushed at the battle of Byczyrna (24 Jan).
1591	Anti-Calvinist mobs at Vilnius (Lithuania's largest town) and Kraków led to the closure of the Calvinist church at the latter.
1595	Synod at Toruń when the Lutherans withdrew from the union agreed at Sandomierz.
1611	Anti-Calvinist incidents at Lublin, Poznań and Vilnius.

Approximate numbers of protestant worshipping congregations in Poland (excluding Lithuania and Livonia) in c.1600

Protestant group	Numbers	Town centres	Noble protectors
Lutherans	800	Gdańsk, Elbing, Königsberg, etc.	Ostroróg, Górka, Tomicki
Calvinists	250	Pińczów, Secymin, Kiejdany, etc	Oleśnicki
Bohemian Brethren	64	Poznań, Leszno	
Anabaptists	c.80		
Unitarians	250	Raków	Kiszka, Sienieński

SECTION SEVEN

Jean Calvin, Geneva and the refugee reformation

7.1 The 'refugee reformation'

One of the consequences of the hostile reactions to the reformation delineated in the previous chapter was the creation of the 'refugee reformation'. This became the bedrock upon which Calvinism was built. It is sometimes referred to as the 'second generation' protestant reformation, or even (in Germany) as the 'second reformation' (*Zweite Reformation*) of the sixteenth century (see page 74). The experience of exile, voluntary or imposed, has a great effect upon those who suffer it in the twentieth century. Its effects in the sixteenth century, when so much of an individual's sense of belonging and identity depended upon family roots and locality, were infinitely greater. Although a good many of those who are accounted 'religious refugees' in the sixteenth century were, in reality, economic migrants, there is no doubt that, no matter what their individual motives, the experience was painful and formative. Jean Calvin, the French reformer who eventually made Geneva a haven for exiles like himself, expressed these experiences better than any other reformer. His 'language of Canaan' (as Calvinist opponents in sixteenth-century France would term it) developed powerful images which would leave an indelible imprint upon those whose personal condition made them susceptible to its effects. The world was a 'labyrinth' and 'abyss' (*abyssus*) in which we would be inevitably entrapped and drowned. The only way out was by meek acceptance (*docilitas*) of the 'hope' of faith (*invocatio*) in God who would be our father (by adoption), our true king (reigning through providential decree), our teacher, our Lord of Hosts (whose final victory was assured, despite the apparent temporary suffering and defeat) and our Judge.

7.2 Background to Calvin's exile from France

Historians have often remarked on the remarkable obscurity and scantiness of materials from Calvin himself relating to his own intellectual and spiritual development prior to his exile from France in the winter of 1534–35. This is in comparison with the huge outpouring of his writings, and their consistency of tone and underlying dynamics thereafter. Beyond the bare chronological details of his educational formation and some associated reconstruction of the evangelical circles in which he moved in the early 1530s, it has been difficult for Calvin's biographers not to draw on the unsupported testimony of his detractors (especially Jérome Bolsec*, whose *Life of Calvin* (1576) was influential) about this period, or to make extravagant inferences about a 'sudden conversion' which he might have experienced on the slender evidence of an autobiographical phrase used by Calvin in the preface to his *Commentary on the Psalms*, published in 1557. From all that we know, however, Calvin's intellectual evolution was progressive, responsive to the changing climate of repression within France, and gradually more expressive of the senses of alienation which became the mainspring of his mature theology.

?1523   Calvin attended the faculty of arts at the university of Paris (?*Collège de Montaigu*). He was taught Latin grammar by Mathurin Cordier (d.1564).

1526/7/8   He withdrew from the university of Paris to study civil law at the university of Orléans.

1531   Calvin graduated from Orléans with a licentiate in law and returned to Paris.

1532   Publication of his commentary on Seneca's treatise *On Clemency* (*De clementia*) (April). Calvin returned to Orléans to continue his legal studies (May).

1533   Calvin returned to Paris (Oct). The rector of the university of Paris, Nicolas Cop, presented a controversial inaugural lecture (1 Nov) (see page 117); a copy of it (possibly dating to 1534) exists in Calvin's own handwriting. Calvin left Paris (late Nov) and (eventually) retired to Angoulême to stay with Louis du Tillet, a noted humanist scholar.

1534   Calvin resigned his chaplaincy at Noyon (May). The affair of the placards (Oct) (see page 117). Calvin retired with Louis du Tillet to Basel (late 1534) and adopted the pseudonym 'Martinus Lucianus' (the latter an anagram of 'Caluinus').

1535   Calvin completed writing the first edition of the *Institution of the Christian Religion* (23 Aug).

7.3 Calvin's writings

7.3.1 The Institution of the Christian Religion

Calvin's most substantial single published work was the *Institution* [generally rendered in English, following the original sixteenth-century English translation, as the 'Institutes'] *of the Christian Religion* (*Christianae religionis institutio*). It was the most sustained presentation of the fabric of reformed protestant Christianity in the sixteenth century, 'at once a handbook of the Christian religion, a history of Christian doctrine, a detailed presentation of its creed, an elaboration of protestant Biblical theology, a manual of ethics and a guide to sixteenth-century controversy'. It was first published shortly after Calvin's exile from France at Basel in the Latin edition of March 1536. The full title (translated) was: *The Institution of the Christian Religion, Containing almost the Whole Sum of Piety and Whatever It is Necessary to Know in the Doctrine of Salvation. A Work very well worth reading by all persons zealous for piety.* . . . It went through numerous expanded editions both in Latin and French so that, by the final Latin edition in Calvin's lifetime (that of 1559), it was a treatise many times larger than the original. Calvin had to struggle hard to retain the overall coherence of the work as it expanded its size. The treatise became a fundamental work for trainee Calvinist pastors and theologians in the sixteenth century and was translated into many vernacular languages. A summary of the imprints of the *Institution* provides only an imperfect guide to the spreading influence of Calvinism in the later sixteenth century.

7.3.2 Latin and French editions of the Institution in the sixteenth century

Latin:
1536 Thos. Platter & Balthasar Lasius, Basel
1539 Wendelin Rihel, Strasbourg
1543 Wendelin Rihel, Strasbourg
1545 Jean Gérard, Geneva
1550 Jean Gérard, Geneva
1553 Robert Estienne, Geneva
1554 Adam & Jean Rivery, Geneva
1559 Robert Estienne, Geneva
1561 Wendelin Rihel, Strasbourg
1561 Antoine Reboul, Geneva
1568 François Perrin, Geneva
1576 Thos. Vautrollier, London
1576 François le Preux, Lausanne
1577 François le Preux, Lausanne
1584 Thos. Vautrollier, London
1585 Eustache Vignon & Jean le Preux, Geneva
1589 Christoph Raben, Herborn
1592 Jean le Preux, Geneva

French:
1541 Michel du Bois, Geneva
1545 Jean Gérard, Geneva
1551 Jean Gérard, Geneva
1554 Adam and Jean Rivery, Geneva (repr.)
1554 Philibert Hamelin, Geneva (repr.)
1557 Jaquy, Davodeau and Bourgeois (repr.)
1560 Jean Crespin, Geneva
1561 Conrad Badius, Geneva (repr.)
1561 Jacques Bourgeois, Geneva (repr.)
1562 Jaques Bourgeois, Geneva (repr.)
1562 Pierre Philippe, Caen (repr.)
1562 no printer or place of pub. (rep. twice)
1563 Louis Cloquemin, Lyon
1563 Sébastien Honorati, Lyon
1564 Thos. Courteau, Geneva
1565 Jean Martin, Lyon
1565 Pierre Haultin, Lyon
1566 François Perrin, Geneva
1596 Jean Wessel, Bremen

The Internal Organization of the Institution

1536	1539	1543-50	Sections from previous edn.	1559 Chapters
1. Law			**Bk I**	**Chapters**
a. Knowledge of God	**1. Knowledge of God**	1. Knowledge of God	[1]	1–10
			[3]	11–12
			[6]	13–14
b. Knowledge of man	**2. Knowledge of man**	2. Knowledge of man	[2]	15
				16
c. Law & decalogue	3. Law	3. Law	[2]	17
d. Justification		**4. on vows: monasticism**	[2]	18
2. Faith			**Bk II**	
Apostles' Creed	4. Faith: Ap. Creed	5. Faith: Ap. Creed	[2]	1–5
			[3]	**6**
a. Part i	a. Part i	6. Creed		**7–8**
b. Part ii	b. Part ii	7. Creed (ii)		**9**
c. Part iii	c. Part iii	Creed (iii)	[14]	10
d. Part iv	d. Part iv	8. Creed (iv)	[11]	11
			[11]	12–16
			[7]	**17**
Election & predestination	**5. Repentance**	9. Repentance	**Bk III**	
	6. Justification	10. Justification	[7]	1
	7. O.T. & N.T.	11. O.T. & N.T.	[5]	2
	– likenesses	– likenesses	[9]	3–5
	– differences	– differences	[21]	6–10
		12. Christian freedom	[10]	11–18
		13. Human traditions	[12]	19
	8. Predestination	14. Predestination	[15]	20
	Providence	Providence	[14]	21–24
3. Prayer	9. Prayer	15. Prayer	[8]	25
			[15]	
			[13]	
4. Sacraments	10. Sacraments	16. Sacraments	**Bk IV**	
a. general			[8]	1–9
b. baptism	11. Baptism	17. Baptism	[15]	10
c. Lord's Supper	12. Lord's Supper	18. Lord's Supper	[4]	11–12
	13. Christian freedom	19. 5 false sacraments	[16]	13
	14. Ecclesiastical power	20. Civil government	[17]	14
5. False sacraments	15. Civil government		[18]	15–16
repentance, satisfaction	16. 5 false sacraments		[19]	17–18
6. Christian freedom, &c			[20]	19
a. Christian freedom	**17. Life of the**	21. Life of the		20
b. Ecclesiastical power	**Christian man**	Chritian man		
c. Civil government				

Bold text indicates new material inserted into older sections

Source: Taken from F.L. Battles, 'Calculus Fidei' in W.H. Neuser, *Calvinus Ecclesiae Doctor* (Kampen, J.H. Kok, n.d. (c.1980)), pp. 85–110, esp. p. 87.

7.3.3 Major translations of the Institution into other European languages (to 1624)

(NB translated and published *extracts* are not generally noted.)

Language	Date	Edition used	Translator
Spanish	1540	1536 Lat (abbrev)	Francisco Enzinas
	1597	1559 Lat	Cipriano de Valera
Italian	1557 (Geneva)	1553 Fr	Giulio Cesare Pascali
Dutch	1560 (Emden) (Dort) – six further editions	1559 Lat	Johannes Dyrkinus
German	1572 (Heidelberg)	1559 Lat	Members of the university of Heidelberg Theological Faculty
	1582 (Heidelberg) 1597 (Hanau)		
Czech	1617	1559 Lat	Jiřík Strejc [Georg Vetter]
English	1561 (London) – 8 further editions	1559 Lat	Thomas Norton

7.3.4 Calvin's Bible commentaries

Old Testament commentaries

Pentateuch

Genesis (1554)
Comparative commentary on the Pentateuch (Harmony) (1563)

Prophets
Hosea (1557)
Isaiah (2nd edition, 1559)
Minor Prophets (1559)
Daniel (1561)
Jeremiah (1563)
Lamentations (1563)
Joshua (1564)
Ezekiel (chs 1–20) (1565)

Psalms
Psalms (1557)

New Testament commentaries
(The dates of the first Latin editions, all printed in Geneva, are given in brackets.)

Gospels
Gospel of John (1553)

'Harmony' (comparative commentary) on the Gospels of Matthew, Mark and Luke (1555)

Acts
Acts of the Apostles (2 vols – 1552; 1554)

Epistles
Epistle of St Paul to the Romans and to the Thessalonians (1540)
Epistle of Jude (1542)
First Epistle of St Paul to the Corinthians (1546)
Second Epistle of St Paul to the Corinthians (1547)
Epistles of St Paul to the Galatians, to the Ephesians, to the Philippians and to the Colossians (1548)
Epistle of St Paul to the Hebrews (1549)
'Pastoral' Epistles of St Paul (to Timothy (1548), Titus (1549), Philemon (1549))
'Catholic' Epistles (1551)
(Collected editions of the Commentaries on all Paul's Epistles appeared from 1550 onwards.)

7.3.5 Calvin's apologetic

Calvin's vast output of apologetic writing encompassed treatises whose objectives were highly diverse. There were those which were intended as mordant satires or critiques of the established church. A further set of treatises was aimed at dangerous trends within reformed protestantism. These included anabaptists, antitrinitarians and spiritual rationalists ('libertines'). There were also tracts which criticized components of Lutheran doctrine and presented the elements of his eucharistic and predestinarian theology. His confessional publications are touched on below (see pages 248–9).

Treatises
These are listed by date of publication or, occasionally, where it is more relevant, by date of composition; the place of publication is Geneva unless otherwise noted. Some minor publications have been omitted.

- *On the sleep of the soul* (*De Psychopannychia*) (composed c.1534; not published in Calvin's lifetime).
- *Epistle to Sadoleto* (1540) – Latin response to a reasoned appeal to Genevans to return to the orthodox church from Cardinal Jacopo Sadoleto*.
- *Little Treatise on Holy Communion* (*Petit Traicté de la saincte Cene de Nostre Seigneur Jesus Christ*) (1541) – a short exposition justifying (with scriptural references) Calvin's position on the eucharist.
- *Treatise on Relics* (*Advertissement tresutile du grand proffit qui reviendroit à la Chrestienté, s'il faisoit inventoire de tous les corps saintz, et reliques . . .*) (1543) – a critique of the practice of venerating relics.
- *Treatise on Free Will against Pighius* (1543) – a detailed theological exposition of predestination and free-will, drawing on Luther's writings.
- *Against the Nicodemites* (*Excuse de Jehan Calvin, à Messieurs les Nicodemites, sur la complaincte qu'ilz font de sa trop grand rigueur*) (1544) – an attack on outward conformity.
- *Against the fantastic sect of the libertines* (1545)
- *Treatise upon Scandals* (1550)
- *On eternal Predestination* (*Congrégation sur l'élection éternel*) (1551) – Calvin's defence of a doctrine which was becoming the focus for criticism.
- *Defence of the orthodox faith concerning the Holy Trinity* (1553) – Calvin's answer to the antitrinitarianism which he had found in the works of Servetus, and which was the reason for his supporting the prosecution of him for impiety.
- *Declaration for the maintenance of true faith against Servetus* (1554)
- *Second Defence against Westphal* (1556) – the beginnings of open hostility between Calvin and the orthodox ('gnesio-') Lutherans, represented by Joachim Westphal (1510–74), the Lutheran pastor at Hamburg (see page 220).
- *Second Defence of the holy and right faith in the matter of the Sacraments* (1556)
- *Last Warning from Jean Calvin to Joachim Westphal* (1557)
- *Clear exposition of the wholesome doctrine of the true partaking of the flesh and the blood of Jesus Christ* (1561)

7.4 Geneva and Jean Calvin

Internal factions continued to dominate the institution of the reformation after Calvin's first appearance in the city in 1536, as before (see pages 99–100). Shifting factional pressures within the city led to his and

Guillaume Farel's* departure less than two years later. The reluctance of his return to Geneva from Strasbourg in 1541 was, at least in part, the consequence of his forebodings about the struggle which would be required to impose a coherent reformation in the city. The political disputes focused on the annual elections of the four syndics of the city as well as its inner governing council (*Petit Conseil*). These posts were restricted to the *bourgeois* of the city, a privileged position enjoyed by natives of the city and those few who could afford to purchase the status. The remainder of the citizens were either inhabitants (*habitants*) or subjects (*sujets*). The latter was the status accorded to those who lived in the rural parishes outside the city but subject to its jurisdiction. The former was enjoyed by legal resident aliens in the city, such as the refugees from France and elsewhere who congregated in Geneva in increasing numbers from the late 1540s. They had no rights to vote, to carry weapons or to hold any position of civil authority within the city. However inhabitants did have the right to be pastors, to teach in the schools and to play a full part in its church. It was partly on the basis of their increasing influence in the city that Calvin's growing authority within the Genevan reformation rested.

7.4.1 Chronology of the Calvinist reformation at Geneva (1536–64)

Calvin's first residence
1536

2 Feb   Bern forces entered Geneva; they withdrew later the same year and Geneva's independence was guaranteed subject to financial retribution.

Feb   Reform-minded city magistrates ('syndics') elected.

19 May   The inner governing council (*Petit Conseil*) summoned a 'general council' of the city to approve the 'new reformation of the faith'; this was held on 25 May.

Aug   Calvin persuaded by Guillaume Farel* to stay in Geneva and assist in the permanent establishment of the reformation there.

Oct   Lausanne Disputation organized by Bern; Guillaume Farel, Calvin and Pierre Viret* attended from Geneva. Calvin's oratorical skills and patristic knowledge deployed to considerable effect.

Nov   Calvin drafted and presented his *Confession of Faith* to the Genevan syndics and inner governing council; Calvin appointed as a preacher and pastor to the church of Geneva.

1537

16 Jan   Presentation of the 'Articles on the Government of the Church' to the Genevan magistrates – a draft of ecclesiastical ordinances

to produce a 'well-ordered and regulated church'. The draft stressed the importance of regular (monthly) communion[†], the importance of retaining excommunication[†] as a way of maintaining ecclesiastical discipline[†]; the significance of an ecclesiastical tribunal to enforce that discipline. The Psalms were to be sung regularly and the young people instructed in the faith and publicly examined on their learning. Finally, new regulations for marriage were proposed.

Feb   New syndics appointed who were all supporters of Farel ('Guillermins' or 'Farets') as opposed to their opponents (the 'Articulants' or 'Artichauds').

Nov   The inner governing council tried to impose Calvin's *Confession of Faith* on the population at large and give the clergy power to excommunicate those who infringed it. The larger councils of the city rejected the proposal.

1538
Feb   Newly elected (more conservative) syndics abandoned the proposals contained in the *Confession* and insisted that Farel and Calvin accept the church order of the canton of Bern, on pain of expulsion. Pro-'Guillermin' members of the inner governing council were suspended and accused of intriguing against the state.

21 April   Farel and Calvin ordered to leave Geneva: Calvin retired to Strasbourg.

Calvin's second residence
1540   Pro-Farel ('Guillermin') faction elected as syndics (Feb). Leaders of the pro-Bernese faction ('Artichauds') executed, exiled or fined (June). Calvin invited back to Geneva (Oct).

1541   Calvin returned under protest to Geneva (13 Sep).

1541–42   Definitive establishment of the Calvinist church organization at Geneva:
             Nov 1541 – *Ecclesiastical Ordinances of the Church of Geneva*.
             1542 – *Second Catechism* (see page 251).
             1542 – *Form of Ecclesiastical Prayers and Hymns* laid out the revised Genevan liturgy.

1542   Regular meetings of the Genevan consistory and the Company of Pastors began.

1543   Serious outbreak of plague in the city (April); several pastors refused to tend victims (with resulting tensions). The spread of the plague was blamed on witches. Plague attenuated the political influence of the 'Guillermin' faction which supported Calvin.

First sustained period of Genevan hostility to Calvin 1545–46

1545–46   The 'Trolliet affair'; Calvin refused to accept Jean Trolliet (a Genevan *bourgeois*) as minister in the church despite pressure from the city magistrates.

1546

Jan–Mar   Attack on Calvin by Pierre Ameaux, a maker of playing-cards whose living had been affected by the religious changes imposed by the consistory. Calvin eventually gained a public and humiliating penitential apology for the 'libels' uttered against him. Other disputes fomented between Calvin and other powerful Genevan *bourgeois* led to riots in the streets against the 'French' pastors and Calvin in particular in the early summer of 1546.

Nov   Ordinances of Genevan Council regulated Christian names to be used at baptism.

Dec   Heads of enquiry drafted by the Company of Pastors for annual parochial visitations in the villages subject to Genevan jurisdiction.

Fears for Genevan security, 1546–48

1546

July–Sep   Rumours of imperial troops amassing against protestant cities in Germany during the Schmalkaldic War (see page 62) provoked fears for Geneva's security.

1547

June   Arrest of Jacques Gruet for attacking the French ministers by means of a libellous placard pinned to a pulpit.

26 July   Execution of Gruet; in the course of his trial he implicated other Genevan *bourgeois* in active hostility towards the French ministers.

22 Sep   Arrest of the captain of the city guard, Ami Perrin (leader of the 'Libertin' faction), for conspiring with France against the Genevan state. He was eventually removed from the inner governing council (*Petit Conseil*) but released.

1548   News reached Geneva that Konstanz had fallen to imperial troops and that Bern was in danger of capitulation (Oct).

1549

April   Geneva in expectation of imminent attack from imperial troops.

May   A doctrinal compromise agreed with the churches of Zürich and Neuchâtel (the *Consensus Tigurinus* – see page 249).

July   Street riot against 'French' refugees in the city following a sermon from Calvin.

Geneva and the influx of French exiles 1549–55

late 1540s   Establishment of the *French Bursary* (*Bourse Française*) to provide funded relief for poor refugees from France.

1551   Jérome Bolsec* presented his criticisms of Calvin's views on predestination before the Company of Pastors (16 Oct). Bolsec condemned to banishment by the Genevan magistrates for his critique of predestination (22 Dec).

1551–52   Recurring debates within the inner governing council to limit access for refugees to the rights of *bourgeois* within Geneva.

1552   French troops invaded the duchy of Lorraine (Spring) and seized Toul, Metz and Verdun, threatening Strasbourg. This produced nervous reactions in Geneva.

1553   Arrest of Michel Servetus in Geneva (13 Aug) (see page 114). Servetus condemned by the city magistrates, after taking advice from the churches of Basel, Bern, Zürich and Schaffhausen, to be burned alive (25 Oct). Calvin attempted to have the sentence commuted to beheading but Servetus was burned the following day.

Final period of Genevan hostility to Calvin (1555)

1555

Feb   Election of pro-Calvin syndics.

18 April   The inner governing council began granting *bourgeois* status to increased numbers of suitable (rich) refugees (57 new *bourgeois* created by 2 May).

16 May   Riot engineered by Calvin's enemies against these changes. Many arrested by the magistrates and the remainder took flight.

24 May   Ami Perrin, Calvin's opponent and the leader of the 'Libertin' faction, was condemned for his part in the riot. Other prominent anti-Calvin faction leaders were executed, fined or exiled in the course of the summer.

Calvin's triumph

1555   First despatch of pastors from Geneva to the Calvinist congregations in France (see page 182).

1556–59   French refugees who had been newly promoted to the status of *bourgeois* entered the lower Genevan councils and reinforced Calvin's authority in the city.

1557   Théodore de Bèze* recalled from the academy at Lausanne to serve as the rector for the foreshadowed Genevan academy.

1559   Inauguration of the Genevan academy (5 June). Calvin became a *bourgeois* of Geneva (25 Dec).

1560   French noble refugees in Geneva implicated in plots against the French monarchy.

1560–62   Many requests for pastors from French congregations and much demand for the pamphlets produced from Genevan presses (see page 272).

1564   Calvin bade farewell to his fellow pastors (28 April). Calvin died (27 May). Théodore de Bèze elected moderator of the Congregation of Pastors (*Vénérable Compagnie des Pasteurs*) as his replacement.

7.4.2 Notable refugees in Geneva

1548   Jean Crespin*
        Théodore de Bèze*
1549   Laurent de Normandie (Noyon)
        Jean Budé (Verace)
1550   Guillaume Trie (Lyon)
        Galeas (Galeazzo) Caracciolo (Marquis de Vico) (Italy)
        Antoine Prévost (Vaneau)
        Robert Estienne*
1551   Jean-François Chastillon (Saillon en Vally)
1553   Claude d'Anduze (Veyrac, Languedoc)
        Pierre, François and Jean d'Aireboudouze (Anduze, Languedoc)
1554   François Budé (Villeneuve)
        Regnault and Jean Anjorrant (Jolly and Paris)
        Jean Morély* (Paris)
        John Knox (Scotland)

7.4.3 Genevan missions

The following are the numbers of pastors despatched by the Company of Pastors from Geneva. The majority were despatched to France, with exceptions being noted in brackets.[1]

1555:   5 (4 to Piedmont)
1556:   5 (2 to Piedmont, 2 to Brazil)
1557:   16 (4 to Piedmont, 1 to Antwerp)
1558:   23 (1 to Turin)
1559:   32
1560:   13 (1 to London)
1561:   12
1562:   12

[1] Figures from E. William Monter, *Calvin's Geneva* (New York, John Wiley and Sons, 1967), p. 135.

7.4.4 Admission to the status of bourgeois at Geneva

Date	Numbers admitted	Total revenue (in Savoyard écus)
1535	61	280
1536	11	112
1537	22	90
1538	23	111
1539	14	213
1540	31	171
1541	21	192
1542	17	66
1543	28	110
1544	8	71
1545	7	68
1546	9	36
1547	138	725
1548	10	42
1549	6	32
1550	8	42
1551	15	80
1552	10	113
1553	24	104
1554	6	30
1555	127	1592
1556	144	1014

Source: Figures from William G. Naphy, Calvin and the Consolidation of the Genevan Reformation (Manchester, Manchester University Press, 1994), p. 216.

7.5 Refugee foyers

Geneva was by no means the only point of refuge for the flow of protestant religious exiles from the hostile reactions which the reformation had provoked in various parts of Europe. The populated and prosperous Rhineland quadrant (see page 264) and north-west Germany (along with southern England) became the major points of refuge. Much depended, however, on the degree to which particular cities permitted 'strangers' (Fr: étrangers; G: Welches) to take up residence. In general, city fathers were cautious and wary towards any significant immigration and guilds were hostile to potential competition. Where the 'strangers' succeeded, at least for brief periods, in settling in significant numbers, they established their own churches, worshipping in their own languages and with their own pastors. These 'stranger churches' were particularly attracted to Calvin's incorporation of the experience of exile into his theology. For his part, he took a particular interest in the well-being and survival of these congregations. They became the first 'Calvinist' churches in Europe outside Geneva.

7.5.1 Stranger churches

Switzerland
Geneva

	—	Italian church
	—	English church
	1558–61	Spanish church
Zürich		
	—	French church

Germany
Basel

	1555–58	English church
	1547–?	French church
Cologne		
	1554–55	French church
Duisburg		
	1554–58	English church
Emden		
	—	Dutch church
Frankenthal		
	1562–69	Walloon church
Frankfurt-am-Main		
	1554–58	English church
	1554–62	French church
	1555–62	Walloon church
The Liepvre Valley		
	1550(?)–62	French church
Strasbourg		
	1538–63	French church
	1557–58	English church
Wesel		
	1545–57	French church
	1555–57	English church
Worms		
	—	English church

England
London

1550–53	Dutch church	
1560–	French church	

Other emigrant settlements and churches were also located at Canterbury, Winchelsea, Rye and Norwich (French) and Sandwich, Maidstone, Colchester and Norwich (Dutch).

7.5.2 Approximate strength of the exile communities[2]

French	c.1560

Switzerland:

Geneva	10,000
Zürich	5,000

Germany:

Basel	800
Frankfurt	1,000
Strasbourg	2,000

England:

London	1,000

Dutch	c.1560	c.1570

Germany:

Aachen	1,000	3,000
Emden	2,000	5,000
Frankfurt	2,000	1,500
Hamburg	—	2,000
Wesel	1,000	7,000

England:	1,400	9,700

---

[2] Figures from G. Parker, *The Dutch Revolt* (Harmondsworth, Penguin, 1977), p. 177; P. Denis, *Les églises d'étreangers en pays rhénans (1534–1564)* (Paris, Faculté de théologie de Liège, 1984).

SECTION EIGHT

Reformation from within

8.1 Catholic reformation

The term 'counter-reformation' (G: *Gegenreformation*) is a neologism coined by nineteenth-century German historians to delineate catholic reactions to the reformation. It has never been adopted without question because the presuppositions which underlined it were not entirely accepted, especially by catholic historians. Their objections have now been integrated into the historiography of the subject. Research has shown how the changes in the catholic church during the sixteenth century were not simply the result of the protestant challenge. For this reason, historians have increasingly preferred the term 'catholic reformation' to describe efforts to reform the church, efforts which often predated the protestant reformation and sometimes offered complementary solutions to the complex problems which the protestants had highlighted and to which they had proposed one (but not the only) solution.

So catholic reforming endeavours in the sixteenth century have to be set in the context of older efforts to reform the church *in capite et in membris* attempted by the councils of Konstanz and Basel (see page 26). The reforming attempts within the regular orders to return to the stricter observance of their rules also provide the background to the new catholic foundations of the sixteenth century. In a handbook of this kind, it is difficult to convey the subtle shifts in attitudes, the generational shifts in perceived expectations and their impact in the public domain, which explain so much of the changes within this complex religious world. One English historian tried to encapsulate these in what he described as 'the spirit of the counter-reformation'.[1] Such a spirit is less easy to document than the new catholic foundations and the sessions of the remarkable council of Trent[†]. But the stress upon new catholic foundations should not allow us to ignore the continuing process of internal reform of older orders which intensified in the sixteenth century. The latter was particularly noticeable in Spain, as

[1] H. Outram Evennett, *The Spirit of the Counter-Reformation* (Cambridge, Cambridge University Press, 1968).

reflected in the reform of the Carmelite order, inaugurated by Teresa of Ávila*, as well as the orders of Augustinian hermits, the Trinitarians and the Mercedarians (a Spanish order, founded in the thirteenth century, devoted to caring for the sick and liberating Christians captured by the Moors).

8.2 New catholic foundations

8.2.1 The capuchins

An order founded in the Italian Marches by Matteo da Bascio (d. 1552) (an 'observant'[†] Franciscan from Urbino) and the brothers Lodovico and Raffaele Tenaglia da Fossombrone. They were dedicated to the strict observance of the Franciscan rule. The name derived from the pointed Franciscan hood (*capuccio*) which they wore; but their beards and sandals also made them distinctive figures. Through the aristocratic patronage of Caterina Cibo, duchess of Camerino, a cousin to Pope Clement VII, they gained a papal bull on 3 July 1528 (*Religionis zelus*) allowing them to become the 'Minor Friars of the Eremitic Life'. The order's constitution was issued and confirmed by Pope Paul III* in 1536. Although it was modified numerous times subsequently (1552, 1575, 1608) the initial rule laid out the objectives of the order. Christ and St Francis provided the two models of Christian living in this world – with both offering a pattern of creative tension between action and contemplation. The order's mission was to spread the gospel wherever that was needed.

That was translated into an endeavour which, in the course of the sixteenth century, was almost as remarkable as that of the Jesuits. The order spread rapidly despite early internal disputes (Ludovico Tenaglia was eventually expelled) and the opposition from the other Franciscans. The third general of the order, Bernardino Ochino*, converted to protestantism in 1541 and almost provoked its early suppression. In 1574, however, Pope Gregory XIII* permitted its expansion outside the Italian peninsula. It rapidly became established in France and elsewhere. By 1596, it had 7,230 members and 660 convents, divided into 30 provinces. At the close of the first century of its existence as an order, there were 16,967 members in 1,260 convents, dispersed amongst 42 provinces, and its growth continued until the middle of the eighteenth century.

Capuchin devotional works reflected much of the prevailing trends in catholic reformation spirituality. Giovanni da Fano's *The Art of Union* (*Arte de la Unione* (1536)) was the first of a continuum of treatises on mystic prayer which continued through the sixteenth century.

Capuchin provinces (to 1620)

	Foundation date of province	No. of houses by 1596	No. of Capuchins attached to houses
Italian peninsula			
Ancona	1528	50	486
Rome	1529	39	410
Assisi	1530	39	427
Florence	1532	27	287
Reggio	1532	26	236
Bari	1535	20	182
Bologna	1535	36	430
Venice	1535	29	410
Milan	1535	29	366
Genoa	1535	36	367
Naples	1535	34	429
Foggia	1535	17	141
Bari	1535	20	182
Salerno	1560	26	235
Aquila	1575	23	207
Cosenza	1584	21	162
Brescia	1587	21	284
Lecce	1590	25	230
Turin	1619	—	—
Sicily, Corsica and Sardinia			
Palermo	1534	25	360
Bastia	1540	5	41
Siracusa	1574	25	329
Messina	1574	29	389
Cagliari	1591	4	38
France			
Paris	1574	13	111
Lyon	1575	8	100
Toulouse	1582	7	59
Marseille	1588	7	86
Nancy	1602	—	—
Tours	1610	—	—
Annecy	1611	—	—
The Spanish peninsula			
Barcelona	1578	20	226
Valencia	1605	—	—
Saragossa	1607	—	—
Madrid	1609	—	—

	Foundation date of province	No. of houses by 1596	No. of Capuchins attached to houses
The Habsburg lands, The Holy Roman Empire and the Netherlands			
Antwerp	1586	10	132
Innsbruck	1593	—	—
Prague	1600	—	—
Graz	1608	—	—
Cologne	1611	—	—
Namur	1616	—	—
Besançon	1618	—	—
The Swiss Cantons			
Luzern	1581	9	66

8.2.2 The Theatines

The Theatines were founded in Rome in 1524 as the 'Clerks Regular of the Divine Providence'. The order was the brain-child of two members of the Roman Oratory of Divine Love[†], Thomas de Vio (Cajetan*) and Gian Pietro Carafa (later Pope Paul IV)* and two associates, Bonifacio de' Colli and Paolo Consiglieri. At the time, Carafa was bishop of Chieti (or, in Latin, 'Theatinus' – hence their name). This was not a 'regular' or 'enclosed' order but a community of priests. It was specifically directed towards providing an environment for reformed secular clergy, devoted to observing canon law and engaged in charitable endeavours with the poor and the sick. The Theatines were not allowed to own any property or to beg. They took oaths to observe a strict austerity in their personal life and the Italian 'Chietini' still denotes religious asceticism. They were distinguishable from other secular clergy only by their white socks. Their foundation house at Rome was dispersed by the ravaging of the city in 1527 and they retired to Venice. Other houses were established in Naples and in other Italian cities. They became particularly noted for their ministry to the *incurabili* (i.e. those suffering from syphilis). There were eventually Theatine clergy in Spain, Portugal, France and central Europe as well as a congregation of Theatine nuns, founded in Italy in 1583. The distinctive nature of the foundation and its objectives had an impact in the catholic reformation well beyond what the numbers of its foundations would imply. Their spirituality received its characteristic expression in Lorenzo Scupoli's influential and popular treatise, *Spiritual Combat* (*Combattimento Spirituale*, 1589).

8.2.3 The Italian Oratory of Divine Love

The first Oratory emerged from the local organizations of priests in Genoa and elsewhere which were inspired by the devotional programmes and social conscience of Caterina Fieschi Adorna (St Catherine of Genoa (1447–1510)). A notary and lay patron of Catherine, Ettore Vernazza, founded the earliest Oratory of Divine Love in Genoa in 1497. It was characterized by lay dominance and its religious observances. The latter included spiritual exercises, a common prayer life, the frequent reception of the sacraments and an evident charitable commitment to the poor and dispossessed. The Genoese Oratory was responsible for the foundation of the first hospital in Italy for the victims of syphilis (*incurabili*). Similar confraternities were established in the numerous cities of northern Italy as well as at Rome and Naples. That at Rome emerged in the 1510s and, although disbanded in the wake of the Sack of Rome (1527), it was refounded and became an important influence on prominent figures in the catholic reformation in Italy. Its effects on Gian Matteo Giberti*, the bishop of Verona, and on the early founders of the Theatines[†], should not be underestimated. The Roman community met in the oratory at the church of San Girolamo, from which room its name probably derived. In 1575, the Roman Oratory was turned into a congregation. By that date, its popularity was considerably advanced through the influence of Philip Neri*. The congregation was finally sanctioned in constitutions approved by Pope Paul V in 1612.

8.2.4 The French Oratory (l'Oratoire de Jésus-Christ)

Modelled on the example of the Roman Oratory, the French Oratory was founded in 1611 by Pierre de Bérulle* at Paris. It would eventually differ from its Italian predecessor by being more centralized in its organization and by concentrating on the running of seminaries for the training of priests and on its colleges. It was through the latter that the order would exercise such a considerable influence on the catholic reformation in France and the Spanish Netherlands in the seventeenth century.

8.2.5 The Ursulines (The Company of Saint Ursula)

Formally established in Brescia in 1535, the Company of St Ursula was composed of the followers of St Angela Merici as a society of consecrated virgins dedicated to charitable works and Christian education but living in their own homes. Their rule, approved by the pope in 1536, emphasized their virginity and laid down a discipline of regular fasting, a life of prayer, frequent confession and attendance at mass[†], and simple living. In its initial form, the company lay in the hands of older women acting as supervisors (*colonelles*) to younger ones, with four men to act as spiritual guides. As so often tended to happen in the new catholic foundations of the sixteenth century, the death of their dominant founder was followed by a period of internal division and external questioning. In due course, the order was reorganized to fall into the pattern of rigidly enclosed orders for nuns outlined by Pope Pius V in 1566 (in the bull[†] *Circa Pastoralis*). The Ursulines adopted a habit, instituted a rite of initiation for new adherents and, by the end of the century, had begun to establish their own convents and convent schools for young girls, more separated from the world at large. Some of these changes came about partly through the influence of Carlo Borromeo*, archbishop of Milan. By the end of the sixteenth century, there were Ursuline foundations in several cities of northern Italy. In addition, the movement had spread to France and the Spanish Netherlands (where they also specialized in educating young girls). It was here that Mary Ward (1585–1645) came under their influence and went on to establish her own religious congregation along similar lines.

8.2.6 The Barnabites (Clerks Regular of St Paul)

The Barnabites gained their popular name from the church of St Barnabus in Milan, where they were founded by Antonio Maria Zaccaria (d. 1539), an aristocrat from Cremona whose lay fraternity at Milan, known as the *Amicizia*, became the inspiration for religious reform. The rule (authorized by the pope in 1533) was shaped by that of St Augustine. In addition, a place was allowed for laymen to join and a parallel order was also founded for women ('The Angelic Sisters of St Paul'). In common with the other new foundations of the period, the Barnabites devoted themselves to social welfare amongst the poor, the ill and the abandoned. The order spread only slowly from Milan to other cities in Italy, but it never established a permanent presence outside the Italian peninsula in this period. Its spirituality reflected the interests of its founders and its extended devotion, known as the 'Forty Hours', was based on meditations around the writings of St Paul, the image of Christ and the eucharist.

Barnabite houses in Italy in the sixteenth century

Milan	1530
Pavia	1557
Cremona	1570
Monza	1571
Casale	1571
Rome	1575
Vercelli	1576
Pisa	1595
Bologna	1599
Novara	1599

8.2.7 The Jesuits (The Society of Jesus)

The Society of Jesus was founded by Ignatius Loyola* and his companions. It had begun to take shape in 1534 when Ignatius persuaded six
other students studying with him at the university of Paris to take vows
of chastity, poverty and obedience. They dreamt of travelling to Palestine to convert the Muslims for Christ or, failing that, to offer their
services to the pope in whatever task best suited their abilities. They left
Paris for Venice, by which time Loyola's associates (they had grown to
ten) became ordained as priests and began to call themselves the Company of Jesus (It: *Compagnia di Gesù*; Lat: *Societas Iesu*). No ship left for
Jerusalem during these years, however, because of the war with the Turks
and so they were obliged to continue to Rome to found a new kind
of moral crusading order to support the papacy and catholic doctrine
against heresy and to undertake missionary work amongst the heathen.
They expected to be able to advance such objectives by preaching, by
leading people through the *Spiritual Exercises* (see page 193), by teaching, hearing confessions, converting individuals to Christianity and per-
forming welfare works. Their model was the itinerant apostolic ministry
described in the New Testament. The order was formally approved by
Pope Paul III* on 27 Sep 1540 (in the bull *Regimini militantis ecclesiae*).

Much has been made of the supposedly 'special' militaristic features
of the Jesuit order, but this was partly a matter of surface texture, less
distinctive than we might suppose. Jesuits were required to be priests
and some were obliged to take an additional vow beyond the normal
vows of those in holy orders or in a monastic rule. This committed them
to going, without question or prevarication, wherever the pope might
require them to serve, in order to save souls. Jesuits were forbidden
from taking on an ecclesiastical dignity on pain of mortal sin, unless
they were required to do so by the pope. There would be no Jesuit
bishops in the catholic reformed church, although there would be several cardinals. Many of the militaristic elements were introduced at a
slightly later date in the *Constitutions* (see pages 193–4) by which the
government of the Jesuit order was laid down and the rules governing
the training of new members defined. The more subtle distinctive elements of the Society of Jesus at the beginning lay in the conception of
a religious order which was dedicated to itinerant ministry. This meant
that the Jesuits were released from the common discipline in the regular orders of reciting the canonical hours and saying mass together.
This gradually led to profound differences from other orders in the
way in which Jesuits were trained and prepared for their tasks. Unlike
the mendicant orders[†], the Jesuits took with them Ignatius' *Spiritual
Exercises*. Gradually they created a new form of outreach – that of the
temporary 'retreat' from the world. This also, in time, made the Jesuit

impact qualitatively different from the other new catholic foundations of this period.

The *Spiritual Exercises* (Lat: *Exercitationes Spirituales*; Sp: *Ejercicios Espirituales*)

Ignatius Loyola's* famous devotional handbook was drawn up during his stay at the monastery at Manresa. It was then revised and expanded until 1540, when it was virtually complete, being only changed in small details for its first publication at Rome in 1548. It was structured around four 'weeks' or parts, which were designed to provide a practical programme of prayer and meditation for a month's seclusion and sustained contemplation. This programme was to be administered by a Jesuit 'spiritual director'; personal use of the *Exercises* for individual meditative purposes was strongly discouraged. The first week (*deformata reformare*) is devoted to a frighteningly precise and progressive consideration of human sin and its manifold consequences. The second week (*reformata conformare*) invites the participant to consider the richness and glory of the kingdom of Christ. The third week (*conformata confirmare*) concentrates on Christ's suffering and Passion in vivid and explicit detail. The fourth week (*confirmata transformare*) celebrates the risen and transcendant Lord. In the prayers and accompanying mental exercises for each week there is an effective engagement of all the senses and imaginative grasp of the individual in a developmental way towards the goal of overall religious transformation. Although designed for sustained use over a month in what would come to be called a religious retreat[†], it was also possible to follow the *Exercises* through a period of ten days. In the fundamental supposition that God talks directly to individuals, as well as in its detailed devotional advice, the *Spiritual Exercises* drew directly on the mystic writers of the fourteenth and fifteenth centuries (see pages 38–9).

The Constitutions (*Constitutionales*)

The Constitutions of the order were based on the original foundation proposal (*Formula Instituti*) which had been presented to Pope Paul III* in 1539. The first edition of 1541, drawn up by Loyola himself and his secretary Juan de Polanco (1516–76), was completely reworked after Loyola thoroughly studied other monastic and mendicant rules and consulted his companions. In 1550, the new version was put into practice for a trial period and Jerónimo Nadal was entrusted with extensive powers to visit the now-scattered order to explain it to them and collect comments. These were eventually worked into the final form which was agreed at the General Congregation of the order in 1558.

The Constitutions established the order as a kind of elective monarchy in which the general (*Praepositus generalis*) was elected for life by the General Congregation summoned specially for the purpose. The general had almost unlimited authority to nominate all superiors, to receive regular reports from them, and to issue decisions on the basis of those reports – but he was expected to take advice from his assistants (to whom groups of provinces were assigned as their specialisms). The order abandoned any equivalent of regular chapter meetings such as those of the other regular orders[†]. During an interregnum after the death of an incumbent general, the vicar-general of the order was required to summon the assistants, the provincial superiors and two elected delegates from each province to elect a new general.

The Constitutions also laid down the rules governing the reception and training of new members. Successful completion of the initial two years as a 'novitiate' was marked by taking the initial simple vows of the order. Then followed an intensive study of philosophy and theology, lasting at least seven years, when the Jesuit was a 'scholastic'. During this period, the recruit might be called upon to act as a tutor or teacher in a college as well as study; but he could be dismissed at any stage. After being ordained and successfully completing the 'scholasticate', the member then completed a final year as a 'novitiate' (known as the 'tertianship'). He would then be admitted to perpetual profession of the Jesuit vows as a 'spiritual coadjutor' or, after several more years, be permitted to take the four vows as a 'professed' Jesuit in the strict sense. The 'professed' Jesuits were the smaller group who occupied its higher offices in the sixteenth century and effectively ran the order.

Generals of the Jesuit order (1541–1615)

Ignatius Loyola	1541–56
Diego Laínez	1558–65
Francis Borgia	1565–73
Eberhard Mercurian	1573–80
Claudio Acquaviva (Lat: *Aquaviva*)	1581–1615

Jesuit provinces in 1556

Italy	Castile
Sicily	Andalusia
Upper Germany	Portugal
Lower Germany	Brazil
France	India
Aragon	Ethiopia

Total: 12 provinces (by 1618, this had risen to 32 provinces)

Jesuit establishments in Europe, 1540–1615

The decision to concentrate on educational establishments, which became apparent in the period from the opening of the first school at Messina in Sicily in 1548 and 1560, fundamentally changed the way that the Jesuit order operated in Europe. The acquisition of college fabric and the inevitable issues of accountability and administration which followed it led to the elaboration of the Constitutions. At the same time, a majority of the order became in due course engaged in teaching the full range of secular subjects in the broad curriculum summarizing Jesuit educational practice, the *Ratio Studiorum*. The order not only gained a well-earned reputation for its intellectual command but also became noted for its willingness to engage with and absorb the humanist learning current during the foundation of the order.

Although only a minority of Jesuit collegians went on to become members of the order, the effects of a Jesuit education on those who attended the college are attested by many of its students. In 1563, the Sodality of the Blessed Virgin, a kind of associateship ('third order'), was established at the Roman College by the Jesuit Jan Leunis. It encouraged boys to regular communion and confession as well as acts of social welfare. In time, it spread to other Jesuit colleges (being institutionalized as a confraternity by Gregory XIII) and provided a way by which former students could continue their attachment to the order. In addition to colleges, however, there were other Jesuit establishments which should not be ignored. These included residential houses for members of the order as well as establishments for social welfare of which the most remarkable was the *Casa Santa Marta* founded in Rome in 1543 for reformed prostitutes.

In retrospect, the greatest successes for the Jesuits in their educational and pastoral outreach lay in Portugal, the Southern Netherlands and in Germany. In Spain, they encountered the hostility of other orders and the suspicion of the monarchy. In France, they contended with the Gallican[†] suspicions amongst the *parlement* of Paris. Openly-voiced doubts about their loyalty to the French monarchy were made more plausible by the case (in certain, specific circumstances of a 'tyrant' king oppressing God's people) for deposing a king (if necessary by force), which had been made by the Jesuits Juan Mariana* and Roberto Bellarmino (Eng: *Bellarmine*)*. These led to the expulsion of the Jesuits from most of France in 1595 by orders of the *parlements*. They were subsequently reinstated in 1603. They were also briefly expelled from Venice in June 1606 on grounds of their potential conflict of loyalties. In southern Germany, by contrast, the extraordinary missions of the Dutch Jesuit Peter Canisius* (D: *Kanijs*) in Austria and Bavaria did much to shape the impact of the Jesuits. Several of the new catholic institutions of higher education established in Germany in the sixteenth century would be run by the Jesuit order (see pages 268–9). In northern Europe, the success of the Jesuit mission to Poland occurred at a critical moment in the evolution of the Polish commonwealth. Arriving in 1564, their schools attracted the sons of protestant as well as catholic families. It was the Polish Jesuit Piotr Skarga whose popularized version of Bible stories (*The Lives of the Saints* (*Żywoty Świętych*), 1579) became a sixteenth-century classic of the genre. In established protestant northern Europe and orthodox Russia, their efforts made less headway. The ambitious efforts of Antonio Possevino* in Sweden and Russia were eventually unsuccessful and the Jesuit mission to England, led by Robert Parsons and Edmund Campion in 1580, would become subsequently entangled in a dispute with the resident catholic minority.

Distribution of Jesuit establishments in Europe

	Colleges	Residential houses and other establishments
Italian peninsula, Sicily, Sardinia and Corsica		
1540–56	19	—
1557–80	22	7
1581–1615	38	4
Spanish peninsula, the Azores, Madeira and the Balearic islands		
1540–56	17	1
1557–80	23	5
1581–1615	37	7
France		
1540–56	—	—
1557–80	8	1
1581–1615	22	9
The Southern (Spanish) Netherlands		
1540–56	1	1
1557–80	8	—
1581–1615	18	9
The Holy Roman Empire (including Austria and Bohemia) and the Swiss cantons		
1540–56	4	—
1557–80	19	1
1581–1615	23	21
Eastern Europe (Poland, Hungary and Transylvania, and Croatia)		
1540–56	—	—
1557–80	5	1
1581–1615	22	14

The *Ratio Studiorum* and Jesuit culture

The *Ratio Studiorum* (*Plan of Studies*) provided a fixed directive for the objectives and curriculum of Jesuit colleges. Although finally put into force in 1599, it had been in preparation for the previous 15 years. The document defined the goal of Jesuit education as 'to stimulate the knowledge and love of Our Creator and Redeemer'. Its curriculum was based on the 'Paris Method' (i.e. the humanist curriculum in use in the faculty of arts at the university of Paris). A thorough grounding in written and spoken Latin (and, to some degree, Greek as well) was the first objective. A philosophical training was built on top of that (with theology following on for those who stayed on beyond the equivalent of the sixth form). It provided specific methods of instruction (*praelectiones*). The interest and engagement of students was stimulated by competitions. Latin plays and dramatic presentations were put on by students and open to the public to foster the link between parents (including local notables) and the school. These plays focused on appropriately adapted Bible stories, whilst engagingly youthful saints were held up as models for emulation by students at the colleges. Music was also actively encouraged and, in time, the strength of Jesuit investigation of natural philosophy (i.e. the natural sciences) was also reflected in its colleges and academies.

By the end of the sixteenth century, Jesuit theologians came to dominate the scholarly printed output of the catholic world in various domains. Its theologians (Roberto Bellarmino*, Francisco de Toledo, Francisco Suárez*, Luis de Molina* and Juan Maldonado*) were leading figures in catholic dogmatics (systematic theology), apologetic (anti-protestant (mostly) thematic debate) and casuistry (the application of catholic doctrine to particular circumstances). The latter became an accepted course in the curriculum for theology at the college in Rome (*Collegium Romanum*). This was part of the route by which Jesuit casuistry developed by the end of the century a distinctive system of moral theology, known as 'probabilism'. This was based on a generous view of human freedom and the principle that, if a particular course of action was held to be morally questionable, it would be acceptable to follow a 'probable' argument in favour of it, despite the possibility that the opposing opinion might command more legal weight.

(For Jesuit missions overseas, see pages 279–84.)

8.2.8 The Schools of Christian Doctrine (The Doctrinaires)

The doctrinarians were founded by César de Bus, a priest from the Comtat Venaissin, the independent papal enclave around Avignon. After a life of military activity he was ordained and devoted himself to charitable works and preaching in the Rhône valley. In 1592, he founded the 'secular priests of Christian Doctrine' at L'Isle (moving to Avignon the following year). The congregation was approved by Pope Clement VIII* in 1597. Its educational and charitable endeavours spread widely in southern France in the course of the seventeenth century. He also founded a complementary order of women.

8.3 The council of Trent

Earlier efforts in the sixteenth century to convene a council of the church, the traditional means by which abuses would be remedied and reform instituted, had not succeeded. For the papacy, the fear lest a council become a tool in the hands of one of the secular powers in Europe and emasculate papal authority was real. The Fifth Lateran Council (see page 28) had demonstrated the dangers. It was only with the accession of Pope Paul III* that renewed efforts were made to convene a council which would not fall prey to this fundamental problem. Even so, it took a decade before the eventual council emerged; and even then it was regarded as something of a miracle that it eventually began its deliberations.

8.3.1 Reforming endeavours under Paul III before the council of Trent (1534–45)

1534	Election of Alessandro Farnese as Pope Paul III* (13 Oct). At his first consistory (13 Nov), he announced his intention to hold a general council of the church and to promote to the rank of cardinals only those of proven ability.
1535	Pope Paul III encouraged the Theatines† to establish the order in Rome and granted privileges to the Barnabites. The Capuchins were also confirmed as an order against the opposition of the Observants† (25 Aug 1536).
1536	
Jan	Emperor arrived in Rome and urged the calling of a general council of the church.
8 April	Decision to summon a general council to Mantua agreed in an extraordinary congregation of cardinals in Rome whilst the emperor was still resident there. The French king objected to the decision.
Nov	The 'Commission of cardinals and other prelates concerning the reform of the church' established by Paul III* began its deliberations. Its nine members represented different strands

of reform within the catholic church – Gasparo Contarini*, Gian Pietro Carafa*, Jacopo Sadoleto*, Reginald Pole, Archbishops Federico Fregoso and Girolamo Aleandro, Bishop Gian Matteo Giberti*, Abbot Gregorio Cortese, and Tommaso Badia, a papal official.

Dec   Promotion of Gian Pietro Carafa, Jacopo Sadoleto, Reginald Pole to the cardinalate.

1537

Feb   Papal envoy sent to Schmalkalden to negotiate with German protestant princes over their possible attendance at a general council – returned rebuffed.

9 March   Report (The 'Counsel for the reform of the church' – *Consilium de emendanda ecclesia*) of the Commission presented to the papal consistory. It presented a concise account of the abuses in the church and ascribed many of them to the malignant effects of an abuse of papal power. Rome was targeted as responsible for the abuses in the church. The document had no immediate effect on the directions of papal policy. But it gained notoriety when a text of it was printed in Rome, with a German translation in the following year accompanied by a preface from Luther.

April   The council which was due to meet at Mantua was prorogued until the following November over a dispute with the duke of Mantua as to its location. Archduke Ferdinand of Austria proposed Trent as a venue; Vicenza eventually gained general acceptance.

Oct   Proposed council further prorogued until May 1538.

1538

Jan   A further commission of nine cardinals was appointed to prepare for the forthcoming council.

March   Further promotions of reforming cardinals – including Girolamo Aleandro.

June   Renewed prorogation of the council at Vicenza (where papal legates had already arrived) was announced by the papacy as a result of the sustained opposition of the French king and the noncommittal attitude of Archduke Ferdinand and the emperor.

1539   Definitive suspension of the Mantua–Vicenza council (31 May).

1540

April   Emperor Charles V summoned the imperial diet to Speyer and (April) planned to hold a council there to resolve the religious division in the Empire along the lines of a national (German) council. Cardinal Giovanni Morone* was despatched to Germany to act as papal legate. An initial conference at Hagenau (July) was prorogued until October and ordered by the emperor to reconvene at Worms.

Sep   Papal approval for the Jesuit order.

1541

Dec–Jan   The conference at Worms took place but was adjourned after four days' discussion of original sin in order to continue at the forthcoming imperial diet at Regensburg.

Jan   Cardinal Contarini* was despatched to Germany to replace Morone as papal legate at forthcoming discussions at Regensburg.

5 April   The diet of Regensburg opened with sustained discussions between Lutheran delegates at the diet and Contarini. These ended without agreement (2 May), but with a catholic statement of position presented to the emperor (the 'Ratisbon (Regensburg) Book') along with protestant counter-articles. The assembled German prelates at the diet urged the necessity of a general council of the church.

1542

May   Reform decrees announced in his diocese at Verona by Gian Matteo Giberti* with papal encouragement.

8 July   The reconvening of a general council once more agreed by the papal consistory; Pope Paul III* met Emperor Charles V at Lucca (Sep) and preparations for a reconvened council were advanced by the appointment of Contarini* and Aleander as commissioners to make proposals for its organization. Mantua was proposed as the place for its meeting but the French king contested the direction of events.

July   Renewed warfare between France and Spain; Pope Paul III remained neutral and despatched commissioners (Sep) to Trent to prepare for the council.

Nov   Arrival of the three papal legates at Trent for the start of the council, but only a few bishops were present; the French king and the emperor refused passports to those due to attend from their territories.

1543   After frustrating delays, the council was suspended *sine die* and those bishops in attendance at Trent were told to return home (July).

1544   Peace of Crépy between Emperor Charles V and François I (Sep).

Suspension of the council was rescinded (19 Nov) and the first session was scheduled for 15 March.

1545   New legates to the forthcoming council appointed (Feb). Council finally solemnly opened (13 Dec).

8.3.2 Sessions of the council of Trent

Sessions	Place	Date of commencement	Pope
1–8	Trent	13 Dec 1545–March 1547	Paul III
9–11	Bologna	21 April 1547–Jan 1548	Paul III
12–16	Trent	1 May 1551–April 1552	Julius III
17–25	Trent	18 Jan 1562–Dec 1563	Pius IV

8.3.3 Debates and Decisions

The discussions of the council of Trent were structured in a complex fashion. There were both particular meetings ('congregations') of theologians and plenary sessions ('general congregations'). Decisions were presented and eventually agreed as chapters and canons. Rejected views were 'anathemitized' (from the Greek, meaning 'suspended' or 'cut off'). No attempt is made here to follow the negotiations in detail, but the general evolution of discussions is evoked with the various sessions dated by the month or months in which they took place.

Sessions 1–8
1546

Jan   Decision to tackle simultaneously the two tasks outlined for the council in its bull of convocation (22 May 1542) – the definition of catholic belief and the reform of the church.

April   (4th session) Agreement to accord apostolic traditions[†] the same reverence as scripture (*pari pietatis affectu*). 'This truth and way of living are contained in written books and in unwritten traditions, which were received by the Apostles from the mouth of Christ himself, or were received by the same Apostles at the dictation of the Holy Spirit, and, as it were, passed on from hand to hand until they came down to us. So, following the example of the orthodox fathers, this Council receives and venerates, with equal pious affection and reverence, all the books both of the New and Old Testaments ... together with the said traditions, as well those pertaining to faith as those pertaining to morals, as having been given either from the lips of Christ or by the dictation of the Holy Spirit and preserved by unbroken succession in the catholic church'. The canon[†] of scripture was agreed at the same time and the Vulgate[†] was agreed as an adequate translation of the Bible for general use.

June   (5th session) Decree on original sin[†] agreed – framed in order to oppose the protestant reformers' beliefs on the survival of original sin after baptism†. Canon 5 stated: 'If anyone should deny that the guilt of original sin is remitted through the grace of our Lord Jesus Christ conferred in baptism, or should assert that thereby everything which can truly and properly be called sin is not taken away, but only covered or not imputed, let him be anathema'.

1547

Jan   (6th session) After long discussions from September 1546 onwards, a substantial draft of the chapters on the catholic teaching on justification† was agreed. 33 chapters were devoted to condemning protestant errors. 16 were concerned to present a positive picture of human will in collaboration with divine grace. Together these create the possibility of human merit. They have to be presented together because of an inward process of sanctification of man through grace which provides the essential basis for justification.

Canon 12: 'If anyone should say that justifying faith is nothing other than trust in the divine mercy which remits sins for Christ's sake, or that we are justified by such trust alone, let him be anathema'.

Canon 26: 'If anyone should say that for their good works, performed in godly wise, the just ought not to expect and hope for an eternal reward from God, through his mercy and the merits of Jesus Christ – if they persevere to the end in good living and keeping of the divine commandments – let him be anathema'.

Canon 32: 'If anyone should say that the good works of a justified man are so exclusively the gifts of God that they are not also the good merits of the man himself; or that the justified man, by the good works that he does through the grace of God and the merits of Jesus Christ (whose living member he is), does not truly merit an increase of grace and eternal life ... let him be anathema'.

March   (7th session) The subjects under discussion were contained in 30 canons on the sacraments, baptism and confirmation as well as 15 chapters on aspects of administrative reform in the church. After prolonged debate a decree on the observance of the duty of residence was concluded with a majority vote in favour of imposing the condition with a fine of a quarter of the annual revenue of the diocese for unjustified absence of over six months. The same session prohibited the holding of more than one bishopric by one person (episcopal pluralism) and decreed new regulations for ordinations. These decrees were only accepted by majority vote. At the same time, the decrees on the sacraments† were agreed unanimously. The seven sacraments of the church were upheld and it was accepted that the sacraments conveyed grace through being actually administered to an individual (*ex opere operato*). The council thus opposed protestant notions of the efficacy of the sacraments as dependent upon an individual's faith in God's promises.

March   (8th session) The decision to move the council to Bologna was taken because of the appearance of plague at Trent. Extensive debates on the sacrament of penance[†].

Sessions 9–11   –

Sessions 12–16
1551

Sep   (12th session) Ten articles on the eucharist extracted from protestant writings and condemned.

Oct   (13th session) Decrees defining the doctrine of the Real Presence[†] and transubstantiation[†] were agreed but the question of administering the eucharist[†] 'in both kinds'[†] was postponed. 'Since Christ our Redeemer said that which he offered under the appearance of bread was truly his body, it has therefore always been held in the church of God, and this holy Council now declares afresh, that through consecration of the bread and wine there comes about a conversion of the whole substance of the bread into the substance of the body of Christ our Lord and the whole substance of the wine into the substance of his blood. And this conversion is by the Holy Catholic Church appropriately and properly called transubstantiation'.

Nov   (14th session) Complex decrees on penance[†] were agreed which upheld the significance of confession[†], reinforced the sense of absolution[†] as a quasi-judicial decision on sins and restated the significance of satisfaction[†]. A further decree on extreme unction[†] retained it as a true sacrament[†]. A delegation of protestant theologians to the council demanded renewed discussion of subjects previously agreed and demanded that bishops present be released from their oaths of allegiance to the papacy. They also advanced the view that general councils should have supremacy over the pope.

1552

Jan   (15th session) The divine institution of the episcopacy was discussed.

(16th session) Protestant confessions were presented before the council and discussed.

April   The suspension of the council discussed and agreed.

Sessions 17–25
1562

Jan   (17th session) Papal legates tabled a decree (which was accepted) that the decisions taken at the council were always to be 'in the presence of the papal legates' (*proponentibus legatis ac praesidentibus*).

Feb   (18th session) Safe-conduct granted to protestants to attend the council.

April   (19th session) Controversial debate over a proposed decree to make the duty of residence a matter of divine obligation (*de iure divino*). The decree (proposed by the Spanish delegates) was opposed by those who saw it as an attack upon the powers of the papacy to grant dispensations for non-residence. The latter (narrowly) won the vote and the decision was left to the pope; this encouraged the papal representative to proceed with further discussions on church reform.

July   (21st session) Agreement that to administer the eucharist[†] to the laity 'in both kinds'[†] was not a matter of divine obligation. The office of indulgence-seller (*quaestor*) was abolished.

Sep   (22nd session) 9 articles on the sacrifice of the mass[†] were agreed along with nine canons on abuses in the celebration of the mass[†]. These developed the notions that it was both a memorial as well as a re-presentation of Christ's sacrifice on the cross. A further 14 articles on discipline within the church were discussed, of which 11 were agreed.

1563

Nov1562–   (23rd session) Decrees on the sacrament of holy orders, on
July   papal supremacy, on the elimination of some ceremonies, on vernacular preaching and Bibles, on the duty of bishops, including that of residence (the latter without any mention of *ius divinum*) were agreed. Various articles reforming the privileges of the Roman curia were also agreed.

Nov   (24th session) Decrees on matrimony published. Clandestine marriages (i.e. those contracted without witnesses and the consent of parents for those under the age of consent) were agreed to be unlawful and invalid. Lawful marriages must be registered in a parochial register. The celibacy of the priesthood was affirmed. Decrees on the reform of church organization were finally agreed following extensive memoranda submitted by various delegations. These were then amalgamated into a consolidated set of proposals by the papal representative and agreed in 21 articles. At this session, the regulations for the proper nomination of cardinals and bishops were laid down. The procedures for regular diocesan synods (to be held every three years) were also enunciated. Bishops were enjoined to hold visitations in their dioceses.

Dec   (25th session) Decrees on purgatory[†], indulgences[†] and the veneration[†] of images[†], saints and relics[†] were promulgated. Further and final chapters on the reform of church organization were agreed including the reform of cathedral chapters and the overhaul of parochial organization and parish preaching. Bishops were held to be responsible for all those in posts involving the care of souls in their dioceses; no exemptions to this were to be allowed in future. Some general decrees on the reform of the regular orders[†] were accepted. The questions relating to the index of prohibited books, the publication of a catechism and the revision of the breviary and missal were left to the papacy.

8.3.4 Papal legates to the council

Sessions 1–11   Cardinal Joannes Maria Del Monte
Cardinal Marcello Cervini (Pope Marcellus II)
Cardinal Reginald Pole

Sessions 12–13   Cardinal Pighino
Cardinal Lippomani

Sessions 14–25   Cardinal Girolamo Seripando* (–17 March 1563)
Cardinal Ercole Gonzaga (–2 March 1563)
Stanislaus Hosius
Luigi Simonetta (–30 April 1563)
Cardinal Giovanni Morone*
Cardinal Bernardo Navagero

8.3.5 Spokesmen (oratores) for princes at the council

The emperor
Early sessions   Francisco di Castelalto
Antonio Queta
Wolfgang, count of Salm, Bishop of Passau
Final sessions   Sigismund of Thun
Anton Brus von Müglitz, archbishop of Prague

King of France
Early sessions   Claude d'Urfé
Jacques de Ligny
Pierre Danès

Final sessions	Louis de Saint Gelais, seigneur de Lansac
	Arnaud du Ferrier
	Guy du Faur, sieur de Pibrac

King of Spain

Early sessions	Diego Hurtado de Mendoza
	Francisco Alvárez de Toledo
Final sessions	Ferdinando d'Avalo
	Fernandez Vegil de Quinones

Spokesmen for other princes

| Early sessions | Representatives for the king of Poland, the duke of Savoy and the duke of Tuscany; also the Knights of Malta |
| Final sessions | Representatives for the king of Poland, the duke of Savoy, the duke of Tuscany, the Knights of Jerusalem, the king of Portugal, the republic of Venice, the seven (catholic) Swiss cantons, the duke of Bavaria |

8.3.6 Other representatives at the council of Trent

	Early sessions (13 Dec 1545– 2 June 1547)	Final sessions (18 Jan 1562– 4 Dec 1563)
Patriarchs and archbishops	12	34
Bishops (and substitutes)	95	247
Abbots and generals of regular orders	9	16
Papal theologians	5	7
Theologians despatched by the Holy Roman Emperor, the king of Spain and other princes	11	33
Canon lawyers and other lawyers	12	25
Theologians representing the regular orders:		
Dominicans	10	19
Minims	39	25
Augustinians	18	18
Carmelites	20	8
Others	19	4
Apostolic commissioners	6	1

[†] secretaries, masters of ceremonies, scribes, notaries etc.

8.3.7 Prelates attending the final sessions of the council of Trent

Prelates attending the final sessions of the council of Trent

Location of bishopric	Prelates in attendance	Delegation by proxy
Italy	187	2
Spain	31	4
France	26	1
(Greece, Croatia, Bosnia and Dalmatia)*	10	
Germany	2	4
Portugal	3	
Ireland	3	
The Netherlands	2	
Poland	2	
Hungary*	2	
England*	1	
Moravia	1	

* Some of these bishoprics were at the time expropriated either by the protestants or the Turks.

8.4 Rome during the reformation

8.4.1 Papal succession

Innocent VIII (Giovanni Battista Cibò) (29 Aug 1484–25 July 1492)
Alexander VI (Rodrigo de Borgia y Borgia) (11 Aug 1492–18 Aug 1503)
Pius III (Francesco Todeschini) (22 Sep–18 Oct 1503)
Julius II (Giuliano della Rovere) (1 Nov 1503–21 Feb 1513)
Leo X* (Giovanni de' Medici) (11 Mar 1513–1 Dec 1521)
Adrian VI (Adrian Florensz Dedal) (9 Jan 1522–14 Sep 1523)
Clement VII (Giulio de' Medici) (19 Nov 1523–25 Sep 1534)
Paul III* (Alessandro Farnese) (13 Oct 1534–10 Nov 1549)
Julius III (Giovanni Maria Ciocchi del Monte) (8 Feb 1550–23 Mar 1555)
Marcellus II (Mercello Cervini) (9 April–1 May 1555)
Paul IV* (Gian Pietro Carafa) (23 May 1555–18 Aug 1559)
Pius IV* (Giovanni Angelo Medici) (25 Dec 1559–9 Dec 1565)
Pius V* (Michele Ghislieri) (7 Jan 1566–1 May 1572)
Gregory XIII* (Ugo Boncompagni) (14 May 1572–10 Apr 1585)
Sixtus V* (Felice Peretti) (24 Apr 1585–27 Aug 1590)
Urban VII (Giambattista Castagna) (15–27 Sep 1590)
Gregory XIV (Niccolò Sfondrati) (5 Dec 1590–16 Oct 1591)

Innocent IX (Giovanni Antonio Fachinetti) (29 Oct–30 Dec 1591)
Clement VIII* (Ippolito Aldobrandini) (30 Jan 1592–5 Mar 1605)
Leo XI (Alessandro Ottaviano de' Medici) (1–27 Apr 1605)
Paul V (Camillo Borghese) (16 May 1605–28 Jan 1621)

8.4.2 Permanent nuncios (see page 14)

Only gradually were the nunciatures, established in the early sixteenth
century primarily as diplomatic agencies, transformed into instruments
for ecclesiastical reform. The process was further advanced under Gregory
XIII*, for whom the pressures for institutional change and the need for
a sophisticated political response to the protestant reformation coalesced
most readily with the necessity of negotiating the acceptance of the disciplinary decrees of the council of Trent with the secular rulers of catholic Europe. This was by no means an easy task. In France, for example,
they were never formally promulgated by the monarchy because of
Gallican[†] objections. The nuncios also became gradually more important in ensuring that episcopal nominations were properly investigated
and sanctioned by the papacy.

	Date (where available)
Kingdom of France	c.1500
Kingdom of Spain	1505
Naples	1511
Republic of Venice	pre-1513
Holy Roman Empire	1513
Teutonic Order (Prussia)	1530
Duchy of Florence	1560
Kingdom of Poland	1572
Milan	—
Genoa	—
Duchy of Savoy	—
Kingdom of Portugal	—
Canton of Luzern	1579
Graz	1580
Cologne	1584
Salzburg	—
Styria	—
Spanish Netherlands	1594/97

8.4.3 The Roman congregations (Sacrae Cardinalium Congregationes)

Like other sixteenth-century monarchies, the papacy reorganized its governing structure in the course of the sixteenth century. The pressures

upon the papal curia[†] were not dissimilar to those which affected secular rulers. These included a greater functional scope, expanded expectations for their effectiveness, an enlarged governing mechanism and a greater degree of specialism in certain areas of papal affairs. The additional complexity for the papacy lay in the existence of the cardinals, whose constitutional position within the church had never been established to the mutual satisfaction of everyone. The position of the cardinals was gradually altered in the sixteenth century by new papal creations which increased their overall numbers, and especially those from Italian backgrounds. This process was accelerated as the position of cardinals in Rome with non-Italian bishoprics became difficult to sustain alongside the decision of the council of Trent requiring bishops to reside in their dioceses. By the second half of the sixteenth century, the overwhelming majority of cardinals would be drawn from Italian bishoprics. Their purpose was increasingly to act as a team of specialist advisors to the papacy. This latter function was enshrined in the engagement of cardinals in the work of the church through commissions and committees known as 'congregations'.

This process had begun with the college of cardinals appointed to supervise the inquisition by Pope Paul III. Others were added in due course until they were regularized by Pope Sixtus V* in 22 Jan 1588 (by the bull[†] *Immensa Dei*) into boards or committees, called on to provide competent advice, especially in legal and other technical matters. Sixtus V had already defined various fundamental aspects of the college of cardinals in 3 Dec 1586 (by the bull *Postquam Verus*). He reiterated that their appointment lay entirely in the hands of the papacy and limited the numbers in the sacred college to 70. Since they were bishops, 30 years of age was the minimum for those appointed. Illegitimate sons were absolutely excluded, as were those who had fathered illegitimate children. A candidature from a bishop who was the blood-relative of an already-serving cardinal would be automatically excluded from consideration. He stipulated that there should be at least four doctors of theology. The counter-reformed sacred college of cardinals took on its definitive shape in response to this constitution.

Although the involvement of the cardinalcy in the decision-making process of the church was an important one, it should be remembered that the secretaries of state became highly significant in papal decision-making in the sixteenth century. Their emergence is still a subject of some obscurity. It occurred in the first half of the sixteenth century when the private secretary of the pope was no longer an individual picked out from the papal chancery but a personal nominee (and often a relative) of the pontiff. Pope Paul III illustrated the trend by appointing his grandson Alexander Farnese to the post. Blood-relations in the post of papal secretary ensured that the necessarily high degrees of confidence accorded the individual, and the discretion expected of him, were not readily abused. By the end of the sixteenth century, the secretaries of state were generally close relations of the pope, the cardinal-nephews, and even the reform-minded Popes Pius V* and Sixtus V found themselves using their relatives to assist them in the political aspects of their rule. The cardinal-nephews functioned as the equivalents of the 'favourites' whose positions in the informal structures of power were also important at other courts in western Europe.

There were initially 15 'congregations' of papal advisors laid down by Pope Sixtus V in 1588. They each consisted of a cardinal prefect and a number of officers, of whom the majority were cardinals. Six of the boards were concerned primarily with the administration of the Papal States. The remainder involved the church at large. This established the permanent organization of these departments in the curia as follows:

- For the **Holy Office** (Inquisition) (*congregatio pro S. inquisitione*). The executive direction of the Holy Office had already been established as a congregation in 1558.
- For the **Signature of Grace**. This board was established to examine individual petitions for favours in areas which were beyond ordinary ecclesiastical jurisdiction and competence.
- For the **erection of churches and consistorial provisions** (*congregatio pro erectione ecclesiasiarum et provisionibus consistorialibus*). The executive which prepared all the decisions for the papal consistory. In time, it would oversee bishops to ensure that they carried out their responsibilities, and receive their reports as well as prepare for and announce apostolic visitations. It would also become responsible for the curriculum in seminaries.
- For the **abundance of supplies and prosperity** of the church's temporal dominions.
- For **sacred rites and ceremonies** (*congregatio pro sacris ritibus et cæremoniis*). This committee was responsible for the liturgy of the church and for the granting of all privileges connected with the religious ceremonies of the church. It was also entrusted with the important discussion of proposals for beatification and canonization and the veneration of saintly relics. One of its officials became popularly known as 'the devil's advocate'.
- For the **equipping of the papal fleet** and maintaining it for the defence of the church's dominions.
- For the **Index of Forbidden Books** (*congregatio de reformando indice et corrigendis libris*). This had been created in 1571 by Pius V and organized into its definitive form the following

year. Its brief was to censure and condemn all books which it considered dangerous to the faith and morality of the church. Its jurisdiction extended to all catholics and it could both give permission for an individual to read a book which had been condemned and permit the publication of expurgated editions of what had been initially proscribed. Its functions were closely related to that of the inquisition.

– For the **execution and interpretation of the council of Trent** (*congregatio super executione et observatione S. Concilii Tridentini*). This followed on directly from the canon of the 25th session of the council that the papacy should monitor the implementation of its decrees. The canon was put into practice by Pius IV in his decree of 1564 which commissioned eight cardinals to undertake the task. This became the congregation formalized by Sixtus V in 1588.

– For the **relief of difficulties in the states of the church**.

– For the **university at Rome** (*congregatio pro universitate studii romani*). This committee advised on questions relating to the university at Rome (later the Gregorian University (*Universitas Gregoriana*)) and also, in time, upon the granting of faculties to confer degrees in catholic universities elsewhere in Europe.

– For the **regulation of religious orders** (*congregatio super consultationibus regularium*).

– For the **regulation of bishops and other prelates** (*congregatio consultationibus episcoporum et aliorum praelatorum*). This was merged with the former in 1601.

– For **maintaining roads, bridges and waterways** in Roman jurisdiction.

– For the **Vatican printing press**.

– For **regulating the affairs in the church's temporal dominions**.

The structure was modified and adapted as the particular institutional or political problems facing the church required. So, for example, the congregation 'On the Help Afforded by Grace' (*congregatio de auxiliis*) was established in 1598 by Clement VIII to attempt to settle the theological controversy over grace[†] which had arisen with Jesuit propositions attempting to reconcile the efficacy of grace with human freedom. These propositions had involved an explanation which revolved around God's 'mediate knowledge' of the kinds of 'efficacious grace' which a particular human would freely consent to accept. The Dominicans declared that the Jesuits conceded too much to free will, thus tending towards Pelagianism[†]. The Jesuits complained that the Dominicans did not adequately safeguard human freedom and thus tended towards Calvinist views of predestination[†]. The congregation persuaded the pope to issue a decree (5 Sep 1607) which allowed both parties to continue to defend their own doctrine but not to censure or condemn the other side. The Roman inquisition (Dec 1611) subsequently attempted to prevent the publication of any book concerning efficacious grace. This did not prevent the underlying issues becoming ones of major contention in the Southern Netherlands, France and elsewhere. Already in the sixteenth century, the writings of Michael Bajus (Fr: Michel de Bay; 1513–89), a Catholic theologian from the Southern Netherlands, had attracted controversy for his Augustinian[†] and anti-Pelagian views of original sin, grace and free will. 76 propositions from his works would be censured by Pius V* in his bull of 1567 (*Ex omnibus afflictionibus*). This did not, however, prevent the issues from resurfacing in the seventeenth century in the writings of Cornelis Jansen* which provided the basis for the movement known as Jansenism[†].

The most famous congregation 'Of Propaganda' (*congregatio de propaganda fide*) was not included amongst those established or confirmed by Sixtus V* in 1588. It had its origins in a commission of cardinals under Gregory XIII but was only fully established in 1622. The further congregation for the fabric of St Peter's, established by Clement VIII*, was also in regular existence and had as its responsibility the running of the basilica of St Peter's, the completion of the building works and the maintenance of its fabric.

8.4.4 Papal revenues in the sixteenth century

Papal revenues

Date	'Spiritual' revenues	Temporal revenues	Total
1480 (florins)	105,000	210,979	315,979
1525 (florins)	212,000	263,989	475,989
1576 (scudi)	238,889	706,426	945,315
1592 (scudi)	420,064	1,181,131	1,601,195
1599 (scudi)	395,400	1,045,442	1,440,842
1605 (scudi)	384,000	1,129,027	1,513,027
1619 (scudi)	461,572	1,372,111	1,839,683

Source: Taken from Peter Partner, 'Papal financial policy in the Renaissance and Counter-Reformation', *Past and Present* No. 88 (1980), table 5, p. 49 and table 3, p. 27.
Note that the figures for 1480 and 1525 are quoted in gold florins whilst the rest are in silver *scudi*; but they provide reasonable comparability.

Papal revenues fell into two categories: 'Spiritual' and 'temporal'. 'Spiritual' revenues were those collected from the expedition of bulls, dispensations and the annates received from the church. The immediate effects of the protestant reformation and the council of Trent were to reduce these incomes. However Sixtus V* was able to revive and increase them, partly in order to sustain substantial loans for which these revenues became the security for repayment. Temporal revenues more than made up the temporary shortfall. These were taxes raised from the Papal States and elsewhere, some of which were new. The triennial subsidy (*sussidio triennale*), raised from the clergy of the Papal States and clerical properties elsewhere in Italy by Pope Paul III*, proved to be one of the most lucrative.

These revenues enabled the papacy to advance its revenues and to borrow more heavily. This it did both by selling offices (see page 11) and by issuing papal bonds (*monti*). The bonds issued by Paul III were often at rather unfavourable rates of interest. By the end of the sixteenth century, however, Rome developed a money-market on the basis of its more assured position in the counter-reformation church. Catholic Europe used the services of agents at Rome for securing letters of dispensation and nomination. These agents also acted as bankers and were able to mobilize considerable amounts of credit. The rise in papal borrowing is evident from the ratio of interest paid on funded debt to total papal income:

Papal borrowing

Date	Interest	Total papal income	% papal income spent on debt interest
1526	211,207	594,986	35.5
1576	404,227	945,315	42.8
1592	739,285	1,601,195	46.2
1599	762,094	1,440,842	52.9
1599	845,251	1,839,683	45.9

Source: Taken from Peter Partner, 'Papal financial policy in the Renaissance and Counter-Reformation', *Past and Present* No. 88 (1980), table 5, p. 49 and table 3, p. 27.

The resulting income from the combination of spiritual and temporal revenues as well as greatly increased borrowing was used to fund the diplomatic and political objectives of the counter-reformed papacy.

8.4.5 Rome in the catholic reformation

The developments in Rome inevitably reflected the chronology and trends within the catholic reformation. Although attention inevitably focuses upon the rebuilding of St Peter's and alterations at the Vatican palace, there were many other churches built or rebuilt during the sixteenth and early years of the seventeenth century. These included the church for the new foundations such as the Jesuits (*Il Iésu*), the Theatines (*S. Andrea della Valle*), the Oratorians (*S. Maria in Vallicella*). Individual cardinals also patronized particular parish churches and patrimonial chapels. The developments reflected both the changing economic fortunes of the church and its underlying confidence.

1506   Foundation-stone laid for the new St Peter's to designs prepared by Donato Bramante (18 April); the main piers and interconnected arches for the dome were completed by 1512.

1508   Buonarroti Michelangelo (1475–1564) began work on the frescoes of the ceiling for the Sistine Chapel, which were completed in 1512.

1513   Refounding of the university of Rome (*Universitas Gregoriana*) (Nov).

1514/17   Foundation of the Roman fraternity of the Oratory[†].

1520   Death of Sanzio Raffaello (Raphael, 1485–1520), successor to Bramante as chief architect of St Peter's. Progress in completing the building project slowed down in the 1520s, and then stopped after 1527.

1527   Sack of Rome (May).

1529   Establishment of Capuchins at Rome.

1535   A new team of architects (Baldassare Peruzzi and Antonio da Sangallo the Younger) prepared revised (and scaled down) plans for the rebuilding of St Peter's; work recommenced in 1542.

1542   Institution of the Roman Index[†] and inquisition[†].

1546   Michelangelo appointed chief architect for St Peter's. The design was again radically changed. By 1550, a year of jubilee, some of the dome of the cathedral was constructed.

1551   Appointment of Giovanni Pierluigi da Palestrina (c.1524–94) as choirmaster; his first book of masses was published in 1554. His *Missa Papae Marcelli* for Pope Marcellus II demonstrated the principle that the words of the mass could be clearly audible, even in contrapuntal music (a concern expressed in the decrees of the council of Trent).

1552   Foundation of the Jesuit college (*Collegium Romanum*) (31 Aug).

1564	Michelangelo's death; the south transept of St Peter's was substantially complete and the drum to the dome was standing up to its pilasters. The final cupola, however, was not begun.
1564	General visitation of all parishes in the diocese of Rome ordered by Pius IV*.
1565	Establishment of the Roman seminary.
1566	Publication of the Roman catechism.
1568	Publication of the revised Roman breviary.
1570	Publication of the revised Roman missal.
1585–90	Completion of the dome of St Peter's. The new Vatican library was completed. The Vatican press was established (1587). Substantial changes were made to the city layout of Rome with new boulevards to link the seven churches which were the focus of pilgrimages to Rome. Aqueducts were built to provide a new fresh water supply (the *Acqua Felice* project). The papal palace in Rome (the Lateran palace) was also reconstructed.
1592	Publication of the revised Roman Vulgate edition of the Bible.
1592	Clement VIII ordered a general visitation of all the churches and religious houses in Rome (June); many of the inspections were carried out in person and the visitation was prolonged to 1596; thereafter regular visitations and inspections began (1601, etc).
1594	Consecration of the new altar at St Peter's, over the apostle's tomb (June).
1595	Foundation of the *Collegium Clementinum*, a papal-founded college for Roman noble youth and foreigners.
1600	Jubilee[†] year; 60–80,000 witnessed the opening of the Holy Door (*Porta Santa*) on 31 Dec 1599 as the symbolic completion of the St Peter's rebuilding project.

8.5 Episcopal and parochial reform

8.5.1 The episcopacy and Rome

The relationship between the papacy and the bishops of the church was not formally defined by the council of Trent[†] and it was left to emerging papal decree and evolving practice in the later sixteenth century to define more precisely the changes which were implicit in the counter-reformation. Episcopal nominations became increasingly subject to a formal enquiry into the background (*de vita et moribus*) of the nominee. By a decree of 1591, Gregory XIV insisted that such enquiries were carried out by the relevant nuncio or, in the case of his absence, a stipulated local bishop. The enquiries took the form of replies to a series of standard questions and, although there were probably parts of Europe where nuncios were able to exercise significant degrees of influence over appointments, this was by no means always the case. More significant in terms of the changing relationship with Rome was the decision of Pope Sixtus V* on 20 Dec 1585 to reintroduce the requirement for bishops to pay regular visits to Rome (known as the 'visit to the tomb of the Apostles' – *Visitatio liminum SS. apostolorum*). Bishops were expected to visit Rome and report on their dioceses at regular intervals on pain of being suspended and forfeiting their revenues. In practice, it was not merely the Spanish bishops who negotiated an exemption from appearing in person and sending a representative instead. The canon of the council of Trent requiring the residence of bishops in their dioceses was enforced with increasing rigour by the papacy, especially when it was inspired by the reforming zeal of the Dominican Pope Pius V* or the Franciscan Pope Sixtus V. The latter's repeated edicts on the subject brought protests in consequence. Such decrees were inevitably accompanied by the issuing of specific dispensations from the duty of residence for particular purposes such as the duties at Rome of a cardinal.

8.5.2 Visitations and diocesan synods

The practice of episcopal visitations had not been absent from the church in the later middle ages; it had often occurred as a result of lay pressure. The difference in the sixteenth century was that episcopal visitation became a sign of a reforming prelate and an instrument for halting the spread of protestantism. One of the first acts of the reforming bishop of Verona, Gian Matteo Giberti*, was to undertake a personal visitation of his diocese, including inspections of fabric, regular orders and clerical morals. He opposed those who claimed exemptions to his jurisdiction and introduced confessionals† into churches to safeguard the secrecy of confessions. He also collected information on popular religious practices which he regarded with suspicion. These were all patterns which would be repeated amongst reforming clerics of the later sixteenth century, amongst whom Carlo Borromeo*, archbishop of Milan, was the most conspicuous model. At Milan, Borromeo conducted annual visitations in person and documented the practice for others to copy. His scheme included articles for the investigation of fabric (*investigatio rerum*) and for the congregation and clergy (*visitatio hominum*).

The council of Trent had reinforced the importance of the episcopal visitation in 1563. Bishops at Rome were ordered to take up residence in their dioceses on 1 March 1564. The injunctions of the council on episcopal visitations were turned into regulations by Sixtus V* in the bull of 1585 (*Romanus Pontifex*). This laid down in detail what was expected of bishops when conducting them. It also provided the headings under which the information gained from such visitations should be presented in reports to Rome. Visitors became used to collecting data with highly detailed printed questionnaires asking about the qualifications, personal life and habits of the clergy, the numbers of communicants and the attendance and behaviour of the congregation in divine service as well as their willingness to contribute to parish fabric and funds. In southern Germany, the practice of visitations was evidently a consequence of the council of Trent. The bishoprics of Bavaria (Ingolstadt etc), and Eichstätt (1565), Trier (1569) and Würzburg (1575) all saw episcopal visitations for the first time in over a generation. In Italy, the practice spread in the later sixteenth century with Borromeo's scheme for the conduct of visitations being adopted. In France, the process was delayed by the civil wars and only became regular from the early seventeenth century onwards.

The council of Trent had included a canon requiring bishops to hold annual diocesan synods, over which the bishop should preside. Archbishops were instructed to hold a provincial synod every three years. Although one of the indications of reforming zeal amongst the counter-reformed episcopacy in Europe is the summoning of such synods and the publication of their decrees (often reinforcing those of the council of Trent), the regular holding of such bodies did not become established church practice in the seventeenth-century catholic church.

8.5.3 Seminaries

The council of Trent[†] had already touched on the question of ecclesiastical education in its 5th session (June 1546) when it had reiterated earlier conciliar demands that every cathedral should provide for the teaching of grammar and the Scriptures to clerics and poor scholars. But it was the seminary decree of the 23rd session in July 1563 which proved to be the turning-point. It was based on the accumulating experience of the 1550s within the church of the significance of providing a more effective institutional basis for the recruitment and training of pastoral clergy. The word seminary (Lat: *seminarium* or nursery) was first used by Cardinal Reginald Pole at the Canterbury Synod of 1555–56 where he had proposed that the cathedral schools should provide both staff and scholarships for those training to be priests. The decree stipulated an ability to read and write Latin as necessary for admission at the age of 12. Courses were to be provided in liturgical and biblical studies alongside practical training in the services and rituals of the church. The probationary period at a seminary was a long one (lasting 13 years to the age of 25 when a seminarian finally became a priest).

The significance of the establishment of seminaries should not be overestimated. In many parts of Europe (e.g. Spain), the training of the clergy had been undertaken by, and would continue to take place within, the universities. In others (e.g. Germany and France), the extensive foundation of grammar schools provided an alternative route to the gaining of a good classical education, even for those of poor background. Their curricula did not necessarily provide a student at 14 with the necessary Latin skills, however, to enter a seminary. Many of these grammar schools were subsumed into the educational institutions run by the Jesuits in the second half of the sixteenth century. Although the council of Trent made no mention of the Jesuit colleges, it is evident that their educational programme, and the range of their establishments would make a greater impact in the catholic church than its seminaries, at least in the period to 1618. This fact was recognized by the gradual establishment of pontifical seminaries in Jesuit hands (as at Vienna, Prague, Fulda and elsewhere). The establishment of foreign colleges at the university of Rome with scholarships for trainee priests also provided a stream of well-trained and professionally equipped priests for missions to protestant Europe. These included the German College (c.1572), the English College (1579), the Greek College, the Scottish College, the Maronite College, the Armenian College and the Hungarian College (later merged with the German College).

SECTION NINE

Confessional identities

9.1 Reformation issues

Understanding the protestant reformation requires a comprehension of the underlying approach of protestant reformers to the fundamental theological and ecclesiastical questions of the day. There were substantial differences of emphasis and sometimes of underlying conception amongst protestant reformers. The following glossary provides brief encapsulations of these issues; but it cannot do justice to the complexity and evolution of protestant views in many areas, or to the way in which these developed in conflictual dialogue both with one another as well as with catholic theologians.

Adiaphora ('things indifferent'); Adiaphorists

The concept of ways of behaving or acting which were neither virtuous nor sinful originated in the Stoic writings of antiquity (Cicero, Seneca etc) and was subsequently also found in the works of medieval theologians. It acquired new relevance, however, when Luther argued that 'good works' in themselves had no merit. This rendered many religious rituals superfluous. But, faced with the potential of radical religious change at Wittenberg in 1521–22, Luther said that, if not specifically forbidden by God's word, such practices should be allowed to continue for the sake of the weaker brethren and to retain civil peace. The definition of what constituted these 'things indifferent' (*indifferentia*) was contained in the Augsburg Confession† (1530) but it continued to be a matter of debate amongst Lutherans, especially after the 'Interim' imposed by Emperor Charles V at the diet of Augsburg (May 1548) (see page 63). The emperor sought to have this provisional religious settlement imposed throughout the Empire and, at the estates of Saxony, meeting at Leipzig in December 1548, Philipp Melanchthon* and his colleagues from Wittenberg presented a similar version of the emperor's statement. Known to its detractors as the 'Leipzig Interim' it declared certain catholic practices such as confirmation and extreme unction, the mass† (without transubstantiation†) and the veneration† of saints to be 'things indifferent'. Concessions on such things could be made to the emperor without damage to fundamental protestant doctrine. This was fiercely contested by Matthias Flacius Illyricus (1520–75), a professor of

Hebrew at Wittenberg, in his *On True and False Adiaphora* (*De Veris et Falsis Adiaphoris*) of 1549. He became the leader of the orthodox ('gnesio') Lutherans and accused his opponents ('Philippists') of being secret ('crypto') Calvinists and criticized Melanchthon for his 'synergist' views of grace (the belief that the human will cooperates with the Holy Spirit and God's grace to convert humans to God). The controversy threatened to split the Lutheran movement until the peace of Augsburg (1555) lessened the overall significance of some of the questions which were raised. It was not finally resolved, however, until article 10 of the Formula of Concord of 1577 which argued that, in times of persecution, concessions were not to be made, but that otherwise ceremonies not explicitly commanded or forbidden by scriptural injunction might be regarded as matters to be left to the judgment of local churches or individuals.

(The) Antichrist

The idea of an embodiment of all the anti-Christian forces at work in the world was not new in the sixteenth century. It had strong associations with the apocalyptic† traditions of the return of Christ to earth, which would be preceded by cataclysmic change associated with the Antichrist. The notion of Antichrist was utilized, however, by the protestant reformers to embody the papacy and its instruments. Luther made these associations explicit in his pamphlet on *The Babylonian Captivity of the Church* in 1520 and they became a pronounced feature of the protestant pamphlets and woodcuts in Germany during the 1520s. The notion was appropriated in due course by the other reformers and found its way into the orthodox confessional statements of the protestant reformation such as the Augsburg Confession† (1530). For the religious radicals of the reformation, however, Antichrist was to be identified with Luther and Calvin no less than the papacy. By the second half of the sixteenth century, the broadening referential scope Antichrist gave additional weight to the anxieties which fuelled millenarian speculation.

Antitrinitarianism

The doctrine of the Trinity (i.e. that the one God exists in three persons, Father, Son and Holy Spirit, but one substance) had a central place in Christian theology in the reformation. It had been defined by the early church councils in the face of the antrinitarian 'heresies' of Arius (256–336) and others on the subject. That it should resurface during the doctrinal questioning of the reformation is not surprising. It initially made its appearance in the thinking of some early anabaptists (e.g. Ludwig Hätzer (d.1529)), although it was not a central feature of the mainstream anabaptist beliefs. It became more significant amongst the spiritualists (see pages 112–13) and the refugee radicals (see pages 113–14). It was from this background that there emerged the antitrinitarianism for which Michael Servetus* stood accused by Jean Calvin (see page 181) as well as that of Lelio Sozzini (Socinus)* (1525–62) and Fausto Sozzini (Socinus)* (1539–1604), the founders of the unitarian[†] churches.

Arminianism

The Dutch reformed theologian, Jacob Hermanszoon (Lat: *Jacobus Arminius**), professor of theology at the university of Leiden from 1603, was at the centre of conflict almost from the moment of his appointment there. His views became the focus for the most profound rift in the views of the Reformed[†] (Calvinist) protestant tradition in the seventeenth century. In 1604, he presented his already well-developed critique of Calvinist notions of predestination[†] in a series of university theses. These were immediately attacked by his colleague François Gomar (Lat: *Franciscus Gomarus*) (1563–1641) as Pelagian[†] and contrary to the Belgic Confession (see page 249) and Heidelberg catechism (see pages 251–2) of the Dutch church. In 1606, Arminius (by then rector of the university) presented his inaugural address on the theme of 'The reconciliation of religious dissensions among Christians' which pleaded for graciousness in the conducting of controversy and called for a conference before the magistrates who had the right (according to the Old Testament) to settle such issues. This was regarded as Erastian[†] by his critics (Arminius had studied with Thomas Erastus at Basel) and rejected. The issues split the faculties at the university of Leiden and soon became more publicly aired. Arminius was invited by the states of Holland and West Friesland to address them in 1608 and his lecture was published. Then, shortly after his death, a statement of his teaching was drawn up at Gouda in 1610 by 46 ministers who supported his views on predestination. Known as the Remonstrance, it presented his revisions of orthodox Calvinist views of predestination under five headings. It rejected both the Supralapsarian and Sublapsarian views of strict (or 'double') predestination[†] (that the 'elect' were destined for Heaven and that the 'reprobate' were doomed to hell). It questioned the view that the saints could not fall from grace. The Remonstrance generated both religious and political controversy. Its supporters ('Remonstrants') were suspected of favouring peace with Spain and the continuation of the Eleven Years' Truce (signed in 1609). The Remonstrants were eventually condemned at the Synod of Dort[†] (1618–19); but Arminianism continued to be a divisive set of views amongst orthodox Calvinists in Europe, especially in England, Scotland, France and the Netherlands.

Ban   *See* (Church) Discipline.

Baptism

Protestant reformers were agreed in retaining baptism as one of the sacraments of the church. In other respects, however, there were fundamental differences of liturgical practice and underlying theological understanding. Luther's first baptismal service (1523) and his revised version (1526) eliminated most (but not all) of the exorcisms of the traditional rite together with the blessing of the font. It included a prayer about how God used water (in the Flood at the time of Noah) as an instrument of salvation, and a reference to Christ blessing children. Children were fully 'dipped' in the water, suggesting that baptism was a complete rebirth. The rite was designed to indicate that, for Luther, it was not the water which had the power of salvation but the word of God acting in and through it. The ceremony was one in which a child could, through 'infant faith', accept the grace which it gave and go on to reflect it in his/her daily life. Luther completely rejected the idea that stillborn children, or unbaptized infants went into limbo, an accessory to purgatory.

Amongst the other reformers, the baptismal rite prepared by Calvin for use at Geneva was unambiguous in its theological implications. Baptism should take place during Sunday worship as a sacrament in which the sign of Christ's life and death for us is communicated to us all. Exorcism was completely omitted as superstitious. The ceremony did not apparently involve 'dipping' but only 'pouring' the water over the child's head. The question of the Christian name was accorded considerable significance, Calvin being particularly concerned (because of its theological implications for his eucharistic[†] notions) about the relationship between the name of something and the thing signified. An introductory homily on the importance of infant baptism indicated the significance of the debate with anabaptists.

The radical reformers made even more fundamental inroads into the traditional perception of baptism, rejecting infant baptism as having no scriptural authority and as the instrument of the Antichrist[†]. True baptism, according to the Schleitheim Confession (1527) (see pages 250–1) was the logical outcome of repentance, faith and conversion and was therefore for adult Christians. Anabaptists adopted Jesus' own adult baptism and the logic underlying *Matthew* 28:19–20 ('Go . . . teach all nations, baptizing them . . .') as the scriptural authority for their views. The significance of adult baptism for anabaptists themselves lay even more in the communal solidarities that the ceremony embodied. Since they linked the repentance, confession and conversion of a particular believer to baptism, the rite became a moment when the individual committed himself to the congregation which received him. In some anabaptist communities, the ceremony itself was less important than this underlying rite of reception. In some German and Dutch communities it was carried out in the open air, in rivers, ponds or in barns. There was a tendency to stress the significance of complete immersion as a sign of washing away completely the old person and assuming the new life in Christ.

(The) Bible   (*See also* 'Sola Scriptura')
The return to the scriptures of the Old and New Testaments formed a central focus of the protestant reformation in its doctrine and ecclesiastical practice. But how passages of the Bible should be interpreted was the subject of intense scrutiny and considerable debate amongst the protestant reformers. The development of textual criticism (philology) in the early sixteenth century and the practical demands amongst protestant clergy for guides on the scriptural materials relevant to particular subjects about which they might be preparing sermons led to different ways of interpreting the Bible ('biblical exegesis').

What constituted the 'canon' of scripture grew more defined and strictly circumscribed in the course of the reformation. The so-called 'Apocryphal' books of the Bible were gradually excluded from the canon by protestant confessions in the sixteenth century in a fashion which was rejected by the council of Trent[†]. At the same time, doubts about the canonical status of some of the New Testament books (especially *II Peter, II* and *III John, Jude* and *James*) were suppressed.

The protestant reformers rejected the complex divisions introduced by medieval biblical commentators into the task of exegesis. In their place, they tended to stress the significance of placing a text into its historical context and elucidating the linguistic complexity of particular phrases. At Wittenberg, Luther's collaborator Philipp Melanchthon* published a series of commentaries in which the thematic components of particular passages were highlighted so that they could form the subject of extended comparison between particular 'common places' (*loci communes*). At Zürich, Zwingli's *Prophezei* meetings emphasized the etymology, grammar and rhetoric in passages before putting them into a historical perspective. Martin Bucer's* commentaries, however, tended to divide the scriptures into small sections and then comment on each section from a variety of different standpoints in order to achieve a thorough understanding of the 'topic' of the passage. Calvin tended to make use of a similar method in his extensive Bible commentaries (see page 176). The protestant reformation resulted in an unparalleled and sustained output of biblical commentary. It drew on the new scholarly editions of the scriptures themselves and developed new forms of layout and presentation of commentaries themselves. In many different ways, protestant biblical exegesis became the handmaid of its preaching and propaganda.

The catholic Bible remained the Latin version compiled by St Jerome and known as the 'Vulgate' (from the Latin: *editio vulgata*). It was pronounced the only authentic Latin text of the scriptures by the 4th session of the council of Trent (April 1546 – see page 201). An edition of the Vulgate was issued by Pope Sixtus V* in 1590 with the intention of producing a definitive printed version. There were, however, so many errors that it had to be extensively revised and reprinted in 1592 under the auspices of Pope Clement VIII* in what is generally known as the 'Sixto-Clementine Vulgate'.

Bishops   *See* Episcopacy.

(The) Church

For the protestant reformers, the true church existed separately from the Roman hierachy and independently of any apostolic succession. It was upon the scriptural references (especially *John* 6:45 – 'Every man therefore that hath heard, and hath learned of the Father, cometh unto me'; and *1 Cor.* 12:27 – 'Now you are the body of Christ . . .') that Luther developed his distinctive early notion of the 'priesthood of all believers' existing within an invisible, true church in the spirit of Christ, and linked indivisibly to the suffering church of Christian saints and martyrs through the ages. At the same time, Luther argued that this church was manifested through the visible marks of the true church, especially baptism†, the eucharist† and the preaching of the true word of God. Calvin accepted these formulations too. His ideal church was the hidden community of saints (the elect), chosen by God, whom God alone could identify. The ideal was never realizable in full by any institution on earth, but where the word of God was properly preached and the sacraments properly administered, then the church had something of the doctrine and spirit of the true invisible church about it. He accepted that the real church would necessarily include 'many hypocrites' in its midst; this strengthened the need for the church to have a 'discipline' to sustain it as a 'school' or 'nursery' for true faith.

For anabaptists, the church was composed of those who had made a solemn vow at their (adult) baptism. It therefore constituted a visible church of the saints, evident not only in the preaching of right doctrine and the scriptural use of sacraments but also in the life of voluntary discipline undertaken by its members. This entailed a degree of separation from the world and, in many cases, a striving to live in accordance with the biblical precepts of (especially) the New Testament. For many (though not all) anabaptists, the commandment of love meant rejecting the ways of the world, sometimes living with goods in common or refusing oaths to secular authorities. If this entailed conflict and suffering, this was not to be rejected, for the true church was a suffering community, living in the last days before the advent of the millennium. It is not surprising that this degree of 'exclusivism' within anabaptist thinking about the church should have led to internal dissension and splits of the kind which marked its history in the sixteenth century.

Communion   *See* (The) Eucharist.

(The godly) Community

The possibility that there might arise within a universal church a smaller group of enthusiastic believers was actively discussed by the protestant reformers, and sometimes promoted with scriptural authority. This group would not necessarily, the reformers stressed, correspond to the 'saints' or the 'elect' because the latter were known only to God. Nor would the existence of a 'leaven' in the 'lump' automatically lead to their forming an exclusive sect within a particular community. Luther's views on the matter were much less developed than those of Martin Bucer* at Strasbourg, who evolved an elaborate picture of how a church community should function. It was an educative society in which those who had progressed the furthest had an obligation to assist others on the journey, and that society would need to have a discipline to protect the godly in this task. It is often held that Calvin adopted his ideas on order and discipline in the 'godly community' at Geneva from Bucer.

To anabaptist brethren, the idea of a godly community, 'brothers in Christ', was fundamental to the sense of 'exclusiveness' which made adult baptism into a rite of initiation. The tendency amongst the brethren to extend the notion of godly community into one which practised the community of property was evident at a relatively early stage. On the basis of *Acts* 2:44–5 ('And all that believed were together and had all things common; and sold their possessions and goods, and parted them to all men, as every man had need'), and also *Acts* 4:32, 'community of goods' on the basis of the household became an undoubted feature of early Swiss anabaptism and a much-criticized (by opponents) element of the Münster rising. Among the anabaptists of Moravia, however, there grew up amidst the splits of the late 1520s the 'community people' (*Gemainschaffter*), an initially small group of dissident and banished anabaptists at Austerlitz, who chose voluntarily to share what little they possessed with others in their congregation in order to assist the most needy. From this group eventually emerged the Hutterite communities which would become the leading anabaptist group in Moravia by the end of the sixteenth century. The characteristic feature of the Hutterites was their community houses (*Bruderhof*) in which they lived together, often more than 40 to a house. Particularly criticized by contemporaries were their child-rearing practices, which involved removing children from their mothers as soon as they were weaned and placing them under the care of nursery sisters. Amongst Dutch anabaptists, 'community of goods' tended to be interpreted, especially after Münster, as mutual aid for those in distress within their communities.

Confession

Protestant reformers coalesced in their rejection of any idea that confession was a compulsory discipline required of individuals. They denied the theological understanding underlying such a requirement and criticized its effects as oppressive. Over the role for voluntary confession and absolution of sin by a pastor, however, they were divided. Luther regarded confession (before a friend, a neighbour, or a pastor) as an essential sacrament. The process of a pastor's hearing of the faith of an individual communicant was laid out by Luther in his widely adopted *Examination* (*Verhör*) of 1523, which tended to become a precondition for admission to the Lord's Supper in many Lutheran churches. For Zwingli, Bucer and Calvin, however, confession was regarded in a still more critical light. Zwingli would allow no more than the efficacy of brotherly and sisterly Christian counselling. Bucer regarded it as a matter of individual conscience and practice rather than general church discipline. Calvin, too, did nothing to build confession within the formal structure of his church.

Consubstantiation   *See* (The) Eucharist.

Covenant

Some medieval theologians had used the concept of a covenant to describe God's ordained power of salvation (see page 32). This was extensively reworked by protestant theologians, especially by Heinrich Bullinger* at Zürich (Zwingli's successor). The covenant was made with God's chosen people (his church). Scriptures contained his promise to be their God, if they would be his people. Later in the sixteenth century, protestant theologians investigated further what the latter part of this proposition might mean and utilized the term 'covenant of works' to describe the commandments which a godly people must uphold. The political use of the idea of covenant appeared within the arguments about whether (and in what circumstances) one could legitimately resist legitimately constituted authority (see pages 239–40). For anabaptists, the term 'Covenant' (G: *Bund*) was much used to describe the commitment of the brethren to the godly community.

Death

The protestant reformers agreed in the abolition of the last rites as a sacrament and abandoned all notions of purgatory. Along with the latter were abolished anniversary masses for the dead. Rituals for the dead should be kept modest, sombre and restrained. The result was a substantial shift in the perceived relationship between the living and dead, with the latter being unable to be assisted by the former, save in the process of dying. Both Luther and Calvin advised on how to console individuals in the last extremity and stressed the importance of family and close friends praying with a dying person to accompany them to the point of death. Thereafter, it was more the case that the dead could affect the living rather than the reverse. We should use the examples of those who lived and died well as patterns for living in the faith. That this became widely preached is apparent from the many collections of funeral sermons and model lives (and deaths) which gradually appeared in print in the later sixteenth century. Although the protestant reformers may have frowned on elaborate funerary rituals, there is a good deal of evidence to suggest that, in practice, the reformed churches allowed them to continue without too much interference into the seventeenth century. One strand amongst the radical reformers rejected the notion that souls of the departed were judged immediately. They preferred to imagine that they went into a period of sleep until the final day of judgment ('psychopannychism' or the 'sleep of souls'). The doctrine was criticized by Calvin in an early treatise (see page 177).

(The) Decalogue (The Ten Commandments)

Although the Ten Commandments had a prominent position within the moral teaching of the medieval church, this was still further heightened by the protestant reformers who used the Decalogue as the basic structure for catechismal teaching and moral discipline. Calvinist Reformed churches tended to have the Ten Commandments painted, or on boards, prominently displayed on the walls of their churches. The commandments were differently enumerated in the Zwinglian and Calvinist traditions from the traditional distribution. The prohibitions of false and idolatrous worship are counted as two whilst the last commandment forbidding covetousness brings together what is treated as two separate injunctions by the catholic church and by Lutherans. This doubtless affected the degree to which notions of 'idolatry' were given prominence within the 'Reformed' (Calvinist) tradition.

(Church) Discipline

Protestant reformers were united in accepting the need for church discipline. They differed over how they saw it contributing to individual salvation. For Luther, the 'inner discipline' of an individual's life was primarily influenced by education, preaching and inculcation of religious values. Church discipline was more a matter of maintaining public order by legal sanction, necessary for the maintenance of a Christian society but not fundamental to salvation. Lutheran churches retained some elements of episcopal government and their consistories (at Wittenberg and elsewhere) utilized the power of excommunication to maintain church discipline. For Zwingli, Bucer and Calvin, however, church discipline (the 'sinews of the church' (Lat: *nervus ecclesiae*)) was fundamental to salvation since it was only within that public community that individual Christians were educated and inculcated with the true values of Christian living. So the stress upon the necessity and visibility of church 'discipline' was much more evident within the Reformed (Calvinist) tradition. There were practical issues which made the matter of church discipline of particular concern. Protestant Europe had either to reform or replace the old system of ecclesiastical courts and the canon law which formed the basis of their jurisdiction. This was particularly urgent in the case of the laws relating to marriage. At Zürich, Zwingli proposed in 1525 (initially as a temporary measure) the establishment of a marriage tribunal (G: *Ehegericht*) composed of six judges (two of whom would be from the clergy) to settle matrimonial cases and other related moral matters. The court became copied widely (by Bern, Basel, Schaffhausen, and various south German cities). It formed the basis for the consistory court (Fr: *consistoire*) at Geneva established by Calvin in 1541. The functions of the consistory court at Geneva, however, were more broadly conceived. It had the duty to investigate, to admonish and, if necessary, to exclude temporarily from communion (the 'ban') or to excommunicate. All unbecoming conduct potentially lay within its remit, including sexual offences, gambling and dicing, extravagant behaviour such as dancing or immodest dress, blasphemy, swearing and superstitious practices or popish customs. The stress upon 'discipline' in the Reformed tradition was reflected in the adoption of the Genevan consistory court (with local variations) in France, the Netherlands, Scotland and the various Calvinist polities of Germany in the second half of the sixteenth century. These were sometimes accompanied by ecclesiastical regulations known as a 'discipline' which gave some precision to the organizational framework of the churches and often stipulated what matters should be of particular concern to the consistories. The French discipline was, after much discussion, presented in a modified form to the synod at La Rochelle (1571) and adopted at that of Nîmes in 1572. This became the model for the Scottish 'Book of Discipline'. Other local disciplines included that for the Pyrenean principality of Béarn under Jeanne d'Albret (1571) and for Guernsey (1581; 1611).

The anabaptists also strongly maintained the fundamental importance of church discipline. God's church (D: *gemeente Godts*) was the body of true believers (G: *Bundgenossen*) who had made a covenant with God at their baptism and surrendered (G: *gelassen*) themselves to his will. A discipline was the means by which the purity of the true believers would be maintained and it became a much-debated element within anabaptism as it was used to exclude elements from their midst. The anabaptists extended the use of temporary exclusion (the 'ban') and permanent exclusion ('excommunication') to include 'shunning' (the complete breaking off from contact with an individual held no longer to be a true believer). Shunning was even extended to the breaking of all ties between husband and wife. It was doubtless because anabaptists were frequently a persecuted minority for whom the problem of informers and spies was a reality that this was a significant issue.

Questions of church discipline were also influenced and shaped by the relationship between the various churches and the political institutions around them. In the Lutheran churches of the German states, church discipline was overwhelmingly sustained by, in and around the state. Visitations were conducted by superintendants on the instruction of ecclesiastical councils under the authority of the prince. Consistory courts exercised authority under princely jurisdiction and cases could be appealed to the ecclesiastical councils. Within the Reformed (Calvinist) traditions, the patterns were more complex. At Zürich, appeals were possible from the matrimonial tribunal to the city magistrates (the 'Great Council'). At Geneva, the Ecclesiastical Ordinances of 1541 stipulated that the consistory courts were not to meddle in matters of civil jurisdiction. In cases where there was a need to impose civil punishments or constrain witnesses to appear, the matters should be reported to the city magistrates for them to judge and sentence as they thought appropriate. In time, and in practice, the Genevan magistrates and consistory courts collaborated widely over the pursuit of moral discipline. Such collaboration was only possible at a local level in those states where strong Calvinist minorities did not succeed in controlling the state at a national level. So in France, the Netherlands and in the Calvinist principalities of the Holy Roman Empire, the issue of consistorial discipline became one which made the Calvinists an 'exclusive' community and reinforced their independence from the state. The debate over this issue surfaced in Germany around Erastianism[†].

(The) Consistory   *See* (Church) Discipline; Presbyterianism.

(The) Elect   *See* Predestination.

Episcopacy
There was no uniform view amongst the reformers about what should be done with the episcopal fabric of the traditional church. For Luther, with the priesthood of all believers[†] as his starting-point, ministry came in many different forms and the office in which it was exercised was a rather minor matter. There was no apostolic succession, which was a papal invention. The origin of ministry lay in the vocation given to individuals by God to be apostles, evangelists and prophets. The authority of ministry lay in being publicly called to the office created under an ecclesiastical ordinance. So there would be Lutheran bishops in the Holy Roman Empire during the first generations of the reformation, a few of

whom were catholic consecrated bishops who had accepted the reformation, and the remainder being bishops under the local ecclesiastical ordinance of the particular principality. The latter, however, gradually died out and, by the end of the sixteenth century there were no more Lutheran bishops in Germany, although they continued within the Lutheran-inclined Scandinavian churches as well as in England (where apostolic succession was also preserved).

Calvin positively eliminated the office of bishop both in his basic understanding of ministry (as presented in the last book of the *Institution*) and in the practice which he recommended at Geneva and elsewhere. Following Bucer, he identified four separate forms of ministry which had existed in the early church (these were: pastors (*pastores*), teachers (*doctores*), elders (*seniores*) and deacons (*diaconi*)). Episcopal functions were redistributed around these four ministries. Most Calvinist churches in Europe followed this model, albeit with some local variation; but it was possible for Calvinist-inclined churches in central Europe (Hungary, Transylvania) in the sixteenth century to retain some episcopal structure without compromising their doctrinal affiliations.

Erastianism

This is the view, named after Thomas Lüber (Lat: *Erastus*) (1524–83), which argued that civil authorities should exercise sovereignty within the state, and that this sovereignty extended also over the church. The church should exercise no rival coercive authority and its claims to exercise the right of exclusion ('excommunication') should only occur with the consent of the civil magistrate. Thomas Erastus was appointed professor of medicine at Heidelberg in 1558, having been born at Baden in Switzerland and having studied medicine and philosophy. In the 1560s, the Calvinists of the Rhine Palatinate, led by Kaspar Olevianus (a student of Calvin's), sought to introduce a 'Holy Discipline' into the Palatinate church with the backing of the elector. In 1568, Erastus drew up his objections. In an already reformed protestant state, no one should be excluded from the Lord's Supper, even if they had been found guilty of some moral misdemeanour. They should be punished in the civil courts for such offences. The Elector Palatine should follow the example of the Old Testament kings and seek to rule over his people through church and state. He sent his views to Heinrich Bullinger* at Zürich (from whom they won support) and Théodore de Bèze* at Geneva (who wrote an extensive rebuttal of them). The debate did not become openly divisive of the Calvinist communities in Europe because neither side sought publicity for their positions. Erastus' theses and accompanying treatise were only published six years after his death in London (in 1589). By this time the basic trends in church–state relations had begun to solidify in many of the Reformed states of Europe and, whilst the arguments of strict Calvinists continued against the basic tenets of Erastus, it was his views which tended to prevail in practice within the Calvinist polities.

(The) Eucharist

The debates about the eucharist (also referred to as 'Holy Communion', 'the Breaking of Bread' and 'the Lord's Supper' in different confessional traditions) were complex and divisive during the reformation. They were based on a limited range of scriptural references but they went to the heart of how scripture should be interpreted and revealed fundamental underlying issues about how holy power was to be understood. Many of the confessional colloquies of the sixteenth century turned upon the interpretation of this issue. It had observable consequences in the liturgies of the various churches of the period which in turn reinforced confessional divisions (for the eucharistic prayers in the Roman rite, the Lutheran mass and the Zwinglian order-book, see pages 252–7).

To medieval theologians, the elements of bread and wine were miraculously changed into the very body and blood of Christ (the 'Real Presence') at the moment when the priest uttered the words of consecration. They explained the process as 'transubstantiation' (*transubstantio*). By this, they meant that the 'substance' (the reality within) the bread and the wine was 'transformed' into the substance of the body and blood of Christ leaving only the 'accidents' (or superficial properties – what could be seen, touched or tasted) unchanged. In common with some later medieval philosophers and theologians, Luther was prepared to accept the notion of a 'Real Presence' but rejected 'transubstantiation' as a means to explain it. For Luther, the fact of the 'Real Presence' had undisputed biblical attestation. It was analogous to the fact that Christ incarnate (both God and Man) had been on earth. Christ's body and blood were not to be equated with the bread and the wine but they lay 'in, with, and under' it in ways that God had not intended to be fully understood. Those who ate and drank the sacrament, became one body ('incorporated') with all the saints.

Others, however, went much further than Luther. In a series of tracts in 1524, Karlstadt* rejected the 'Real Presence' of Christ at the Lord's Supper and suggested that when Christ said '*This* is my body' he was pointing at his body (and not at the bread). The following year, Huldrych Zwingli suggested in a published letter that the word 'is' should be taken to mean 'signifies'. He expanded on the idea in his *Commentary on True and False Religion* (*De vera et falsa religione* . . .) of the same year. Those who ate and drank at the Holy Supper were commemorating Christ's sacrifice, celebrating their redemption by his passion. A sacrament was a sign that a believer had grace and belonged to the church. Communion was therefore a solemn and important sacrament, but did not need to be a regular part of Sunday worship. Indeed, Zwingli arranged for communion to be available not more than four times a year. Zwingli refused to accept that the body and blood of Christ could be in any way connected with the material objects of the bread and the wine. To make such a connection was to engage in superstition[†]. If the bread and wine were a eucharistic sacrament, it was because, in our hearts and minds, we could envisage them as representing the body and blood of Christ. The rejection of the 'Real Presence' led to supporters of Zwingli being often described by contemporaries as 'sacramentarian'[†].

It is difficult for us to appreciate fully why such issues should have mattered so much, especially to those in positions of authority. But we should remember that Zwingli was proposing a radical shift in how holy power was conceived. It further desacralized the material world and invested holy power within the consciences of individual people and the authority of collective worship. That had profound implications for how other forms of power were to be regarded. Zwingli's views were reflected in the attitudes and practices of the anabaptists who also stressed that the Lord's Supper was a thanksgiving and commemoration. Some radical reformers (Sebastian Franck and Kaspar von Schwenckfeld) even suspended or abandoned the eucharist altogether.

Luther's critique of Karlstadt* and Zwingli emerged in a series of polemics in the years 1526 and 1527. Their views were 'errors' and 'poison'. They had twisted the scripture away from its natural meaning and misunderstood Augustine. In the famous meeting between Zwingli and Luther at the colloquy of Marburg in October 1529, a meeting convened by Landgrave Philipp* of Hesse to settle the bitter dispute over the eucharist, the differences were highlighted but not resolved. In addition to Luther and Zwingli, the conference was attended by Philipp Melanchthon*, Johannes Oecolampadius* and a dozen other leading reformed theologians. To concentrate their minds, Luther wrote in chalk on the table at the beginning of the discussions on 2 October: '*Hoc est corpus meum*' ('This is my body'). The following debate revealed fundamental differences about how scripture was to be interpreted as well as over the doctrine of the 'Real Presence'.

Some of the theologians at Marburg (especially those from Strasbourg — Martin Bucer*, Jakob Sturm* and Caspar Hedio) tried without success to broker a compromise. This would be the role that Calvin inherited. The compromise rested on trying to align the reality of what is signified with its sign. The Lord's Supper was a commemorative act, a sign; but with it came the reality for those who participated in it of communion with Christ and participation ('incorporation') in his body. So, although he rejected Luther's teaching that Christ was 'in, with and under' the bread, Calvin also held that participation with Christ in the eucharist became a reality in that the Holy Spirit brought Christ into the heart of the true believer, or, equally, lifted the heart of the believer to Christ in Heaven. But this was something to be experienced rather than analysed and explained. This became the basis of the careful formulations which were worked out between Calvin and Heinrich Bullinger* in the theological agreement concluded at Zürich in 1549 and known as the *Consensus Tigurinus* (see page 249).

This notion of a mysterious union with Christ appeared in subsequent reformed confessions in Europe, although to different degrees and not always very clearly. In practice, the Reformed[†] (Calvinist) churches of Europe had quite wide differences in eucharistic practice too. In many Reformed churches, only those who had sworn to the confession and discipline of the church were accepted at the Lord's Supper and this was enforced by giving communicants tokens (Fr: *méraux*) to present to sidesmen as they went forward to communion. There were issues of whether one stood or knelt, and whether the elements were passed from hand to hand – important ways of reinforcing a basic sense of the sacrament as a commemorative meal and not a sacrifice. The issue of whether the bread should be in the form of a wafer (often with the image of a cross on it) or a plain loaf became significantly indicative of eucharistic divisions at a popular level as well as amongst theologians, especially in later sixteenth-century Germany.

Excommunication   *See* (Church) Discipline.

Grace
St Augustine's theology of grace became the fundamental starting-point for all protestant thinking on this complex subject, which had implications for how the eucharist[†] and other sacraments were conceived, and much else besides. Augustine's insistence on the necessity for God to initiate our salvation was shared by all the reformers, even if they had very different ways of interpreting how this happened. For Luther, the process is utterly dependant on Christ. We receive grace when we believe in Christ. His righteousness becomes ours at that moment. In this mystical union with Christ, which goes beyond any attempt at rational explanation, the believer receives forgiveness and renewal of life, and is justified. This is what happens when we receive the real body and blood of Christ at the eucharist and also when the word of God is received within our hearts.

For Zwingli, the process was conceived rather differently. Grace is received by us through Christ, but it is Christ as the Holy Spirit who works in our hearts by means of the example of his life and our own experience of what the Holy Spirit does in our own lives. So, at the eucharist, we have a sign and confirmation of the Holy Spirit already working within us, but the sign does not, of itself, convey any grace. Calvin was impressed with Luther's formulations and used the image of Christ being 'ingrafted' in us through our faith in the loving kindness of God, from whom we, like lost sheep, receive a grace which we do not deserve. The fact that he went on to outline a doctrine of absolute predestination was, for Calvin, both a natural extension of this doctrine of grace and also no radical departure from that of Luther. For later Calvinists, this juxtaposition was uncomfortable, and this resurfaced in the debates about grace launched by Arminius*. How Calvin explained the process of 'ingrafting' was highly complex, and is still a subject of debate amongst theologians. It depended on how he interpreted a 'sign'. The preaching of the word and the offering of the sacraments 'represent' (i.e. 're-present') God's grace to us in a way which means that they are neither merely a symbol nor an active agent (crudely conceived) for conveying grace.

The radical reformers often developed their own theologies of grace and it is difficult to discern the elements which might be held entirely in common by them. They tended, however, to emphasize still further the significance of the Holy Spirit as the instrument for conveying grace. They also tended to see grace in terms of a spiritual union with Christ which was utterly transforming of an individual's life and, once the experience had overtaken the whole world, this would be how the millennium[†] would be achieved.

Iconoclasm

Iconoclasm (the rejection of objects or individuals invested with religious significance) was a fundamental feature of the protestant reformation from its inception. Holy relics, shrines, statues, altars, consecrated hosts, chalices and stained-glass windows were as vulnerable to its destructive energies as individual monks and priests. Its manifestation, however, differed markedly in accordance with the particular divisive anxieties raised by the protestant reformation in its adversaries. It also depended on the degree of seriousness with which the problem of 'idolatry' in the traditional church was viewed by the reformers themselves. Luther was relatively tolerant of images, regarding it as more important to remove the idolatry from people's hearts. Karlstadt*, by comparison, encouraged iconoclastic destruction at Wittenberg in December 1521 by arguing that the veneration of images was idolatry which polluted the whole community. Similar iconoclastic incidents occurred in Zürich as Zwingli and his partners attacked images. The magistrates in Zürich, however, prudently ordered the 'purification' of the city's churches in a move which would be mirrored in many Rhineland cities. Calvin's hostility to images did not extend (like that of other Genevan-trained ministers) to enciting iconoclastic destruction, but his attitude towards the idolatry which images and relics contained was unambiguous. This undoubtedly had its impact in the early years of the French civil wars where iconoclasm was a major part of the popular sectarian disturbances which engulfed its cities in the 1560s. The same was also true for the 'iconoclastic fury' which overtook the Netherlands in 1566.

Justification by faith (Lat: *Sola Fide*)

This was the fundamental theological conceptual change imparted by the protestant reformation. It lay close to the heart of how Luther (and, with notably different emphases, subsequent protestant reformers) regarded salvation. The term 'justification' (Lat: *iustificatio*) occurred within the New Testament, especially in the Pauline writings, as a metaphor to explain how human beings are 'made righteous' by God. The basic features of Luther's distinctive doctrine of justification were all in place by 1520. Citing passages by St Paul, Luther held that man is the recipient of God's mercy through faith alone (Lat: *sola fide*). Salvation cannot depend on human merit or upon good works or upon the church. Our faith is a gift of grace from God who mysteriously elects to save us and it works in a mysterious way in us. Luther talks about faith as a 'trust' (Lat: *fiducia*) in God's promises, as revealed to us in Christ. Through this trust, although sinners, we nevertheless have a hope of righteousness which God imparts to us.

For none of the other protestant reformers did the doctrine of justification by faith have the same resonance as an explanation of salvation as for Luther. It is difficult to find much sustained interest in the notion in the writings of Zwingli, who was more concerned with the educative processes by which God makes us instruments for moral actions. Bucer also sought to concentrate on how we learn to live and act in faith. Calvin, however, came the closest to providing a framework for harmonizing these rather divergent elements. He did so by stressing that our faith in Christ enables Him to live in us as a real and living force and becomes the route by which we can share in the benefits of His passion. We 'possess' Christ and he becomes 'ingrafted' into our beings and lives, transforming, justifying and sanctifying them at one and the same time.

Marriage

Although the protestant reformation did not seek fundamentally to alter the institution of marriage, by rejecting its sacramentary character it changed its nature. The rejection of clerical celibacy also contributed to the changes in attitudes towards marriage which were reflected in the writings of the reformers. Luther wrote of marriage both as a human necessity (for the satisfaction of sexual hunger) and also as a state in which, like other human states, there was the possibility of its being endowed with grace from God. Where a marriage no longer met the satisfaction of sexual hunger, then the possibility for divorce had to exist – especially in cases of impotency, adultery, abandonment and violence. But the practical need to provide for divorce did not mean that Luther positively advocated it. On the contrary, every effort should be made to encourage reconciliation and forgiveness to strengthen the bonds of an existing marriage. These views were not significantly different from those advocated by Zwingli and Calvin. If there was any difference, it probably lay in the establishment of marriage tribunal courts and consistory courts in Reformed[†] (Calvinist) regions to replace the old episcopal courts and canon law regulations with new institutions. But both in Lutheran and Reformed traditions, the old canon law regulations on the forbidden degrees of marriage were slimmed down to the obligatory 'second degree' laid down in *Leviticus*. If the 'magisterial reformers' were largely agreed on the subject, the anabaptists may have had something more distinctive to offer in the concept of a 'marriage within the covenant'. Because of the need for both spouses to be within the community of the saints, marriage potentially became a strong symbol of how the covenanted saints (D: *bundgenooten*) should relate to one another. The protestant picture of marriage, and the corresponding significance placed upon the 'household' as a place where religious instruction and education should take place within a paternally-dominated setting, was reflected in the growing body of literature (G: *Hausvaterliteratur*) of an improving kind on how the godly household should be organized.

Music

There were few areas which revealed more clearly the divisions between the reformers than in their attitudes to devotional music. Luther regarded music as a divine skill and one which, second only to that of language, should be allied with the word to be the handmaid of the Gospel. He introduced the German hymn and wrote several metrical psalm chorales; and the Lutheran *Deutsche Messe* allowed for the use of vernacular polyphonic ('many-parts') chorales sung by choirs and using biblical or devotional texts. Zwingli, by contrast, found no biblical or theological reason to include any music within religious services. The early church had apparently made no use of it, it was inextricably linked with the patterns of worship of the traditional church, and he regarded its inclusion as likely to detract from the preaching of the word and the corporate prayer which should lie at the centre of shared worship. The organs were left in place within the churches at Zürich but they were used outside the formal liturgical services. Calvin's attitude to devotional music was influenced to a considerable extent by his experience of congregations singing Lutheran metrical psalms at Strasbourg. It led to the greatest innovation in popular devotional music in the protestant reformation. Calvin prepared a selection of psalms for use in the French stranger church in Strasbourg, which was published in 1539. It was based on the poetic versions in French prepared by the court poet Clément Marot (c.1496–1544). By his death, Marot had completed 50 such Psalms and the arrangements were completed by Théodore de Bèze* to become the great Genevan Psalter of 1562. This was just one of many versions of metrical psalmody in the vernacular to appear in the protestant reformation. Although Calvin thought they should be sung unaccompanied by a congregation and to a simple repeated one-line ('monophonic') melody, they were in fact quickly set to a variety of harmonizations. For the practical use of devotional music in the reformation was diverse and conservative musical practice was sometimes used as a mask for more radical liturgical experimentation.

Outward conformity

How should the true believer behave when finding himself in a minority amongst his local community or, worse, persecuted for his faith? The problem was one which greatly exercised the protestant reformers. Although there was a good deal of scholastic discussion of the circumstances in which it was permissible to conceal the truth (which was not the same as lying), there were obvious dangers for the Christian community in encouraging hypocrisy. Calvin rejected outright the justifications for outward conformity. In his treatise against the 'Nicodemites' (after the Pharisee named Nicodemus who kept his faith hidden through fear) and elsewhere Calvin rejected all the arguments which might allow 'feigners and dissemblers' to 'keep themselves in the favour of the world'. Amongst his fellow protestants in France as well as for evangelical[†] protestants in Italy, however, the practical need to disguise convictions behind a façade of participation in catholic worship was uppermost. This led to discussions about whether it was right to seek flight from persecution in order to be able to hold one's beliefs in peace. For anabaptist brethren, the practical problems were still more pressing. The stress upon a religion of the spirit, which did not depend on any form of external observance for its validation, led anabaptists to be able to justify outward conformity without any scruples of conscience. For David Joris*, for example, Heaven and hell lay within, rather than outside, man. Throughout the latter part of his life, he lived as a respectable patrician in Basel under an assumed name as well as having a second identity as an anabaptist leader. The elements of religious observance required of him in his public identity had nothing to do with his life of the spirit. Such dualism gave the established churches, both catholic and protestant, considerable unease. In the catholic world, the problem was most acute in respect of the converted Jews (Sp: *marranos*) and Moors (Sp: *moriscos*).

Philippists   *See* Adiaphora.

Presbyterianism

The name derived from the Scottish terminology for the system of church government associated with the Calvinist reformation in Europe. Calvin's church discipline[†] was developed to provide an ascending and interlocking pattern of ecclesiastical courts, comprising both clergy and lay elders. At the level of the parish or congregation, the minister and elders together met as the consistory[†] (in Scottish terminology, a 'session'). The consistory provided the base unit for church discipline (see pages 227–9). Above it came a regular meeting of representatives from individual churches, called a 'classis' (or, in France, a 'colloque'; in Scotland, a 'presbytery') to deal with common problems. Then, above that, lay more occasional regional synods (in France, 'synodes provinciaux') and, at the top, the national synods (or, in Scotland, 'general assemblies'). The basis of the presbyterian pattern of government was laid by Calvin in Geneva in his reformulation of church government at a local level. Following Bucer, he identified four separate forms of ministry which had existed in the early church (these were: pastors (Lat: *pastores*), teachers (*doctores*), elders (*seniores*) and deacons (*diaconi*)). But the interlocking and ascending pattern of presbyteries and synods was, in reality, a development outlined in the French ecclesiastical discipline (Fr: *Discipline ecclésiastique*) of 1559.

Predestination

Predestination (from the Lat. *praedestinare* 'to foreordain') is the belief that certain individuals (the 'elect') are chosen in advance for eternal salvation. On the basis of the Pauline scriptures, St Augustine had developed it as a mystery which the human mind had to accept but which could not be further investigated. It was evident in the works of all the major reformers, but later developments somewhat caricatured it as a doctrine of unique significance to Calvin alone. In reality, Luther's views on the subject were not significantly different from those of Calvin. But Calvin was forced by his opponents to explore and justify 'this terrible decree' in greater detail at the same time as Philipp Melanchthon* was softening the Lutheran approach to the same issues. Calvin argued not merely that some ('the elect') were foreordained to salvation, but also that the remainder of fallen humanity ('the reprobate') were foreordained to damnation. This is sometimes referred to as 'double predestination'. In the later sixteenth century, the need to train pastors and provide simpler materials for instruction of the laity in doctrine tended to simplify (and thus to distort) the complex issues raised by predestination. Calvin's successor at Geneva, Théodore de Bèze*, insisted that it was a doctrine contained in scripture and thus not one which could be avoided. He produced the famous *Table of predestination* (*Tabula praedestinationis*) (1555) as a one-page diagrammatic representation of double predestination. It foreshadowed the later sixteenth-century debates about the order of predestination, especially about whether God had foreordained who should be saved before the Fall of Adam ('supralapsarianism' or 'antelapsarianism') or afterwards ('sublapsarianism'). Such issues were earnestly discussed amongst Calvinists at the Synod of Dordrecht (Dort) in 1618 which led to the Arminian divisions of the seventeenth century.

'Priesthood of all believers'   *See* (The) Church.

Psychopannychism   *See* Death.

Real Presence   *See* (The) Eucharist.

(Rights to) Resist established authority
The political divisions provoked by the protestant reformation led to the reformulation of traditional arguments in favour of legitimate resistance to established authority. These eventually provided a more profound religious and constitutional basis for such arguments than had existed previously in European political thought. For both Luther and Calvin, the strong traditions of pacific acceptance of divinely constituted civil authority in Christianity could not readily be contradicted. But from the beginning Luther promoted (and demonstrated by his own actions) the possibility (and necessity) of passive resistance to legitimately constituted authority in circumstances where it was constraining individuals to act against their consciences. However, it was amongst the lawyers in the chanceries of Saxony and Hesse that constitutional theories of resistance began to develop following the decisions of the diet[†] of Augsburg in 1530 (see pages 61–2). They argued that the emperor could be resisted on legitimate grounds by the princes. In the imperial constitution, he was an elected monarch and the princes (who elected him) had rights of self-defence against a tyrannical emperor. They had legitimately constituted rights as 'inferior magistrates' in the empire to advance 'true religion' amongst their subjects, if necessary against the emperor's will. Although not immediately put to the test, the doctrine of the 'inferior magistrate' became exploited in due course after the Schmalkaldic War of 1546–47. The city of Magdeburg refused to accept the Augsburg Interim imposed by the emperor after his military success and it was besieged. During the siege, the ministers and magistrates of the city issued the 'Magdeburg Confession' – in reality, a manifesto of the rights of lesser magistrates to resist legitimate authority. This tendency would flourish whenever the right conditions prevailed in the later sixteenth century.

These occurred in England (during the recatholicization of Mary Tudor, 1553–58), in France during the wars of religion (1562–98) and during the Dutch Revolt (especially post-1572). To the rights of lesser magistrates were added new elements. These included the fundamental religious right, which was extended to the 'people' (generally taken to mean the rights invested in the corporate entities of the people or region, the estates or parliaments), to resist ungodly or idolatrous rulers. This was justified on biblical (Old Testament) grounds. This fundamental religious right was vested in the people by a contract, or covenant, which God had made with his chosen people and a parallel contract which he made with the ruler. A ruler who broke the latter contract could expect to lose the obedience of his (godly) people as well as divine protection. These arguments were first deployed by English writers in opposition to the rule of Mary Tudor. They were further developed by French 'monarchomach' ('monarch-hater') writings during the French civil wars. These were generally published after the massacre of St Bartholomew (see page 119) although they had often been written before the event. They included Beza's *On the Right of Magistrates* (*Du droit des magistrats*) of 1574, François Hotman's *Franco-Gallia* (*Frankish (Free) Gaul*) of 1573, and the *Vindiciae contra Tyrannos* (*Vindication against Tyrants*) of 1579. The latter was published under the pseudonym 'Etienne Junius Brutus'. It may have been a composite work in which the French Huguenot scholar-soldier Philippe du Plessis Mornay is likely to have played a part. These theories were not the exclusive preserve of protestants. When the circumstances were right (as in the catholic opposition to Elizabeth I's rule in England, or during the Catholic League in France), similar arguments – sometimes borrowed without acknowledgement from protestant sources – were also to be found advanced by catholics. They formed the justifications openly utilized to defend the assassination of the Valois king Henri III in 1589.

For anabaptists, the arguments centred around the separation of the communities of brethren and their shared faith from the authority of the magistrate. Most early anabaptists refused to countenance any authority which would require them to order judicial execution ('the sword'). They therefore refused to swear any oaths in a court of justice or civic context and rejected all forms of military obligation. This rejection was, if anything, reinforced after the events of Münster but it tended to become a sustained, passive non-recognition of the powers that be.

Sabbath; Sabbatarianism

Strictly speaking, sabbatarians rejected the celebration of Christian Sunday in favour of the Jewish Sabbath (Saturday). Such a view was expressed periodically in the sixteenth century, especially amongst millenarian anabaptists who sought a conversion of the Jews to Christianity prior to the coming of the millennium. In a looser sense, the term is applied to those who demanded a strict observance of Sunday as a day of rest. This became a marked feature of Puritan thinking in seventeenth-century England.

Saints; saints' days

The medieval practice of venerating saints and invoking their assistance in specific ways was universally rejected by the protestant reformers. It had no biblical basis, they argued, and diverted attention from faith in Christ as the universal redeemer. The community of saints, however, continued to be represented by the reformers as all the godly of past ages in union with Christ. The practical effects of this critique appeared in the rapid decline in the cult of saints and their relics. Yet Lutheran Germany retained a good number of the significant feast-days ('solemnities') of the traditional church calendar (see pages 1–3) and had no objection to local saints' names being used at baptism. In Zwinglian, Calvinist and anabaptist Europe, however, these elements tended to be actively forbidden or discouraged by ecclesiastical authorities.

Sin

The protestant reformers profoundly transformed the notion of sin. This was the result of their fundamentally different conceptions of the human psyche. The medieval conception of human beings was reordered. This medieval conception had been one in which (generalizing loosely) a superior, rational faculty lay in control of the sensual and potentially sinful lesser corporal elements of the body, including the emotions and the senses. It was these lesser elements which contained the roots of human sins, which were duly dissected into the sins connected with particular senses and emotions. In its place the reformers placed a more balanced and holistic conception of the human psyche. Mind and body lay in a profound interrelationship one with another. Both were integrally touched by the original sin which was part of our human nature. That sin was indivisible, all-embracing and all-pervasive. Only faith in Christ, by which believers were given the grace to be better than their fundamentally sinful nature, could transform us. But that faith reached us at least as much by the word of God appealing to our emotions as to our rational faculties. So, for Luther, we were at one and the same time 'justified and sinful' (*simul iustus et peccator*); by faith, the 'sin that rules us' (*peccatum regnans*) could be transformed into the 'sin that is ruled' (*peccatum regnatum*). For Zwingli, the dominant metaphors were those of sin as a fundamental and inherited 'disease' of 'self-love' from which only the grace of Christ saves us. For Calvin, the language was even more graphic. Sin was unbounded lust ('concupiscence'), a 'pollution' to which we as human beings were 'enslaved'. Only the grace of Christ could set limits to the bounds of our lust and prevent us from mixing up ('polluting') the holy with our sin. In both the Lutheran and Calvinist traditions, these uncompromising and graphic analyses of original sin were at the heart of internal discussion and dissension. This surfaced particularly in the 'synergistic' controversy in Germany (see 'Adiaphora', page 220).

Sola Scriptura ('Scripture alone')

Protestant reformers were not the first theologians to regard Scripture as the prime validator of doctrine. They were, however, the first to place Scripture in direct opposition to the traditions and practices of the church. They did so because, so they argued, the medieval church had granted itself the authority to determine what Scripture said and how it should be interpreted. By contrast, the reformers regarded all traditions within the church as only carrying weight if they conformed to Scripture.

The reformers further argued that Scripture had within it the guiding lights and inspiration by which it should be interpreted. *Sola scriptura* was also a principle of biblical exegesis. Scripture was the holy word of God and inspired by the Holy Spirit. However, there was an assumed distinction between the substance of the Scriptures (*res*) and the words (*verba*) they contained. The latter might be lost in translation without affecting the former, whose 'truth' and 'certainty' would still be capable of being conveyed to our consciences and minds despite the limits of our capacities for understanding them.

'The Sword'   *See* (Rights to) Resist established authority

Superstition

The battle launched by the protestant reformers against what they perceived as 'superstition' was central to their preoccupations. Following St Augustine (and medieval theologians), they defined superstition as not merely the credulous notions of the unlearned but the dangerous worship of false gods. The latter extended to idolatry, divination, sorcery and magic. Luther's fundamental critique of the path to salvation offered by the traditional church was that it relied on objects and routines ('works') which made God into an 'idol and even a puppet'. Purgatory was, according to Luther, 'a pure devilish fantasy'. The sacraments had become invested with magical associations by the Roman church. In Luther's view, the 'words are revered more than they are believed'; 'salt and holy water have been given as great a power as holy baptism itself'. The practice of fasting gave an unjustified confidence in human merit; it was pure 'idolatry' and part of the 'impious worship' of the old church. The invocation of saints was 'an abuse introduced by Antichrist' into the church which made people 'consider the saints as their saviours, able to

assist them individually and imputing to each saint a particular virtue
... this is pure idolatry'. The veneration of relics, indulgences and
pilgrimages 'turned many people away from Christ and led them to put
their confidence in their own works, and so it has made them idolatrous
...'. The result, according to Calvin, was to risk mixing up the holy with
the profane ('pollution') and to encourage hypocrisy towards the sacred.
Calvin was particularly concerned to develop the critique against the
veneration of relics (in his *Treatise on relics* (1543)) and judicial astrology
(in his *Advertisement against astrology* (1549)). The latter was dangerous
paganism and on the increase. Papal superstition was not, therefore,
merely an institutional failing. It threatened the very fabric, the 'institution', of the Christian religion and was the work of the devil. This critique was the more powerful amongst contemporaries because it appeared
to reinforce many fundamental and common anxieties about the threats
assailing Christendom, especially the apparent rise in witchcraft (see
pages 276–8).

Toleration

The reformation created religious pluralism, which in turn generated
the first sustained debate in Europe about what we would know as religious 'toleration'. The word 'toleration', however, had a negative conno-
tation in the sixteenth century. It meant tolerating an abuse which one
was powerless to prevent rather than advancing a cause that was worthy
in itself. For the latter, the terms 'charity' (*caritas*), 'concord' (*concordia*)
and peace (*pax*) were more regularly adopted. Erasmus* became the
beacon figure later in the sixteenth century in the advocacy of religious
reconciliation (*concordia*) on the basis of a return to the original Scriptures, the avoidance of needless theological speculation and the delineation of a limited number of evidently fundamental Christian doctrines.
Arguments for the liberty of conscience which were advanced by the
mainstream protestant reformers (Luther, Calvin) could also be used to
justify a more sustained tolerance of the religious opinions of others.
They figure in the most famous advocacy of religious toleration in the
sixteenth century, that composed by Sébastien Castellio*. Writing from
Basel in the wake of the trial and execution of Michael Servetus*, Castellio
published his *On heretics and whether they should be punished* (*De haereticis
an sint persequendi*) (1554). Castellio collected the views of earlier Christian writers as well as the protestant reformers about the importance of
the freedom of religious conscience. He then presented his own conclusion that to persecute heretics was presumptuously to undertake God's
work for him. Castellio's views would survive amongst the religious
radicals of the later sixteenth century, especially amongst the unitarian
churches in Poland and in the northern Netherlands in the early seventeenth century.

Meanwhile, the political effects of religious and sectarian division in middle Europe in the second half of the sixteenth century encouraged the growth of more prudential justifications for the state to tolerate a limited diversity of opinions. Some of these arguments were advanced by protestants whose primary aim was the abolition of persecution and who argued that the limited toleration of their right to worship constituted no fundamental threat to the survival of the state. Other arguments were to be developed by lawyers and statesmen for whom civil 'peace' was more significant than religious 'concord'. These were to be found most notably stated by the chancellor of France during the earlier years of the French civil wars, Michel de l'Hôpital (1503–73; chancellor, 1560–68) and the 'politique' thinkers in France whose writings and influence he inspired. By 1618, there were a limited number of practical examples of religious pluralism imposed by political authority (the peace of Augsburg (1555); the pacification of Nantes (1598) etc) which could be used to prove that, whatever the arguments for or against, the practicalities of pluralism did not automatically lead to the dissolution of the state or society.

Unbelief
The definition of 'unbelief' in the sixteenth century was rather different from that which is encompassed by modern perceptions of 'atheism'. In the sixteenth century, the most common (though not exclusive) defining characteristics of 'atheism' (though it was a new word for the vernacular languages in the sixteenth century) were not an absence of belief in a God or gods, but the absence of a belief in (and respect for) the divine economy of rewards and punishments in heaven and hell, the absence of a belief in divine providence and retribution. As the Genevan-trained Pierre Viret put it in 1564: 'It is common to call by this name [atheists] not only those who deny all divinity, if indeed anyone so wicked can be found among men, but also those who make fun of all religion, like the deists'. In the light of this definition, it is understandable why protestant reformers were so concerned that the religious debates and divisions of their age were an open door to encouraging atheism to flourish. The final edition of Calvin's *Institutes* (1559) was concerned to the point of obsession with the problem of the 'unbelievers' (Fr: *incrédules*). Calvin was not, however, alone and the catechisms of the sixteenth century (including the Tridentine catechism – see page 252) define atheism in a way which indicates that it was a precisely conceived and apparently dangerous reality. Atheism lay, however, in the eye of the beholder, and the degree to which atheism may be said to have been a significant problem in the sixteenth century, is the subject of current scholarly debate. There was certainly what was perceived as a dangerous trend to mock the gods in writings inspired by the classical writer Lucian of Samosata (most famously represented in the works of the French

writer François Rabelais (1483–1553)). There were also trends in rationalist natural philosophy, especially prevalent in Italian scholarly circles, which tended to minimize (or even eliminate) the capacity of God to intervene in the natural laws governing his universe. The appearance of antitrinitarian views in the reformation (see pages 220–1) – which were seen by many mainstream theologians as impious – was taken as a further sign of the imminent dangers of atheism which the reformation had provoked.

9.2 Reformation colloquies

The word 'colloquy' was utilized in the sixteenth century to delineate the formal attempts to achieve religious 'concord' (*concordia*) and reconciliation of the divisions provoked by the reformation. The word 'colloquy' (*colloquium*) evoked a 'friendly meeting of minds' rather than the reality of the colloquies in sixteenth-century Europe, which generally became the moments for highlighting doctrinal division.

9.2.1 Augsburg, 1530

The discussions between leading Lutheran theologians (including Philipp Melanchthon*) and catholic theologians (including Johann Eck*) which succeeded the presentation of the Augsburg Confession[†] to the imperial diet. There was a broad measure of agreement on many of the statements in the confession and some willingness to compromise displayed by the Lutherans, but the discussions of communion 'in both kinds'[†], the doctrine of the mass[†], the marriage of priests and the problem of the alienation of monastic properties produced fundamental disagreement. The colloquy reported to the diet on the four controversial points and these were specifically held over until a general council of the church (confidently anticipated to be held shortly) was convened.

9.2.2 Hagenau/Worms/Regensburg (Lat: Ratisbona), 1540–41

The failure to assemble a general council which would address the religious problems of the Empire lay behind the efforts (at Emperor Charles V's and King Ferdinand's behest) to make progress on the points of disagreement which had emerged in 1530. In the initial meetings at Hagenau, much of the discussion was devoted to deciding whether the Augsburg Confession could still be regarded as the sole basis for negotiation. When the theologians were reconvened at Worms (Nov 1541), the protestants proposed a modified version of the Augsburg Confession (the 'Variata') as the basis for debate. Eck* and Melanchthon* were, once more, the principal spokesmen. Some progress was made in a good atmosphere and the ground prepared by the drafting of a document which would replace the Augsburg Confession as the basis for future discussions (known as the 'Book of Regensburg (Ratisbon)'). These would take place at the diet of Regensburg, which opened in April 1541. In the presence of the papal legate Gasparo Contarini*, the theologians at Regensburg agreed, or came close to agreement, on the majority of clauses in the draft document. They disagreed fundamentally, however, on the sacrament of the eucharist and the question of authority within the church. A draft document was submitted to the diet from the theologians along with some protestant counter-articles. The resolution of these remaining issues was, once more, held over to the holding of a general council.

9.2.3 Regensburg, 1546

A further colloquy was organized under the auspices of the emperor and attached to the diet of Regensburg, which opened in January 1546. It would be suspended in March without definite conclusion because of the impending Schmalkaldic War, which would bring to an end all further hope for religious reconciliation through a colloquy in Germany.

9.2.4 Poissy (September 1561)

The only substantive attempt to produce religious reconciliation in France along similar lines to those attempted in the Holy Roman Empire in the 1530s and 1540s occurred on the eve of the French civil wars at the small village of Poissy, to the west of Paris. It was convened by the Regent of France, Catherine de Médicis, governing in the place of her infant son, Charles IX. It brought together leading theologians from Geneva (especially Théodore de Bèze*) as well as (for the catholics) Charles de Lorraine, the cardinal of Lorraine and Diego Laínez, the general of the Jesuit order. The colloquy lasted for about a month but ended in failure. The conclusion of the council of Trent's† deliberations in 1563 effectively ended further attempts to seek reconciliation of the theological differences raised by the reformation by means of a colloquy.

9.3 Reformation confessions

The traditional church had utilized the Apostles', Nicene and Athanasian creeds as the statements of its fundamental beliefs, with specific issues of disagreement being occasionally resolved by councils of the church. One of the most distinctive novelties of the protestant reformation was therefore the appearance of the 'confession' as a way of defining distinctive doctrines and demonstrating religious solidarity in the face of conflict. These confessions became more and more numerous, with individual towns and regions developing their own confessional statements and requiring their clergy and people to adhere to them under oath of obedience. In the Holy Roman Empire, political fragmentation and the peculiar devolved nature of the religious peace of Augsburg (1555) led to a process of confessional identities being sharpened and more defined, partly because of the close proximity of religious pluralism and partly because the divisions followed those between one principality and another. Some German historians have called this process 'confessionalization' (G: *Konfessionalisierung*). Only those confessions which secured a wide degree of common currency are noted here.

9.3.1 Lutheran confessions

The Augsburg Confession (*Confessio Augustana*)
Date: June 1530 (published 1531)
Principal authors: Martin Luther*, Philipp Melanchthon* and others
Background: The confession originated with an invitation from the elector of Saxony to his protestant theologians to summarize their doctrines with references to Scripture for the forthcoming diet[†] at Augsburg (see page 61). The resulting document became known as the *Torgau Articles* and it formed the seven chapters of the second part of the confession. The first part was an expansion of the 15 Articles which Luther had drawn up after the colloquy at Marburg (see page 232) on 5 October 1529. It provided a documented statement of the chief articles of faith as well as a reasoned statement of the abuses in the catholic church which had to be abolished. It became the principal Lutheran confession and was widely adopted in the first two generations of the reformation.

Formula of Concord (*Formula Concordiae*)
Date: 1577 (subscribed); 25 June 1580 (published on the fiftieth anniversary of the Augsburg Confession)
Background: This confession brought to an end several decades of controvesy within the Lutheran movement after Luther's death. The orthodox ('gnesio') Lutheran theologians were based at the universities of Magdeburg and Jena. Their adversaries, the 'Philippists' or synergistic and crypto-Calvinists, drew on theologians at the universities of Wittenberg and Leipzig for their leadership. The issues raised by the adiaphoristic controversy[†] were eventually resolved by the Formula of Concord which aimed to produce an agreed statement of doctrine (*corpus doctrinae*) for all Lutherans. Laid out in 13 articles which concentrated on the various issues under dispute, the Formula of Concord became a basis around which Lutherans could unite in opposition to Calvinists and the radical reformation groups in the Empire. Some Lutheran states (e.g. Sweden) never formally gave their allegiance to it.

9.3.2 Reformed confessions

The Confession to Charles V (*Ad Carolum Romanum imperatorem Germaniae . . . Fidei Huldrychi Zwinglii Ratio*)
Date: 1530
Author: Huldrych Zwingli
Background: Zwingli wrote this confession to present to the diet of Augsburg in 1530. It provided a clear statement of Zwingli's views on the Lord's Supper, predestination, original sin, the church, and the sacraments. It was not accepted at the diet but it influenced other reformed confessions at a later date.

Tetrapolitan Confession (*Confessio Tetrapolitana*)
Date: 9 July 1530
Authors: Wolfgang Capito, Martin Bucer* and Caspar Hedio for the cities of Strasbourg, Konstanz, Memmingen and Lindau
Background: Various imperial cities in southern Germany sought to prepare arguments in writing in defence of their respective beliefs at the diet of Augsburg in 1530 (see page 61). Although the statement was not accepted by the diet, and although the four cities went on to adopt the Augsburg Confession[†] in the following year, the articles of the Tetrapolitan Confession continued to be of significance for its formulations of doctrine on the Lord's Supper and on images.

The First Confession of Basel (*Confessio Fidei Basiliensis Prior*)
Date: 1534
Author: Johannes Oecolampadius*
Background: A short formula of confession prepared for the city and designed to offer some compromise in the growing divide between Luther and Zwingli. Proposed in September 1531, it was subsequently revised in 1532 and published in 1534 by the government of Basel with an introduction by the mayor of the city. It was typical of many civic confessions of faith and influenced Calvin when he came to draw up the confession for the city of Geneva.

The First Helvetic Confession (*Confessio Helvetica prior . . .*)
Date: 1536
Authors: Heinrich Bullinger* and others
Background: This is the first Reformed confession which was drawn up to serve all the protestant cantons of Switzerland. Its 26 articles offered a weaker formulation of Zwinglian views on the eucharist[†].

The Genevan Confession
Date: 1536
Authors: Guillaume Farel* and Jean Calvin*

Background: Short confession which followed the internal pattern of the Augsburg Confession by beginning with fundamental theological definitions and then dealing with matters of dispute with catholics. It did not have as great an impact as the Genevan catechism of 1541.

The Zürich Consensus (*Consensus Tigurinus*)
Date: 1549
Authors: Jean Calvin* and Heinrich Bullinger*
Background: A common confession between Zürich and Geneva, drawn up after lengthy preliminary exchanges and delicate negotiations between Heinrich Bullinger and Jean Calvin. Its 26 propositions offered an agreed compromise formula on the doctrine of the eucharist and other disputed issues, and it was subsequently adopted by other churches in Switzerland. Bern, however, refused to sign it. The confession has often been seen as of significance in marking the coalescence of the Zwinglian and Calvinist reformations.

The Hungarian Confession (*Confessio Czengerina*)
Date: 1557
Authors: Various
Background: A Reformed Hungarian confession, framed at the synod in Czenger. The confession was replaced by the Heidelberg Catechism and then by the Second Helvetic Confession, which were adopted in 1567.

The Gallican Confession (*Confessio Fidei Gallicana*)
Date: 1559
Authors: Jean Calvin; Antoine de la Roche Chandieu (1534–91), and possibly others
Background: The confession agreed at the first national synod of the French protestants in May 1559. It was based on a draft sent by Calvin and then altered and expanded by the synod. The confession and its preface were presented to the French king in 1560 and to the colloquy at Poissy in 1561. It existed in two versions, a shorter one in 35 articles and a longer one in 40 articles (the latter being designated the 'true confession' in 1571).

The Belgic Confession (*Confessio Belgica*)
Date: 1561 (French); 1562 (Dutch)
Author: Gui de Brès* and others
Background: This confession was drawn up in imitation of the Gallican Confession and largely followed its conceptual framework, albeit without some of its more polemic elements. It was composed in 37 articles and was presented (in vain) to Philip II in 1562. It was formally adopted later by the synods of Antwerp (1566), Dort (1574), Middelburg (1581), Veere (1610), and again by the synod of Dort (in April 1619).

The Second Helvetic Confession (*Confessio Helvetica Posterior*)
Date: March 1566
Author: Heinrich Bullinger and others
Background: A confession written to provide a clear exposition of Reformed faith for the elector palatine, Friedrich III, who arranged for its publication in Latin and German. A French translation was also published and, in due course, this became one of the best-known and highly regarded confessions from the Reformed (Calvinist) tradition of protestantism. It was laid out in 30 chapters.

The Bohemian Confession (*Confessio Bohemica*)
Date: 1575
Background: A confession drafted to present to the Bohemian estates at Prague and then to Emperor Maximilian II. It was composed of 25 articles and a preface to the emperor. Although often categorized as a 'Reformed' (Calvinist) confession, it was based on the Augsburg Confession[†] with the article on the eucharist altered to conform to the views later expressed by Melanchthon.

The Canons of Dordrecht
The 93 canonical statements drawn up at the closing session of the Synod of Dordrecht (Dort) in May 1619 which confirmed the doctrinal statements in the Belgic and Heidelberg Confessions and reflected the articles agreed at the synod the previous month confirming a strict Calvinist interpretation of questions of predestination and grace.

9.3.3 Other confessions

The Form of Profession of the orthodox catholic faith (*Forma professionis ortodoxae fidei catolicae*)
Date: 1564
Authors: A group of cardinals who drew up the document which was then issued by Pope Pius IV in two separate papal bulls.
Background: A summary of the conclusions of the council of Trent[†] on the major controversial theological questions posed by the reformation.

The 'Schleitheim Confession'
Date: 1527
Author: Michael Sattler*
Background: Although often referred to as a 'confession', that word is not used in it. Entitled the 'Brotherly Union of a Number of the Children of God Concerning Seven Articles', it stated a number of specific matters of fundamental belief which set the anabaptists apart from the 'papists and antipapists'. It was never officially adopted as a statement of anabaptist

faith, and did not seek to set out (even if that had been possible) the full range of their doctrines.

9.4 Catechisms

The term 'catechism' was derived from the Greek 'to instruct'. It was applied by the protestant reformers to books of instruction in the faith which were extensively utilized to teach the elements of the faith to the unlearned or the young. These were extremely numerous. Only the more renowned (and more theologically demanding) catechisms have been noted here.

Great Catechism (Ger: *Grosser Catechismus*)
Prepared by Martin Luther after his visitations of Saxon parishes where he recorded the prevailing ignorance. Based on the sermons he had given in 1528, it was published in 1529 and provided statements of fundamental truths which were intended as a detailed 'teaching manual' for the educated reader, fathers and pastors in their instruction of their children or congregations.

The Little Catechism (*Der Kleine Catechismus* . . .)
A shorter and simpler version of the Great Catechism for more popular usage. It was first published at Wittenberg in 1529 and would be used in schools, churches, and homes, not only in Saxony, but elsewhere in Germany during the protestant reformation. It existed in two 'tables', the first of which was intended for children and the second for adults. The latter contained a preface, morning and evening prayers and devotional exercises for the family.

The Genevan Catechism (*Catechismus Genevensis* or *Catechismus Posterior*)
This was a revision of the original confession prepared by Jean Calvin for use at Geneva in 1536. It was published in French in 1542, and in Latin in 1545. Although in question and answer format, it was a long and detailed catechism, divided into five parts (faith, the law, prayer, the word of God and the sacraments). It is difficult to believe that it was originally intended for use by anyone other than the adults who attended the Sunday catechism classes at Geneva. Although it may not have served as an elementary educational instrument, it became widely consulted by those training for the ministry and, in time, one of the basic documents of the Reformed (Calvinist) tradition.

The Heidelberg Catechism (*Der Heidelberger Catechismus*)
This catechism was prepared by a commission at the instigation of Friedrich III to produce a textbook for religious instruction in schools

and churches throughout the Rhine Palatinate. It was published in Heidelberg in 1563 and became the most widely consulted Reformed (Calvinist) catechism. It was divided into 129 questions and answers, which were (in its later editions) distributed around each of the Sundays of the year. It was thus designed as an organized and developing course in elementary protestant theology. The first Sunday dealt with 'our only consolation'. The next three Sundays were concerned with 'our misery' and so on. It drew on many of the earlier catechisms already in circulation and modified some of Calvin's specific doctrines to a certain degree. The published catechism was complemented by around 700 scriptural citations in the margin which were designed as lessons to be read alongside the service each week.

The Canisius Catechism (*Summa Doctrinae Christianae per quaestiones tradita et ad capitum rudiorum accomodata* or *Catechismus Major*)
This was the famous manual of religious instruction for use by the Jesuits devised by Peter Canisius*. It was originally published in 1555 but it was reprinted over 130 times before the end of the sixteenth century and translated into many different languages. A smaller version was produced for children in 1556 (the *Catechismus minimus*) and then (in 1559) an intermediate one for those approaching adulthood (the *Parvus catechismus*). These were often published with illustrations. In addition to the traditional questions and answers on the Apostles' Creed, the Lord's Prayer and the sacraments (divided into the Sundays of the year), the Canisius catechism also included sections on practical divinity and how to live a good Christian life.

The Roman Catechism (*Catechismus ex Decreto Concilii Tridentini . . .*)
The council of Trent[†] had recommended that a new catechism should be prepared for religious instruction in harmony with the decrees of the council. This was drafted by a council, supervised by Carlo Borromeo* and published in 1566. It was mainly intended for use in preparing parish priests and provided a systematic presentation of catholic theology for their instruction.

9.5 Eucharistic prayers

The eucharistic prayers utilized in the rites of the Lutheran, Calvinist and Roman churches in the age of the reformation are given below (only the central prayers of the eucharist have been indicated).[1]

[1] These are extracts from translations made from B. Thompson, *Liturgies of the Western Church* (Philadelphia, Westminster Press, 1961), pp. 75, 77, 85, 134–5, 153–5 by Dr Susan Hardman Moore. I am very grateful for her permission to reproduce them here.

Roman rite	Deutsche Messe, 1526	Zurich Liturgy, 1525
The celebrant, bowing low over the alter, says silently: And so, through Jesus Christ, your son, our Lord we humbly pray and beseech you, most gracious Father, to accept and bless these offerings, these oblations, these holy, unblemished, sacrificial gifts. We offer them to you in the first place for your holy Catholic Church. . . . We pray you, God, to be pleased to make this offering wholly blessed, a thing consecrated and approved, worthy of the human spirit and of your acceptance, so that it may become for us the Body and Blood of your dearly beloved Son, our Lord Christ. *He takes the host in his hand and consecrates it, saying:* He, on the days before he suffered death, took bread into his holy and worshipful hands, and lifting up his eyes to you, God, his Almighty Father in heaven; and giving	*The office and Consecration follows in this fashion:* Our Lord Jesus Christ, in the night in which he was betrayed, took bread: and when He had given thanks, He brake it and gave it to His disciples, saying: 'Take, eat; this is my Body which is given for you: do this as often as you do it, in remembrance of me'. After the same manner also, He took the cup, when He had supped, and said: 'Take and drink you all of it. This is the Cup, a new Testament in my Blood, which is shed for you for the remission of sins. Do this, as often as you drink it, in remembrance of me'. It seems to me that it would be in accord with the institution of the Lord's Supper to administer the Sacrament immediately after the consecration of the Bread, before the Cup is blessed, for both Luke and Paul	*The server says:* Dear brothers. In keeping with the observance and institution of our Lord Jesus Christ, we now desire to eat the bread and drink the cup which He has commanded us to use in commemoration, praise and thanksgiving that He suffered death for us and shed His blood to wash away our sin. Wherefore, let everyone call to mind, according to Paul's word, how much comfort, faith and assurance he has in the same Jesus Christ our Lord, let not anyone pretend to be a believer who is not, and so be guilty of our Lord's death . . . *The Lord's Prayer is said. Then the server prays as follows:* O Lord, God Almighty, who by your Spirit has brought us together into one body in the unity of faith, and has commanded that body to give you praise and thanks for your goodness and

Roman rite

thanks to you, he blessed it, broke it, and gave it to his disciples, saying: Take, all of you, and eat of this, for this is my body.

The bell is rung three times as he genuflects and shows the Sacred Host to the people and genuflects again.

He now consecrates the wine, saying:

In like manner, when he had supped, taking also this godly cup into his holy and worshipful hands, and again giving thanks to you, he blessed it, and gave it to his disciples, saying: 'Take, all of you, and drink of this for this is the chalice of my blood, of the new and everlasting covenant, a mystery of faith. It shall be shed for you and many others, so that sins may be forgiven.

He genuflects, saying:

Whenever you shall do these things, you shall do them in memory of me

He then shows the chalice to the people, genuflecting after doing so. The bell is again rung three times.

Deutsche Messe, 1526

say: He took the cup after they had supped, etc. During the distribution of the Bread the German Sanctus could be sung, or the hymn *Gott sei gelobet* (*God be praised*), or the hymn of Jan Hus *Jesus Christus unser Heiland* (*Jesus Christ our saviour*).

Then shall the Cup be blessed and administered; while the remainder of the hymns are sung, or the German *Agnus Dei* [*Lamb of God*]. Let there be a chaste and decorous order, not men and women mixed up with each other, but the women after the men ... We do not want to abolish the Elevation but retain it because it goes well with the German Sanctus and signifies that Christ has commanded us to remember Him. For as the Sacrament is elevated in a material fashion and yet Christ's body and blood are not seen in it, so he is remembered and elevated by the word

Zurich Liturgy, 1525

free gift in delivering your only begotten Son, our Lord Jesus Christ, to death for our sins. Grant that we may do the same so faithfully that we may not, by any pretence or deceit, provoke you, who are the truth, and who cannot be deceived. Grant also that we may live as purely as becomes your body, your family and your children, so that even the unbelieving may learn to recognize your name and glory. Keep us, Lord, that your name and glory may never be reviled because of our lives. O Lord, ever increase our faith, which is trust in you, who lives and reigns, God for ever and ever, Amen.

The way Christ instituted this supper. The server reads as follows:

'On the night in which He was betrayed and given up to death, Jesus took bread ...' [*from 1 Cor. 11:24–26*].

Then the designated servers carry round the unleavened bread, from

Roman rite	Deutsche Messe, 1526	Zurich Liturgy, 1525
He continues:	of the sermon and is	*which each one of the*
Calling therefore to	confessed and adored	*faithful takes a morsel*
mind the blessed	in the reception of	*or mouthful with his*
Passion of this same	the Sacrament. Yet it	*own hand, or has it*
Christ, your Son, our	is all apprehended by	*offered to him by the*
Lord, and also his	faith, for we cannot	*server . . . And when*
resurrection from the	see how Christ gives	*those with the bread*
grave, and glorious	his body and blood	*have proceeded so far*
ascension into	for us and even now	*that everyone has eaten*
heaven, we your	daily shows and offers	*his small piece, the other*
servants, Lord, and	it before God to	*servers then follow with*
with us all your holy	obtain grace for us.	*the cup, and in the*
people, offer to your		*same manner give it to*
sovereign Majesty, out		*each person to drink.*
of the gifts you have		*And all of this takes*
bestowed upon us,		*place with such honour*
a sacrifice which is		*and propriety as well*
pure, holy and		*becomes the Church of*
unblemished, the		*God and the Supper of*
sacred Bread of		*Christ. Psalm 113:1–9*
everlasting life, and		*is recited antiphonally.*
the Cup of eternal		
salvation. Deign		
to regard them		
with a favourable		
and gracious		
countenance, and to		
accept them as it		
pleased you to accept		
the offerings of your		
servant Abel the Just,		
and the sacrifice of		
our father Abraham,		
and that which your		
great priest		
Melchisedech		
sacrificed to you,		
a holy offering,		
a victim without		
blemish.		
Bowing low over the		
altar, he says:		

Roman rite	Deutsche Messe, 1526	Zurich Liturgy, 1525

Humbly we ask it of
you, God almighty.
Bid these things to
be carried by the
hands of your holy
angels up to your
altar on high, into
the presence of your
divine majesty. And
may those of us who
by taking part in the
sacrifice of this altar
have received the
Body and Blood of
your Son, be filled
with every grace and
heavenly blessing ...
*The administration to
the congregation
proceeds, after the
celebrant has
communicated. The
prayer of confession and
absolution are repeated
... The celebrant,
taking the ciborium
from the altar, holds up
a consecrated Host, and
says:*
Behold the Lamb of
God, behold him
who takes away the
sins of the world.
*He then says three
times:*
Lord, I am not
worthy that you
should enter beneath
my roof, but say only
the word and my
soul will be healed.
He then goes to give

Roman rite	Deutsche Messe, 1526	Zurich Liturgy, 1525
Holy Communion to each communicant. . . . *When all have communicated he returns to the altar and places the ciborium in the tabernacle. The congregations may now sit. Wine is poured into the chalice. The celebrant drinks it and says:* That which our mouths have taken, Lord, may we possess in purity of heart; and may the gift of the moment become for us an everlasting remedy.		

9.6 Vernacular Bibles in the age of the protestant reformation

The process of translating the Bible into the vernacular languages of Europe had begun before the protestant reformation; but it was immeasurably advanced by protestantism because of the latter's insistence upon individual access to the Scriptures as a means to salvation. No comprehensive survey of the range and variety of vernacular Bibles produced in the sixteenth century is possible here. The following represents the most significant vernacular publications of the Bible during the sixteenth century, listed by vernacular language. Only the first dates of publication are indicated and they were often reprinted and altered in later editions in ways which are not indicated here:

9.6.1 Czech

Biblij Czeská w Benátkach tisstená or Venetian Bible (1506)
Published at Venice by Pieter Liechtenstein of Cologne, it was a revised version of an earlier translation, published in 1488.

Czech Bible (1533)
Published at Námesti (Prague), it was a new translation of the Bible, based on Erasmus'* Latin version, rather than the Vulgate.

Biblj České (the 'Kralice Bible') (New Testament, 1564; and further sections thereafter)
Published at Kralice (Moravia), this was the translated Bible for the Bohemian Brethren. The New Testament was translated from the Greek by the distinguished Bible scholar Jan Blahoslav (1523–71). The translators borrowed heavily from the Antwerp Polyglot Bible of 1569–72, and also relied on various Latin commentaries.

9.6.2 Danish

Christian II's *New Testament (Nye Testamente)* (1524)
This was the first translation of the New Testament into Danish. It was published at Leipzig and based largely on Luther's German version of 1522 (with some influence from Erasmus' Latin version as well). The publication included various woodcut illustrations.

The *Christian III Bible* (The 'Danish Reformation Bible') (1550)
This full translation of the Bible was published at Copenhagen. It was based on Luther's 1545 German Bible and included woodcuts and marginalia.

9.6.3 Dutch

The Dutch Bible (1526)
Translated by Jacob van Liesveldt of Antwerp and published there, this translation was the first in Dutch ('Low German') to be based on Luther's German translations.

Den Gheheelan Bybel (The 'Authorized' Catholic Bible in Dutch) (1548)
Translated by Nicolaas van Winghe and published at Louvain, this version, based on a translation of the Vulgate, was intended to meet the enthusiasm for vernacular Bibles in the Low Countries.

The *Biestkens Bible* (*Biblia, Dat is de gheheele Heylighe Schrift* . . .) (1558)
This was the Mennonite Bible, published at Emden, and based on Luther's German Bible (in the 1554 edition).

9.6.4 French

La saincte Bible en Francoys (*The Antwerp Bible*) (1530)
The translation attributed to Jacques Lefèvre d'Etaples* and published at Antwerp by Simon de Colines. The New Testament was published in 1523 and the Old Testament in 1528. The introduction to the New

Testament was protestant in tone, but the translation followed the Vulgate with some corrections from the Greek.

The *Neuchâtel Bible* (also *La Bible de Serrières*) (1535)
This was the first authentic protestant version of the Bible in French, translated by Pierre Robert Olivétan (Fr: Louis Olivier. Lat: Olivetanus – 'midnight oil'). It was published originally by Pierre de Wingle and formed the basis for all subsequent French Bibles, including the Geneva Bibles, in the sixteenth century.

The *Louvain Bible* (1550)
A catholic translation of the Bible into French, undertaken by Nicolas de Leuze (with assistance from others) and authorized for publication by the faculty of theology of the university of Louvain. It frequently borrowed from earlier (protestant) translations.

9.6.5 German

The German Bible (1518)
A translation of the Vulgate by Johann Mentelin, published at Augsburg.

The German New Testament (1522)
Martin Luther's first published work of Bible translation (with Melanchthon's* assistance). It was published at Wittenberg in a folio edition with numerous woodcuts and wood-cut initial letters. It was substantially based on Erasmus' Latin version and associated works.

The German Old Testament (published in several parts, beginning with the Pentateuch in 1523)
Martin Luther's translation with assistance from Melanchthon and others.

The High German Lutheran Bible (1534)
The complete Bible with numerous woodcuts and marginalia in Luther's version. It was substantially revised and published in two volumes in 1539–41.

The Zürich Bible (1530)
This was the translation into Swiss-German by Zwingli* and colleagues at Zürich. It was largely based on Luther's German Bible.

9.6.6 Hungarian

The Hungarian New Testament (1541)
This was the first translation of the New Testament into Hungarian. It was undertaken by János Sylvester (H: Erdösi), a Lutheran who studied

at Wittenberg under Philipp Melanchthon*, and published at Sárvár on the estates of the evangelically inclined Count Tamás Nádasdy.

The Complete Hungarian Bible (The 'Károlyi Bible') (1590)
This became the official Hungarian protestant Bible. It was translated by Gáspár Károlyi (c. 1529–92) and published with the financial support of Sigismund Rákóczy of Transylvania.

9.6.7 Italian

Brucioli's Bible (1532)
This was the Italian translation undertaken by Antonio Brucioli (c.1495–1566) from Florence and published at Venice.

The Diodati Bible (1607)
Giovanni Diodati (1576–1649), the noted Hebrew and Greek scholar at Geneva, translated this Bible, which became the standard protestant Bible in Italian.

9.6.8 Polish

The Polish Bible (1561)
This was the first complete Bible in Polish. It was a catholic version, based on the Vulgate, and translated by the confessor to King Zygmunt II August.

The Brest Bible (Radziwiłł's Bible) (1563)
The Bible translated by Polish Calvinists including Jan Łaski and published at Brest Litovsk in the Grand Duchy of Lithuania with the financial backing of the Grand Hetman of Lithuania, Prince Nicholas Radziwiłł.

9.6.9 Spanish

The Spanish New Testament (1543)
This was an Antwerp publication of the translation by Francisco de Enzinas, based on Erasmus' Greek text. It was suppressed by the inquisition in Spain and placed on the Index in 1559 both because of its unorthodox marginalia and because Enzinas printed in capitals the verses of *Romans* 3 which were exemplary of Luther's justification by faith.

The Spanish Old Testament (Ferrara Bible) (1553)
This was a curious version of the Old Testament in Spanish, based on a translation from the Hebrew, and published by a Jewish press at Ferrara.

The Spanish New Testament (1556)
A Calvinist translation by Juan de Valdés and based on the original Greek, published at Geneva by Juan Pérez de Pineda.

The Complete Spanish Bible (The *Bear Bible*) (so called because of the woodcut device on the title-page of a bear) (1569)
The first complete Bible translated into Castilian from the original texts (albeit with borrowings from earlier editions, especially for the New Testament). It was produced by Casiodoro de Reina (Lat: Cassiodorus Reinius) (c.1520–94), a refugee Spanish priest who had converted to protestantism. It was published at Basel.

9.6.10 Swedish

The Swedish New Testament (1526)
Published at Stockholm by the royal press, this was the first Swedish translation of the New Testament. It was based on Luther's German New Testament, although Erasmus' Greek version and the Vulgate were also consulted in the preparation of the work.

The Swedish Bible (*The Gustav Vasa Bible*) (1541)
This was the first complete translation of the Bible into any Scandinavian language. Published at Uppsala, it was the work of Olaus and Laurentius Peterssen (Petri)*.

9.7 Multilingual scholarly editions of the Bible

There were numerous Latin, Greek and Hebrew editions of the Bible produced in the sixteenth century for scholarly purposes, too many to analyse here. Of particular importance, however, were the multilingual ('polyglot') Bibles with parallel or interlinear texts in the classic languages for comparative scholarly evaluation and study. Of these, the great monuments to sixteenth-century Biblical scholarship were:

The Complutensian Polyglot Bible (1514–17)
Produced by a team of scholars and published at the expense of Cardinal Francisco Jiménez de Cisneros at Alcalá, it had the Bible in its respective Hebrew, Latin (Vulgate) and Greek texts in parallel columns with a Chaldaic paraphrase added at the foot of the page for the Pentateuch. An appendix contained a Hebrew and Chaldaic vocabulary and Hebrew grammar.

The Plantin Bible (*Biblia sacra, Hebraice, Chaldaice, Graece, & Latine*)
(1569–71)
Prepared by a team of scholars, this beautiful multilingual edition
was printed by Christoffel Plantijn (Plantin) (1520?–89), the famous
Antwerp printer. It included a Chaldaic dictionary and grammar.

9.8 Protestant martyrologies

Historical martyrologies were a recognized genre from the early middle
ages. Protestant writers adapted the form to serve the purposes of jus-
tificatory apologetic. By presenting the stories of the bravery of ordinary men and women in extraordinary circumstances, the martyrologists
demonstrated the power of protestant faith. If the seeds of the true
church lay in the blood of martyrs, then the proof that the true church in
the age of the reformation lay in protestant hands was to be found in
the sufferings of their persecuted congregations. In the history of Christian persecution, too, might be found some indications of the proximity
of the coming millennium. This led both protestant and catholic historians to an intensive study of ecclesiastical history. The results of the
former appeared most notably in the *History of the Christian Church* (*Historia
Ecclesiae Christi* (Basel, 1559–74)). This huge work was prepared by a
team of Lutheran scholars led by Matthias Flacius Illyricus (1520–75)
and it presented the history of the Christian church divided up by centuries from its beginnings to 1400. It became known as the 'Centuries
of Magdeburg' and was answered in time by the catholic scholar Cesare
Baronius (1538–1607) in his *Ecclesiastical Annals* (*Annali Ecclesiastici*
(Rome, 1588–1607)).

Jean Crespin*, *The Book of Martyrs* (*Le Livre des martyrs*)
(Geneva, 1554)
The work included a brief history of the Christian church from its
beginnings, tracing the growth of papal corruption and tyranny. It then
outlined the various heretical movements of the middle ages which were
presented as antecedents to the protestant reformation. The work provided a European perspective on the protestant martyrs and included
references to events in England as well as France. Subsequent editions
of this frequently republished work brought it up to date, with events in
France up to and during the civil wars especially highlighted.

Adriaen Cornelis van Haemstede (c.1525–62), *The History and Death
of the Pious Martyrs* (*De Reschiedenisse ende den doodt der vromer
Martelaren . . .*) (1559, revised 1565)
Published at Emden, this martyrology concentrated on events in the Low
Countries and France in the 1550s. The French section was extensively

borrowed from Crespin, but the material concerning the Netherlands provides an important account of the developments in the protestant reformation there during this critical period.

The Sacrifice of the Lord (Het Offer des Heeren) (1562)
Published in either Emden or Amsterdam, this was the first anabaptist martyrology.

Ludwig Rabus, *History of the Martyrs (Historien der Martyrer . . . Darinn das Erster und Ander Buch von den Heyligen Auserwölten Gottes Zeugen, Bekennern und Martyren* (8 vols., 1554 and succeeding editions))
The early sections trace the history of true religion from the time of Adam whilst the later parts recount the history of the medieval church up to the time of Hus and the Lollards. Space is also devoted to the history of contemporary protestantism, with lengthy biographies of the chief reformers, including Luther and Zell.

Matthias Flacius Illyricus, *Catalogus Testium veritatis qui ante nostrum aetatem reclamarunt papae . . .* or *Catalogue of Witnesses to the Truth, who have cried out against the Pope before our time* (Basel, 1556)
Contains materials which were borrowed by later protestant martyrologists.

SECTION TEN

Background contexts

10.1 European population densities

10.1.1 European population densities in c.1600

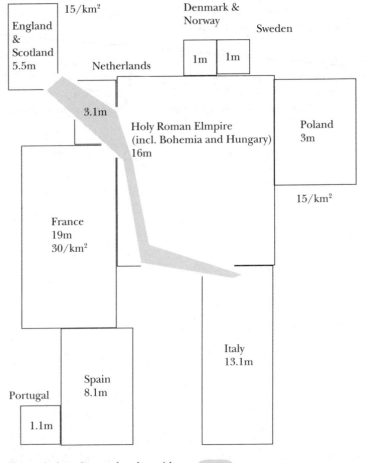

England & Scotland 5.5m — 15/km²

Netherlands — 3.1m

Denmark & Norway — 1m

Sweden — 1m

Holy Roman Elmpire (incl. Bohemia and Hungary) 16m

Poland 3m — 15/km²

France 19m 30/km²

Portugal 1.1m

Spain 8.1m

Italy 13.1m

Europe's densely-populated corridor: (over 50/km²)

10.1.2 Population of continental Europe, by territory and region (1500–1650)

Population of continental Europe (in millions)

Territory	1500	1550	1600	1650
Scandinavia	1.5	1.7	2.0	2.6
Netherlands	0.95	1.25	1.5	1.9
Belgium	1.4	1.65	1.6	2.0
Germany	12.0	14.0	16.0	12.0
France	16.4	19.0	19.0	20.0
Switzerland	0.65	0.8	1.0	1.0
Italy	10.5	11.4	13.1	11.3
Spain	6.8	7.4	8.1	7.1
Portugal	1.0	1.2	1.1	1.2
Austria (with Bohemia)	3.5	3.6	4.3	4.1
Poland	2.5	3.0	3.4	3.0

Source: Figures taken from Jan de Vries, European Urbanization, 1500–1800 (London, Methuen, 1984), table 3.6.

10.1.3 Numbers of cities by categories of size (1500–1650)

Northern European cities

Category	1500	1550	1600	1650
100,000–999,000	1	1	2	3
40,000–99,000	5	10	15	16
20,000–39,000	24	24	34	38
10,000–19,000	59	61	68	61
5,000–9,000	255	(250)	250	237
Total	344	346	369	355

Mediterranean European cities

Category	1500	1550	1600	1650
100,000–999,000	3	2	6	7
40,000–99,000	9	13	14	8
20,000–39,000	13	22	25	15
10,000–19,000	40	40	56	49
5,000–9,000	108	111	116	104
Total	173	188	217	183

Source: Figures taken from Jan de Vries, *European Urbanization, 1500–1800* (London, 1984), table 4.2.

10.2 Universities and academies

10.2.1 Europe's universities on the eve of the reformation

The majority of Europe's universities, the centres for advanced studies in theology, law and medicine, were founded in the middle ages. By 1500, there were some 78 institutions, which had increased from about 45 in 1400. In general, therefore, they were old foundations. Paris (with its famous theological faculty, the Sorbonne[†]) was established in the twelfth century. Germany, however, stood out in the growth of new universities in the fifteenth century with the creation of 12 new schools at places like Leipzig (1409), Basel (1456), Freiburg (1457), Ingolstadt (1472) and Wittenberg (1502).

During the fifteenth and sixteenth centuries, even the older foundations acquired new characteristics. In particular, university education became an important stage for anyone growing up in the upper echelons of society. The universities found no difficulty in attracting increasing numbers of the sons of Europe's nobility as well as educating its future state officials, lawyers, physicians and clergy. Moreover, their students became imbued with the humanist[†] values which gradually permeated through the faculties. Humanism was more easily accepted in the newer universities and resisted to a certain extent in the older seats of learning such as Paris, Cologne and Salamanca. Yet, by the end of the fifteenth century, the influence of the new learning in the universities was almost overwhelming. More difficult to delineate is the effects of humanism on its students and teachers; but the impact of humanist changes in social and cultural values is certainly not to be underestimated. It is not surprising that the reformation should originate in a new university town.

The buoyancy of university matriculations in the first half of the sixteenth century, despite the catastrophic disturbance during the years of the early reformation, is recorded in the following statistics for yearly attendance at German universities:[1]

1501–5	3,346
1506–10	3,687
1511–15	4,041
1516–20	3,850
1521–25	1,994
1526–30	1,135
1531–35	1,645
1536–40	2,307
1541–45	3,121
1546–50	3,455
1551–55	3,670
1556–60	4,334

10.2.2 Newly-founded Lutheran universities

Many of the Lutheran universities were, like Wittenberg, older foundations which became Lutheran in the course of the reformation. The impact of the reformation was felt in the abolition of certain faculties or parts of the curriculum. The teaching of canon law was generally abandoned. The theological textbooks (the most familiar was Peter Lombard's *Sentences*) were replaced. There were a few new foundations as well. They were almost all on German soil in the period to 1620 and were typically the result of patronage from Lutheran princes. Proud of their Lutheranism, these new foundations tended to be the focus for strictly orthodox Lutheranism and for a revived scholasticism in the second half of the sixteenth century:

Liegnitz (1526)
Marburg (1527–1606/7)
Königsberg (1544)
Jena (1558)
Helmstedt (1575)
Giessen (1607)

---

[1] Figures from Franz Eulenburg, 'Die Frequenz der deutschen Universitäten von ihrer Gründung bis zur Gegenwart', *Abhandlungen der philologisch-historischen-Klasse der königlichen sächsischen Gesellschaft der Wissenshaften* 24 (Leipzig, 1904), pp. 55 and 102–3 as presented in the *New Cambridge Modern History* vol. II (second edition) (Cambridge, Cambridge University Press, 1990), p. 471.

10.2.3 Newly-founded Calvinist universities and academies

More significant were the new foundations under Calvinist auspices. The Genevan academy, which had been envisaged many years before, finally opened its doors in 1559. It provided something of a model for such institutions, especially in Germany. Because the peace of Augsburg had excluded the Calvinists from a formal place in the Holy Roman Empire, new Calvinist institutions of higher education could not, therefore, claim university status. But older universities (e.g. Heidelberg) could become Calvinist and continue to give degrees like their Lutheran counterparts. In France, similarly, the Calvinist academies established after the pacification of Nantes (1598) did not have degree-awarding status. In the Dutch republic, however, the new foundations were symbols of the new state and given university status. They all tended to attract students from across Europe to their doors. The following were the newly-established Calvinist institutions of higher education. Those which functioned as degree-awarding universities (even if not continuously so during the period from their foundation to 1620) are indicated by (u):

Zürich (Switzerland)	(1525)	
Sárospatak (Hungary)	(1530)	
Debrecen (Hungary)	(1550)	
Geneva	(1559)	(u)
Nîmes (France)	(1562)	
Orthez (Béarn)	(1566)	
Leiden (Dutch Rep)	(1575)	(u)
Neustadt (Germany)	(1578)	
Franeker (Dutch Rep)	(1585)	(u)
Herborn (Germany)	(1584)	
Burgsteinfurt (Germany)	(1591)	
Montpellier	(1596)	
Montauban (France)	(1600)	
Sedan (Germany)	(1601)	
Die (France)	(pre-1600)	
Saumur (France)	(1604)	
Marburg (Germany)	(1606/7)	(u)
Bremen (Germany)	(1610)	
Groningen (Germany)	(1614)	(u)

10.2.4 Newly-founded catholic universities and institutions of higher education

Those institutions which functioned as degree-awarding universities (even if not continuously so during the period from their foundation to 1620) are indicated by (u):

Dillingen (Germany)	(1554)
Würzburg (Germany)	(1561/1582) (u)
Douai (Sp. Netherlands)	(1562) (u)
Braunsberg (Prussia)	(1568)
Zamość	(1574) (u)
Pont-à-Mousson (Lorraine)	(1572)
Olmütz (Bohemia)	(1576) (u)
Jilnins (Poland)	(1578)
Graz (Germany)	(1586) (u)
Paderborn (Germany)	(1614) (u)
Molsheim (Germany)	(1618) (u)
Rinteln (Germany)	(1619) (u)
Salzburg (Austria)	(1621) (u)

10.3 Printing

10.3.1 Printing centres for incunabula books in Europe, 1491–1500

Holy Roman Empire and Switzerland	76
Italian peninsula	62
France	36
Spanish peninsula	23
England and Scandinavia	9
E. Europe	7

10.3.2 Main centres for German printing in the sixteenth century[2]

	Number of printers
Cologne:	92
Nuremberg:	62
Strasbourg:	57
Basel:	54
Wittenberg:	38
Frankfurt-am-Main:	37
Augsburg:	31
Leipzig:	29
Erfurt:	28
Vienna:	22

[2] J.L. Flood, 'Le livre dans le monde germanique à l'époque de la Réforme' in Jean-François Gilmont, La Réforme et le livre. L'Europe de l'imprimé (Paris, Les Editions du cerf, 1990), pp. 29–104; table, p. 41.

10.3.3 The linguistic division of Latin and German books published at Strasbourg, 1480–1599[3]

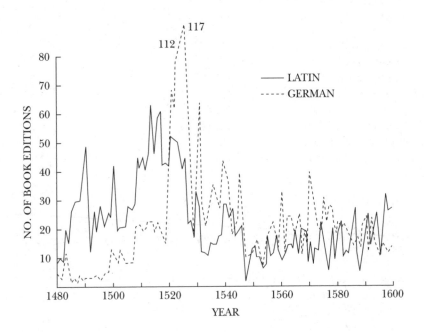

10.3.4 Lutheran printers and printing centres, 1518–29

The following statistics are based on an analysis of the editions published by or about Luther during the years from 1518 to 1529 to be found extant in the magnificent Gustav Freytag collection of sixteenth-century pamphlets in the city and university library of Frankfurt-am-Main. The unidentified printers and places of printing, as well as the partial nature of the sample, limit the significance of the evidence.[4]

Major printers used by Luther and by others publishing about him:	Number of pamphlet editions
Jörg Gastel	16
S.Grimm and M. Wirsung	12

[3] From Miriam U. Chrisman, *Lay Culture, Learned Culture: Books and Social Change in Strasbourg, 1480–1599* (New Haven, Yale University Press, 1982), figure 1.

[4] From Richard G. Cole, 'Reformation printers: unsung heroes' in *Sixteenth Century Journal* vol. xv (1984), pp. 331–2.

Johann Grünenberg	15
Jobst Gutknecht	27
Gabriel Kantz	11
Melchior Lotter	68
Hans Lufft	62
Silvan Otmar	41
Melchior Ramminger	17
Georg Rhau	32
Christian Rödinger	17
Niclaus Schirlentz	61
Wolfgang Stöckel	21
Unknown	665
Total sample:	1,065

Major printing centres for the publication of works by Luther and his friends	Number of pamphlet editions
Altenburg	18
Augsburg	140
Bamberg	10
Basel	61
Erfurt	52
Leipzig	62
Munich	17
Nuremberg	90
Strasbourg	75
Tübingen	4
Ulm	5
Wittenberg	181
Zürich	23
Zwickau	24
Unknown	473
Total sample:	1,235

10.3.5 The rise of Genevan publishing, 1536–72[5]

The following list showing the number of titles produced each year is based on extant and dated titles in the Bibliothèque Publique et Universitaire de Genève:

[5] From statistics in R.M. Kingdon, *Geneva and the Coming of the Wars of Religion in France 1555–1563* (Geneva, Dvoz, 1956), pp. 98–9; cf William Monter, *Calvin's Geneva* (New York and London, John Wiley, 1967), p. 179.

	Number of titles		Number of titles
1536	3	1555	20
1537	3	1556	19
1538	5	1557	41
1539	7	1558	28
1540	5	1559	41
1541	6	1560	38
1542	4	1561	48
1543	15	1562	35
1544	17	1563	28
1545	20	1564	28
1546	3	1565	26
1547	6	1566	34
1548	12	1567	19
1549	11	1568	20
1550	18	1569	21
1551	22	1570	19
1552	21	1571	11
1553	20	1572	12
1554	28		

10.3.6 Types of protestant religious literature published at Strasbourg (1519–60)

These percentages are based on a sample of 818 editions[6] and have been rounded up.

Anticatholic polemic	42
Protestant internal debates	8
Devotional manuals for the laity	3
Collections of hymns/popular chants	8
Protestant manuals for the clergy	8
Protestant doctrinal theology	20
Sermons	11

10.3.7 The Index of Prohibited Books

The main published indexes of prohibited books in the sixteenth century:

[6] From M.U. Chrisman, 'L'édition protestante à Strasbourg' in Jean-François Gilmont, *La Réforme et le livre. L'Europe de l'imprimé* (Paris, Les Editions du cerf, 1990), pp. 217–38, esp. p. 234.

Index of the University of Paris: 1544; 1545; 1547; 1549; 1551; 1556
Index of the University of Louvain: 1546; 1550; 1558
Index (It: *Catalogo*) of the Venetian state: 1549; 1554
Index of Milan: 1554
Index of the Portuguese Inquisition: 1547; 1551; 1559; 1561; 1564; 1581; 1597
Index of the Spanish Inquisition: 1551; 1559; 1564; 1571; 1583; 1612
Index of Liège: 1568; 1569
Index of Antwerp: 1569; 1570; 1571
Index of Rome: 1559; 1564; 1590; 1593; 1596
Index of Munich: 1569; 1582
Index of Parma: 1580

10.4 The enemies of the Christian community

10.4.1 Patterns of moral regulation

Moral regulation – what some historians have called the imposition of 'social discipline' by religious elites – predated the protestant reformation. The term social discipline may be misleading, however, for it was often as much a case of enforcing religious uniformity as social discipline. Moral enforcement also often depended upon the degree to which (and the conditions within which) local communities were prepared to accept the terms of such social discipline. The reformations of the sixteenth century generally created a heightened awareness of the significance of religious conformity. It also probably increased shared anxieties which may have fostered the desires for a greater degree of social discipline at various levels of society. The categorization of moral offences is, however, inevitably imprecise. The following figures, which indicate the regional differentiation in the enforcement of religious and moral conformity, should be used with that imprecision in mind:

Religious and moral enforcement in the consistory courts of the Rhine Palatinate and in southern French consistory courts around 1600

Category of offence	France				Palatinate		
	Montauban (%)	Castelmoron (%)	Meyrueis (%)	Cardaillac (%)	Bacharach (%)	Neckarelz (%)	Germersheim (%)
Religious conformity	23.0	27.0	21.5	47.0	22.0	47.5	67.0
Refusal to attend church services	2.6	1.1	1	12.3	7.2	15.6	22.7
Blasphemy	2.4	1.1	2.1	10.9	5.9	10.2	19.0
Sunday observance	0.9	0	9.6	0	1.4	4.1	7.6
Consorting with catholics	9.4	10.9	2.1	2.7	1.3	0.8	1.0
Magical practices	1.2	0	1.0	0	1.4	2.4	1.0
Obedience towards parents	1.1	6.5	2.1	0	4.2	2.0	0
Family dissension	5.8	4.3	5.5	0	0	0	0
Marital problems	2.1	4.5	1.0	4.0	12.9	11.0	5.3
Verbal or physical violence	26.5	34.0	55.9	23.2	6.7	2.0	0
Drunk and disorderly; frequenting taverns	1.4	0	1.0	0	8.1	3.2	1.0
Gambling	3.6	2.1	0	4.1	0	0	0
Extra-marital sex	7.5	5.4	7.5	15.0	5.1	0.8	4.2
Dancing	14.1	2.1	5.3	0	0	0	0

Source: J. Estèbe and B. Vogler, 'La genèse d'une société protestante: étude comparée de quelques registres consistoriaux languedociens et palatins vers 1600', *Annales E.S.C.* vol. 36 (1976), pp. 362–88.

Numbers represent % of total cases for each consistory court. Not all cases are categorized, whilst others may be cited in several categories. The percentages are therefore not intended to add up to 100% but to provide a comparative perspective across different communities of the varying significance attached to particular offences.

Moral regulation in the city of Emden: two samples

Category of offence investigated	1558–62 (%)	1596–1600 (%)
Offences against religion and the ecclesiastical ordinances	27.6	14.0
Offences against local ordinances	5.2	2.6
Cases involving marriage, family and educational matters	7.4	12.3
Sexual misdemeanours	8.0	8.8
Anti-social behaviour	26.9	51.8
Cases involving household dissension	12.3	5.3
Capital offences	1.2	1.8
Cases involving accepted social conventions and honour	2.3	0
Cases of self-censure of the consistory court	3.4	0
Unspecified	5.6	3.5

Source: Heinz Schilling, 'Sündenzucht und frühneuzeitliche Sozialdisziplinierung. Die calvinistische presbyteriale Kirchenzucht in Emden vom 16. bis 19. Jahrhundert' in Georg Schmidt (ed.), *Stände und Gesellschaft im alten Reich* (Stuttgart, Franz Steiner Verlag, 1989), pp. 265–302.
The above statistics are based on a lengthy investigation of the cases of moral regulation which came before the ecclesiastical and civil authorities of Emden, an important city for the reformation in northern Germany. Figures shown represent percentages for the sample years in question.

Moral regulation in Geneva: a sample from the consistory court records, 1542, 1546, 1550

Category of offence	1542		1546		1550	
	Number	(%)	Number	(%)	Number	(%)
Interpersonal disputes	98	(30.7)	170	(40.5)	238	(40.3)
Public disputes	8	(2.4)	40	(9.5)	66	(11.2)
Morality violations	52	(16.3)	144	(34.3)	188	(32.0)
Religious irregularities	161	(50.2)	58	(13.8)	86	(14.6)
Others	1	(0.3)	8	(1.9)	6	(1.0)

Source: From William G. Naphy, *Calvin and the Consolidation of the Genevan Reformation* (Manchester and New York, Manchester University Press, 1994), table 14, p. 109.

Moral regulation in Italy: the sample of the Venetian inquisition

Offences	1547–85		1586–1630	
	Number of defendants	% total	Number of defendants	% total
Heresy and suspected heresy	960	(78.1)	252	(30.9)
Prohibited books	93	(7.6)	48	(5.9)
Prohibited meats	23	(1.2)	12	(1.5)
Blasphemy	17	(1.3)	41	(5.0)
Abuse of the sacraments and illegal celebration of the mass	11	(0.9)	16	(2.0)
Sexual misdemeanours	21	(1.7)	46	(5.6)
Magic	59	(4.8)	319	(39.1)
Offences against the Holy Office	10	(0.8)	8	(1.0)
False witness	14	(1.1)	7	(0.9)
Others	21	(1.7)	67	(8.2)
Total	1,229		816	

Source: Details from E. William Monter and John Tedeschi, 'Towards a statistical profile of the Italian Inquisitions, sixteenth to eighteenth centuries' in Gustav Henningsen and John Tedeschi (eds), *The Inquisition in Early Modern Europe* (Dekalb, Illinois, Northern Illinois University Press, 1986), appendix 1, p. 144.
The above table details the number of defendants for the period indicated and not the number of trials. Several trials involved more than one individual. The cases are listed by the primary charges for which these individuals are asked to answer.

10.4.2 Witchcraft

The offence of witchcraft (sorcery, or *maleficium*) was conceived of and punished before the reformation but its repression became a matter of major concern in Europe mainly in the century of sectarian tension after the reformation (1560–1660). The notion of a pact between the devil and a witch (*pactum diabolicum*) only gradually coalesced during the later medieval period. It was accepted particularly by lawyers and judges for whom it lessened the difficult problems of judicial proof within witchcraft trials. A number of treatises on demonology further highlighted the potential dangers of the crime, which became increasingly prosecuted before secular as well as ecclesiastical courts in the sixteenth century. Protestant reformers accepted the possibility and reality of witchcraft. The protestant reformation's stress upon the active providence of God in the world may well have heightened the fears of the equally active intervention of the Devil on this earth. It is equally likely that the protestant reformation removed various remedies which had been available to ordinary people through the cults and religious practices of the pre-reformation church. They may thus unwittingly have created an increased recourse to magical remedies. Many supposed witches died in local witch-hunting 'crazes' where an individual case sparked off a cluster of other indictments. The possible explanations for these events, and for the broader phenomenon of increased witchcraft prosecution, have been increasingly closely examined by European historians. The resulting research has taught us a great deal, especially about the elements of social dysfunctionality within local communities, but it has also left us with a number of unanswered questions.

Approximate estimates of numbers of individuals tried for witchcraft in the period 1500–1700[7]:

Holy Roman Empire:	50,000
Poland:	15,000
Switzerland:	9,000
French-speaking Europe:	10,000
Spanish and Italian peninsulas:	10,000
Scandinavia	4,000
Hungary, Transylvania, the Balkans and Russia:	4,000

Regional execution rates in witchcraft trials:

Region	Dates	Persons tried (fates known)	Executions	% Executed
Freiburg	1607–1683	162	53	33
Geneva	1537–1662	318	68	21
Neuchâtel	1568–1677	341	214	63
Pays de Vaud	1537–1630	102	90	90
Luxemburg	1509–1687	547	358	69
County of Namur	1509–1646	270	144	54
Guernsey	1563–1634	78	33	46
Dunkirk region	1542–1679	187	90	48

Source: Brian P. Levack, *The Witch-Hunt in Early Modern Europe* (Harlow and New York, Longman, 1994), p. 20 (table 1).

[7] Estimates from Brian P. Levack, *The Witch-Hunt in Early Modern Europe*, 2nd edition (Harlow and New York, Longman, 1994), pp. 20–1.

Regional chronologies of witchcraft

The following are the totals for those investigated for witchcraft in the stated localities or regions:

	Geneva	Estonia*	Norway
pre-1540	5	2	—
1541–50	13	5	—
1551–60	9	0	0
1561–70	83	0	4
1571–80	14	0	25
1581–90	5	7	17
1591–1600	24	11	16
1601–10	49	6	21
1611–20	57	22	73

Source: The sources for this table are contained in E. William Monter, *Witchcraft in France and Switzerland* (Ithaca and London, Cornell University Press, 1976), appendix one, pp. 208–15 and Bengt Ankarloo and Gustav Henningsen (eds), *Early Modern European Witchcraft* (Oxford, Clarendon Press, 1990), pp. 267 and 371.
* The Estonia figures are calculated to a marginally different decennial pattern (1520–29: 1530–39: 1540–49 etc) and have not been altered for the purposes of this table.

10.5 Europe's wider horizons

10.5.1 Ottoman sultans, 1512–1617

	Regnal dates
Selīm I	1512–20
Sulaimān I (The Magnificent)	1520–66
Selīm II	1566–74
Murād III	1574–95
Mehemmed III	1595–1603
Ahmed I	1603–17

10.5.2 The Turkish threat in the Mediterranean

(For the Turkish threat in Hungary, see pages 156–7.)

1528   Capture of Algiers by the Knights of Malta (see page 24) and the establishment of a Christian garrison at Tripoli. The community of corsairs (privateers or *Ar'tāife*) at Algiers became the allies of the Ottomans under the leader Khair ad-Dīn (d.1546), who became the Ottoman naval commander in the Mediterranean.

1534   Capture of Tunis by the Ottomans.

1535   Turkish fleet active in the Adriatic and attacked Corfu.

1538   Naval defeat by the Ottomans of the joint naval forces of Emperor Charles V, the pope and Venice at Prevesa (by the gulf of Arta) on 28 Sep. Ottoman naval supremacy secured in much of the eastern Mediterranean.

1541   Emperor Charles V launched an armada against Algiers which was defeated by storms.

1543   Khair ad-Dīn seized and burnt the town of Reggio in Calabria, off the Italian coast and captured Nice.

1551   Tripoli captured from the Knights of Malta by the Ottomans under their naval commander Torghūd Re'īs. Ottomans began to establish elements of naval supremacy in the western Mediterranean.

1560   Ottomans seized the island of Djerba; Philip II ordered the construction of a much enlarged Mediterranean fleet.

1565   Ottomans launched a naval expedition to besiege Malta; despite hard fighting, they were forced to withdraw.

1570   Cyprus fell to an Ottoman invasion; the conjoined naval forces of King Philip II of Spain, the papacy and Venice were unable to act swiftly enough to prevent the fall of the island.

1571   The battle of Lepanto (off the coast of Greece) (7 Oct); the Christian fleet under the united command of Don John of Austria almost completely destroyed the Ottoman fleet. Cyprus remained in Ottoman hands but Tunis was briefly captured by Don John (Oct 1573).

1574   Ottomans recaptured Tunis (July) and reinforced the corsair communities there, and at Tripoli and Algiers. They would remain the key threat to Christian Europe in the western Mediterranean in the early seventeenth century.

10.6 Christian missions in the age of discovery

10.6.1 Christian missions and the Spanish New World

The discovery of America, followed by the conquest of central and south America, created a vast domain for conversion and assimilation into European Christianity. It led to a considerable extension of the institutions of the traditional church. It also generated debates about the status of the subject peoples and the process of missionary endeavour. One of the great theorists of the latter was the Jesuit José de Acosta*.

1492   Christopher Columbus (1451–1506) discovered America, which he imagined to be a part of Asia, and thus called the 'West Indies'.

1493   Papal decision (bull[†]: *Inter Caetera Eximiae Devotionis*) (3–4 May) which recognized Spanish rights to the newly discovered regions and drew a demarcation line between the Spanish and Portuguese New World 100 leagues west of the Azores and the Cape Verde Islands. All lands to the west of the line were to lie within the patronage (Sp: *padronado*) of Spain. In return for recognizing Spanish rights, the papacy imposed an obligation upon the Spanish crown of promoting the spread of Christianity in the new lands.

1494   Treaty of Tordesillas; extended the line about 270 leagues further to the west – which enabled the Portuguese to lay claim to Brazil in due course.

1500   First Franciscan mission to the Caribbean.

1508   By the papal bull (*Universalis Ecclesiae*) Pope Julius II granted the Spanish crown rights to found dioceses in the New World and to nominate all benefice-holders, including bishops.

1509/10   First Dominican mission to the Caribbean; beginnings of Dominican concern to protect the Indians, especially through Bartolomé de Las Casas (1474–1566), who became a Dominican in 1522. He denounced the abusive treatment of the Indian population in the conquest of the New World and was instrumental in securing legislation from the Spanish crown for their protection.

1513   Vasco Nuñez de Balboa (1475–1517) crossed the Panama isthmus to reach the Pacific ocean.

1519–21   Hernando Cortés (1485–1546) dismantled the Aztec empire in central America by force.

1532–36   Conquest of Peru by Francisco Pizarro (1475–1540).

1536   Conquest of Colombia by Quesada.
         First college of higher education in Mexico.

1539   Dominicans concentrate missionary work in Peru; creation of Dominican province there.

1555   Council of Mexico refused orders (see page 5) to Indians and half-castes.

1568   First Jesuit activity in Peru.

The Reductions (Sp: *Reducciones*)

A particular feature of South American missionary activity was the establishment of villages where Christianized Indians lived, segregated from European immigrants, under the authority of missionaries. These were Indians who had been 'reduced' to Christian obedience, as opposed to the larger numbers of natives who remained untouched by it. Although they were by no means the only missionaries to utilize the arrangement, the Jesuits became best known for it by their Reductions in the dense forests of the Pampas and the Gran Chaco of Paraguay. These were undertaken with the approval of the Spanish crown, which granted the Jesuits the mandate for the Paraná territory. The Jesuits began to carry it out systematically in around 1610.

Establishment of dioceses in the Spanish Americas, 1500–1620
(Archdioceses are indicated in bold.)

Caribbean

Puerto Rico	1511
Santo Domingo	1511 (**1547**)
Concepción de la Vega	
(Santo Domingo)	1512–27
Santiago de Cuba (Cuba)	1518

Central America

Panama	1513
Taxcala (Mexico)	1519
Mexico City	1530 (**1547**)
Guatemala	1530
Antequera	1535
Michoacán	1536
Chiapa	1539
Guadalajara	1548
Yucatán	1561
Durango	1620

South America

Coro	1531
Cuzco	1537
Lima	1541 (**1547**)
Popayán	1546
Quito	1546
La Plata	1552 (**1609**)
Arequipa	1556
Santiago de Chile	1559
Concepción	1561/1603
Santa Fé de Bogotá	1564
Trujillo	1577
Santa Cruz de la Sierra	1605
Huamanga	1611
Buenos Aires	1617

Missions to the Spanish Philippines

The Philippines came to have a unique place within the history of European Christian missions overseas in the sixteenth century. Firstly, the native Philippino population practised a religion based on local animist cults which put up no resistance to Christian evangelism. Secondly, because Philippine discovery was rather later than that of the Americas the missionaries had learnt lessons from their experiences and mistakes which they were able to put into practice. Thirdly, because commercial activity with Europe on any scale was impossible the practical pressures towards slavery and forced labour of the natives were removed. The missionaries proclaimed themselves the 'protectors' of the Indians and were able to shield them more effectively than anywhere else in colonized overseas empires from the excesses of the colonizers. The effects created the largest success for overseas missions anywhere in the sixteenth century.

1569	Spain took possession of the Philippine islands.
1571	Foundation of Manila.
1575–78	Arrival of missionaries: (Augustinians, 1575; Franciscans, 1577; Dominicans, 1578).
1579	Foundation of the bishopric of Manila.

Estimated numbers of conversions of the Philippino population in the sixteenth century:

1585	400,000
1595	700,000
1620	2,000,000

10.6.2 Missions under Portuguese patronage

Unlike the Spanish overseas empire, the first overseas empire of the Portuguese in the Far East encountered powerful, advanced civilizations with well-established religious belief-systems, buttressed by their institutional and social fabrics. It was not possible to undertake substantial colonization, but merely to establish trading posts around factories and forts. The commercial instincts predominating in these trading posts made the preaching of the missionaries ring hollow. Missionary endeavour could create a Christian minority, but it could not create a Christianized population; when it was tried, the ecclesiastical authorities in Europe suspected those involved of accepting too readily the native religions and cultures which they encountered.

1498	Vasco da Gama (c.1468–1524) reached India via the Cape of Good Hope.

1500 Pedro Alvares Cabral (1460–1526) discovered Brazil.
Pope Alexander VI subjected the region from the Cape of Good Hope to the Indies to the authority of an apostolic delegate (in the bull *Cum sicut maiestas*) (March).

1511 Goa was established as the capital of the Portuguese Far East and the sea-routes to the Moluccas ('spice islands') came mainly in to Portuguese hands.

1514 Leo X granted (in the bull *Dum fidei constantiam*) the Portuguese the rights to nominate to all sees, churches and benefices (July).

1541 Francis Xavier* was nominated by Paul III as 'legate' for the Indies and left Lisbon for Goa.

The establishment of bishoprics in the Portuguese overseas empire
(Archbishoprics are indicated in bold.)

Funchal (Madeira)	1514 (**1534**)
Santiago de Cabo Verde (Cape Verde Island)	1534
São Tomé (Guinea)	1534
Sã Salvador de Agra (India)	1534
Goa (India)	1534 (**1557**)
Cochin (India)	1557
Malacca (Malaya)	1557
Macao (China)	1576
Funai (Japan)	1588
Angamale (**Cranganur** from 1609) (India)	1600 (**1608**)
Mailapur (India)	1606

10.6.3 Christian mission to Japan

The success of the Japanese mission in the half-century to 1620 should not be underestimated because of the subsequent persecution. The latter culminated in the Shimabara Revolt of 1637–38 and the closure of Japan to European influence thereafter. Missionary endeavour was undertaken in the sixteenth century without the support of the Portuguese state and despite the localization of power within a partially dissolved Japanese state. It was the first moment on a systematic basis in which European missionaries abandoned their normal methods of spreading the faith. Instead they sought a substantial degree of accommodation (in so far as it was possible) with local religious concepts and accepted social practices. This led to internal conflicts, especially within the Jesuit order which was at the forefront of the Japanese missionary effort.

1542–43 Discovery of Japan by the Portuguese.
1548–49 First Portuguese expedition; Francis Xavier* arrived (1549–51).

1563   First Japanese local ruler (Daimyo) baptized.

1587   First imperial order (on the instructions of Tokugawa (regent) Hideyoshi) to expel all missionaries; order not carried out, but further conversions had to be carried out with discretion.

1597   First mass martyrdoms of Christians and missionaries at Nagasaki (Feb).

1603   Beginnings of apostasy amongst Japanese Daimyos.

1613–14 Imperial decrees against Christians, and ordering the banishment of Europeans.

Jesuit 'visitors' to Japan
Francis Xavier
Cosmas de Torres
Francisco Cabral
Alessandro Valignano

Estimated size of Christian congregations in Japan
1551   1,000
1570   20–30,000
1580   150,000
1600   210,000

10.6.4 Christian mission to China

As with Japan, the Christian mission to China took place without significant involvement from the Portuguese state and under the leadership of the Jesuits. The platform for these efforts was laid, however, when the Portuguese acquired the Gozan peninsula from the Chinese and founded the city of Macao in 1554. It proved extremely difficult to gain access to imperial China. Once there, however, the Jesuits appreciated the significance of appealing to established imperial authority and accommodating as many of the local customs and as much of the belief-system within Christianity as possible. This led to even sharper internal debates than those raised by the Japanese mission.

Jesuit missionaries to China (dates of first appearance in China)
Francis Xavier* (1552)
Michele Ruggieri and Matteo Ricci (1583)

Estimated size of Christian congregation in China
1605   200 (Nan-ch'ing and Beijing)
1608   2,500 (Nan-ch'ing, Beijing and Shanghai)
1615   5,000 (Nan-ch'ing, Beijing and Shanghai)

SECTION ELEVEN

Biographies

The following are not complete biographies of the individuals mentioned. The brief entries provide a conspectus of the person's significance within the protestant reformation and an outline of the highlights of a particular career. Those canonized by the catholic church are only indicated as such if the canonization took place within the period 1500–1630.

Acosta José de (1540–1600): The Spanish Jesuit missionary who spent 17 years in Peru from 1570 to 1587 studying Indian languages and culture. When he returned to Spain he published his great work on missionary endeavour, *On securing the salvation of the Indians* (*De procuranda Indorum salute*) (1588) and the debate which it aroused led to his imprisonment (1592–93). But he was released in due course and became head of a college at the university of Salamanca. His great survey of the natural history of Spanish America was published in 1590, a testimony to Jesuit precocity in scientific enquiry.

Aleandro Girolamo (Lat: *Aleander*) (1480–1542): An able Italian humanist of Venetian origins, who was a famous Sorbonne theologian before becoming a papal diplomat and cardinal. In his earlier life, he knew and appreciated the works of Erasmus. In 1519, he was invited by Pope Leo X* to be papal librarian and charged with a number of significant papal missions. These included being sent to Germany to enforce the bull against Luther in 1520 and appearing as his opponent at the diet of Worms in 1521 (see page 57). Aleandro was principally responsible for the text of the edict of Worms which the diet agreed to in May 1521. Thereafter his various missions involved combating protestant heresy, whether as nuncio† in Venice (1533–35) or Vienna (1538). He became archbishop of Brindisi (1524) and a cardinal (1538).

Andreae Laurentius (Sw: *Lars Andersson*) (c.1470–1552): Swedish protestant reformer and statesman. He was archdeacon at Strägnäs and assumed responsibility for the diocese after the execution of its bishop in 1520. He was a supporter of the proclamation of Gustav Vasa's kingship of Sweden in 1523 and became the royal secretary. Along with Olaus Peterssen* he was responsible for all the religious reformation of Sweden in the 1520s and 1530s. His vision of the reformed church was of a lay institution, which was not subservient to the state. The church belonged to the local congregation and the latter should have rights to administer its wealth after the reformation. But he was arrested and sentenced to death in 1540 for opposing excessive royal power in the church. The sentence was not carried out and he lived out the remainder of his life in retirement at Strägnäs.

Arminius Jacobus (D: *Jacob Hermanszoon*) (1559–1609): A controversial Dutch protestant theologian. He studied at the great Calvinist academies of Utrecht, Leiden, Geneva and Basel before returning to Amsterdam in 1588 to be ordained minister. His criticism of the prevailing Dutch Calvinist notions of predestination[†] led to his gaining notoriety and his supporters secured his election to the university of Leiden in 1603 (see page 143). After his death, his supporters in the Netherlands upheld his views and were attacked as theologically unsound and politically suspect. The dispute culminated in the synod of Dort. They became known as 'Arminians' (see page 221).

Béda Noël (c.1470–1537): A leading figure in the Sorbonne and a strong early adversary of the protestant reformation. He attacked Erasmus and other Christian humanists whose exegetical methods he regarded as dangerous to church unity. He regarded them as laying the foundations upon which Luther would build. He organized the condemnation of Erasmus by the university of Paris in 1528 and orchestrated the campaign which led to the execution of Louis de Berquin* for heresy in 1529. It was partly through his influence that the internal divisions of the Sorbonne[†] were gradually surmounted and the faculty became the guardian of religious orthodoxy.

Bellarmino Roberto (Eng: *Robert Bellarmine*) (1542–1621): A cardinal and counter-reformed theologian and controversialist. Originally from Tuscany and with a maternal uncle as a pope (Pope Marcellus II), Bellarmine became a Jesuit, studying at the Roman College, Padua, and finally Louvain, where he studied protestant doctrines of grace and free will, published a compact Hebrew grammar, and engaged in theological controversy. In 1576, he returned to the Roman College to take up a new chair in controversial theology. His lectures there formed the basis for his great refutation of protestant theology, the *Controversies* (*Disputationes de controversiis Christianae fidei . . .*) which appeared during the years from 1586 to 1593. Bellarmine became involved in many theological issues. He revised the Sixtus V Latin Bible for Clement VIII (see page 224) and produced two very popular catechisms. He was elected a cardinal in 1599 against his wishes and made bishop of the remote Italian diocese of Capua in 1602. He went to reside there and became a model counter-reformed bishop. In his last years, he served on the inquisition in Rome and personally told Galileo Galilei (1564–1642) in 1616 of the inquisition's decision forbidding him to teach that the earth revolved around the sun.

Berquin Louis de (c.1490–1529): A French humanist who initially enjoyed the protection of François I and his sister Marguerite*. He was known for translating various shorter writings of Erasmus and suspected of favouring the protestant reformation. The suspicions were confirmed when books by Luther, Melanchthon* and Karlstadt* were found by the *parlement* of Paris in 1523 along with Berquin's translations of them on the shelves of his library. His translations were condemned by the Sorbonne† and he was imprisoned, only being released after the king's intervention. He was arrested once more in 1526 on a charge of heresy and, although he managed to frustrate the judges for a few years, he was eventually sentenced to death and burned at the stake on 17 April 1529.

Bérulle Pierre de (1575–1629): Cardinal, theologian, diplomat and leading figure of the counter-reformation in early seventeenth-century France. He was born in Champagne, was ordained priest in 1599, and directed his efforts towards spiritual guidance and the processes of conversion. His efforts to establish the reformed Carmelites in France and to found the French congregation of the Oratory (1611) incurred opposition from, amongst others, the Jesuits and the secular clergy. His spiritual writings, amongst which the most famous was the *Grandeurs of Jesus* (*Grandeurs de Jésus*) (1623), reflected the characteristic tone to the French catholic reformation of the earlier seventeenth century.

Bèze Théodore de (Lat: *Beza*) (1519–1605): The leading French Calvinist theologian and scholar of his day and Calvin's colleague (and later successor) at Geneva. He was originally from Burgundy and educated in law at the university of Orléans. He took up refuge in Geneva in 1548 and was condemned by the *parlement* of Paris and burned in effigy in 1550. After a period of teaching at Lausanne he returned to Geneva in 1559 to be the rector to the new Geneva academy (see page 268). In 1561, he represented the Huguenots at the colloquy of Poissy (see page 246). After Calvin's death he became his biographer and successor in Geneva. His enormous surviving correspondence provides a record of the fortunes of the Calvinist churches in Europe. His new Latin translation of the New Testament (1556) and the famous critical edition of the Greek New Testament (1565) were enduring monuments to his biblical scholarship.

Biel Gabriel (c.1420–95): A medieval theologian who influenced Luther. Educated at Heidelberg, Erfurt and Cologne, Biel joined the Brethren of the Common Life[†] before being involved in the foundation of the university at Tübingen. He was a nominalist[†] in the tradition of William of Ockham*. His works included a commentary on the *Sentences* of Peter Lombard, the standard medieval theology textbook, and an exposition of the canon of the mass. Both were available in printed editions before the protestant reformation.

Bockelson Jan (Jan van Leyden) (1509–36): The 'king' of anabaptist Münster. He was the son of a village notable from near Leiden and became a journeyman tailor who spent some time as an apprentice in England before marrying the widow of a ship-proprietor. He was influenced by the Melchiorites in the Netherlands and then met up with Jan Matthys*, and spent some time in his house in November 1533. It was at this date that he received his new baptism and was commissioned as an 'apostle'. Arriving in Münster in mid-January 1534, he acted as Matthys' lieutenant before becoming the acknowledged and charismatic leader of the revolt. He was captured alive after its disintegration. The bishop had him extensively interrogated and displayed before he was publicly tortured to death in Münster on 22 January 1536. The bodies of Bockelson and two associates executed with him were displayed in cages suspended from the tower of the church; the cages are still to be seen there.

Bolsec Jérome (c.1524–84): A French physician from Paris who became a protestant in the late 1540s and a consultant to one of Calvin's friends who lived just outside Geneva. Bolsec voiced his objections to Calvin's theology of predestination[†] in October 1551 and was imprisoned and put on trial for heresy. Although he received some support in letters from neighbouring cantons (especially Bern) he was found guilty and exiled for life from Geneva on 23 December 1551. He disagreed profoundly with the burning of Servetus and criticized the Bernese authorities for supporting that decision. He eventually returned to catholicism and published an influential but highly prejudiced account of Calvin's life.

Borromeo (Saint) Carlo (1538–84): Archbishop of Milan, cardinal and leading figure in counter-reformed Italy. Born the younger son of an Italian noble from the region near Lake Maggiore, he studied at the university of Pavia before becoming a secretary to his uncle, Pope Pius IV, a cardinal and archbishop of Milan. As a cardinal-nephew he was a conscientious secretary, involved in the concluding sessions of the council of Trent, and wrote the new Roman catechism (see page 252). After Pius V's death in 1565, he concentrated his efforts on implementing Tridentine changes in his archdiocese of Milan. His visitations (see pages 216–17) generated considerable local hostility but he persevered. He was canonized in 1610.

Brandenburg Albrecht von (1490–1545): Archbishop of Magdeburg (1513) and Mainz (1514), elector of the Holy Roman Empire, and close relative of the electors of Brandenburg. In return for acquiring these sees, Albrecht agreed to give Pope Leo X* 24,000 ducats, part of which he expected to recoup from the sale of papal indulgences in the Magdeburg archdiocese. It was these sales, organized by Johann Tetzel*, which led Luther to send the letter to Albrecht in which he enclosed his 95 theses in October 1517. The archbishop took over two years to reply to it. He was an admirer of Erasmus and a great patron of the arts. In the early years of the reformation he remained neutral and only after 1525 did he join the anti-Lutheran leagues (see page 87). He was made a cardinal in 1518.

Brant Sebastian (1457–1520): A humanist poet, best known as the author of the *Ship of Fools* (*Das Narrenschiff* (1494)), which satirized contemporary social failings in vernacular German with the underlying message that true wisdom is not to be found on this earth.

Brenz Johannes (1499–1570): Lutheran reformer at the imperial city of Schwäbisch-Hall in the critical years of the reformation (1522–48) and then the distinctive protestant theologian in the duchy of Württemberg. Initially an Erasmian enthusiast, he was won over to Luther's opinions whilst a student at the university of Heidelberg in 1518, where he was a student of Johannes Oecolampadius*. He played a substantial role in a wide range of theological treatises in defining (alongside Philipp Melanchthon*) Lutheranism. He was particularly influential in shaping its ecclesiastical institutions. His church ordinances for the duchy of Württemberg in 1559 provided a widely-admired model for the organization of the Lutheran church polity in Germany.

Brès Gui de (?–1567): Protestant preacher in the French-speaking (Walloon) Netherlands and the author (or one of the authors) of the Belgic Confession (see page 249). He was a painter (on glass) from Mons who converted to protestantism in the 1540s and became prominent in organizing the churches 'under the cross' in the Southern Netherlands on the French border. By 1559 he had become pastor of the leading congregation in the Southern Netherlands at Tournai and was active in trying to restrain the headier elements from foolhardy demonstrations or rebellion. During the first revolt of the Netherlands he was preacher at Valenciennes and succeeded in persuading the authorities not to invite the French Huguenots to come to its aid during the siege of the city. He was executed for his pains when it eventually surrendered to the Habsburg besiegers.

Briçonnet Guillaume (c.1470–1534): Guillaume Briçonnet was from a family of senior officers to the French monarchy. His father had been a distinguished French cardinal. He received a humanist education in Paris from Josse Clichtove*, from whom he learnt to appreciate the works of Jacques Lefèvre d'Etaples*. Whilst entering royal service, he also became abbot of the wealthy Paris abbey of St Germain (in 1507) and (in 1515) bishop of Meaux, a diocese not far from Paris. He used his positions in royal service and in the church to become a patron of French humanists and turned his bishopric into a focal point for reforming endeavours. He became the confidant of Marguerite d'Angoulême* and a distinctive (but not unique) reforming figure in the French church. However, his position became compromised and his influence waned with the dispersal of the Meaux group in the later 1520s.

Bucer Martin (G: *Butzer*) (1491–1551): The distinctive and important Strasbourg protestant reformer. Like Johannes Brenz who was almost his exact contemporary there, Bucer was influenced first by Erasmus and then by Luther during his student days at the university of Heidelberg in 1517–18. Exploiting the diverse influences in the crossroad city of Rhineland Strasbourg (where he arrived in 1523), Bucer absorbed protestant theological influences from other sources besides Luther (especially Zwingli* and Oecolampadius*). His theology developed from a sense of the divine order which had been destroyed at the Fall. Humanity yearns for that divine order which can only be satisfied in the crucified Christ. Christ's life and death demonstrate to us the profound order which God offers us, and which we glimpse in the mutual support and creative challenges of Christian community. Within such a rightly ordered community, there are those empowered to encourage this process of support and edification and others who are at the beginning of their spiritual journey towards the divine order. His theology was expressed in a series of biblical commentaries which originated in lectures in the cathedral at Strasbourg in the later 1520s, as well as in his treatise *On the kingdom of Christ* (*de regno Christi*).

After the colloquy of Marburg in 1529 (see page 232), Bucer became more prominent through his attempts to broker a theological compromise over protestant divisions concerning the eucharist. One of his earliest, and unsuccessful, efforts was the *Tetrapolitan Confession* which he submitted to the diet of Augsburg in 1530 (see page 248). At the same time he was called on to organize the protestant churches in various towns, especially in and around the upper Rhineland. His attempts to recover protestant unity in the 1530s were mirrored by efforts to draft a book of concord which would serve as a the basis for wider reconciliation at the time of the colloquy of Regensburg in 1541 (see page 246). However the threat to the independence of Strasbourg led him to oppose the Augsburg Interim of 1548 and to seek exile in England in 1549, where he was appointed regius professor of divinity at Cambridge and where he died.

Bullinger Heinrich (1504–75): Swiss protestant reformer and successor to Zwingli at Zürich. He stabilized the Zürich reformation following Zwingli's death in 1531, gaining a reputation as a hugely prolific writer, preacher and correspondent. He was the driving force behind the First Helvetic Confession of 1536 which was designed to secure the adherence of all the protestant cantons of Switzerland (see page 248). His most influential publications were his considerable collections of sermons as well as his treatise on the covenant[†] (*De testamento seu foedere Dei unico et aeterno*) of 1534, the first major protestant treatment of the subject. He also wrote the first history of the Zwinglian reformation, whose traditions he saw himself as embodying. Calvin and Bullinger struggled to overcome their differences of approach over the eucharist[†], predestination[†] and other issues. They were eventually able to agree to the Consensus Tigurinus of 1549, which is generally taken to mark the overall coalescence between the Zwinglian and Calvinist traditions of the protestant reformation (see page 249).

Burckhardt Georg – see Spalatinus, Georgius

Cajakob Georg ('Blaurock') (c.1492–1529): A student at Leipzig and a priest before 1523. He appeared in Zürich in 1525 where his distinctive blue coat earned him the name '*Blaurock*'. He was clearly an active enthusiast, frequently arrested by the Zürich authorities before being flogged and expelled in early January 1527. He continued to act as a missionary zealot in Bern and in the Tyrol, exploiting the embers of discontent left by the Peasants' War before being burned at the stake at Clausen, Austria on 6 Sep 1529.

Cajetan (Cardinal) (It: *Tommaso Gaetano de Vio*) (1469–1534): Theologian and general of the Dominican order (1508–18). Born at Gaeta in Italy (hence his name), he taught at the universities of Padua, Pavia and Rome and became one of the most versatile of papal apologists. In 1511, he defended papal supremacy before the council at Pisa and, in 1517, he was created cardinal by Leo X*. He was sent as a papal legate to Germany where he encountered Luther at Augsburg (see page 51).

He was a prolific biblical scholar and Thomist (a supporter of St Thomas Aquinas) philosopher. He supported a measure of internal reform in the church but lost his influence within the church towards the end of his life.

Calvin Jean (1509–64): French protestant theologian. Born at Noyon, north-east of Paris, he studied at Paris and possibly Orléans before publishing his first work, a Latin commentary on Seneca's *On Clemency* (*De Clementia*) in 1532, a testimony to his humanist education and training (see page 172). The Affair of the Placards (see page 117) forced him into exile to Basel (1535) where the first edition of his *Institution of the Christian Religion* appeared in March 1536 (see page 173). On his way through the city of Geneva in July 1536, Calvin accepted the invitation of Guillaume Farel* to stay on there as a preacher and professor of theology. His efforts to shape the reformation there led, however, to his being ordered to leave in 1538. He retired to Strasbourg where he became the leader of the French exiled congregation and a friend of Martin Bucer*. Changes in the government of Geneva led to Calvin being invited to return to the city in September 1541. The remaining years in Geneva saw Calvin gradually fashion the Genevan reformation and develop its (and his) reputation as leading the reformation in the generation after Luther's death (see section seven).

Canisius Peter (D: *Peter Kanijs*) (1521–97): The noted Jesuit preacher, theologian and controversialist. He was educated at the university of Cologne before joining the Jesuits. He undertook the *Spiritual Exercises* in 1541 and became the first Jesuit in Germany. He taught at the university of Ingolstadt before becoming a superior at Augsburg during the period of rapid Jesuit expansion in south Germany. He enjoyed the support of the emperor and the dukes of Bavaria in the assistance he provided to the foundation of Jesuit colleges at Augsburg, Ingolstadt, Mainz and elsewhere in southern Germany. It was also at the instigation of the emperor that Canisius wrote his famous catechism, initially published in 1555 (see page 252). His preaching missions were extensive and many thousands of pages of his sermon notes are still extant.

Capito Wolfgang (1478–1541): The German protestant reformer. Educated at Freiburg, Capito initially fell under the influence of Erasmus before moving to Strasbourg, where he led the reformation until he was overshadowed by Bucer towards 1530. They collaborated in the preparation of the *Tetrapolitan Confession* (see page 248) which reflected his own willingness to act as a mediator in the emerging theological differences in the reformation.

Carafa, Gian Pietro   see **Paul IV**

Castellio Sebastianus (1515–63): Castellio was a protestant reformer, born near Geneva, who met Calvin in Strasbourg in 1540 and accompanied him to Geneva. Disagreeing with him over predestination, he left in 1544 for Basel where he eventually was appointed to a professorship in Greek. He published a complete French translation of the Bible and a Latin Bible with critical annotations (1551). But he was best known for his powerfully argued critique against the burning of Servetus at Geneva, published in 1554 (*De haereticis*).

Clement VIII (Pope) (*Ippolito Aldobrandini*) (1536–1605): Pope from 1592. He rose gently through the Roman curia in the Rota and Datary after his education in law at the universities of Padua, Perugia and Bologna. He earned the favour of Pope Sixtus V*, not least for the delicacy of his negotiations in Poland as legate in 1588–89 when he defused a dispute between the Polish king and the Habsburgs. He was a candidate for the succession in all three elections of 1590–91 before finally securing enough Spanish votes to succeed in 1592. His spirituality was much influenced by Philip Neri*, whom he appointed as one of his spiritual advisors. He continued to press forward reforms within the church as laid out at the council of Trent†, especially in the reform of religious houses and his efforts were certainly felt in Rome (see page 215). The revised Vulgate of 1592 (the 'Clementine edition') as well as a new breviary (1602) and missal (1604) were testimony to his desire to encapsulate the reform efforts within the church. He similarly encouraged the severity of the inquisition. The Italian libertine philosopher Giordano Bruno (1548–1600) was amongst over 30 heretics who were condemned to the stake in his pontificate. In international politics, he reluctantly accepted the conversion of the French king, Henri IV (1593) and the pacification of Nantes (1598). His greatest diplomatic achievement was to assist in brokering the peace between France and Spain at Vervins in 1598.

Clichtove Josse (van) (c.1472–1543): A Flemish humanist and critic of corruptions in the church. Although Flemish by origin, Clichtove spent most of his life in Paris where he mixed with the Christian humanists at the university. He became the disciple, and then the collaborator, of Jacques Lefèvre d'Etaples*. He was also called upon to participate in the reforming endeavours of various bishops in the French church, especially Briçonnet*, and campaigned for the reform of the clergy. His treatise *On the Life and Morals of the Priesthood* (1519) would have its impact in due course on various individuals called to the early sessions of the council of Trent†. His vision of the priest was as an individual apart from the world, dedicated to the holy, and an ascetic. The reform of the church depended on the fostering of this vision. He defended himself and Lefèvre from the charge of being fomenters of heresy but, when he discovered how widely Lutheranism was spreading in his native Flanders, he turned to oppose Luther, publishing his *Antiluther* (*Antilutherus*) in 1525 and other works which defended the institutional and ritual fabric of the established church.

Coligny Gaspard II de (1519–72): Political leader of the French protestants (Huguenots[†]). He was a member of the Châtillon family and, after a successful military career in the 1540s, was given the title *amiral de France* in 1552. Shortly afterwards he became inclined to protestantism and assisted the ill-fated attempt to establish a Huguenot colony at Rio de Janeiro in Brazil in 1555 led by Nicolas Durand de Villegaignon (1510–71). He became one of the military high command for the Huguenots in the early civil wars and, after the death of Condé in 1562, their overall commander. He successfully extracted concessions from the French crown for the protestants at the edict of St Germain in 1570 (see page 119) but was wounded in Paris on 22 August 1572. Two days later he was murdered at the beginning of the massacre of St Bartholomew. The responsibility for the initial assassination attempt has never been conclusively assigned, and, although it is clear that the servants of the Guises carried out the later murder, the underlying reasons for the massacre of St Bartholomew go very much deeper.

Condé Louis I (de Bourbon), prince de (1530–69): Noble leader of the French protestants (Huguenots[†]) in the early civil wars. He was a prince of the blood who enjoyed extensive estates in Picardy and Brie, thanks to his marriage in 1551 to the wealthy heiress Eléonore de Roye. He emerged as the leader of the political and military wing of France's protestants in the wake of the conspiracy of Amboise (1560). Condé knew about the plot in advance and was arrested and tried for treason. It was only the death of the young king François II that saved him from execution. Thereafter he organized protestant meetings at court, extracted the concession of an edict of toleration and, as France descended into open civil war, led the Huguenot military forces. He masterminded a further attempt to seize the king in September 1567 which began further military hostilities. He was killed at the battle of Jarnac in March 1569.

Contarini Gaspara (1483–1542): Member of the Venetian ruling oligarchy whose humanist education and close friendship with like-minded patricians at Venice put him at the centre of a group of humanist laymen and clergy with concerns for the reform of the church as a personal crusade and institutional objective. In the 1530s, he sought to win the Lutherans back to the church by sweet reasonableness. He deployed his humanist learning in defence of papal authority and this doubtless helped towards his appointment as a cardinal by Paul III* on 21 May 1535. He brought to the church his Christian humanist credentials, his leadership, his practical governing experience and his commitment to reform. All of these components made their appearance in the *Consilium de emendanda ecclesia* (1537), a critique of the contemporary church which he largely wrote (see page 199). He supported the foundation of the Jesuit order and, shortly before his death, attempted to reconcile the German Lutherans with his church at the colloquy of Regensburg (see page 246).

Cranach Lucas (1472–1553): The German painter and engraver, known as 'the Elder' to distinguish him from his son. He was court painter to the electors of Saxony at Wittenberg, which was where he met and painted Luther and produced numerous etchings and woodcuts.

Crespin Jean (c.1520–72): French protestant publicist and martyrologist. Born at Arras, he studied law and practised in Paris before retiring for religious reasons to Strasbourg (in 1545) and thence to Geneva (in 1548). There he established his printing press and devoted his energies to promoting protestantism in France (see page 262).

Dantyszek Jan (Lat: *Johannes Dantiscanus*) (1485–1548): Polish humanist and Erasmian. Jan Dantyszek was the son of a merchant from Gdańsk (hence his Latin name). He studied law and theology at Kracôw, and became a royal secretary and diplomat to the Polish King Zygmunt I. His literary interests drew him towards an enduring admiration for Erasmus and he became one of the most prominent Erasmians in Poland during Erasmus' own lifetime. He appears never to have been attracted by the protestant reformation.

Denck Hans (c.1500–27): Anabaptist leader. Hans Denck was a well-educated humanist who had been influenced by the Erasmian circle at Basel before coming into contact with the intoxicating ideas of Karlstadt* and Müntzer*. He was expelled from Nuremberg in January 1525 during the Peasants' War for his uncomfortable views and thereafter he wandered between the cities of south Germany, writing and reacting to the early persecution of anabaptists. His many writings reveal traces of the medieval mystics, especially Johannes Tauler. Scriptural truth and the sacraments serve only to strengthen the truth inwardly revealed by the spirit. For that revelation to take place, we must be obedient to God's law and be ready to be filled with God's spirit. He thus disputed Luther's denial of free will, his assertion of the bondage of the will, and his reliance on the primacy of the Scriptures for faith. Denck's writings became the most fruitful and drawn-on lineages of radical spiritualist anabaptism in the reformation.

Dévay Mátyás Bíro (c.1500–45): Hungarian protestant reformer. He was a Magyar, born in Transylvania, who joined the Franciscans before becoming influenced by Luther whilst a student at Wittenberg (1529–30). He returned to Hungary where he spread the new ideas, despite repeated harassment and occasional imprisonment. He was protected by protestant-inclined members of the Hungarian nobility and lived to see the conferences at Oradea Mare and Debrecen which established the Hungarian protestant churches. By that date, however, he was engaged in controversy over his interpretation of the 'Real Presence' in the eucharist+. By then his theological formulations, always independent, had matured towards those of Melanchthon* or even the Swiss reformers. He was an able preacher and an important writer of Hungarian prose.

Eck Johann (1486–1543): Catholic theologian and controversialist – Luther's most gifted opponent. He was professor at the university of Ingolstadt (from 1510) and had humanist credentials. But Luther's attack on indulgences[†] led to his confronting him in the public disputation at Leipzig in June 1519. In 1520, he was appointed a papal legate to Germany and was sent to despatch the bull excommunicating Luther (*Exsurge Domine*). He continued to write in defence of papal supremacy and against the reformation in the 1520s and was invited by Emperor Charles V to provide a refutation of the Augsburg Confession of 1530.

Erasmus Desiderius (1466–1536): The great Christian humanist of the early sixteenth century. His life as a wandering scholar brought together many diverse novel elements within late medieval Christianity which, on their own, would remain of only limited impact but which, briefly and precariously, he was able brilliantly to fashion into a powerful amalgam. He was born an illegitimate child in Rotterdam and sent to live with and be educated by the Brethren of the Common Life[†] at Deventer. In 1487, he entered the religious life with the Augustinian canons at Steyn, a vocation which he later strongly rejected. In 1485, he went to the university of Paris to study theology and, once more, he found much to criticize in the scholastic theology which he encountered there. In 1499, he embarked on what would become a lifetime of study and travel which would put him in direct contact with Italian humanism and various heterodox currents within contemporary Christendom. These he gradually reflected in writings and publications which became the best-sellers amongst the commonwealth of letters of his day (see pages 34–5). Of the need for reform, Erasmus left no doubt. His witty and effective satires against a worldly and corrupt church and an ineffective monasticism first earned him his audience. The remedy he proposed for Christendom was the 'philosophy of Christ' (*philosophia Christi*). The term was a conscious adaptation of the late medieval mystic 'imitation of Christ' to suggest an implicit love of the wisdom to be found in the Word of God (once it had been shorn of its scholastic excrescences and made widely accessible). Erasmus had a great belief in the power of the Word incarnate to transform the lives of individuals and, through them, of society at large. It reflected his commitment to the significance of education, and his conviction that it was a force through which all could be made new.

Erasmus' success was at its height on the eve of the Luther affair. But it earned him numerous critics. As the Lutheran affair took root in Germany, he was also attacked by protestants. His most significant debate, however, was with Luther himself. Luther had openly acknowledged his debts to Erasmus during his early controversy with Rome and Erasmus defended Luther's right to be heard. But, by 1520, Erasmus blamed Luther (in a letter which he intended to be widely read in Germany) 'for making everything public and giving even shoemakers a share in what is normally dealt with by scholars as mysteries reserved for the initiated'. When Erasmus finally entered into open debate with Luther, however, it was in 1524 and over the important issue of the freedom of the will. The issue was a central one for Erasmus, who argued that an individual did not have the authority to advocate his views against the consensus of Christendom and thereby to create damaging dissension which would ensure that the philosophy of Christ could not set to work. By the time of his death at Basel in 1536, Erasmus had been discredited among many on both sides of the reformation and his works would end up on the Roman Index.

Estienne Robert (1503–59): French printer, classical scholar and Erasmian. He produced famous editions of the Bible in Latin (1528; 1532; 1540), of the Old Testament in Hebrew (1539–41; 1544–46), and the New Testament in Greek (1550–51). He had the support of the French king François I but his biblical publications led him into conflict with the *parlements.* He moved to Geneva in 1551 and set up his printing press there, publishing many of Calvin's works.

Farel Guillaume (1489–1565): The authentic voice of early French protestantism and the early collaborator of Calvin at Geneva. He studied at Paris with Jacques Lefèvre d'Etaples* before becoming part of the Meaux circle around Guillaume Briçonnet*. Apparently dissatisfied with the pace of change there he moved to Basel where he met Erasmus. It is a sign of Farel's impatience for change that he developed an antipathy for the latter and moved on around the Rhineland. At Montbéliard he declared himself ordained and celebrated communion. At Strasbourg he met Bucer* and other reformers. His journeys took him on evangelical missions to the Vaud in 1527 (part of the Swiss canton of Bern at this date) and thence to Geneva. During his first visit there in 1532, he faced popular violence and was fortunate to escape with his life. His second visit in June 1535 coincided with the decisive steps towards the reformation in the city (see page 100). He invited Calvin to remain and help him in the task in 1536. They collaborated in drafting the *Ecclesiastical Ordinances* and the *Genevan Confession* but the opposition they faced was so great that they were ordered to leave the city in 1538. Farel went to Neuchâtel where he remained pastor until his death. His published writings were almost all in French and consisted of expositions of protestantism adapted for the evangelical communities which were in the process of coalescing in France in the later 1520s and early 1530s. The best known was his *The Lord's Prayer* (*Pater Noster*), a commentary cast in the form of a prayer with a translation of part of Luther's commentary on the Apostles' Creed.

Friedrich III 'the Wise' (Elector) (1463–1525): Luther's princely protector. His own religious inclinations were conventional and serious. In 1493, seven years after he assumed the electorate, he undertook a pilgrimage to the Holy Land in order to add to his relic collection. He founded the new university at Wittenberg in 1502 and was instrumental in inviting Luther to teach there. He continued to protect Luther despite the latter's excommunication and the imperial ban issued against him. In 1523, he even dismantled his relic collection. Luther's contacts with him were mainly through the agency of the elector's secretary, Georg Spalatin*.

Froben Johann (c.1460–1527): Humanist printer at Basel and friend of Erasmus, who published many of his works, including his *New Testament* of 1516. He set new standards for the printed book. He employed the best humanist talent in Germany to prepare works for publication. Beatus Rhenanus (1485–1547) and Wolfgang Capito* proof-read his Latin texts whilst Konrad Pellicanus* prepared Greek texts. His editions of the writings of St Jerome and St Augustine became the standard editions used by the protestant reformers.

Gerson Jean (le Charlier de) (1363–1429): Chancellor of Notre Dame de Paris and the university of Paris and great figure in pre-reformation attempts to reform the church. He attended the council of Konstanz[†], asserting its jurisdictional supremacy over the pope and affirming the rights of doctors of theology to have a voice in its proceedings along with the bishops. He also drew up the famous 'Four Articles' of Konstanz, which became the foundation-stone for Gallicanism[†]. He was dedicated to the reform of the church 'in head and limbs'[†] as a means to eliminate schism and heresy. In numerous writings, many of which had been printed at Basel, Strasbourg and Cologne by the time of the Luther affair, he provided theoretical justifications for conciliar theory (especially *On the Power of the Church* (*De potestate ecclesiae*), 1417). Theologically, he belonged to the nominalist school which was influential at the Sorbonne†. He also wrote a large number of treatises reflecting a mystical approach to spiritual life, especially *The Mountain of Contemplation* (1397), *Mystical Theology* (*Considerationes de Mystica Theologia*) and *The Perfection of the Heart* (*De perfectione cordis*). His writings were highly regarded by Luther in his formative years.

Giberti Gian Matteo (1495–1543): Catholic reformer and bishop of Verona. His origins were Genoese and mercantile. He studied at the university of Bologna and used the favour of Pope Leo X* to become the secretary and friend of Cardinal Giulio de Medici. At Rome, he made his mark as an early reformer by insisting that cardinals wear clerical dress and shave off their beards. He was made bishop of Verona in 1524 and his leadership of the pro-French faction at the curia in the years before the Sack of Rome (1527) ruined any chances of his becoming a cardinal. He retired to his diocese and in time turned it into an exemplary model of what might be achieved to reform the clergy and reinvigorate spiritual life. He attracted to his service able collaborators, conducted pastoral visitations in person, established a printing press and visited convents and monasteries in his diocese. His appointment to the commission to produce a blueprint for church reform in 1536 was a recognition of his success (see page 199).

Glait Oswald (var: Glaidt) (1490–1546): A Franciscan monk who became one of the earliest evangelical Lutheran preachers in Austria in the early 1520s. Expelled from Austria in 1525, he retired to Moravia and was attracted to the anabaptists by Balthasar Hubmaier* in 1526. The following year he was preaching the anabaptist cause in Liegnitz, Silesia, which was where he prepared his treatise *On the Sabbath*, the first protestant defence of sabbatarianism†. His argument for the Sabbath was based in part on the patterns of world time from the Creation to the Second Coming. He continued to preach on the significance of Sabbath-day observance when he returned to Moravia, with a significant effect on the lifestyle of Moravian anabaptism. He was arrested, tortured and executed by orders of a court in Vienna in 1546.

Góis Damaio de (1502–74): Portuguese humanist who became a close friend to Erasmus. He was brought up in the service of the royal court of King Manoel I. A good many of his formative experiences were as a diplomat, commercial agent and then scholar in residence in various locations in Europe. He returned to Portugal in 1548 to become the keeper of the royal archives and to write the official history of King Manoel. In 1571, however, he was arrested and imprisoned by the inquisition and died in disgrace.

Grebel Konrad (c.1497–1526): Called by Zwingli the 'ringleader' of the Zürich radicals. He had initially supported Zwingli and joined his group studying Erasmus' Greek New Testament in 1522. By October 1523 he was disillusioned with the pace of change. In 1524, he was in touch with Thomas Müntzer* and Karlstadt* and shared their reductionist vision of a church made up solely of the godly. Infant baptism[†] was, by September 1524, seen by him as a sign of the godless old church. Although he was responsible for rebaptizing Blaurock in January 1525, he never deliberately left the church at Zürich and may not have seen himself as establishing a separate 'sect'.

Gregory XIII (Pope) (*Ugo Buoncompagni*) (1502–85): Pope from 1572. Like so many of the counter-reformed popes, he was trained as a lawyer. After studying and teaching at the university of Bologna, he entered the service of Pope Paul IV*. He took part in the closing sessions of the council of Trent[†], shortly after which he was made a cardinal. His election to the pontificate in 1572 owed much to the support of the Spanish for his candidacy. In international affairs, his pro-Spanish background compromised him in the eyes of many and weakened his effectiveness. His efforts to coordinate military efforts against the Turks in the Mediterranean were largely unsuccessful. So too were his measures against England's Elizabeth I. His support for the reforming measures outlined at Trent (and, in addition, his encouragement for the Jesuits) would prove, however, to be more long-lasting.

Gregory of Rimini (d.1358): A philosopher and Augustinian monk. He studied in Paris, Bologna, Padua and Perugia, eventually being elected a general of the Augustinian order. His philosophical teachings reflected the nominalism of William of Ockham and took it still further. He argued that whatever man achieved (works) would remain sinful without God's grace and that unbaptized children incurred eternal damnation (earning him the title 'the infant torturer' (*tortor infantium*)). His work on the *Sentences* of Peter Lombard was published at Paris in 1482 and variously thereafter before the reformation.

Haller Berthold (1492–1536): Swiss reformer at Bern. He was educated at conservative Cologne but became an adherent of Zwingli at Zürich and unilaterally refused to celebrate the mass at Bern where he was a city priest. By the late 1520s, Haller was the recognized leader of the reformation in Bern, a noted anabaptist antagonist and sacramentarian[†] city reformer.

Hätzer Ludwig (c.1500–29): Not strictly an anabaptist, although he was expelled from Zürich in January 1525 along with the anabaptists. He was a university-trained chaplain to whom the Zwinglian reformation opened the door to a refreshing individualist and spiritualist perception of religious change. Active in Zürich, Konstanz, Basel and Strasbourg, he translated the books of the prophets into German and expressed mystical and antitrinitarian[†] views. He was executed for adultery at Konstanz on 4 Feb 1529.

Hofmann Melchior (1495?–1543): A furrier and lay preacher in Estonia and Latvia, Hofmann was an enthusiastic evangelist of the reformation in the Baltic cities of the Hansa whose ideas did not always conform with Luther's. He was expelled from Livonia (1526), Sweden (1526), Lübeck (c.1527) and the duchy of Holstein (1529), before finding a home in the combustible radicalism of Strasbourg in the early 1530s where he converted to anabaptism and fell in with the visionary prophetesses, Barbara Rebstock and Ursula Jost. Their predictions of the last days became his. His public advertising of the coming millennium[†] led to his arrest and imprisonment in April 1530. His writings, however, were smuggled out of prison and, in print, found their audience in the Rhineland and the Low Countries. In due course, he too escaped and undertook successful missions to Emden and Amsterdam (where he undertook mass rebaptisms). He had already announced in 1526 that he expected the world to come to an end in 1533 and this became the predominant theme of his pamphlets in these years. He returned several times to Strasbourg and was arrested there in 1533 on the grounds (not entirely justified) that he had threatened civil rebellion. He died in prison there in 1543. His followers ('Melchiorites'), anticipating the coming millennium, were initially incited to rebellion by Hofmann's intoxicating message (Jan Bockelson*) and then later diverted into inward spiritual quest (Obbe Philips*).

Hubmaier Balthasar (c.1485–1528): Early anabaptist leader. He was born near Augsburg and, unlike many of the anabaptist leaders, had a formal education, studying for a time under Johann Eck*. Attracted by Zwingli's teaching, he went to Zürich in 1523 but joined the radical brethren soon after, becoming a preacher to the rural community of Waldshut in Austria. It was there that he probably drafted the famous demands of the peasants (as well as approving a set of ordinances) which circulated very widely. After the Peasants' War, he returned to Zürich but found that his life was in danger and joined other anabaptists in emigrating to Moravia. There he settled at Nikolsburg (Cz: *Mikulov*) and attracted a sizeable following; but he was eventually arrested by the Habsburg authorities and condemned and burnt at the stake in Vienna. In his later writings, Hubmaier developed his ideas on baptism[†], the eucharist[†], the ban[†], free will and the sword. He made use of his formal education to construct a coherent theology which explained why infant baptism was idolatry[†] and portrayed adult baptism as the beginning of a lifetime process in the regeneration of the soul. He believed in an established church and, unlike many anabaptists, argued for the legitimacy of governing authorities. In his last treatise *On the Sword* (*Von dem Schwert*) he regarded rebaptized Christians as the only humans properly qualified for the post of magistrate.

Hut Hans (c.1490–1528): A sexton and clerk by trade, Hans Hut was born in southern Germany (Haina) and lived in the Würzburg region. He was much influenced by the writings of Karlstadt*, Denck* and Müntzer*, and took part in the battle of Frankenhausen at the climax of the Great Peasants' War. Much of his own apocalyptic writing derived its force from the reading and experience of the two years 1524–25. He preached that the end of the world would come soon (1528) and that (adult) baptism was a way by which the elect would be 'sealed' ready for the end-time. Beyond this baptism, he saw little need for further elaborate organization, since the end-time was close. The elect[†] would know, however, who they were because, for them, the order of creation had already begun to be overturned. The elect would already see themselves as part of suffering, serving humanity through their suffering since, through it, the world would be purified. The world did come to an end for Hut in 1528; he died as a result of smoke poisoning in an attempt to escape from jail in Augsburg on 6 December.

Hutten Ulrich von (1488–1523): An imperial knight from Franconia whose humanism inspired him to publicize the Lutheran reformation. His education, like his subsequent travels, was extensive (especially in Italy). His friends included Erasmus* and Reuchlin*. Hutten placed his considerable polemic skills at the service of Luther after 1519 and turned to writing in German. The bull of excommunication against Luther also named von Hutten. Protected by the leader of the so-called Knights' War, Franz von Sickingen, he continued his somewhat impetuous support until the collapse of that movement and the death of his protector made him flee to Basel and then to Zürich, where he died.

Jansen Cornelis Otto (Lat: *Cornelius Jansenius*) (1585–1638): Bishop of Ypres and founder of Jansenism+. He was educated at Louvain and Paris, where he became the principal of a college. It was there that he met Jean du Vergier de Hauranne (1581–1643), later abbot of Saint-Cyran, who would be his collaborator. In 1617 he became director of a newly-founded college at Louvain university which was where, over a decade later, he would begin to compose the *Augustinus*, a work which, when it was published two years after his death, would challenge the theological consensus over the issues of grace and justification arrived at by the council of Trent[†].

Joris David (c.1500–56): A Dutch artist (painting on glass) and lay preacher who became attracted to Lutheran views in the 1520s and was arrested for distributing evangelical literature in his native Delft. His subsequent banishment brought him into contact with the apocalyptic anabaptism of Melchior Hofmann*. He was rebaptized in the winter of 1534–35 by Obbe Philips* and, in the wake of the Münster uprising, argued that the godless would be punished by God's angels in due time. In December 1536, he had visions of the apocalyptic 'third David' who (like the 'second David', Christ) would come to earth (in the Netherlands), and establish the kingdom and restore the 'children of God' to their rightful inheritance. This coming would only occur after the inner sanctification of the 'children of God' in preparation for it. Under intense pressure from the authorities, he moved to Antwerp, where he had the support of a patrician family. He eventually retired to Basel and lived there in style under the pseudonym 'Johan van Brugge' leaving the remnants of his followers (the 'Davidites') to be absorbed amongst the Mennonites.

Karlstadt Andreas (Rudolf Bodenstein von) (1480–1541): Protestant reformer, collaborator and (later) critic of Luther. Karlstadt was Bodenstein's birthplace (hence his name). His early years in the university of Wittenberg were as Luther's colleague, where he studied and published Thomist philosophy (the philosophy of Thomas Aquinas). He was awarded a theological doctorate in 1513 and this was the beginning of the first of a series of radical awakenings which characterized his life and writings (see page 46). Having been initially unpersuaded by Luther's Augustinian theology, he joined him in the late 1510s and accompanied Luther to the Leipzig disputation (see page 53). In 1521 he wrote treatises against clerical celibacy and monastic vows. In early 1522 he took over the reformation at Wittenberg and persuaded the city council to sanction ordinances which set about creating a New Jerusalem of social and biblical order in the town. The abolition of images was essential to his vision and, when Luther returned in March 1522 to put a stop to the changes which were in hand, Karlstadt was challenged, marginalized and his activities restricted. In 1523, he retired to a rural parish in Thuringian Saxony to enable him both to advance his ideas of a communally-based reformation and to have his treatises published (at Jena). Eventually, in September 1524, Karlstadt was exiled from Saxony and he led a wandering life in the upper Rhine region, publishing treatises on infant baptism[†] and on the eucharist[†] which indicated his affinity with views later known as anabaptist. During the Peasants' War he was an active leader in Franconia at Rothenburg and, when the revolt was crushed, he was granted asylum by Luther at Wittenberg so long as he did not express his views in public. He was eventually able to escape from Saxony in 1529 and, with the help of Zwingli, he managed to find a post at Zürich where he became a preacher and teacher. He ended his life as a professor of biblical theology at the university of Basel. His theology was distinctive, powerful, and left its mark on mystics in Germany later in the sixteenth century. We have been all created in the image of God; with that image we have the capacity to create a community of the godly on this earth if we surrender our will to that of the divine within us. The majority of his large numbers of treatises were published in German and widely read. The emphasis on Luther during the early years of the German reformation tends to relegate Karlstadt's significance to an undue extent.

Knipperdollinck Berndt(1490?–1536): Anabaptist leader. Cloth merchant from Münster with protestant leanings whose part in the opposition to the bishop of the city in 1528 had led to his imprisonment and torture. His initial support for Jan Matthys was critical to the gathering anabaptist presence in the city. His house provided the headquarters where Rothmann's pamphlets were published. He was tortured and executed along with Bockelson on 22 January 1536.

Krzycki Andrzej (Lat: *Andreas Critius*) (1482–1537): Polish humanist, churchman and Erasmian. In 1515, he was appointed secretary to the Polish king and, in 1525, he was promoted to the bishopric of Przemyśl with a further elevation to the see of Płock two years later. Two years before he died he became archbishop of Gniezno. His humanist talents were displayed in his poetry and his patronage. His house near Kraków was known as 'Tusculum' and had a reputation as a republic of letters in its own right. Erasmus was treated as an honorary member of the academy. He treated protestantism as an offshoot of this humanism and felt no inconsistency in inviting Melanchthon* to his court in the early 1530s. Several of those in his entourage would become the Polish protestants of the next generation, especially Jan Łaski*.

Łaski Jan II (Lat: *a Lasco: Lascius*) (1499–1560): Polish protestant reformer. He was the nephew of Jan Łaski, archbishop of Gniezno and was educated at his uncle's court. In an extensive European tour in 1524–26, he spent time at the French court and formed connections with Marguerite d'Angoulême* there. He then went to stay with Erasmus at Basel, funded his library and began his lifelong affection for Erasmus' approach to the religious problems of the day. He also began his contacts with other Rhineland reformers. After his return to Poland, he was elevated to a bishopric and became embroiled in the Hungarian civil war with his brother. He failed to secure the archbishopric of Gniezno which had been promised him in 1530 and left Poland in 1539 to live in the Netherlands. In 1542, he broke openly with the catholic church and was appointed as the minister of Emden and the superintendent of the church of East Friesland. In 1544, he prepared a confessional statement for the Friesland church and attempted to mediate in the controversy over the eucharist[†]. These efforts led to his being relieved of his position at Emden (in 1549) and his retirement to England. At the invitation of Cranmer, he became the minister to the stranger church of London in 1550. In 1556, he was permitted to return to Poland where he attempted to unite the disparate protestant elements in the country. But he faced a royal mandate which limited his rights to preach and only in Little Poland, where he directed the Calvinist church, did he achieve any great measure of success.

Lefèvre d'Etaples, Jacques (Lat: Jacobus Faber Stapulensis) (c.1460–1536): The distinguished French humanist and biblical scholar. He was born, as his name indicates, at the seaport of Etaples in Picardy and studied in Paris. Much of the early part of his life was spent in studying philosophy, the writings of the medieval mystics, the hermetic texts of natural magic and other neo-Platonic texts which we now know to come from the early Christian centuries. In each case, his studies took him back to the detailed study of the texts. But his interests gradually shifted towards the study of the biblical texts themselves. In 1509, whilst the librarian at the abbey of St Germain-des-Près, he published, in a synoptic form, the five Latin versions of the psalter, the Quincuplex Psalterium. This heralded a series of commentaries on the Pauline Epistles (1512), the Gospels (1521) and the so-called 'Catholic' Epistles (1527). These works had a considerable impact on the protestant reformers and were extensively used by them. Although often claimed as a 'proto-protestant', Lefèvre himself never declared himself an adherent of reform. His correspondence indicates his knowledge of, and private admiration for, some of the protestant reformers' writings; and his retirement to Strasbourg in 1525 was a powerful statement about the kind of reactions to heresy which he deplored. He subsequently enjoyed the protection of the king's sister, Marguerite of Navarre, whose eclectic and personal approach to the questions raised by the reformation he probably shared. In the event, his greatest contribution to the protestant reformation may have been the French translation of the Bible ascribed to him (published at Antwerp in 1530) which became the inspiration for the more famous Olivétan Bible.

Leo X (Pope) (*Giovanni de' Medici*) (1475–1521): Pope from 1513. The second son of Lorenzo de' Medici, he was the head of the family by the time of the lengthy conclave which elevated him to the papacy. He had the background of an Italian prince and ruled the Papal States in a similar fashion, declaring war on the duchy of Urbino in 1517 and attempting to seize Ferrara in 1519. At the same time, he had been educated in theology and canon law at Pisa and enjoyed a humanist's eye for promising artists and men of letters. He inherited the fifth Lateran council and brought it to a conclusion in 1517 without tackling any of the major problems of reform in the church; but he was sufficiently aware of the strands of internal reform in the church to encourage the Oratory of Divine Love at Rome (see pages 189–90). Given his background and perspective, it is not surprising that he should have comprehensively misunderstood the significance of the Luther affair.

Loyola (Saint) Ignatius (c.1491/5–1556): The founder of the Jesuits. He was the son of a noble family from the Basque country whose military career ended abruptly when his right leg was badly wounded at the siege of Pamplona (1521). Whilst convalescing at Loyola he underwent a profound spiritual awakening which would be reflected in the rest of his life. He made a general confession and exchanged his clothes with those of a beggar. He spent the following year in a monastery at Manresa (near Barcelona), where he led a life of prayer and mortification and experienced the desolation and the consolation which are the twin features of the *Spiritual Exercises*, which he probably began to write at this time.

From Manresa, Ignatius went to Rome and thence to Jerusalem, living purely off begging. On his return, he studied at Barcelona, Alcalá, Salamanca (1524–28) and then Paris (1528–35). It was there that he gathered around him six companions whom he guided through the full *Exercises*. They took a mutual vow of poverty, chastity and a pilgrimage to Jerusalem if possible. In due course, they accompanied Ignatius to Venice where he and several of the others were ordained priests. Being prevented from travelling to Jerusalem by the Turkish threat in the Mediterranean, they went to Rome where their new order was sanctioned by Paul III* in 1540. The remainder of Ignatius' life was spent in organizing and shaping the Jesuit order (see pages 192–3). He was canonized in 1622.

Luther Martin (1483–1546): The founder of the protestant reformation. He was born at Eisleben in Saxony, the second son of a miner from Thuringian Saxony and the daughter of a well-established family of local notables from Eisenach. He was educated at the cathedral school in Magdeburg, at Eisenach and at the university in Erfurt (1501–5) where he studied philosophy. In 1505, he entered the monastery of the reformed

Augustinians at Erfurt. The remaining details of his career, writings, and of the 'Luther affair' are to be found elsewhere in this volume (see in particular section three).

Maldonado Juan (1533–83): Spanish biblical theologian and Jesuit. He was educated at the university of Salamanca, entered the Jesuit order at Rome in 1562 and was sent to teach in Paris. He engaged in controversies and earned enemies amongst the theologians at the Sorbonne before undertaking an extensive visit of the Jesuit establishments in France. It was on the basis of experiences in France that, in late 1580, he returned to Rome and assisted in the drafting of the Jesuit curriculum of studies, the *Ratio Studiorum* (see page 197).

Mantz Felix (c.1500–27): Zürich's first anabaptist 'martyr'. He was the illegitimate son of a Zürich canon who was in contact with Müntzer* and Karlstadt* and supervised some of the latter's publications in Basel in 1524. Large numbers of these tracts were distributed by Mantz in and around Zürich that year. He submitted a protest to the Zürich authorities in December 1524 on the subject of infant baptism[†] which may have been drawn from Karlstadt's writings. During his temporary expulsion from Zürich in 1525, his missionary efforts took him to Basel and elsewhere in Switzerland. After escaping from prison in March 1526, he was eventually recaptured by the Zürich authorities in December and put to death for breaking his undertaking not to continue rebaptizing.

Marguerite d'Angoulême (also Marguerite of Navarre) (1492–1549): The sister of the French king, François I, Marguerite used her royal connections to protect French humanist biblical scholars like Lefèvre d'Etaples*, Gérard Roussel and Louis de Berquin*. Her own religious beliefs reflected a pattern of bold and individual spiritual journeying which drew on various elements of Christian humanism and the emerging protestantism (as it was filtered through to her). Her *Pater Noster* ('Our Father') was a paraphrase of an early Lutheran text and there is a strong possibility that she encouraged the printing of Lutheran translations and assisted in their diffusion within France. She patronized an evangelical Lenten sermon of Roussel* in 1533 and her poem on *The Mirror of the Sinful Soul* would be initially condemned by the Sorbonne[†] (although this was later withdrawn).

After the affair of the placards of 1534, Marguerite withdrew to the ancestral lands of her husband and set up court at Nérac where she established an important evangelical community. Lefèvre d'Etaples* stayed there until his death in 1536. Jean Calvin also spent some time there in 1534, as did the poet Clément Marot (c.1496–1544). She corresponded with like-minded reformers in Strasbourg and remained the protector and inspirer for French reformers whilst never officially departing from the established faith.

Mariana Juan (1536–1624): The outstanding Spanish Jesuit political philosopher and historian. He studied at the university of Alcalá before joining the Jesuit order in 1553. He taught theology at Rome, Palermo and Paris before returning to Toledo to devote himself to writing. His Latin *History of Spain* (1592) portrayed the origins of its contemporary greatness; but his best-known work was *On the state and its origins* (*De rege et regis institutione*) in 1598, a remarkable treatise in which Mariana elaborated the view that resistance to tyrants was justifiable. The assassination of Henri IV, the first Bourbon king of France, was held to have been inspired by the teachings of the Jesuits, and especially of Mariana. In reality, his political philosophy was disowned by Acquaviva, the general of the order.

Marpeck Pilgram (c.1495–1556): Anabaptist leader. Pilgram Marpeck was born to a family of small-town notables in the Tyrolean mining town of Rattenburg. He served as mining inspector and town councillor before his sympathies for anabaptism in 1527 led to his resignation of his office and his abandonment of his property to travel to Bohemia where he was apparently baptized into the anabaptists and became an elder. He was in Strasbourg by 1528 and was arrested for having anabaptist meetings in his house. He published two tracts and a confession in 1531; in December that same year he confronted Martin Bucer* in the Strasbourg *Rat* chamber on the role of the civil authorities in matters of faith. His rejection of any powers of constraint of conscience led to his expulsion and retirement to Switzerland. For the following decade he organized anabaptist congregations in southern Germany and wrote occasional tracts. For the last decade of his life, he was resident in Augsburg where, although he was periodically warned by the authorities about his illegal activities, he managed not to be prosecuted.

Like many other laymen who became engaged in the theological controversies of the sixteenth century, Marpeck drew on a rich cocktail of sources for his beliefs. In addition to Luther, Zwingli and Bucer, he evidently knew the writings of the German medieval mystics. Central to his thinking was the notion of a community which had been sanctified by the Holy Spirit, offered to all who would receive it willingly as a result of Christ's sacrifice for the old and sinful world. It raised questions about precisely how Christ had become flesh, which would be pursued in several anabaptist contexts in the sixteenth century. In the sanctified community, (adult) baptism became a 'covenant of good conscience' through which the individual gradually becomes a member of the sanctified community where social welfare and mutual charity was fundamental. The state could never impose a godly community from without; its efforts to do so created Pharisees rather than Christians. But he advocated the payment of taxes and obedience to the civil power as a necessary evil to be tolerated. Many of his writings have only been discovered and ascribed to him relatively recently. He has been described as 'the major spokesman and theorist of responsible, pacifistic, evangelical Anabaptism'.[1]

Matthys Jan (var: Matthijsz) (?–1534): A Dutch anabaptist who had originally been a baker. He was apparently influenced by Melchiorite (see entry for Melchior Hofmann above) prophecy to become an anabaptist. In November 1533, he announced his revelation that the time of troubles was coming to an end and that the baptism of the true church of believers should begin. Together with five apostles he went through Holland preaching that God would shortly establish the millennium[†] and destroy all earthly tyranny. Under the threat of persecution, he left for Münster and, with the help of Berndt Rothmann*, he gained control of the city.

Melanchthon Philipp (Ger: *Philipp Schwartzerdt*) (1497–1560): Luther's collaborator at Wittenberg. He was from a respectable merchant family and the great nephew of Reuchlin*. Educated at Heidelberg (1509–12) and Tübingen (1512–18) he was appointed professor of Greek at Wittenberg in 1518 (see page 46). He rapidly won Luther's confidence and accompanied him to the Leipzig disputation in 1519. His most famous published contribution to protestant reformation literature in the sixteenth century was his *Loci theologi* or *Loci communes* (*Theological common-places*) which took the humanist technique of establishing the *topoi* or 'topics' of a particular passage as the way into understanding its fundamental meaning, and then applied it to the Bible. It was regularly revised in his lifetime and appeared in its definitive German edition in 1555. In it, Melanchthon's awareness of the way in which the gospel of Christ 'fulfils' the law is amply explored. But Melanchthon also produced textbooks on Aristotelian philosophy and assisted Luther in his translations of the Bible (see page 259).

Melanchthon's significance as an administrative organizer of the reformation should not be underestimated. He acted as advisor for the protestant reformation in numerous localities outside Saxony (e.g. Nuremberg, 1525–26) and was often called upon as a mediator in local disputes. His careful and moderate logical mind was appreciated by Luther at the colloquy of Marburg and it is not surprising that he should have been chosen to be the leading protestant representative at the diet of Augsburg (1530) and to draft the Augsburg Confession (see

---

[1] G.H. Williams, *The Radical Reformation* (Philadelphia, Westminster Press, 1962), p. 273.

pages 245 and 247). He remained a moderate voice in the Lutheran reformation and, when the protestant princes were overwhelmed by Charles V's forces in the Schmalkaldic War (1546–47), he gave his approval to the Augsburg Interim (1548). The result was that he became embroiled in a bitter dispute with more diehard Lutherans over the concept of adiaphora[†] and this, despite his best endeavours, split the German Lutheran movement for the remainder of his lifetime and beyond (see page 220).

Molina Luis de (1535–1600): A Spanish theologian and Jesuit, who taught at Coimbra and Evora universities. His controversial work on questions of free will and divine grace, published in 1588 (*Concordia liberi arbitrii cum gratiae donis*), emphasized the divine foreknowledge implicit in free human actions. This became termed 'Molinism' and the views became adopted by many Jesuits and defended in controversies with the more orthodox and conservative Dominican theologians.

Morély Jean (c.1524–c.94): French protestant theologian from a wealthy Parisian family who advocated a congregational organization for the French protestant church. His *Treatise on discipline and Christian government* (*Traicté de la discipline et police chrestienne*) was published at Lyon in 1562. In it, Morély proposed that the reformed church had not gone far enough in vesting authority in the assembly of the faithful and criticized the oligarchy created by the consistory court system. His proposals were discussed and dismissed in the national synod of Orléans in 1562 and he eventually fled to England in the wake of the massacre of St Bartholomew.

Morone Giovanni (1509–80): Italian cardinal and reformer. Born into a Milanese family, he was made bishop of Modena in 1529 before being sent as papal legate to Germany in 1536. By then, Morone had become identified with the small wing of reformers within the church protected by Pope Paul III*. He was created cardinal in 1542 and participated in the preparations for the council of Trent[†]. He fell from favour under Pope Paul IV* and was charged with heresy and imprisoned. Released by his successor, Pope Pius IV, he presided over the final sessions of the council of Trent in 1563, by which time his own brand of catholic reform had become the accepted consensus.

Müntzer (var: Münzer), Thomas (pre 1491–1525): Militant radical of the early German reformation. Many of the details of his itinerant life are known to us only through incidental references. Born at Stohlberg in the Harz mountains of central Germany, his university studies took him to Leipzig and then Frankfurt an der Oder, where he graduated. He became an ordained priest and acted as chaplain, confessor and occasional preacher in various locations, including Wittenberg in 1518–19. In

May 1520, possibly on Luther's recommendation, he became a preacher in the Saxon town of Zwickau. This is where his reading of the late-medieval German mystics (especially Johannes Tauler) led him to stress the importance of the spirit within, and his own role in the forthcoming apocalyptic events of the age. He was dismissed for supposedly causing a breach of the peace and went to Prague, preaching there and publishing his famous 'Prague Protestation' (or 'Prague Manifesto') of November 1521. In this, he proclaimed that the church had become a whore and that it was his mission to restore it to its pristine spirit. His wanderings continued, but the most creative period was that spent as reforming preacher in the Saxon walled enclave town of Allstedt from March 1523 through to August 1524. Here he instigated a reformation of the spirit, composed his German liturgy, and attacked Luther for his 'contrived faith' – a faith without suffering and works to prove it. He even preached before Duke Georg of ducal Saxony and his son in the castle church of Allstedt in a sermon on the second chapter of Daniel in which he intimated that he was a second 'Daniel' who could interpret dreams in terms of the apocalyptic events to come. Faced with growing opposition, he formed a defensive Christian League (*Bund*) as an embodiment of the covenant of the saints with God. This idea resurfaced the following year when, having been expelled from Allstedt, he rallied the council and other followers in Mühlhausen to support the peasant rebellion. On 10 May, he placed himself at the head of a peasant band and marched to Frankenhausen. He interpreted the events of the Peasants' War as the beginning of the apocalypse, convinced that God would put power in the hands of the oppressed and faithful remnant. Basing himself on the model of Gideon (in Judges 6–8), he took on the role of army commander. On 15 May, his troops were slaughtered outside Frankenhausen, Müntzer himself was taken captive, and (on 27 May) he was beheaded outside the walls of Mühlhausen. His memory survived, however, not least for Luther himself, for whom Müntzer remained a warning of radical dangers. His name and writings were subsequently invoked by various anabaptist leaders, especially Hans Hut* and Hans Denck*.

Myconius Friedrich (1490–1546): German protestant reformer. In 1524 he joined Luther's cause and became the leading reformer in Gotha. In 1529, he accompanied Luther to the colloquy of Marburg.

Neri (Saint) Philip (1515–95): Catholic reformer and devotee of the Roman Oratory. The son of a Florentine family who studied at Rome before abandoning his formal education for the priesthood in 1538 to begin a life of religious devotion and practical social welfare. In 1548 he organized a fraternity to assist pilgrims and the poor, and founded a hospital. He was eventually ordained in 1551 and gathered round him a congregation of priests for prayers, devotion and discussion. From this activity grew the revived Oratory, a community which devoted itself to afternoons of prayer, preaching and study (see pages 189–90). Although initially it attracted the suspicions of the papacy, it was recognized in 1575 as a congregation and given a church in Rome to rebuild. He eventually became the spiritual advisor to Clement VIII and was canonized in 1622.

Ochino Bernardino (1487–1564): Italian evangelical religious reformer. Born in Siena, he joined the Franciscans and became their general but, in 1534, transferred to the newer order of the Capuchins. He soon became their vicar-general (1538) but fell foul of the authorities for supporting Lutheran doctrines of justification†. In 1541, in a spectacular defection, he fled to Geneva to avoid the inquisition. In 1545, he became the pastor of the Italian church at Augsburg but, in 1547, went to England where he wrote a dialogue criticizing papal authority (*The Usurped Primacy of the Bishop of Rome*) and one which attacked Calvin's views on predestination (*Labyrinth*). In 1553 he moved once more, this time to Zürich and became a pastor there in 1555. But in 1563 he was forced once more to depart, this time for his radical views on marriage and polygamy. He died in Moravia.

Ockham (William of) (c.1285–1347): An Oxford philosopher and theologian from Ockham in Surrey. He was a Franciscan and a controversial figure during his lifetime, being accused of heresy and (at one stage) excommunicated and imprisoned. He wrote in exposition of the imperial authority to depose a pope and his political theories played a part in the conciliar movement. But it was his logical writings which earned him the title 'head of the nominalists' (*Princeps nominalium*). His logical *Tractate* (*Tractatus logice*) was printed at Paris in 1488 and many of his other works were published in Lyon and elsewhere in the years before the protestant reformation.

Oecolampadius Johannes (G: *Johan Huszgen*) (1482–1531): Swiss protestant reformer at Basel. Originally from the Rhine Palatinate, he studied law at Bologna and theology at Heidelberg, Tübingen and Basel. He fell under the influence of the humanist Jakob Wimpfeling* and adopted his Latin pseudonym (meaning 'shining light'). In 1515, he was appointed city preacher at the cathedral of Basel and also worked for Froben* in preparing the Erasmus edition of the New Testament for the press. He was an enthusiastic supporter of Luther and became a pastor at Basel. After his death, his position was filled by Oswald Myconius*.

Oldenbarnevelt Jan van (1547–1619): Dutch statesman who served as Grand Pensionary in Rotterdam from 1576, which made him a member of the states of Holland. He supported the Union of Utrecht of 1579 (see page 130), persuaded the estates to offer Prince Maurice of Nassau the title of stadholder in 1584 on the death of William the Silent* and, in 1586, was appointed Land's Advocate of Holland. This was the office which, with skill and enormous dedication, he turned into the leading political authority in the union. He was particularly significant in foreign affairs. But it was his signature of the 12-year truce with Spain in 1609 which led to disagreements with Maurice of Nassau, divisions which were exacerbated by the debates between supporters and opponents of Arminius*. In August 1618, he was arrested and charged with treason by the estates-general. He was executed at The Hague.

Orange (William of) ('the Silent') (1533–84): Stadholder of the United Provinces and military leader of the protestant northern states of the Netherlands. He was born at Dillenburg in Germany and educated as a protestant. He inherited the Nassau fortune from his cousin in 1544 and joined the catholic court of Emperor Charles V. He helped to negotiate the peace of Cateau-Cambrésis (1559) and was appointed governor of the northern provinces of the Netherlands when Philip II returned to Spain. In 1561, William married Anna, the daughter of the Lutheran Mauritz of Saxony. This led to a sharpening of his religious views and, in 1563, he joined with Counts Egmont and Horn to protest against the religious changes of Granvelle, the minister of Regent Margaret of Parma. Although he attempted to repress the disorders provoked during the iconoclastic riots in Antwerp in March 1567 he subsequently renounced his office and retired to his ancestral home in Dillenburg. Thereafter he attempted an ambitious campaign to liberate the Netherlands. The first attempted invasion (Autumn 1568) failed ignominiously. That of 1572 only succeeded when William marched to support the sea invasion of the Beggars and assumed the leadership of the movement as stadholder of Holland, Zeeland and Utrecht. He resided mainly at Delft and, in October 1573, became a member of the Calvinist church. The remainder of his life was spent in fighting campaigns against the Spanish in which his brothers Louis and Henry both lost their lives. He himself was assassinated in 1583 by a catholic fanatic, Balthasar Gérard.

Paul III (Pope) (*Alessandro Farnese*) (1468–1549): Pope from 1534. He was brought up in the Medici household and was made a cardinal in 1493. He served four different popes before himself being unanimously elected. He is often accounted a proponent of reform, especially because of his initial pronouncement committing him to a general council, his shrewd promotion of reform-minded cardinals and the final opening of the council of Trent during his pontificate. Yet it was not a consistent path towards reform. In his personal life, he fathered four children, three of whom were legitimized, and one of whom (Pier Luigi) became duke of Parma and Piacenza. The latter would be assassinated in 1547 on the orders of the Habsburg governor of Milan, an event which reinforced Paul III's anti-Habsburg convictions. He appointed two of his own grandsons as cardinals. In international affairs, he struggled to maintain papal neutrality in Habsburg–Valois rivalries which threatened the holding of a general council. As the remarkable Titian portrait of him implies, he was, by the time of his pontificate, an old man struggling to encompass and control the forces of change in a new order.

Paul IV (Pope) (*Gian Pietro Carafa*) (1476–1559): Pope from 1555. He was from an eminent Neapolitan noble family and received a humanist education at Rome, thanks to his uncle (Cardinal Oliviero Carafa), before being named bishop of Chieti in 1504. By the time he was elected pope, he had made some contributions to the cause of ecclesiastical reform. In 1524, he had assisted in the founding of the Oratory of Divine Love (see pages 189–90) and the establishment of the Theatines (see page 189). In 1542 he assumed responsibility for the reinvigorated Roman inquisition and gradually turned that institution into an agency for the repression of heresy and the discrediting of his own rivals. He eventually secured the pontificate thanks to the support of Cardinal Alessandro Farnese, Pope Paul III's great grandson. It was in order to acknowledge this fact that he chose the name of Paul IV. During his pontificate, it has been said that the papacy 'changed course and lost course'. He certainly increased the role of the inquisition in Roman affairs. He refused to reconvene the council of Trent†, preferring to work for reform on a piecemeal basis from within. He gained a deserved reputation for unpredictable, but severe, measures against non-conforming clerics. Monks found outside their monasteries were sent to the galleys or had their property confiscated. He used the inquisition as a means of settling old scores and published the Roman Index. He was suspicious of the Jesuit order and attempted to force on the order changes to its constitutions. He imposed draconian restrictions on the Jewish community in Rome, including penal levels of taxation and the creation of a rigid ghetto. In international affairs, he tried to oppose the Habsburgs in Naples but failed. He rejected any attempt to compromise with the protestants and opposed the peace of Augsburg in Germany (1555). When he died in August 1559 (in the midst of a three-day fast), crowds rejoiced and the statue of himself which he had ordered to be erected on the Capitoline hill was torn down and the head thrown into the Tiber.

Pellicanus Konrad (Konrad Kürsner) (1478–1556): A humanist from Alsace and friend of Erasmus. He was taught Hebrew by Johannes Reuchlin* and published the first Hebrew grammar. He became a protestant, a professor of theology at Basel and a leading biblical commentator and scholar.

Peterssen Laurentius (Lat: *Petri*) (1499–1552): Swedish protestant and archbishop of Uppsala (1531–52). He was the younger brother of Olaus Peterssen* and supported him within the emerging Lutheran church of Sweden.

Peterssen Olaus (Lat: *Petri*) (1493–1552): Swedish protestant reformer and brother of Laurentius. He is often referred to as the 'Martin Luther of Sweden'. He studied at Uppsala, Leipzig and Wittenberg, being present at the latter whilst Luther was giving the lectures on the Pauline epistles which outlined his new thinking. He returned to Sweden in 1518 and was appointed an archdeacon in the diocese of Strengnäs. It was there that Gustav Vasa was acclaimed king of the newly-independent Sweden in 1523, and Peterssen soon became (thanks to an introduction to his court from Laurentius Andreae*) town clerk at Stockholm and its city preacher. In 1525, with royal protection, he married and, during the following decade, wrote the first protestant translations of the Bible and accompanying protestant divinity and polemic in vernacular Swedish (see page 261). Later in life, Peterssen opposed Gustav Vasa's attempts to centralize royal control of the church. For this, and more immediately for failing to reveal information about a possible rebellion against the king which was given him in confidence during a confession, he was accused of treason and sentenced to death. The sentence was relaxed and he continued to work for the establishment of a moderate Lutheran church polity in Sweden until his death.

Philips Dirk (Dietrich) (1504–68): A Franciscan and younger brother of Obbe Philips* from Leeuwarden who became one of the leading anabaptist figures of the Netherlands. He was rebaptized in around 1533 by a disciple of Jan Matthys* but stood aside from the Münster uprising. In its aftermath, his influence on disillusioned Dutch anabaptism grew and, for a period in the 1540s and 1550s, it was preeminent. He preached in and around the Netherlands, being active for a time in Emden. As an elder of the Dutch anabaptists, he argued strongly for a strict interpretation of the ban[†] and enforced it in disputes with Frisian anabaptists and others.

Philips Obbe (c.1500–68): A Dutch anabaptist and lay medical practitioner who was rebaptized by his brother Dirk Philips* and influenced by Melchior Hofmann*. He played a significant role in Dutch anabaptism until about 1540; his numerous adherents became known as 'Obbenites' – although they later were subsumed into the Mennonites.

Phillip of Hesse (Landgrave) (1504–67): German prince and early supporter of Lutheranism (see page 69). He married Christina of Saxony in 1523 and gave his allegiance to Luther's cause in 1524. He was active in suppressing the peasants' revolt and, in 1526, began the reform of the church in his own principality. A year later, he founded the new protestant university of Marburg (see page 268). His efforts to reconcile the differences between Zwingli and Luther failed at the colloquy of Marburg in 1529. But he played an essential part in the inception of the Schmalkaldic League of 1530 to unite the protestant princes of north Germany (see pages 87–8). In 1540, he married Margaret von der Saal. Although recognized by Luther, it was a bigamous match which alienated many of his erstwhile princely supporters. In the Schmalkaldic War, he was defeated and imprisoned by the emperor, only to be released in 1552. Despite his later failures, he was an able administrator and one of the most politically adept German princes to support Lutheranism in the early years.

Pirckheimer Willibald (1470–1530): Nuremberg patrician and noted humanist polymath. His erudition, and the piety of his sisters (who belonged to the Sisterhood of the Common Life[†]) earned them the admiration of both Erasmus and Luther. He was an important figure amongst the literary circles of the city and a friend of the artist Albrecht Dürer. Luther stayed in his house on his return from Augsburg in 1518. Although he wrote in defence of the evangelical reformation, he sought its eventual reconciliation with the church.

Pius IV (Pope) (*Giovanni Angelo Medici*) (1499–1565): Pope from 1559. Although a Medici by name he was no relative of the more famous Florentine princely family. He was born in Milan and studied at Bologna before entering the papal secretariat. He was promoted to the nominal archbishopric of Dubrovnik (Lat: *Ragusa*) in 1545 and was made a cardinal in 1549. He fell from favour under Pope Paul IV*, partly because of his pro-Habsburg inclinations. His election in 1559 was mainly the result of an evenly-divided electoral college which took over three months to decide upon his name as a compromise candidate. His first actions as pontiff were to arrest (and, in one instance, order the execution of) the family favourites and protégés of his predecessor. He reconvened the council of Trent[†] and promptly supported its decrees, issuing a new catechism and revising the Index of prohibited books. He promoted reform-minded cardinals and made his nephew, Carlo Borromeo*, his leading advisor. In international affairs, he relied on Spanish hegemony but was cautious in his response to the unfolding civil war in France and the accession of Elizabeth I in England.

Pius V (Pope) (*Antonio ('Michele') Ghislieri*) (1504–72): Pope from 1566. He grew up as a shepherd and became a Dominican at the age of 14 (giving himself the name 'Michele'). He came to the notice of Pope Paul IV* for his rigorous pursuit of heretics as inquisitor in northern Italy. He made him cardinal in 1557 and Inquisitor General the following year. He was chosen after a 19-day conclave in which the influence of his predecessor's cardinal-nephew, Carlo Borromeo*, proved crucial. His pontificate was as austere as his personal life, and one of the outstanding reforming pontificates of the sixteenth century. He reduced the papal court, issued stricter instructions for the observance of holy days in Rome and tried to stamp out nepotism in the Roman curia. He appointed a commission in 1567 to investigate all episcopal appointments, revised the Roman breviary (1568) and Missal (1569) before setting up a commission to revise the Vulgate Bible (1570). He ensured that the decrees of the council of Trent[†] were despatched and enforced in the catholic world overseas, in the new dioceses in Mexico and the Far East. He supported the work of the inquisition and built a new palace for it. He completed the attack upon the Jewish community in Rome advanced by his predecessor Pope Paul IV* with their expulsion from everywhere save the ghettos at Rome and Ancona. In international affairs, his rigorous attitudes did not always produce the desired results. His excommunication of Elizabeth I of England antagonized other princes in Europe. His support for Catherine de Médicis' military campaigns against the Huguenots[†] was nullified by the edict of pacification of 1570. His relations with Philip II of Spain were made more difficult by his attempts to undermine the Spanish crown's control of the church. His great success was the 'holy league' with Spain and Venice whose naval forces defeated the Turks at Lepanto (see page 279).

Possevino Antonio (c.1533–1611): Jesuit missionary. Born in Mantua, he became a Jesuit in 1559 and was given delicate responsibilities in protestant territories. These included a mission to the Waldensians in the Alps in 1560, to French protestant regions (1563–70), Sweden (1579) and Russia (1580). His missions to Sweden and Russia did not have the effects which he desired and he retired to Padua to teach at the local Jesuit college.

Renée (of France, duchess of Ferrara) (1510–74): Prominent protestant patroness. She was the daughter of King Louis XII and Anne of Brittany and she married Ercole d'Este, duke of Ferrara in 1534. She patronized humanists and evangelical reformers. In 1536, Calvin visited her court and it was partly under his influence that she became a protestant. Her husband took away her children and she was imprisoned in 1554. She formally recanted and was released shortly afterwards but she declared her protestant sympathies again and, after the duke's death, returned to France to live at Montargis.

Reuchlin Johannes (1455–1522): A German humanist and Hebraist. His initial interest in Hebrew scholarship was partly inspired during a visit to Italy. He acquired his knowledge of the language, however, from a physician in the court of Emperor Maximilian. Although his Hebrew grammar and edition of the penitential Psalms were most acclaimed by the protestant reformers, he esteemed his works on the Cabbala (Jewish mystical writings) his most important. Although his name was often linked with the Lutheran reformation, he never supported it openly.

Röubli Wilhelm (Reublin) (c.1484–1559): Anabaptist. By origins he was a priest from Rottenburg (Germany) who came to Zürich from Basel, where he had apparently learnt of Zwingli's teaching. He was an effective preacher who, after his expulsion from Zürich in 1525, went to Waldshut, Strasbourg, and elsewhere in southern Germany, possibly exploiting the remnants of Peasant War sentiments in his successful rebaptizing missions.

Rothmann Berndt (1495?–1535): Anabaptist leader. He was by origins a catholic priest, the son of a blacksmith, and the evangelical preacher at Münster who drafted the city's church ordinances of 1533. By the end of that year, however, he had written his first anabaptist tract, declaring infant baptism[†] idolatrous (8 Nov 1533). He knew the prophecies of Melchior Hofmann* and was influenced by them in late 1533. On 5 January 1534, he received his adult baptism from the apostles of Jan Matthys* sent from Amsterdam and set about about finding the true church of Christ in the city. His published treatises during the rising give clear documentation of the development of Münster anabaptist thinking.

Roussel, Gérard (c.1500–55): French evangelical reformer and bishop of Oloron. His early career as a student of Jacques Lefèvre d'Etaples* and a member of Guillaume Briçonnet's* circle at Meaux left an indelible mark on his later thought. He took refuge in Strasbourg with Lefèvre in 1525; it was under the protection of the king's sister, Marguerite of Navarre* that he returned and was appointed (in 1536) bishop of Oloron. The latter appointment prompted a hostile letter from Calvin for his desertion from the cause of reform; but Roussel continued to believe that reform was possible 'from within' the French church. Whether he ever attempted to put his ideas into practice in his own diocese, however, is not known. He was killed by a noble who attacked him in the pulpit while he preached.

Ruiz de Virués Alonso (c.1480–1545): A Spanish Benedictine who became a great admirer and advocate of Erasmus in Spain. He eventually translated some of his works into Spanish. He became a court preacher to Charles V and travelled with him to Germany. But in 1534 he was indicted before the inquisition for heresy and imprisoned in Valladolid, eventually securing his release a year later to become bishop of the remote Canary Islands.

Sadoleto Jacopo (1477–1547): Humanist scholar and catholic reformer. Having received a fine humanist education he joined the papal secretariat and, in 1517, was appointed bishop of Carpentras (Provence, France). In 1536, he was made a cardinal by Pope Paul III* and prepared some of the agenda for the council of Trent†. He was amongst those of his generation who tried unsuccessfully to heal the divisions provoked by the protestant reformation.

Sartorius Johannes (1500?–57?): Dutch Christian humanist who became rector of the school at Amsterdam before being removed for his evangelical sympathies in the aftermath of the Münster uprising (December 1535). He became a country schoolmaster and continued to publish his Latin school-texts which indicated his admiration for Erasmus as well as some influence from the *devotio moderna*†.

Sattler Michael (c.1490–1527): Anabaptist leader. Born near Freiburg, he became a Benedictine before leaving the order, marrying and settling in Zürich where he was amongst the earliest anabaptists. In 1525 he was expelled from the city and went to Strasbourg. In February 1527 he presided over the meeting of anabaptists which determined the Schleitheim Confession (see pages 250–51). Shortly afterwards, he and his wife were arrested and taken to Rottenburg where he was burnt at the stake and his wife drowned.

Savonarola Girolamo (1452–98): A Florentine Dominican whose reputation as a biblical scholar and preacher was considerable. His apocalyptic thinking was supported by substantial learning. Outside Florence, he began to preach (in 1485) his fundamental message that the church would soon be cleansed and reformed. In 1491, he was appointed prior to the convent of San Marco in Florence and preached to large crowds his vision of a mighty king who would descend upon the sinful people of Italy and cleanse the church. Florentines should seek individual repentance to avoid God's wrath. With the French invasion of Italy in 1494, his prophesies seemed about to be realized and he was influential in the banishment of the Medici from Florence and the installation of the Florentine republic. Over the following three years, he tried to prepare

Florence for the approaching end of time. He called for harsh penalties against homosexuals and blasphemers, and tried to have the Jews expelled or converted. With opposition to his changes mounting, however, he was arrested, tortured, forced to confess to false prophecy, and executed on 23 May 1498.

Sepúlveda Juan Ginés (de) (c.1490–c.1573): Spanish humanist. He studied at Alcalá and Bologna. He defended the natural rights of the Spanish monarchy to wage war and enslave the American Indians on the grounds of conquest. He engaged in a famous debate in 1550 at Valladolid against Bartolomé de Las Casas on the matter.

Servetus Michael (c.1509–53): Born in northern Spain (Villaneuva), he studied in Toulouse, becoming then (or later) a physician. His wandering life thereafter took him to Strasbourg, Basel and Paris before he settled in Lyon and Vienne where he worked as a publisher's assistant. He was immensely well-read and highly intelligent and had the humanists' delight in undermining previously accepted notions and fusing different traditions. On the basis of neo-Platonic and mystic influences, he questioned the accepted Galenic physiological notions of the bloodstream. He also developed a radically novel way of interpreting the Bible. Drawing on Rabbinic sources, he questioned the doctrine of the Trinity. Although he published under pseudonyms or anonymously, the authorities in Vienne became aware of his identity and tried him for heresy. He escaped to Geneva en route for Italy but was again discovered and burned at the stake for his antitrinitarian views. The trial was highly controversial and Calvin's role in it much debated. Although his books were seized in France and burned at Geneva, copies of them survived and were taken to Poland, Lithuania and Transylvania. They were translated into Polish and Hungarian and acted as the somewhat unlikely foundation-stones for the unitarian+ beliefs underpinning the Polish Brethren and the Hungarian unitarian church in the sixteenth century.

Simons Menno (c.1496–1561): A priest from Friesland, the Netherlands, who became a Dutch anabaptist leader. His many followers became known as 'Mennists', and later as 'Mennonites'. His brother died in a Friesland rising in support of the Münster affair in 1535; his own conversion to anabaptism followed soon after and he was ordained an elder by Obbe Philips* before 1540. He spent the remainder of his life being chased by the authorities and in hiding. He lived partly in Groningen, Holland, and partly in the duchy of Holstein. His opposition to elements of Melchiorite anabaptism, especially its resistance to the secular power, the propositions in respect of polygamy and the imminent visible kingdom of Christ on this earth, led him to articulate a distinctively more moderate and quietist vision. 'Spiritual resurrection' around the 'new birth' in Christ was the central plank for the baptized brethren who together made up the true church of regenerate souls who were bearing the cross of Christ. He accepted the necessity for the ban[†] of those brethren whose behaviour or beliefs did not conform but apparently urged its lenient use. This did not, however, prevent increasing divisions amongst the Dutch anabaptists in the 1550s.

Sixtus V (Pope) (*Felice Peretti*) (1520–90): Pope from 1585. He was a Franciscan who became papal nominee on the Venetian inquisition in 1557. His rigidity led to his being recalled in 1560. He was made a cardinal in 1570. He was one of the most effective reforming popes of the sixteenth century. He enforced the council of Trent's decrees with measures on clerical discipline and the reform of the central administration of the church (see pages 208–12). In the Papal States he repressed brigandage and carried out extensive visitations of all the churches and colleges in Rome. Through the expansion of its credit and increased fiscality, he financed ambitious public works projects in Rome, imported grain in bad years to feed the local population, funded a fleet to protect its commerce against the North African corsairs, and hoped to have sufficient resources to influence international affairs. In the latter, his attentions were dominated by events in England. He offered to underwrite part of the costs of the Armada for Philip II. Meanwhile, in France, he wanted to support the Catholic League without encouraging Spanish ambitions.

Sozzini Fausto (*Socinus*) (1539–1604): Nephew to Lelio Sozzini* and much indebted to his uncle for his antitrinitarian ideas. He retained the patronage of the Grand Duke Cosimo I of Florence until the latter's death in 1587 providing that he did not subscribe in public to his unorthodox notions. His initial works therefore circulated in manuscript and found a following amongst unitarians in Transylvania and Poland. When he finally visited Poland in 1583, he was lionized by the Polish Brethren. Following the death of his Florentine protector and the seizure by the inquisition of his property, he decided to stay in Poland and became a key unifying force in the Polish Brethren's movement. His antitrinitarian doctrines were more uncompromising than those of Servetus*. Christ was an entirely human and historical figure with no preexistent divinity.

Sozzini Lelio (*Socinus*) (1525–62): Notable antitrinitarian. The son of a law professor at Padua, he travelled widely in northern Europe, refining his religious views and acquiring a reputation as a persistent and tiresome doubter. On the death of his father, his portion of the inheritance was confiscated by the inquisition on the grounds of his suspected heresy. He spent the last years of his life in Switzerland and wrote an exposition of the first chapter of the Gospel of St John which implicitly rejected the notion of the Trinity. His views were developed by his nephew Fausto.

Spalatinus Georgius (*Georg Burckhardt*) (1484–1545): German humanist and secretary to Elector Friedrich the Wise. He had studied under Luther and acted as his intermediary with the elector. He accompanied the elector to the diet of Worms to act as his advisor and, under his successor (Johann Friedrich) drew up plans for the implementation of the Lutheran reformation of the Saxon church. He translated some of Luther's writings into German from Latin.

Spengler Lazarus (1479–1534): A humanist lawyer and supporter of Martin Luther in Nuremberg. He studied law at the university of Leipzig and when he returned to his native city of Nuremberg he joined the literary circle that called itself the *Sodalitas Celtica* in honour of the humanist Conrad Celtis (1459–1508), the renowned German humanist poet. The group later changed its name to the *Martinianer* after Martin Luther's visit to the city in 1518.

Staupitz Johannes von (c.1490–1524): The vicar-general in Germany of Luther's Augustinian order. He had been invited by Elector Friedrich the Wise* to assist in the setting up of the new university of Wittenberg and became the first dean in its faculty of theology. In 1503, he became vicar-general of the order and it was in this capacity that he took a protective interest in Luther, whom he chose to succeed him at Wittenberg. He refused to discipline him for his attack upon indulgences. In his last years, he was abbot of the wealthy Benedictine abbey of St Peter at Salzburg and began to preach against the protestant reformation.

Sturm Jakob (1489–1553): Sturm provides a rich example of the influence of Erasmian ideas on the significant urban magistrature of the Rhineland. He was from a patrician family from Strasbourg and had studied under Jakob Wimpfeling* before falling under the spell of Erasmus in the later 1510s. By the early 1520s, he was a supporter of the evangelical[†] reformation and, in January 1524, he entered the city government of Strasbourg (*Rat*). In 1526, he was its chief magistrate (*Stettmeister*) and in charge of the city's external affairs. This brought him into contact with the other Lutheran principalities of the German empire and he played a key role in the negotiations leading to the Schmalkaldic League. He was one of the leading lay figures who argued for limiting the toleration of radical sectaries in Strasbourg and for the creation of its state church. But his humanist leanings showed through most clearly in his support for the Latin school (*Gymnasium*) established in the city in 1538, whose reformed curriculum, devised by his namesake Johannes Sturm (1507–89), became a model for other protestant colleges in Germany and elsewhere.

Suárez Francisco (1548–1617): Spanish Jesuit philosopher. He was born into a family of lawyers from Granada, studied at Salamanca (1561) and joined the Jesuits (1564). From 1571 he taught philosophy and theology in various universities and later at the Jesuit Collegium Romanum (1580–85). From 1597 until his death he was professor of theology at the university of Coimbra (Portugal). It was there that he published his major philosophical work (*Disputationes Metaphysicae* (1597)) in which he dealt with the questions of human free will which would become identified with the Jesuits more generally. In later works, he tackled the delicate questions of political obedience, arguing that the people are the original possessors of political authority. He regarded the state as founded on a contractual basis, with its people being entitled by their contract to live their lives with liberty.

Sztárai Michael (H: *Mihály*; Lat: *Starinus*) (1520–75): Hungarian reformer and protestant missionary. He was of noble extraction and had been a Franciscan friar. By the 1540s he was a school-teacher and it was as a propagator of the protestant faith, especially in Turkish-occupied parts of Hungary that he would be best remembered. He gradually organized a Lutheran church in eastern Poland with parishes and church officials, much to the disquiet of Turkish officials. His methods of evangelizing were unorthodox, making use of popular songs and contemporary jokes in his sermons. He translated some of the Psalms into Hungarian and rendered some of the biblical stories as epic dramas for the stage.

Teresa (Saint)(of Jesus) of Ávila (1515–82): Spanish mystic and religious reformer. She was educated by Augustinian nuns and, despite family pressure, entered the Carmelite convent at Ávila in 1533. From 1557 onwards, she began to have mystical experiences which propelled her towards founding a new convent in 1563 where poverty and strict seclusion from the outside world would be more completely maintained. In 1567, she was granted permission to found further convents for her new order of 'Discalced' (i.e. wearers of sandals) Carmelites and, by the time of her death, there were 17 reformed houses for women and a further 15 for men. Her success, and the suspicions aroused by her mystical writings engaged the opposition of those in authority in the Spanish church but she retained the protection of King Philip II and (later) Pope Gregory XIII. Her reputation as a mystic rests on a series of four remarkable works, amongst which the *House of Perfection* (*Casa de perfección*) and *The Interior Castle* (*Las morados o el castillo interior*) are masterpieces of Christian mystical writing. She was canonized in 1622.

Tetzel Johann (1465–1519): German preacher and indulgence-seller. He was a Dominican who was appointed in 1516 to sell indulgences in aid of the rebuilding of St Peter's in and around Magdeburg. His flair for publicity attracted Luther's response in the 95 theses (see page 49).

Torquemada Tomás de (1420–98): Grand Inquisitor of the Spanish inquisition. His activities helped to shape the institution. He conducted an energetic campaign against the crypto-Jews (*marranos*). He demanded that the state expel all the remaining practising Jews in order to assimilate the *marranos* properly. It was through the publicity which he gave to the accusation against the Jews that they were practising ritual murder that he assisted in achieving their expulsion from Spain in 1492 (see page 153).

Valdés Alfonso de (c.1500–33): Valdés was a humanist royal secretary of Charles V, originally from the Castilian province of Cuenca. In 1526, he became secretary to Charles V's chancellor, Mercurino di Gattinara, by which time he was a correspondent of Erasmus and enthusiastic advocate of his ideas. On Gattinara's death, he took over the chancellor's role as mediator at the diet of Augsburg in 1530. By his death, he was regarded with suspicion by the inquisition.

Vergara Juan de (1492–1557): A student at the Spanish humanist cradle, the university of Alcalá, where he became a collaborator on the Complutensian Polyglot Bible before being appointed secretary to Cardinal Francisco Jiménez de Cisneros*. He met Erasmus on a trip to the Low Countries in 1520–22 and was also present at the diet of Worms of 1521 where Luther resisted the will of the emperor. He continued to correspond with Erasmus in the 1520s but at the expense of becoming a marked man to the officials of the inquisition. He was arrested in 1533 and accused of being a closet Lutheran, Erasmian and illuminist. Although he was partially cleared of the charges in 1535, he had to pay a substantial fine and retire to monastic seclusion for a year.

Vio Thomas de – see (Cardinal) Cajetan.

Viret Pierre (1511–71): French protestant reformer. He was a disciple of Guillaume Farel* with whom he was a minister at Neuchâtel and Geneva. In the early 1560s he was despatched to southern France where his distinctive preaching against idolatry made its mark in outbreaks of iconoclasm[†]. His *Christian instruction* (*Instruction chrétienne*) of 1564 argued the case for a right of resistance to established authority on religious grounds for individuals.

Vives Juan Luís (1492?–1540): Although born in Valencia, Spain, Vives lived most of his life in the Low Countries. It was at Bruges (Brugge) that he joined a group of humanist church reformers and published, with Erasmus' help, a commentary on Augustine's *City of God*. But it was in education and charitable endeavour that he most accurately represented Christian humanist objectives and influenced poor relief policy. Although he was widely read by both catholics and protestants, some of his works were held suspect and placed on the Roman Index.

Wimpfeling Jakob (1450–1528): Humanist professor of poetry and rhetoric at the university of Heidelberg who became cathedral preacher at Speyer and an early protestant reformer in Alsace. He enjoyed close friendship with Sebastian Brant* and Geiler von Kaisersberg. He used his humanist credentials to attack contemporary abuses, especially amongst the clergy.

Xavier (Saint) Francis (1506–52): Spanish Jesuit and missionary, known as the 'Apostle of the Indies'. He was amongst the original companions of Ignatius Loyola* at Paris. Ordained at Venice in 1537, he set out for the East Indies in 1541 and began a series of highly successful missionary visits to Ceylon, Malacca (1545) and the Moluccas (1546). His more ambitious expedition to Japan set off in 1549. In 1552 he set off for China but died on an island close by the Chinese mainland. He was canonized in 1622.

Zell Katharina (1497/8–1562): Protestant reformer at Strasbourg. She wrote some fascinating treatises on theological matters, challenging accepted categorizations of women in relation to theology and the reformation. She married Matthias Zell* in 1523 and defended the legitimacy of clerical marriage. She corresponded with Luther as well as other reformers.

Zell Matthias (1477–1548): Protestant reformer at Strasbourg. After a period of study at Freiburg, he taught theology in the city and became a priest. But he devoted himself to the protestant reformation from 1521 and became a highly popular preacher.

Zwilling Gabriel (c.1487–1558): Protestant reformer, iconoclast and pastor at Torgau. He studied at Prague and Wittenberg where he became Luther's companion in the Augustinian convent. During Luther's enforced absence from the town in 1521 he collaborated with Karlstadt* in promoting rapid changes in the church which led to outbreaks of iconoclasm. When Luther returned, he quelled the enthusiasms and Zwilling was sent to serve as a pastor at Torgau.

Zwingli Huldrych (1483–1531): Swiss protestant reformer. He was born at Wildhaus in the canton of St Gall, the son of the local mayor, and educated at Bern (1497–98), Vienna (1500–2) and Basel (1502–6). Soon after gaining his MA he was ordained and became the pastor at Glarus where he continued his humanist studies and learnt some Hebrew. He then became chaplain to the Swiss mercenaries in Italy and was present at the battle of Marignano (1515), where they were defeated. In 1518, he was invited to become a priest in the principal church at Zürich, where he remained until his death.

He began preaching on the New Testament in 1519. His sermons reflected his fundamental rethinking of the significance of the Gospel message. By that date Zwingli was aware of the significance of Luther's attacks on indulgences and the veneration of relics and saints; but he always insisted that he had developed his own opposition to the established religious order by an independent route. Supported by the town council in Zürich, he was not forced to confront any major practical challenge until 1522 when Johann Faber, the vicar-general of the bishop of Konstanz, was sent to Zürich to oppose his attack on abstaining from eating meat in Lent. The progressive divisions which marked out the reformation at Zürich in the 1520s saw Zwingli playing a leading part and helping to shape the particular emphases of the reformation there (see pages 94–7). These included an insistence on removing all traces of idolatry from worship, a greater significance attached to education and indoctrination, which showed through in a more radical recasting of church services and liturgies, and finally an emphasis placed on a public and 'civic' concern for obedience, social discipline and responsibility. By the end of the 1520s, the Zwinglian-influenced reformation had an underlying sense that the Lutheran reformation had not gone far enough.

The reformation in Zürich caused Zwingli to have to face internal opposition from those who wanted to radicalize it still further. His opposition to the advocates of adult baptism formed one of the important themes in the Zürich reformation of the 1520s (see pages 102–3). His controversy with Luther proved to be even more explosive. It began with a letter from Zwingli to a friend in 1524 where he outlined his 'sacramentarian'[†] interpretation of the eucharist and it continued in pamphlets and letters until the colloquy at Marburg (1529) (see page 232). In his final years, Zwingli was preoccupied with the importance of winning over other Swiss cantons to the protestant reformation. His greatest success occurred in the theological disputation at Bern in early 1528. This secured the allegiance of the canton of Bern. But Zwingli died in 1531 serving as chaplain in an army fighting against the Swiss 'forest cantons' (see page 94) who opposed the protestant reformation and the growing hegemony of Zürich and Bern.

SECTION TWELVE

Glossary

12.1 Glossary

This glossary is shorter than might be expected because many definitions have been included within the text proper and may be located by referring to page numbers given in bold type in the index.

Alumbrados   The term was coined in Spain in the early sixteenth century, possibly amongst the inquisitors, for those mystical individuals and groups who were believed to be 'illuminated by the Holy Spirit'. Although the inquisition apparently believed such conventicles to be highly active and influential, in reality there were only a small number of significant, but highly disparate, groups and a further smattering of individuals which the inquisition was eventually able to uncover. (See pages 153–4.)

Annates   The first year's revenue of an ecclesiastical benefice, paid to the papal curia.

Augustine of Hippo (St) (345–430)   Bishop of Hippo, and one of the great 'Doctors of the Church'. His substantial theological and philosophical writings had an enormous impact on the theologians of the protestant reformation.

Concordat   A negotiated agreement between civil and ecclesiastical authorities over matters of ecclesiastical jurisdiction, taxation, or ecclesiastical rights of self-determination.

Conversos   The term used in the Spanish peninsula for Christianized Jews and their descendants and also for converted Muslims – see also '*marranos*'.

Degradation   The depriving of a cleric of his benefice, privileges and orders.

Evangelism; evangelical   The term was already in use in the sixteenth century by the protestant reformers to describe their reliance upon the

'Gospel' of the 'Evangelists' and their desire to return to the Christianity of the earliest days of the faith. The term became used in Germany and Switzerland (G: *evangelisch*) to delineate the Lutheran (as opposed to the 'Calvinist' Reformed[†]) churches. Modern historians use the term to describe the explosive appeal of protestantism's call for a biblical Christianity, open to all, especially in its earliest years. These were the years when protestant preachers and writers found themselves leading a movement with huge social potential but great inner variety.

The term 'evangelism' was also used by scholars in the early twentieth century to describe the groups of protestant-inclined Christians in Italy who accepted the concept of justification of faith, but were unable or unwilling to commit themselves openly to protestantism. The efforts to delineate the disparate trends of religious change in sixteenth-century Italy into the single category of 'evangelism' have inevitably, however, led to criticism. There certainly were individuals and groups who read protestant literature and were influenced by protestant ideas. There were also reforming individuals and groups within the church (sometimes referred to be contemporaries as '*spirituali*' because they criticized other contemporary churchmen for their worldliness) who might, or might not, have been influenced directly by protestant ideas. Finally, there were also study groups and conventicles to be found in various localities in Italy where Bibles were read and works which stimulated individual Christian piety circulated. The groups were held in suspicion by the revived inquisition, and it is as a result of its investigations that we know most about the existence, and gradual effacement, of popular 'evangelism' in Italy (see pages 148–50).

Exorcism   The practice of expelling malign spirits by means of prayer.

Gallicanism, Gallican Articles   The essence of Gallicanism was the assertion of a considerable degree of freedom for the church in France from the ecclesiastical authority of the papacy. It was a claim sustained by leading Sorbonne theologians (such as Jean Gerson*) from the fifteenth century onwards and supported by French lawyers and judges in the parlements. The rights of the Gallican church (hence the name 'Gallicanism' adopted in the later seventeenth century) were based on the prerogatives of the French crown. They were expressed in Charles VII's attempts to apply the canons of the council of Basel[†] unilaterally in France by means of the 'Pragmatic Sanction' of Bourges, issued by the French clergy on 7 July 1438. In the sixteenth century, they emerged in the opposition in the *parlement* to François I's decision to sign the 'Concordat' of Bologna with Pope Leo X* which nullified the 'Gallican' aspects of the 'Pragmatic Sanction' of Bourges whilst gaining papal recognition for the royal rights in the French church which it had also proclaimed.

Huguenot, Huguenots The term, first used as one of abuse by their critics in around 1560, to describe French protestants.

Illuminism See *alumbrados*.

Jansenism The views attributed to Cornelis Jansen*. They were summed up in five propositions extracted from or clearly implied in his large treatise, the *Augustinus* (1640) and condemned by the Sorbonne in 1649. They concerned his interpretation of the theology of grace.

Jubilee In the catholic church, a holy year in which a special indulgence was granted to those who went on pilgrimage to Rome.

Marranos The pejorative word – it means 'pigs' – for the crypto-Jews of Spain and Portugal – i.e. those who adhered to their faith secretly after they had been forced to undergo baptism.

Meaux Circle The individuals who congregated around the reforming bishop Guillaume Briçonnet in his diocese of Meaux, to the east of Paris, and attempted to introduce reform, including regular preaching around passages from the Gospel and ambitious changes to the local social welfare arrangements. The outbreak of iconoclastic[†] incidents and the opposition from the Franciscans and the Sorbonne as well as the parlement of Paris led to bishop Briçonnet being brought to trial in 1525 for allowing heresy to spread in his diocese. Others in the group (including Lefèvre d'Etaples*) found themselves under warrant for arrest and fled and the Meaux experiment was brought to an abrupt end.

Melchiorites The followers of Melchior Hofmann*.

Mennonites The followers of the anabaptist Menno Simons*.

Pelagius A British monk in c.400AD who gave his name to a theology (Pelagianism) which held that mankind took the first steps towards salvation by its own efforts and without the assistance of divine grace. The theology and its associated followers were declared heretical in the early fifth century AD. The charge of Pelagianism was often asserted of one's opponents in sixteenth-century controversies of grace and justification.

Polish Brethren Polish supporters of Jan Hus* (see page 114).

Protestantism The name for the doctrines of the protestant reformation, derived from the 'protestatio' presented by the supporters of Luther to the diet of Speyer (1529) (see page 61) in opposition to the decisions taken by its catholic majority.

'Reformed'   The term commonly used to delineate Calvinist churches and their adherents in the sixteenth century. This corresponded to their own expressions (Fr: *églises réformées*: G: *reformierte Kirchen*) as well as to those used by their opponents. In France, the protestants were often referred to in official documents as 'those of the so-called Reformed religion'.

Sacramentarians   The name given by Martin Luther to those theologians (such as Huldrych Zwingli* and Johannes Oecolampadius*) who maintained that the bread and wine in the eucharist were the body and blood of Christ in only a 'sacramental' or 'metaphorical' sense. The word became widely used, especially in France, to describe all protestants.

Secularization, secularized   In the sixteenth century, these terms apply to lands formerly belonging to the church, which were transferred into lay ownership. These lands included substantial territories in Germany which had formerly belonged to the catholic church and which were secularized in the course of the protestant reformation.

(The) Sorbonne   The theological faculty of the university of Paris.

Tithe   Payments from the laity for the maintenance of the clergy. Theoretically a tenth portion of production, tithes were, in fact, of varying proportions and composed of different elements, depending on the products being tithed and the methods of payment agreed. Many tithes were 'commuted' to fixed money payments by the sixteenth century.

Usury   The exacting of interest for loans. It was formally condemned by various councils of the church on the grounds that money was merely a medium of exchange, 'barren' in itself and incapable of productive good. In reality, 'reasonable' rates of interest (i.e. 5%, or the equivalent of rates of return on land) were allowable and a variety of legal fictions were in existence to permit lending without legal redress. Luther and Zwingli continued to condemn the lending of money for interest. Calvin's views were more complex. Usury was not, of itself, unlawful except in the circumstances where it 'contravenes equity and brotherly union'. Amongst the rich, he accepted that usury was 'freely permitted'.

Veneration   The touching, or kissing, of an object with holy power or associations.

Wyclif, John (c.1330–80)   English theologian and ecclesiastical reformer, whose views were condemned at the council of Constanz (1415) and whose supporters became known as Lollards.

Zwinglianism   The doctrines associated with the Swiss protestant reformer Huldrych Zwingli*.

SECTION THIRTEEN

Guide to further reading

Any comprehensive bibliography to the European reformation giving just the published works in the major European languages over the last twenty years would produce a volume comfortably larger than this. So this has to be a highly selective, and doubtless idiosyncratic and even arbitrary, bibliographical commentary. The author feels rather like a gardener having the privilege of showing someone around the Lord's magnificent estate, large tracts of which he has rarely been able to do more than walk round, let alone dig or plant, himself. It aims to provide an itinerary to the major recent trends in published reformation work. There is an inevitable concentration on works published in English. Books are preferred to articles. English works (and English translations of foreign-language publications) are preferred over those in foreign languages. Asterisks indicate the existence of particularly useful bibliographies in other published works.

13.1 Guides, dictionaries and reference works

The standard reference work to be found on many library shelves has just appeared in a new and thoroughly revised edition: F.L. Cross and E.A. Livingstone (eds), *The Oxford Dictionary of the Christian Church*, 3rd edition (Oxford, 1997). Equally recent and even more invaluable is Hans J. Hillerbrand (ed.), *The Oxford Encyclopaedia of the Reformation*, 4 vols (New York and Oxford, 1996)*. Amongst the atlases, there is nothing which matches Hubert Jedin, K.S. Latourette and J. Martin (eds), *Atlas zur Kirchengeschichte; die Christlichen Kirchen in Geschichte und Gegenwart* (Freiburg, 1975). J.S. Purvis, *Dictionary of Ecclesiastical Terms* (London, 1962) is a handy, brief companion – but not all the definitions hold good for the reformation period.

James E. Bradley and Richard A. Muller, *Church History: An Introduction to Research, Reference Works and Methods* (Grand Rapids, 1995)* provides a general orientation to bibliographies and guides to research. There is an annual supplement to the journal *Archiv für Reformationsgeschichte** which is devoted to an annotated review of the year's publications, much of it in English. William S. Maltby (ed.), *Reformation Europe: a Guide to Research* (St Louis, Center for Reformation Research, 1992)* is as its title suggests. Other literature reviews are more specialized. Lutheran studies are served by Kenneth Hagen (ed.), *Luther Digest: an Annual Abridgement of Luther Studies* (Fort Wayne, Luther Academy, 1993)* as well as by annual reviews in the journal *Lutherjahrbuch*, many of which are in English. Calvin studies rely on the older W. Niesel, *Calvin-Bibliographie, 1901–1959* (Munich, 1961)* and D. Kempff, *A Bibliography of Calviniana, 1959–1974* (Leiden, 1975)*. For Erasmus, there are the critical bibliographies of Jean-Claude Margolin in *Quatorze années de bibliographie Erasmienne, 1936–1949* (Paris, 1969)*, *Douze années de bibliographie Erasmienne, 1950–1961* (Paris, 1963)* and *Neuf années de bibliographie Erasmienne, 1962–1970* (Paris, 1970)*. On Zwingli, there is H.W. Pipkin, *A Zwingli Bibliography* (Pittsburgh, 1972)*. The important specialist bibliography of anabaptism in the reformation era is catered for by Hans J. Hillerbrand (ed.), *A Bibliography of Anabaptism, 1520–1630* (Elkhart, Institute for Mennonite Studies, 1962)* and *A Bibliography of Anabaptism, 1520–1630: a Sequel, 1962–1974* (St Louis, Center for Reformation Research, 1975)*. Thereafter, the extensive reviews section of the journal *Mennonite Quarterly* provides a guide for more recent publications. John W. O'Malley (ed.), *Catholicism in Early Modern History* (St Louis, Center for Reformation Research, 1988)* is a useful synoptic bibliography. Also helpful, albeit now somewhat outdated, is Steven Ozment (ed.), *Reformation Europe: a Guide to Research* (St Louis, Center for Reformation Research, 1982).

There are numerous, generally rather older, valuable encyclopaedias of ecclesiastical history and the church which contain often extensive treatments of particular institutions, individual biographies and theological ideas. *The New Catholic Encyclopedia*, 17 vols (New York, 1967–79) is always valuable as a work of reference. G. Krause and G. Müller (eds), *Theologische Realenzyklopädie* (Berlin, 1977–) is exclusively in German, although the bibliographies are multilingual. The French *Dictionnaire d'histoire et de géographie ecclésiastique*, ed. A. Baudrillart, A. Vogt *et al* (Paris, 1912–) has only reached the letter H. For biographies of individuals, in addition to those contained in the *Oxford Encyclopaedia of the Reformation* already referred to, many relevant entries are to be found in the excellent P.G. Bietenholz (ed.), *Contemporaries of Erasmus*, 3 vols (Toronto, 1985–87). J.N.D. Kelly, *The Oxford Dictionary of Popes* (Oxford and New York, 1986) is brief and summary on the sixteenth-century pontiffs, and no substitute for the wonderful Ludwig van Pastor, *History of the Popes* (translation from the original German edition of Freiburg im Breisgau, 1889–) (40 vols, London, 1891–1953) which is a mine of reference for this period of ecclesiastical history. The *Bibliotheca Dissidentium. Répertoire des non-conformistes religieux des seizième et dix-septième siècles*, ed. André Séguenny (Baden-Baden, 1980–) is now over twenty volumes and contains substantial studies of dissident figures from the reformation period. Harold S. Bender and C. Henry Smith (eds), *The Mennonite Encyclopaedia*, 3 vols (Hillsboro, Kansas, 1955–59) has biographical and thematic entries on the radicals, groupings and ideas which grew out of the protestant reformation.

13.2 General surveys

It is particularly invidious to single out a few of the many recent, and distinguished, general studies of the reformation period. Let us begin with those originating from continental Europe. The monumental *Handbuch der Kirchengeschichte*, 2nd edition (Freiburg im Breisgau, 1967) – translated as the *History of the Church* (ed. Hubert Jedin and John Dolan) contains vol. v (vol. iv of the German edition) by Erwin Iserloh, Joseph Glazik and Hubert Jedin and entitled *Reformation and Counter-Reformation* (London, 1980)* with an extensive bibliography, especially good on German publications. A. Fliche, V. Martin *et al* (eds), *Histoire de l'Eglise depuis les origines jusqu'à nos jours* (1934, n.p. Paris)* is roughly the French equivalent. It was never translated and is now rather dated (vol. xvii is the relevant one by L. Christiani, entitled *L'Eglise à l'époque du Concile de Trente* (1948)). By contrast, the compatriot E.G. Léonard's *History of Protestantism* (ed. H.H. Rowley), 2 vols (London, 1965–67)* retains a good deal of its value. Pierre Chaunu, *Eglise, culture et société. Réforme et Contre-réforme* (Paris, 1984)* was produced as a text for the French *agrégation* examination; it is particularly good at evoking the social and cultural background to the reformation. Jean Delumeau, *Naissance et affirmation de réforme*, 3rd edition (Paris, 1973)* contained an authoritative summary of current debates over the birth of the European reformation. Its counterpart volume was translated as Jean Delumeau, *Catholicism between Luther and Voltaire. A New View of the Counter-Reformation* (London, 1977)* and is similarly orientated towards a summary of the (still current) debate about the fundamental long-term changing relationship between church and people. Pierre Chaunu (ed.), *The Reformation* (Gloucester, 1989) is richly illustrated.

For general surveys by Anglo-Saxon scholars, we are spoiled for choice. Owen Chadwick, *The Reformation* (The Pelican History of the Church, vol. 3) (London, 1972) has now been superseded by E. Cameron, *The European Reformation* (Oxford, 1991)*, an altogether excellent text with a well-informed bibliography. Carter Lindberg, *The European Reformations* (Oxford, 1996) is clear and straightforward. John Bossy, *Christianity in the West* (Oxford, 1985) provides a distinctive interpretative essay on the reformation context. It is best read alongside his articles which develop comparable perspectives. These include 'The mass as a social institution, 1200–1700', *Past and Present*, No. 100 (1983), 29–61; 'The Social History of Confession in the Age of the Reformation', *Transactions of the Royal Historical Society*, 5th Series, vol. xxv (1975), 21–38; and 'Prayers', *Transactions of the Royal Historical Society*, 6th Series, vol. i (1991), 137–48. It may also profitably be compared with the two broad interpretative essays by Jean Delumeau; *La peur en occident, XIVe–XVIIIe siècle: une cité assiégée* (Paris, 1978) and *Sin and Fear: the Emergence of a Western Guilt Culture, 13th–18th centuries* (New York, 1990). By contrast, L.W. Spitz, *The Protestant Reformation, 1517–1559* (New York, 1986) is more confined to the events and developments of the early reformation. George Williams, *The Radical Reformation*, 3rd edition (St Louis, Center for Reformation Research, 1992)* is much more than a general survey, containing more than one could reasonably expect from any one-volume study of the disparate and fissiparous individuals and movements produced during the protestant reformation.

For general surveys of the religious and intellectual thought of the period, there is also a good deal to choose from. A. McGrath, *The Intellectual Origins of the European Reformation* (Oxford, 1987)* is excellent. His *Reformation Thought: an Introduction*, 2nd edition (Oxford, 1993)* contains useful appendices, including a glossary of theological terms. Bernard M.G. Reardon, *Religious Thought in the Reformation*, 2nd edition (London, 1995)* is clear and straightforward. J. Pelikan, *The Christian Tradition: a History of the Development of Doctrine*, vol. 4 (*The Reformation of Church and Dogma (1300–1700)*) (Chicago and London, 1984)* looks at changing theological ideas in a long-term perspective. For political thought in this period, see Q. Skinner, *The Foundations of Modern Political Thought*, 2 vols (esp. vol. 2) (Cambridge, 1978) and also J.H. Burns (ed.), *The Cambridge History of Political Thought, 1450–1700* (Cambridge, 1991). S.E. Ozment, *The Age of Reform, 1250–1550: an Intellectual and Religious History of Late Medieval and Reformation Europe* (New Haven and London, 1980) was a brave attempt at a broad synthesis encompassing the late medieval past, and developed out of his edited volume *The Reformation in Medieval Perspective* (Chicago, 1971). For the humanist background, see C. Trinckaus, *The Scope of Renaissance Humanism* (Ann Arbor, Michigan, 1983) and Anthony Goodman and Angus Mackay (eds), *The Impact of Humanism on Western Europe* (London, 1990). For the complex history of the Bible, see G.W.H. Lampe (ed.), *The Cambridge History of the Bible* vol. 2 (*The West from the Fathers to the Reformation*) (Cambridge, 1969) and vol. 3 (*The West from the Reformation to the Present Day* (Cambridge, 1987).

The reformation was polyvalent and, even at the level of general surveys, it has often made sense to look at it within a geographically delineated area. G.R. Elton (ed.), *The New Cambridge Modern History*, 2nd edition (Cambridge, 1990) is a standard reference work, both for the political background to the period in general and in particular countries. Andrew Pettegree (ed.), *The Early Reformation in Europe* (Cambridge, 1992)* should be complemented by Bob Scribner, Roy Porter and Mikuláš Teich (eds), *The Reformation in National Context* (Cambridge, 1994)*. Both volumes provide up-to-date surveys of the origins and development of the reformation in particular 'national' contexts. Bob Scribner, *The German Reformation* (London, 1986) is a deservedly popular, short introduction to the reformation in that heartland. M. Greengrass, *The French Reformation* (Oxford, 1987) attempts the same for France.

13.3 Published collections of documents and published sources

The reformation has a considerable range of original materials readily available for study in translation, and in modern editions. There are, of course, the works of the protestant reformers themselves. Selections of these are conveniently available in E.G. Rupp and B.J. Drewery, *Martin Luther* (London, 1970); G.R. Potter, *Huldrych Zwingli* (London, 1978) and G.R. Potter and M. Greengrass, *John Calvin* (London, 1983). Calvin's main work is available in a translation by F.L. Battles (ed. John T. McNeill), *The Institutes of the Christian Religion*, 2 vols (Philadelphia and London, 1960). His New Testament commentaries have been retranslated and published in twelve volumes (eds D.W. and T.F. Torrance) (Edinburgh, 1963). Luther's works are extensively available in translation in the American translation, edited by J. Pelikan and H.T. Lehmann, *Luther's Works* (Philadelphia and St Louis, Missouri, 1955–). There are further selections of the major reformers' treatises in translation in the *Library of the Christian Classics* Series, including selections from Luther (vols 15–18); Melanchthon and Bucer (vol. 19); Calvin (vols 20–23); Zwingli and Bullinger (vol. 24); and spiritualists and anabaptists (vol. 25). P. Matheson (ed. and trans.) *The Collected Works of Thomas Müntzer* (Edinburgh, 1988) provides an opportunity to confront the early radical reformer at close quarters. Steven Ozment, *Mysticism and Dissent. Religious Ideology and Social Protest in the Sixteenth Century* (New Haven and London, 1973) is a series of extracts from the more radical writings of the reformation period. Gordon Rupp, *Patterns of Reformation* (London, 1969) sought to document the reformation from the pens of less well-known religious reformers. The political thought of the reformers has also been the subject of particular volumes of edited and selected translations, all with relevant introductions. These include Harro Höpfl (ed.), *Luther and Calvin on Secular Authority* (Cambridge, 1991) and Michael Baylor, *The Radical Reformation* (Cambridge, 1991). A selection of confessional materials is available in A.C. Cochrane, *Reformed Confessions of the Sixteenth Century* (London, 1966) and M.A. Noll, *Confessions and Catechisms of the Reformation* (Leicester, 1991). For the catholic reformation period, the range of documentary materials is less comprehensive. However, H.J. Schroeder *Canons and Decrees of the Council of Trent* (St Louis, 1941) provides a useful comparative edition of this vital and complex document. There are various translations of St Ignatius Loyola's *Spiritual Exercises*. I have used that edited by E.M. Tetlow (New York, 1989) but there is a new Everyman edition also available.

Any mention of the more general documentary collections should perhaps begin with a great classic: B.J. Kidd, *Documents Illustrative of the Continental Reformation* (Oxford, 1911). Though not translated, the extracts included within the collection are so well chosen and introduced that the work has enduring utility. H.J. Hillerbrand, *The Reformation in its Own Words* (London, 1964) provides a documentary collection which extends occasionally beyond the 'magisterial' reformers. Pamela Johnson and Bob Scribner, *The Reformation in Germany and Switzerland* (Cambridge, 1993) is an excellent choice of documentary extracts for teaching purposes. Tom Scott and Bob Scribner (eds), *The German Peasants' War. A History in Documents* (Atlantic Highlands, New Jersey, 1991) is more far-reaching in its scope than its name suggests. Alistair Duke, Gillian Lewis and Andrew Pettegree (eds), *Calvinism in Europe, 1540–1610* (Manchester, 1992) provides an excellent collection of documents for that highly diffuse phenomenon.

13.4 Pre-reformation religion and context

Here is where there has been a considerable degree of historical revision, both about the nature and weaknesses of the late-medieval church, its relationship with the laity, and important questions about popular piety. Many of these questions are prefigured in the surveys by F. Rapp, *L'Eglise et la vie religieuse en occident à la fin du moyen âge* (Paris, 1971)* and F. Oakley, *The Western Church in the Later Middle Ages* (Ithaca, New York, and London, 1979)*. They receive their most recent general treatment in R.N. Swanson, *Religion and Devotion in Europe, c.1215–c.1515* (Cambridge, 1995)*. The debate is somewhat crudely encapsulated in an article by L.G. Duggan, 'The unresponsiveness of the late medieval church: a reconsideration', *Sixteenth-Century Journal*, vol. ix (1978), 3–26.

This historical revision has often proceeded by means of detailed investigations of particular localities. Recent, representative examples of these include F. Rapp, *Réformes et réformation à Strasbourg: église et société dans le diocèse de Strasbourg (1450–1525)* (Paris, 1974); J. Toussaert, *Le sentiment religieux en Flandre à la fin du moyen-âge* (Paris, 1963) and J-L. Gazzaniga, *L'Eglise du midi à la fin du règne de Charles VII d'après la jurisprudence du parlement de Toulouse* (Paris, 1976); see also D. Hay, *The Church in Italy in the Fifteenth Century* (Cambridge 1977). B. Moeller, 'Religious life in Germany on the eve of the Reformation' – translation in G. Strauss (ed.), *Pre-Reformation Germany* (London, 1972), pp. 13–42 – had a considerable impact on the direction of historical investigation and thought by emphasizing the 'popularity' of many religious practices which were subsequently to be condemned by the protestant reformers. W. Christian, *Local Religion in Sixteenth-Century Spain* (Princeton, 1981) also provides evidence for the vitality of local religion on the eve of the protestant reformation.

There are numerous studies of particular ecclesiastical institutions on the eve of the reformation. J.A.F. Thomson, *Popes and Princes, 1417–1517: Politics and Piety in the Late Medieval Church* (London, 1980) looks at relations between the two. On Rome itself, Peter Partner, *Renaissance Rome, 1500–1559* (Berkeley, Los Angeles, and London, 1976) provides a cultural and social portrait. The conciliar movement has generated a substantial literature all to itself. A good deal of it is encapsulated in Anthony Black, *Council and Commune. The Conciliar Movement and the Fifteenth-Century Heritage* (London, 1979). Francis Oakley, *Natural Law, Conciliarism and Consent in the Late Middle Ages* (London, 1984) is particularly useful for analysing the continuity of conciliarism through into the reformation period. Brian Tierney, *Foundations of the Conciliar Theory* (London, reprinted 1968) is the enduring work on the origins and standing of conciliar theory within medieval political and religious thought.

Popular religious thought and practice has also been investigated in a number of thematic contexts. Lionel Rothkrug, *Religious Practices and Collective Perspectives. Hidden Homologies in the Renaissance and Reformation* (a special issue of the journal *Réflexions Historiques*, vol. vii (1980)) investigated the patterns behind the multiplication of shrines in late-medieval Germany. See also, however, C. Zilka, 'Hosts, processions, and pilgrimages in fifteenth-century Germany', *Past and Present*, No. 118 (1988), 25–64. William Christian, *Apparitions in Late Medieval and Renaissance Spain* (Princeton, 1981) also used shrine evidence to investigate that phenomenon. Thomas Tentler, *Sin and Confession on the Eve of the Reformation* (Princeton, 1977) used the surviving confessors' manuals to try to reconstruct attitudes towards sin. See also L.G. Duggan, 'Fear and confession on the eve of the Reformation', *Archiv für Reformationsgeschichte* vol. lxxv (1984), 153–73. The problem of 'anticlericalism' is investigated in the various essays which make up P.A. Dykema and H.A. Oberman (eds), *Anticlericalism in Late Medieval and Early Modern Europe*, Studies in Medieval and Reformation Thought, No. 51 (Leiden, New York and Cologne, 1993). E. William Monter, *Ritual, Myth and Magic in Early Modern Europe* (Brighton, 1983) has an extensive discussion of the problem of 'popular' religion. R. Muchembled, *Popular Culture and Elite Culture in France, 1400–1750* (Baton Rouge, La., 1985) starts from an unambiguous picture of 'popular' religion before the reformation. This is sustained (though in modified fashion) in various contributions to J. Obelkevich (ed.), *Religion and the People, 800–1700* (Chapel Hill, 1979) and A.N. Galpern, *Religions of the People in Sixteenth-Century Champagne* (Cambridge, Mass., 1976).

The history of European late-medieval heterodoxy and dissent has a substantial bibliography all to itself, stretching well beyond the chronological confines of this volume. For our purposes, H. Kaminsky, *A History of the Hussite Revolution* (Berkeley, 1967) and E. Cameron, *The Reformation of the Heretics: The Waldenses of the Alps, 1480–1580* (Oxford, 1984) should be particularly noted, the latter alongside G. Audisio, *Les Vaudois du Lubéron: une minorité en Provence (1460–1560)* (Mérindol, 1984). On the *devotio moderna* and its influence on the reformation, see R.R. Post, *The Modern Devotion: Confrontation with Reformation and Humanism*, Studies in Medieval and Renaissance Theology, vol. 3 (Leiden, 1968). Norman Cohn, *The Pursuit of the Millennium* (London, 1970), formulates a late-medieval millennial tradition which reaches a climax of expression during the early years of the reformation itself.

The question of the impact of the Renaissance on the reformations of the sixteenth century tends to be posed somewhat unequally – more in terms of its influence upon the protestant than the catholic reformation. A. Renaudet's great study, *Préréforme et humanisme à Paris pendant les premières guerres d'Italie (1494–1517)*, 2nd edition (Paris, 1953) makes the case for the profound and challenging effects of humanism upon religious thought in France. L.W. Spitz, *The Religious Renaissance of the German Humanists* (Cambridge, Mass., 1963) makes it more tentatively for Germany. M. Grossmann, *Humanism at Wittenberg 1485–1517* (Nieuwkoop, 1975) provides a case-study. See also, however, James Kittelson, 'Humanism and the Reformation in Germany', *Central European History*, 9 (1976), 303–22. The continuing scholastic context in Germany is stressed in J.H. Overfield, *Humanism and Scholasticism in Late Medieval Germany* (Princeton, 1984). For Luther and humanism, A.G. Dickens, 'Luther and the humanists' in P. Mack (ed.), *Politics and Culture in Early Modern Europe* (Cambridge, 1987) carefully balances Luther's misgivings with his willingness to explore new ways of thinking.

Erasmus studies also have a dynamism which is quite distinctive. The approachable biography by Roland H. Bainton, *Erasmus of Christendom* (London, 1969; reprinted New York, 1982), is still worth reading; but James K. McConica, *Erasmus* (Oxford, 1991) is in the Past Masters series from a present master of Erasmus studies. The most recent and comprehensive study is the recently translated Cornelis Augustijn, *Erasmus: His Life, Works, and Influence* (Toronto, 1991). Erasmus' influence in various parts of Europe is the subject of numerous studies. The most famous is undoubtedly that on Spain by the great French scholar Marcel Bataillon, *Erasme en Espagne* (Paris, 1937). On France, there is M. Mann, *Erasme et les débuts de la réforme française (1517–1536)* (Paris, 1934). For Germany, Peter Bietenholz, 'Erasmus and the German Public, 1518–1520', *Sixteenth Century Journal*, vol. viii (1977), 61–78 is a suitable background to Erasmus' disagreement with Luther. There are several works on the latter. Harry J. Sorley, *Luther Right or Wrong?* (New York, 1968) should be read alongside M. Boyle, *Rhetoric and Reform: Erasmus's Civil Dispute with Luther* (Cambridge, Mass., 1983). See also the latter author's 'Erasmus and the "Modern" Question: Was he semi-Pelagian?', *Archiv für Reformationsgeschichte* vol. lxxv (1984), pp. 59–72. Jerry H. Bentley, *Humanists and Holy Writ* (Princeton, 1983) is a sound study of Erasmus' biblical scholarship. Erika Rummel, *Erasmus and His Catholic Critics*, 2 vols (Nieuwkoop, 1989) is an excellent antidote to excessive Erasmus adulation.

13.5 Magisterial reformers

The biographical approach to the reformation has its historical limitations; but there are exceptional studies of the major protestant reformers and these are often an early point of departure for student reading. Amongst Luther's more recent biographers, Heiko Oberman's translated study *Luther. Man Between God and the Devil* (London, 1990) and H. Bornkamm, *Luther in Mid-career, 1521–1530* (Philadelphia, 1983) are both outstanding works of synthesis and interpretation. Others which ought to be mentioned include John Todd, *Martin Luther. A Biographical Study* (London, 1964); Richard Friedenthal, *Luther* (London, 1970); A.G. Dickens, *Martin Luther and the Reformation* (London, 1967) and *The German Nation and Martin Luther* (London, 1974); S.H. Hendrix, *Luther and the Papacy* (Philadelphia, 1981); Bernard Lohse, *Martin Luther. An Introduction to his Life and Work* (Edinburgh, 1987) and D.C. Steinmetz, *Luther in Context* (Bloomington, Ind., 1986). Two works closely follow and analyse Luther's theological development; W. van Loewenich, *Luther's Theology of the Cross* (London, 1976) and A.E. McGrath, *Luther's Theology of the Cross* (Oxford, 1985). J. Pelikan, *Spirit versus Structure: Luther and the Institutions of the Church* (London, 1968) deals with a critical issue in the evolution of Luther's thought.

On Calvin, there is also a plethora of material to choose from. Amongst the biographies in English, those of William J. Bouwsma, *John Calvin: a Sixteenth-Century Portrait* (Oxford, 1988) and A.E. McGrath, *A Life of John Calvin* (Oxford, 1990) offer contrasting, but rich, perspectives on the reformer. F. Wendel, *Calvin: the Origins and Development of his Religious Thought* (London, 1960) is an older, but still distinguished one-volume study. F.L. Battles (ed.), *John Calvin* (Abingdon, 1966) and W.H. Neuser, *Calvinus Ecclesiae Doctor* (Kampen, c.1980) both bring together disparate series of essays reinterpreting parts of Calvin's life and work. Individual aspects of Calvin's thought are attended to in the following works. For his political thought, see H. Höpfl, *The Christian Polity of John Calvin* (Cambridge, 1985); for economic and social matters, see A. Biéler, *La pensée économique et sociale de Calvin* (Geneva, 1959). For his use of French, see Francis Higman, *The Style of John Calvin in his French Polemical Treatises*

(Oxford, 1967). On his preaching and various aspects of his theology, see T.H.L. Parker, *Calvin's Doctrine of the Knowledge of God*, revised edition (Edinburgh, 1969) and *The Oracles of God: an Introduction to the Preaching of John Calvin* (London, 1962); see also R. Stauffer, *Dieu, la création et la providence dans la prédication de Calvin* (Bern, 1978).

One of the important developments of reformation historiography, however, has been the attention given to the numerous other reformers of the reformation. The process has recovered the 'multi-stranded' and 'polyvalent' nature (to use Bob Scribner's terms) of the movement. To begin with, there is a richer range of works now available to explore the ideas and context of the Swiss reformer, Huldrych Zwingli. These include J. Courvoisier, *Zwingli, a Reformed Theologian* (Richmond, 1964); G.R. Potter, *Zwingli* (Cambridge, 1976); Gerhard Locher, *Zwingli's Thought: New Perspectives*, Studies in the History of Christian Thought, vol. 25 (Leiden, 1981); Illrich Gabler, *Huldrych Zwingli, his Life and Work* (Edinburgh, 1986); J.V. Pollet, *Huldrych Zwingli* (Paris, 1988). Martin Bucer at Strasbourg has also received greater (and overdue) attention. The most comprehensive study still remains available only in German: Martin Greschat, *Martin Bucer. Ein Reformator und seine Zeit* (Munich, 1990). But Christian Krieger and Marc Lienhard (eds), *Martin Bucer and Sixteenth-Century Europe*, 2 vols (Leiden, 1993) provides an embracing collection of studies; see also D.F. Wright, *Martin Bucer: Reforming Church and Community* (Cambridge, 1994). W.P. Stephens, *The Holy Spirit in the Theology of Martin Bucer* (Cambridge, 1970) is a thorough theological evaluation of one crucial aspect of Bucer's thinking. Other magisterial reformers to emerge from the shadows include Johannes Brenz, the Lutheran reformer from Schwäbisch-Hall. His skills as a church organizer have been emphasized by James M. Estes, *Christian Magistrate and State Church: The Reforming Career of Johannes Brenz* (Toronto, 1982). For Philipp Melanchthon, there is Clyde Manschreck, *Melanchthon: The Quiet Reformer* (Westport, Conn., 1958; reprinted, 1975) and E.P. Meiring, *Melanchthon and Patristic Thought: The Doctrines of Christ and Grace, the Trinity and the Creation*, Studies in the History of Christian Thought, vol. 32 (Leiden, 1983). On the early French reformer Guillaume Farel, the collected papers of a colloquium must serve as an introduction to more recent work: Pierre Barthel, Rémy Scheurer and Richard Stauffer (eds), *Actes du colloque Guillaume Farel* (Geneva, 1983). It includes a complete inventory of his surviving correspondence and a bibliography of his printed works. For Théodore de Bèze, Calvin's successor at Geneva, the biography of Paul-F. Geisendorf, *Théodore de Bèze* (Geneva, 1967) may be supplemented with Tadataka Maruyama, *The Ecclesiology of Theodore Beza: The Reform of the True Church* (Geneva, 1978) and Jill Rait, *The Eucharistic Theology of Theodore Beza: Development of the Reformed Tradition*, AAR Studies in Religion, vol. 4 (Chambersburg, Penn., 1972). Shorter studies of the various secondary doctrinal shapers of protestantism are contained in Richard L. Demolen (ed.), *Leaders of the Reformation* (Selinsgrove, 1984) and Jill Raitt (ed.), *Shapers of Religious Traditions in Germany, Switzerland and Poland, 1560–1600* (New Haven and London, 1981).

A firm division between 'magisterial' and 'radical' reformers was never sustainable and that has become still more evident with the emergence of recent studies, where the subtlety and range of their thinking has become clearer. Karlstadt's 'theology of regeneration' is emphasized in Ronald J. Sider, *Andreas Bodenstein von Karlstadt: the Development of his Thought, 1517–1525*, Studies in Medieval and Renaissance Thought, vol. 11 (Leiden, 1974). For Müntzer, the most auhoritative English-language biography is now Tom Scott, *Thomas Müntzer: Theology and Revolution in the German Reformation* (New York, 1989). See also, however, Abraham Friesen, *Thomas Müntzer, a Destroyer of the Godless* (Berkeley, Cal., 1990) for some challenging chapters on the origins of Müntzer's theology. Kaspar von Schwenckfeld has his own modern interpreters, especially R. Emmet McLaughlin, *Caspar Schwenckfeld: Reluctant Radical* (New Haven and London, 1986). The millennial thinking amongst anabaptist leaders is well evoked in K. Deppermann, *Melchior Hoffman: Social Unrest and Apocalyptic Visions in the Age of Reformation* (Edinburgh, 1987).

13.6 Engraven reformation: printing, engraving and the spread of protestantism

Understanding the mechanisms of the extraordinary diffusion of protestant ideas is vital to explaining its unique impact in sixteenth-century Europe. Explanations must ultimately transcend studies of printing, engraving and preaching and embrace the social impact of the reformation – of which more will be said by way of bibliographical orientation later. For the moment, the sophisticated studies of print culture and its relationship to the enduring traditions of preaching and teaching during the early reformation should be noted. For the background to early printing and its impact see the following: Elizabeth Eisenstein, *The Printing Revolution in Early Modern Europe* (Cambridge, 1983); Lucien Febvre and Henri-Jean Martin, *The Coming of the Book* (London, 1976); S.L. Hindman (ed.), *Printing the Written Word. The Social History of Books, c.1450–1520* (Ithaca, 1991); Miriam Usher Chrisman, *Lay Culture, Learned Culture: Books and Social Change in Strasbourg, 1480–1599* (New Haven and London, 1982). For the adaptation of print-culture to the needs of the early reformation see Bob Scribner, *For the Sake of Simple Folk: Popular Propaganda in the German Reformation* (Cambridge, 1981); numerous articles collected together in his *Popular Culture and Popular Movements in Reformation Germany* (London, 1987), and also 'Heresy, literacy and print in the early German Reformation' in Ann Hudson and Peter Biller (eds),

Heresy and Literacy, c.1100–c.1530 (Cambridge, 1994), pp. 255–78; Mark U. Edwards Jr., *Printing, Propaganda and Martin Luther* (Berkeley and London, 1994). The following is a selection of the fascinating, more recent literature emerging on the imagery in early German reformation woodcuts and engravings: C. Andersson, 'Polemical Prints in Reformation Nuremberg' in J. Chipps Smith (ed.), *New Perspectives on the Art of Renaissance Nuremberg* (Archer M. Huntington Art Gallery, University of Texas at Austin, 1985); C. Andersson, 'Popular imagery in German Reformation broadsheets' in G.P. Tyson and S.S. Wygonheim (eds), *Printing and Culture in the Renaissance* (Newark, Del., 1986); C. Andersson and C. Talbot (eds), *From a Mighty Fortress. Prints, Drawings and Books in the Age of Luther, 1483–1546* (Detroit, 1983); Thomas Brady, 'The Social Place of a German Renaissance Artist: Hans Baldung Grien at Strasbourg', *Central European History*, vol. viii (1975), 299–315; R.G. Cole, 'Pamphlet woodcuts in the communication process of Reformation Germany' in K.C. Sessions and P.N. Bebb (eds), *Pietas and Societas. New Trends in Reformation Social History* (Kirksville, Miss., 1985); K. Moxey, *Peasants, Warriors and Wives. Popular Imagery in the Reformation* (Chicago, 1989); R.A. Crofts, 'Printing, reform and the Catholic Reformation in Germany (1521–1545)', *Sixteenth Century Journal* vol. xvi (1985). Amongst the broader studies about the role of art and images in the reformation, that of C.C. Christensen, *Art and the Reformation in Germany* (Athens, 1979) may now be complemented with the same author's case-study on *Princes and Propaganda: Electoral Saxon Art and the Reformation* (Kirksville, Miss., 1992); Carlos M. Eire, *War Against the Idols: The Reformation of Worship from Erasmus to Calvin* (Cambridge, 1986) is a broad and fascinating study of attitudes towards images and the divisions which it provoked amongst the reformers themselves. See also now, however, S. Michalski, *The Reformation and the Visual Arts. The Protestant Image Question in Western and Eastern Europe* (London, 1993).

The question of the enduring significance of preaching becomes linked to that of the lay impact of the early German reformation more generally. S. Karant-Nunn, 'What was preached in German cities in the early years of the Reformation?' in P. Bebb and Sherrin Marshall (eds), *The Process of Change in Early Modern Europe* (Athens, Ohio, 1988); Paul Russell, *Lay Theology in the Reformation. Popular Pamphleteers in Southwest Germany, 1521–1525* (Cambridge, 1986) provides some evidence for what may have been preached from the published pamphlet material. The question of the involvement of the laity is picked up also in H. Robinson-Hammerstein, 'Luther and the laity' in H. Robinson-Hammerstein (ed.), *The Transmission of Ideas in the Lutheran Reformation* (Dublin, 1989); Miriam Usher Chrisman, 'Lay response to the Protestant Reformation in Germany, 1520–1528' in P.N. Brooks (ed.), *Reformation Principle and Practice* (London, 1980).

13.7 The reformation in Germany

At the heart of the protestant reformation lay a 'coalescence' (to use the term adopted by Euan Cameron) of a novel set of ideas with the political and social aspirations of particular groups in society, local polities and government which, when lined up together, inaugurated permanent changes in the way those societies then governed themselves and looked at the world. That process of 'coalescence' has been particularly intensively studied in Germany, whether in the case of the territorial princes, the peasants or the self-governing cities. The general background to the reformation in Germany can be found in a variety of standard accounts, such as Franz Lau and E. Bizer, *A History of the Reformation in Germany to 1555* (London, 1969).

For the princely reformation, there are older accounts of the polities of the German princes, especially F.L. Carsten, *Princes and Parliaments in Germany from the Fifteenth to the Eighteenth Century* (Oxford, 1959). H.J. Cohn (ed.), *Government in Reformation Europe, 1520–1560* (London, 1971) contains several relevant articles. T.A. Brady, 'Princes' Reformation versus urban liberty: Strasbourg and the restoration in Württemberg, 1534' in I. Batori (ed.), *Stadtische Gesellschaft und Reformation* (Stuttgart, 1980), pp. 265–91 is a useful case-study of the tensions between princely and city reformations. T.A. Brady, 'Phases and strategies of the Schmalkaldic League', *Archiv für Reformationsgeschichte*, vol. lxxiv (1983), 162–81 analyses the evolution and internal dynamics of the protestant league in Germany. Henry Cohn, 'Church property in the German Protestant principalities' in E.I. Kouri and Tom Scott (eds), *Politics and Society in Reformation Europe* (London, 1987) deals with an important issue in the princely reformation. M.U. Edwards, *Luther's Last Battles. Politics and Polemic, 1531–1546* (Leiden, 1983) explores Luther's later relationships with the Lutheran princes. H.J. Hillerbrand, *Landgrave Philip of Hesse, 1504–1567* (London, 1967) is a study of one of the most intelligent of the Lutheran German princes. Irmgard Hoss, 'The Lutheran Church of the Reformation: Problems of its organization and formation' in L.P. Buck and J.W. Zophy, *The Social History of the Reformation* (Columbus, 1972), pp. 317–39 gives a good account of the practical difficulties in establishing a Lutheran territorial church.

The Great Peasants' War of 1524–26 has a substantial specialist literature all to itself. Peter Blickle, *The Revolution of 1525* (Baltimore and London, 1981) and *The Communal Reformation* (London, 1992) argues the case for a great 'communal' uprising. This is just one of the 'new viewpoints' represented in R.W. Scribner and G. Benecke (eds), *The German Peasant War. New Viewpoints* (London, 1979). Two helpful review articles by Tom Scott, 'The Peasants' War: a historiographical review', *Historical*

Journal, vol. xxii, (1979), 693–720, 953–74 and 'The common people in the German Reformation', *Historical Journal,* vol. xxxiv, 1990, 183–92 take the debate onwards to our own decade. Various specialist studies illuminate important aspects of the Peasants' War and its relationship to the reformation. H.J. Cohn, 'Anticlericalism in the German Peasants' War', *Past and Present,* No. 83 (1979), 3–31; C. Scott Dixon, *The Reformation and Rural Society. The Parishes of Brandenburg-Ansbach-Kulmbach, 1528–1603* (Cambridge, 1996); Tom Scott, *Freiburg and the Breisgau. Town–Country Relations in the Age of Reformation and Peasants' War* (Oxford, 1986); James M. Stayer, *The German Peasants' War and Anabaptist Community of Goods* (London, 1994).

The greatest efflorescence of scholarship has, however, concerned the protestant reformation and the German cities. The process was greatly stimulated by the appearance of Miriam Usher Chrisman, *Strasbourg and the Reform* (New Haven and London, 1967) and B. Moeller, *Imperial Cities and the Reformation: Three Essays* (Philadelphia, 1972). This was quickly followed by Stephen Ozment, *The Reformation in the Cities* (New Haven and London, 1975). T.A. Brady, *Turning Swiss. Cities and Empire, 1450–1550* (Cambridge, 1985) examined the cities of south-western Germany in the light of the Swiss example. The urban framework of this region and the reformation had already, however, been ably examined by Manfred Hannemann, *The Diffusion of the Reformation in Southwestern Germany, 1518–1534* (Chicago, 1975). Amongst the numerous individual studies of the German reformation in particular cities, the following are noted: L.J. Abray, *The People's Reformation. Magistrates, Clergy and Commons in Strasbourg 1500–1598* (Oxford, 1985); T.A. Brady, *Ruling Class, Regime and Reformation at Strasbourg* (Leiden, 1978); T.A. Brady, 'In search of the Godly city' in Po-Chia Hsia, *The German People and the Reformation* (Ithaca, 1986), pp. 14–31; P. Broadhead, 'Politics and expediency in the Augsburg Reformation' in P.N. Brooks (ed.), *Reformation Principle and Practice* (London, 1980); C. Scott Dixon, 'The German Reformation and the Territorial City', *German History,* 14 (1996); Hans Guggisberg, *Basel in the Sixteenth Century* (St Louis, Miss., 1982); S.C. Karant-Nunn, *Zwickau in Transition 1500–1547: The Reformation as an Agent of Change* (Columbus, 1987); H-C. Rublack, 'Is there a new history of the urban Reformation?' in E.I. Kouri and Tom Scott (eds), *Politics and Society in Reformation Europe* (London, 1987) and also his 'Martin Luther and the urban social experience', *Sixteenth Century Journal,* vol. xvi (1985); Heinz Schilling, 'The Reformation in the Hanseatic cities', *Sixteenth Century Journal,* vol. xiv (1983); R.W. Scribner, 'Civic unity and the Reformation in Erfurt', *Past and Present,* No. 66 (1975); R.W. Scribner, 'Why was there no Reformation in Cologne?', *Bulletin of the Institute of Historical Research,* vol. xlix (1976).

13.8 The reformation in the Swiss cantons and Geneva

For the reformation in its Swiss context, it is easy for the focus upon Geneva to overwhelm the interest which we ought to have in the reformation in eastern Switzerland. N. Birnbaum, 'The Zwinglian Reformation in Zurich', *Past and Present*, No. 15 (1959), 27–47 can be supplemented by R.C. Walton, *Zwingli's Theocracy* (Toronto, 1967). J.W. Baker, 'Church, state and dissent: the crisis of the Swiss Reformation, 1531–1536', *Church History*, vol. lvii (1988), 135–52 examines a key period of evolution. P. Biel, *Doorkeepers at the House of Righteousness. Heinrich Bullinger and the Zürich Clergy, 1535–1575* (Bern, 1991) and Bruce Gordon, *Clerical Discipline and the Rural Reformation. The Synod in Zürich, 1532–1580* (Bern, 1992) both indicate how much we have still to learn about the difficulties of establishing a godly reformed ministry.

For such a small polity, the literature about the reformation in Geneva is massive. For a general history, William Monter, *Calvin's Geneva* (New York and London, 1967) is well-informed and interesting. William G. Naphy, *Calvin and the Consolidation of the Genevan Reformation* (Manchester, 1994) documents the significance of the opposition which Calvin encountered towards his version of a protestant reformation there and how he managed to overcome it. R.M. Kingdon, *Geneva and the Coming of the Wars of Religion in France, 1555–1563* (Geneva, 1956) and *Geneva and the Consolidation of the French Protestant Movement, 1564–1572* (Geneva, 1967) both examine Geneva's role in respect of the emerging French churches. R.M. Kingdon, 'Was the protestant reformation a revolution? The case of Geneva' in R.M. Kingdon (ed.), *Transition and Revolution: Problems and Issues of European Renaissance and Reformation* (Minneapolis, 1974), pp. 53–76 puts the case for the social changes in the city, especially the transformation of the estate of clergy into the much smaller pastoral cadre, amounting to a revolution. The effects of immigration to the city during the reformation may be explored in William Monter, 'Historical demography and religious history in sixteenth-century Geneva' in *Journal of Interdisciplinary History*, ix (1979), 399–427; and Liliane Mottu-Weber, *Genève au siècle de la Réforme. Economie et Refuge* (Geneva, 1987). The assistance dispensed by the Genevan church to new arrivals is carefully examined in Jeannine E. Olson, *Calvin and Social Welfare: Deacons and the Bourse Française* (Selinsgrove, Penn., London and Cranbury, N.J., 1989). For the works on the Genevan consistory, see page 350.

13.9 The reformation in France and the Netherlands

Both the French and Dutch reformations came to be dominated by violent political upheaval. The standard political histories of the period are therefore, of necessity, also histories of their reformations. For France, these include J.H.M. Salmon, *Society in Crisis. France in the Sixteenth Century* (London, 1975) and F. Baumgartner, *France in the Sixteenth Century* (London, 1995); Geoffrey Parker, *The Dutch Revolt* (London, 1977) is the starting-point for the focal political events in the Netherlands. A. Duke, *Reformation and Revolt in the Low Countries* (London, 1991), however, provides a much more detailed and revealing set of studies about the processes of reformation in the Dutch setting and Janine Garrisson, *Les Protestants au XVIe siècle* (Paris, 1988) provides broad background to the reformation in France. Donald Kelley, *The Beginning of Ideology* (Cambridge, 1981) is a remarkable study, which uses France in the sixteenth century for a case-study of how and why ideological movements take shape.

Thereafter, there are individual studies, some concentrating on the evidence gained from the earlier period of persecution and repression which protestantism underwent in both polities, others on the later periods of sectarian tension and church-building. On the evidence from the earlier period, there is an exemplary study by Raymond Mentzer, 'Heresy proceedings in Languedoc, 1500–1560', *Transactions of the American Philosophical Society* (Philadelphia, 1984) which analyses the repression of protestantism in the French Midi. More generally, H. Heller, *The Conquest of Poverty* (Leiden, 1986) presents a linked series of case-studies which are designed to exemplify a Marxist interpretation of the rise of French protestantism. For the Netherlands the conclusions of J. Decavele's study of Flanders are summarized in A. Duke, *Reformation and Revolt . . .* cited above, see also Andrew Pettegree, 'The Exile Churches and the Churches "under the Cross": Antwerp and Emden during the Dutch Revolt', *Journal of Ecclesiastical History*, vol. xxxviii (1987).

On the sectarian tensions of the later century, Denis Crouzet, *Les Guerriers de Dieu*, 2 vols (Paris, 1990) presents a challenging explanatory framework for religious violence in terms of collective psychology. Phyllis Mack Crew, by contrast, in *Calvinist Preaching and Iconoclasm in the Netherlands (1549–1569)* (Cambridge, 1978) provides an altogether more predictable account of the (sometimes unconscious) effects of Calvinist preaching. Denis Richet, 'Aspects socio-culturelles des conflits religieux à Paris dans la seconde moitié du XVIe siècle', *Annales E.S.C.*, xxxii (1977), 764–89 is evocative and interesting on the social roots of Parisian sectarianism. Mark Konnert, 'Urban values versus religious passion: Châlons-sur-Marne during the Wars of Religion', *Sixteenth Century Journal*, vol. xx (1989), 387–405 is an example of the emerging local studies of religious violence, some of which have appeared as excellent monographs of particular cities. These include for France: Philip Benedict, *Rouen during the Wars of Religion* (Cambridge, 1988); Barbara B. Diefendorf, *Beneath the Cross. Catholics and Huguenots in Sixteenth-Century Paris* (Oxford, 1991) and Penny Roberts, *A City in Conflict. Troyes during the French Wars of Religion* (Manchester, 1996). For the Netherlands, there is C.C. Hibben, *Gouda in Revolt: Particularism and Pacifism in the Revolt of the Netherlands, 1572–1588* (Utrecht, 1983) and, for the southern Netherlands, Robert DuPlessis, *Lille and the Dutch Revolt. Urban Stability in an Era of Revolution (1500–1582)* (Cambridge, 1991). For the emerging protestant churches in both France and the Netherlands, there is Janine Garrisson, *Protestants du Midi (1559–1598)* (Toulouse, 1980), an excellent study for the French Midi. As yet, however, there is nothing as comprehensive for the Netherlands.

Other relevant studies include: Natalie Zemon Davis, *Society and Culture in Early-Modern France*, new edition (Cambridge, 1987) and Lucien Febvre, *Au coeur religieux du XVIe siècle* (Paris, 1957) – both sparkling sets of essays; N.M. Sutherland, *The Huguenot Struggle for Recognition* (New Haven and London, 1980), a thorough study of the politics behind the French edicts of pacification, and Andrew Pettegree, *Emden and the Dutch Revolt. Exile and the Development of Reformed Protestantism* (Oxford, 1992).

13.10 The reformation in Scandinavia and Eastern Europe

There are excellent introductory articles on the reformation in these regions in Andrew Pettegree (ed.), *The Early Reformation in Europe* (Cambridge, 1992) and also in R. Scribner, Roy Porter and Mikulás Teich (eds), *The Reformation in National Context* (Cambridge, 1994). They provide up-to-date bibliographies. E.H. Dunkley, *The Reformation in Denmark* (London, 1948) provides a starting-point. See also Ole Peter Grell (ed.), *The Scandinavian Reformation* (Cambridge, 1995). For Sweden, C. Bergendorff, *Olavus Petri and the Ecclesiastical Transformation in Sweden, 1521–1552* (Philadelphia, 1965) delineates the role of someone who, as we have seen, played a key part in the leadership of the Swedish reformation. Poland's reformation took place within a pluralistic religious environment. This is examined in J. Tazbir, *A State without Stakes. Polish Religious Toleration in the Sixteenth and Seventeenth Centuries* (New York and Warsaw, 1973). The best study of the destinies of the various competing religious groups and their social basis in Poland is, however, A. Jobert, *De Luther à Mohila. La Pologne dans la crise de la Chrétienté, 1517–1648* (Paris, 1974). For the reformation in Czech lands, the question is complicated by the existence of the Utraquist church and the Bohemian Brethren. There is a good bibliographical study guide to the substantial literature by J.K. Zeman, *The Hussite Movement and the Reformation in Bohemia, Moravia and Slovakia 1350–1650* (Ann Arbor, Michigan, 1977)*. On Austria, D.P. Daniel, 'Ecumenicity or Orthodoxy: the Dilemma of the Protestants in the Lands of the Austrian Habsburgs', *Church History*, vol. xlix (1980), 387–400 gives a picture of the plight of those inclined to protestantism there. For Hungary, K. Benda, 'La réforme en Hongrie' in *Bulletin de la Société de l'Histoire du Protestantisme Français*, vol. cxxii (1976), pp. 1–53 is the classic summary.

13.11 Confessionalization and the enforcement of religious change

The development of the reformation along confessional lines was not ignored by older historians of the reformation. They tended to take the process for granted and to work (unconsciously) within it. Because of the existence of a certain confessional pluralism in German protestantism, modern German historians have now come to take the process of 'confessional identification' (or 'confessionalization') more seriously. By some historians, it is linked to the complex forces at work behind the forging of more tightly organized principalities and states. The defining of confessional identities was part and parcel of the greater attention to the enforcement of religious change in protestant Europe; and we should link that to the sense (among some of Europe's protestants) that they were embarked upon a task of reformation which proved to be herculean – indeed sisysphean.

The major literature on confessionalization still remains in German: H. Schilling, *Konfessionskonflikt und Staatsbildung: Eine Fallstudie über das Verhältnis von religiösen und sozialen Wandel in der Frühneuzeit am Beispiel der Grafschaft Lippe* (Gütersloh, 1981) and the various contributions to his edited collection *Die reformierte Konfessionalisierung in Deutschland: Das Problem der 'zweiten Reformation'* (Gütersloh, 1987). The argument, however, is contained in elements of the same author's chapter on 'Between the Territorial State and Urban Liberty: Lutheranism and Calvinism in the County of Lippe' in R. Po-Chia Hsia, *The German People and the Reformation* (Ithaca, 1988), pp. 263–83 and in his *Religion, Political Culture and the Emergence of Early Modern Society* (Leiden, 1992). In English, however, there are some good studies of the 'later' or 'second' reformations in various German territorial principalities. C-P. Clasen, *The Palatinate in European History, 1559–1600* (Oxford, 1963) is a useful pamphlet on a state that was of significance for both France and the Netherlands in the second half of the century. Bodo Nischan, *Prince, People, and Confession. The Second Reformation in Brandenburg* (Philadelphia, 1994) is an exemplary study of the processes at work. More generally, Menna Prestwich (ed.), *International Calvinism* (Oxford, 1985)* is excellent as a study of the often divisive impact of Calvinism in Europe.

Questions about the enforcement of the reformation take us to the complex matter of 'social discipline'. Historians have sometimes used the phrase rather unquestioningly to delineate the impact of the protestant reformation, especially in matters of morality. William Monter, *Enforcing Morality in Early-Modern Europe* (London, 1987)* and R. Po-Chia Hsia, *Social Discipline in the Reformation. Central Europe 1550–1750* (London, 1989)* put the emphasis on the complex educative elements of enforcement, and stress that all the organized religions of the sixteenth century were attempting to enforce conformity in a variety of different and often new ways. Gerald Strauss, *Luther's House of Learning. Indoctrination of the Young in the German Reformation* (Baltimore and London, 1978) also emphasized the educative endeavour in the Lutheran reformation. Lorna Jane Abray, *The People's Reformation. Magistrates, Clergy, and Commons in Strasbourg, 1550–1598* (Oxford, 1985); Bruce Tolley, *Pastors and Parishioners in Württemberg during the Late Reformation 1581–1621* (Stanford, 1995); A. Pettegree (ed.), *The Reformation of the Parishes. The Ministry of Town and Country* (Manchester, 1993) all investigate different aspects of the problems of enforcement.

The church, or 'consistory' courts to be found in protestant (especially) Calvinist Europe have attracted a number of research projects which are trying to release the potential richness of this documentation. The results can be seen for Geneva in the following studies by R.M. Kingdon – 'The control of morals in Calvin's Geneva' in L.P. Buck and J.W. Zophy (eds), *The Social History of the Reformation (in honour of H.J. Grimm)* (Columbus, 1972), pp. 3–16; 'Calvin and the establishment of consistory discipline in Geneva: the institution and the men who directed it', *Nederlands Archief voor Kerkgeschiedenis* lxx (1990), pp. 158–72; 'The Geneva Consistory in the time of Calvin' in Andrew Pettegree, Alastair Duke and Gillian Lewis (eds), *Calvinism in Europe, 1540–1620* (Cambridge, 1994), ch. 2. See also William Monter, 'The Consistory of Geneva, 1559–1569', *Bibliothèque d'humanisme et de la renaissance* xxxliii (1976), pp. 467–84. R. Mentzer, '*Disciplina nervus ecclesiae*: The Calvinist Reform of Morals at Nîmes', *Sixteenth Century Journal*, vol. xviii (1987), 89–115 provides a good comparative example from southern France.

The question of success and failure was originally posed by Gerald Strauss in 'Success and failure in the German Reformation', *Past and Present*, No. 67 (1975), 30–63. This article stimulated a debate as well as more detailed investigation of the reports from the Lutheran visiting superintendants, whose evidence Strauss had cited as the basis for the perceived and relative 'failure' of the Lutheran reformation. J.M. Kittelson, 'Success and failure in the German Reformation: the report from Strasbourg', *Archiv für Reformationsgeschichte* vol. lxxiii (1982), pp. 174–86 was a more positive assessment of the achievement of the protestant reformers. Geoffrey Parker, 'Success and Failure during the First Century of Reformation', *Past and Present*, No. 136 (1992), 43–82 expands the discussion to include the whole of protestant Europe.

13.12 The reformation and its social context

L.P. Buck and J.W. Zophy (eds), *The Social History of the Reformation (in honour of H.J. Grimm)* (Columbus, 1972) was a pioneering collection of essays and the social history of the protestant reformation is now a central feature of its historiography. This is true in the sense of historians being more sensitive to, and wanting to understand more about, the social appeal of different elements of protestantism. We have already seen this trend in our survey of recent works so far. It has also affected the studies of the radical reformation and Claus-Peter Clasen, *Anabaptism: a Social History* (Ithaca, 1972) was an excellently documented analysis of the socio-geographical basis of German anabaptism. But it is also true in the sense of historians wanting to know more about the relationship between the reformation and the social transformations of this period – those which led to different attitudes towards men, women and the family for instance. So, for example, there are now some rich and exciting studies on the impact of the reformation on domestic life which touch on the fundamental questions of enforcement and how the reformation became embedded in European experience. Amongst these, we should note: Steven E. Ozment, *When Fathers Ruled: Family Life in Reformation Europe* (Cambridge, Mass., 1983); Lyndal Roper, *The Holy Household. Women and Morals in Reformation Augsburg* (Oxford, 1989); T.M. Safley, *Let No Man Put Asunder: the Control of Marriage in the German South-west: a Comparative Study, 1550–1600* (Kirksville, 1983); various contributions to Sherrin Marshall (ed.), *Women in Reformation and Counter-Reformation Europe. Public and Private Worlds* (Bloomington, 1989); Jeffrey Watt, 'Women and the consistory in Calvin's Geneva', *Sixteenth Century Journal,* vol. xxiv (1993), 429–39.

For the protestant reformation in a broader social context, it is impossible to avoid the enormous outpouring of studies on witchcraft, since the latter poses complex questions about the relationship between the changes brought about by the protestant reformation and the increasing, but patchy, prosecution for witchcraft in Europe during this period. See Brian Levack, *The Witch-Hunt in Early-Modern Europe,* 2nd edition (Harlow, 1994); Stuart Clark, *Thinking with Demons: the Idea of Witchcraft in Early-Modern Europe* (Oxford, 1997); and Robin Briggs, *Witches and Neighbours* (London, 1996).

13.13 The enforcement of orthodoxy and the survival of dissent in Mediterranean lands

It is not merely in Mediterranean lands that recent scholarship has become interested in questions about the enforcement of orthodoxy; but it is here that those studies have their greatest relevance. Attention naturally focuses on the Inquisition. Henry Kamen, *Inquisition and Society in Spain in the Sixteenth and Seventeenth Centuries* (London and Bloomington, 1985)* is an excellent introduction. Gustav Henningsen and John Tedeschi (eds), *The Inquisition in Early Modern Europe* (Dekalb, Illin., 1986)* and William Monter, *Frontiers of Heresy. The Spanish Inquisition from the Basque Lands to Sicily* (Cambridge, 1990)* have a broader scope and are extremely useful.

For the *samizdat* existence of protestantism (often distinguished only with difficulty from other expressions of heterodoxy) in Mediterranean lands, Gordon Kinder, *Spanish Protestants and Reformers in the Sixteenth Century* (London, 1983)* is a fundamental bibliography; John E. Longhurst, *Luther and the Spanish Inquisition. The Case of Diego de Uceda, 1528–9* (Albuquerque, 1953) and *Luther in Spain, 1520–1540* (vol. ciii of the *Proceedings of the American Philosophical Society*, 1959) all provide good leads. Alastair Hamilton, *Heresy and Mysticism in Sixteenth-Century Spain. The Alumbrados* (Cambridge, 1992) is excellent on the illuminists and their religious context. Henry Kamen has argued for a continuing 'alternative tradition' of heterodoxy in Spain in 'Toleration and dissent in sixteenth-century Spain: the alternative tradition', *Sixteenth Century Journal*, vol. xix (1988), 3–23.

Italian protestants became masters at hiding their beliefs behind a mask of conformism. Describing them as 'evangelists' or 'proto-protestants' hardly does justice to the complexity of the position in which they found themelves or the reasons for their continuing to adopt a protestant shadow existence. D. Cantimori, *Italian Heretics of the Sixteenth Century* (Cambridge, Mass., 1979) is a translation of a work which has had a defining effect on the treatment of the subject this century. E-M. Jung, 'On the nature of evangelism in sixteenth-century Italy', *Journal of the History of Ideas*, vol. xiv (1953), 511–27 is also a useful starting-point. P. McNair, *Peter Martyr in Italy: an Anatomy of Apostasy* (Oxford, 1967) is an evocative study of one individual who eventually chose to take up exile in northern Europe; it can profitably be read alongside A.J. Schutte, *Pier Paolo Vergerio: the Making of an Italian Reformer* (Geneva, 1983). J. Martin, 'Salvation and Society in Sixteenth-Century Venice: Popular Evangelism in a Renaissance City', *Journal of Modern History*, vol. lx (1988), 115–28 examines the degree to which proto-protestantism had popular roots. D. Fenlon, *Heresy and Obedience in Tridentine Italy: Cardinal Pole and the Counter Reformation* (Cambridge, 1972) explores the forces which drew many evangelists back to orthodoxy and the mainstream of the catholic church.

A good deal of our discussion of the influence of protestantism in Mediterranean lands revolves around questions about the publication and circulation of literature. We are still making unpredicted discoveries here. Fortunately, we now are beginning to have proper editions of the various indexes of prohibited books in Europe in the series (ed. J.M. de Bujanda), *Index des livres inédits* (Sherbrooke and Geneva, 1986–). C. Griffin, *The Crombergers of Seville* (Oxford, 1988) gives an authoritative and thoroughly researched account of one of the presses responsible for importing protestant works into the Spanish New World. P.F. Grendler, *The Roman Inquisition and the Venetian Press, 1540–1605* (Princeton, 1977) is a thorough account of the attempts to censor an important centre for printing and book distribution in Italy.

13.14 The catholic reformation

Because the catholic reformation was a particularly dispersed and fractured phenomenon, stretching well beyond the chronological confines of this book, it has been difficult to write convincing syntheses for the general reader. For the same reasons, it is impossible to provide a completely satisfactory bibliographical orientation. However, for general introductory purposes, the following are available. N.S. Davidson, *The Counter-Reformation* (Oxford, 1987) is a clear and elegant overview. A.D. Wright, *The Counter-Reformation: Catholic Europe and the Non-Christian World* (London, 1982)* provides a substantial bibliography and is the most sophisticated of the general introductory works available. H. Outram Evennett, *The Spirit of the Counter-Reformation* (Cambridge, 1968) has exercised its charms over a generation of students since its publication. Michael Mullett, *The Counter-Reformation and the Catholic Reformation in early modern Europe* (London, 1984) is a useful student introduction. Louis Châtellier, *The Europe of the Devout. The Catholic Reformation and the Formation of a New Society* (Cambridge, 1987) demonstrates how much is to be gained from a perspective on the catholic reformation which looks beyond institutional and doctrinal confines and also beyond 1620. R.B. Wernham (ed.), *The New Cambridge Modern History*, vol. 3 ('The Counter-Reformation and Price Revolution, 1559–1610') (Cambridge, 1968) gives the essential political background where required.

13.15 The council of Trent and the new orders

The standard history of the council of Trent is H. Jedin, *Geschichte des Konzils von Trent*, 4 vols (Freiburg, 1949–75). The first two volumes alone have been translated into English as *A History of the Council of Trent*, 2 vols (London, 1957–61). Jedin's *Papal Legate at the Council of Trent: Cardinal Seripando* (St Louis, 1947) is a good history of one of its leading figures, especially during the early sessions. His *Crisis and Closure of the Council* (London, 1967) is a good summary evaluation of the later sessions of its work.

On the Society of Jesus, there is a vast specialist literature, to which the indispensable guide is Lásló Polgár (ed.), *Bibliographie sur l'histoire de la Compagnie de Jésus*, 3 vols (Rome, 1981–1990). John O'Malley, *The First Jesuits* (Cambridge, Mass., 1993) provides extensive bibliographical citations and covers virtually every aspect of Jesuit activity in the period to 1565. William V. Bangert, *A History of the Society of Jesus*, 2nd edition (St Louis, 1986) is comprehensive and competent. A. Lynn Martin, *The Jesuit Mind: the Mentality of an Elite in Early Modern France* (Ithaca, 1988) studies Jesuit attitudes and frustrations as depicted in their correspondence. Gabriel Codina Mir, *Aux sources de la pédagogie des jésuites: Le 'Modus Parisiensis'* (Rome, 1968) established the fundamental basis of our knowledge of the origins and development of the Jesuits' educational programme.

For the other new religious orders, H.O. Evennett's contribution on 'The New Orders' in *The New Cambridge Modern History*, vol. II (ed. G.R. Elton) (Cambridge, 1990) is an invaluable comparative introduction. Fr Cuthbert, *The Capuchins: a Contribution to the History of the Counter-Reformation*, 2 vols (Port Washington, New York, reprinted 1971) is still the best introduction to that order. Isidoro de Villapadierna, 'The Capuchins – Hermits and Preachers', *Greyfriars Review*, vol. ii (1988), 93–113 provides a bibliography for the works published on the early Capuchins. Louis Ponnelle and Louis Bordet, *St Philip Neri and the Roman Society of his Times (1515–1595)* (London, 1932), follows the complex career of the individual who inspired the Italian Oratory.

13.16 Catholic missions

S. Neill, *A History of Christian Missions* (Harmondsworth, 1964) includes a general account of overseas missions. C.R. Boxer, *The Church Militant and Iberian Expansion (1440–1770)* (Baltimore, 1978) links catholic missions and the destinies of the Iberian maritime empires. Anthony Pagden, *The Fall of Natural Man: the American Indian and the Origins of Comparative Ethnology* (Cambridge, 1982) examines the contemporary debates (with their theological overtones) about paganism and the possibilities of conversion. Josef Franz Schütte, *Valignano's Mission Principles for Japan*, 2 vols (St Louis, 1980–85) is essential for an understanding of Jesuit missionary endeavour in Japan and China.

There are almost innumerable studies of missionary activity in different areas. The following is a representative selection: C.R. Boxer, *The Christian Century in Japan, 1549–1650* (Berkeley, 1951); Georg Schurhammer, *Francis Xavier: his Life, his Times*, 4 vols (Rome, 1973–82); Luis Martín, *The Intellectual Conquest of Peru: The Jesuit College of San Pablo, 1568–1768* (New York, 1968); R. Ricard, *The Spiritual Conquest of Mexico:*

an Essay on the Apostolate and the Evangelizing Methods of the Mendicant Orders in New Spain, 1523–1572 (Berkeley, 1966); John L. Phelan, *The Hispanization of the Philippines: Spanish aims and Filipino responses, 1565–1700* (Madison, 1959); J. Gerent, *China and the Christian Impact: a Conflict of Cultures* (Cambridge, 1985).

Genealogical tables

1. The Habsburg Dynasty in the Sixteenth Century*

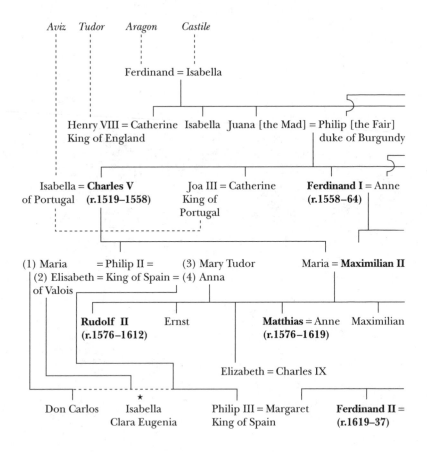

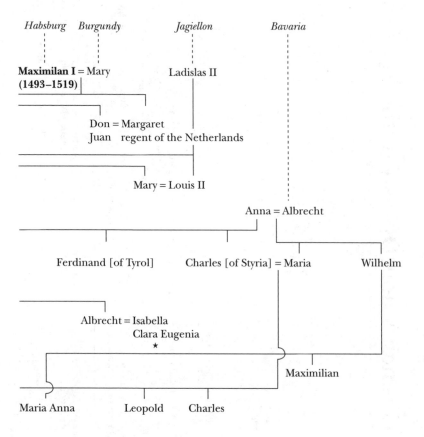

Habsburg *Burgundy* *Jagiellon* *Bavaria*

Maximilan I = Mary Ladislas II
(1493–1519)

Don = Margaret
Juan regent of the Netherlands

Mary = Louis II

Anna = Albrecht

Ferdinand [of Tyrol] Charles [of Styria] = Maria Wilhelm

Albrecht = Isabella
Clara Eugenia
★

Maximilian

Maria Anna Leopold Charles

2. The French Valois Dynasty in the Sixteenth Century

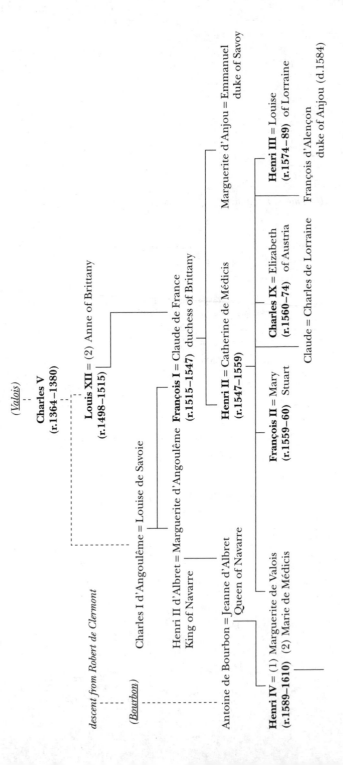

descent from Robert de Clermont

(*Valois*)

(*Bourbon*)

Charles V
(r.1364–1380)

Louis XII = (2) Anne of Brittany
(r.1498–1515)

Charles I d'Angoulême = Louise de Savoie

Marguerite d'Angoulême **François I** = Claude de France
(r.1515–1547) duchess of Brittany

Henri II d'Albret = Marguerite d'Angoulême
King of Navarre

Henri II = Catherine de Médicis
(r.1547–1559)

Marguerite d'Anjou = Emmanuel
duke of Savoy

Antoine de Bourbon = Jeanne d'Albret
Queen of Navarre

François II = Mary
(r.1559–60) Stuart

Charles IX = Elizabeth
(r.1560–74) of Austria

Henri III = Louise
(r.1574–89) of Lorraine

François d'Alençon
duke of Anjou (d.1584)

Claude = Charles de Lorraine

Henri IV = (1) Marguerite de Valois
(r.1589–1610) (2) Marie de Médicis

3. Leading Protestant Dynasties and their Connections in the early seventeenth century*

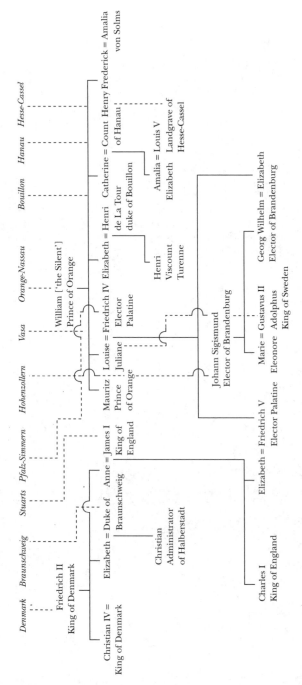

Denmark Braunschweig Stuarts Pfalz-Simmern Hohenzollern Vasa Orange-Nassau Bouillon Hanau Hesse-Cassel

Friedrich II
King of Denmark

Christian IV =
King of Denmark

Elizabeth = Duke of
Braunschweig

Christian
Administrator
of Halberstadt

Anne = James I
King of England

William ['the Silent']
Prince of Orange

Maurits Louise = Friedrich IV Elizabeth = Henri   Catherine = Count Henry Frederick = Amalia
Prince   Juliane   Elector   de La Tour   of Hanau   von Solms
of Orange   Palatine   duke of Bouillon

Henri
Viscount
Turenne

Amalia = Louis V
Elizabeth   Landgrave of
           Hesse-Cassel

Johann Sigismund
Elector of Brandenburg

Marie = Gustavus II
Eleonore   Adolphus
          King of Sweden

Elizabeth = Friedrich V
           Elector Palatine

Georg Wilhelm = Elizabeth
Elector of Brandenburg

Charles I
King of England

* *simplified – many of the dynastic lines are incompletely indicated*

Maps

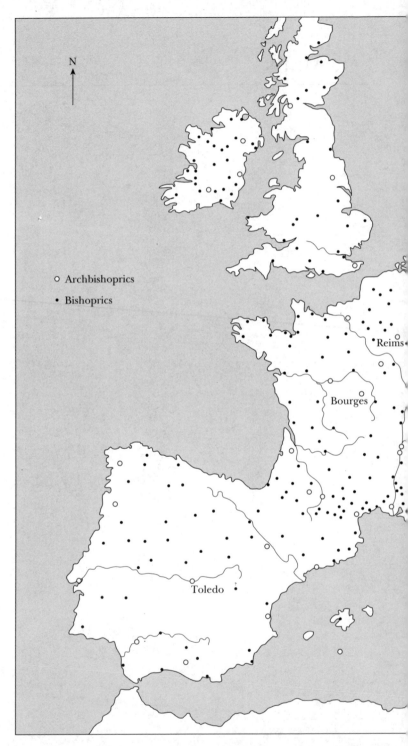

1. Bishoprics and archbishoprics in the Western Church c.1500

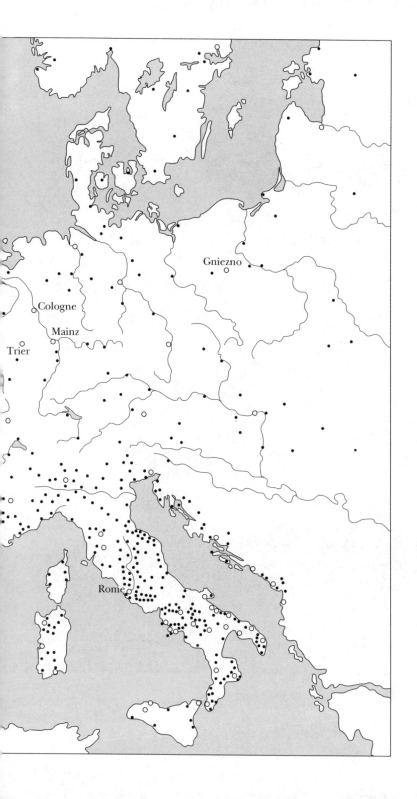

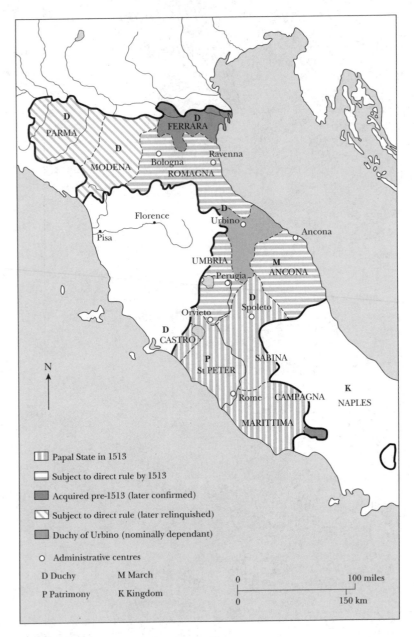

N

Legend	
Papal State in 1513	
Subject to direct rule by 1513	
Acquired pre-1513 (later confirmed)	
Subject to direct rule (later relinquished)	
Duchy of Urbino (nominally dependant)	

○   Administrative centres

D Duchy   M March

P Patrimony   K Kingdom

0   100 miles

0   150 km

2.   The Papal States in the sixteenth century

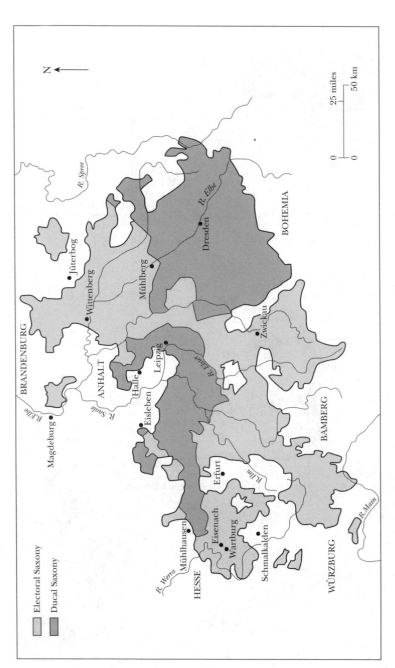

3. Saxony at the time of Martin Luther

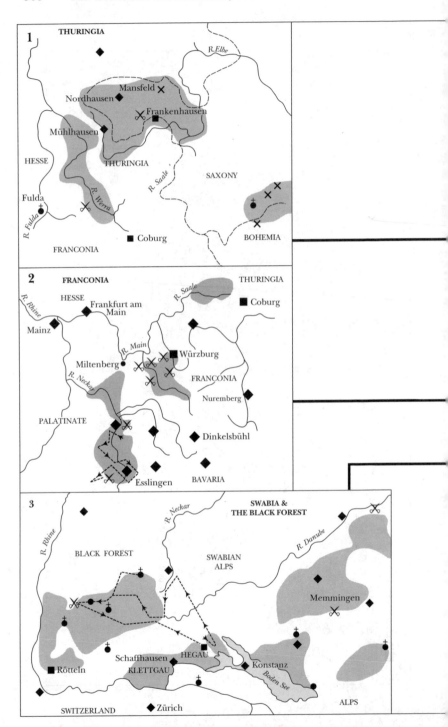

4. The German Peasants' War

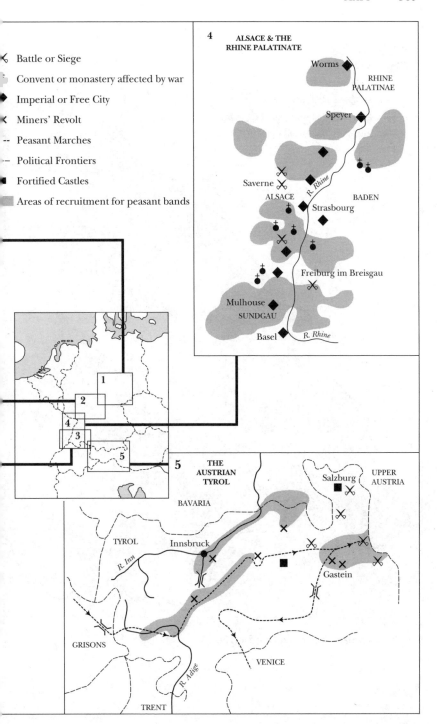

Battle or Siege
Convent or monastery affected by war
Imperial or Free City
Miners' Revolt
Peasant Marches
Political Frontiers
Fortified Castles
Areas of recruitment for peasant bands

4   ALSACE & THE
RHINE PALATINATE

Worms

RHINE
PALATINAE

Speyer

Saverne
ALSACE   R. Rhine   BADEN

Strasbourg

Freiburg im Breisgau

Mulhouse
SUNDGAU

Basel   R. Rhine

1
2
4
3
5

5   THE
AUSTRIAN
TYROL

Salzburg   UPPER
AUSTRIA

BAVARIA

TYROL   Innsbruck

R. Inn   Gastein

GRISONS

VENICE

R. Adige

TRENT

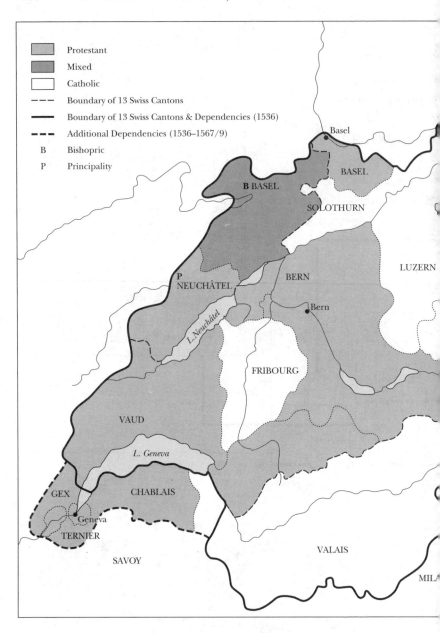

5.   Protestantism in Switzerland c.1564

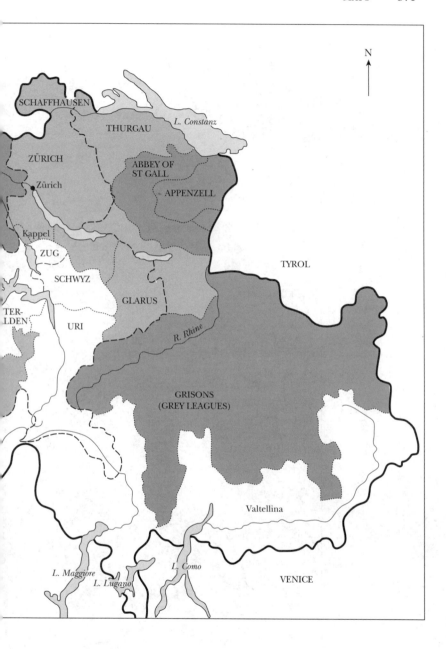

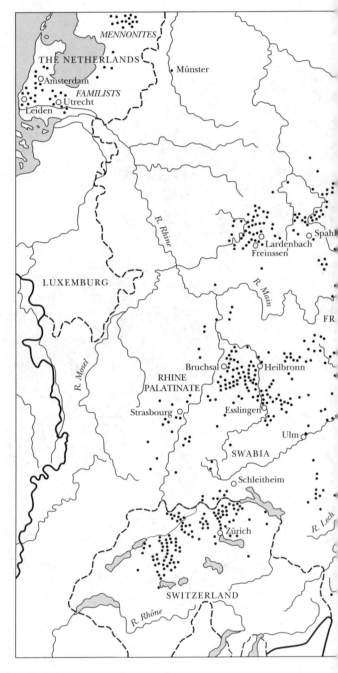

6. Anabaptist and radical communities in Central Europe, c.1550

Boundary of the Holy Roman Empire
Other Political boundaries
Anabaptist Communities

N

Poznan

R. Oder

R. Elbe

THURINGIA

ONIA

SCHWENCKFELDIANS

MORAVIA

Regensburg

R. Danube

HUTTERITES

R. Danube

Augsburg

Linz

BAVARIA

AUSTRIA

Rattenburg

Kitzbühel

Hall

Schwaz

Steinach

R. Mur

Sterzing

OL

R. Drau

STYRIA

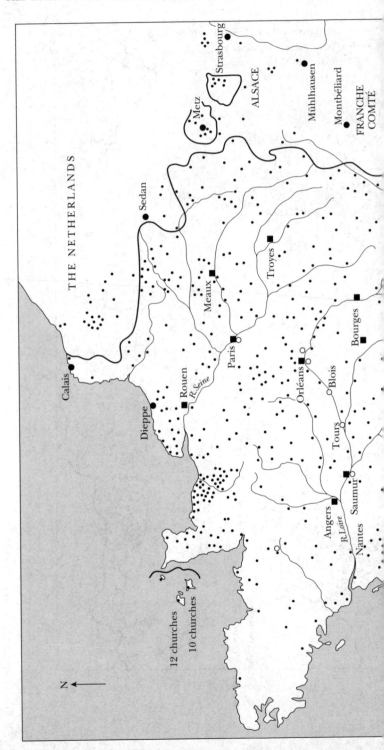

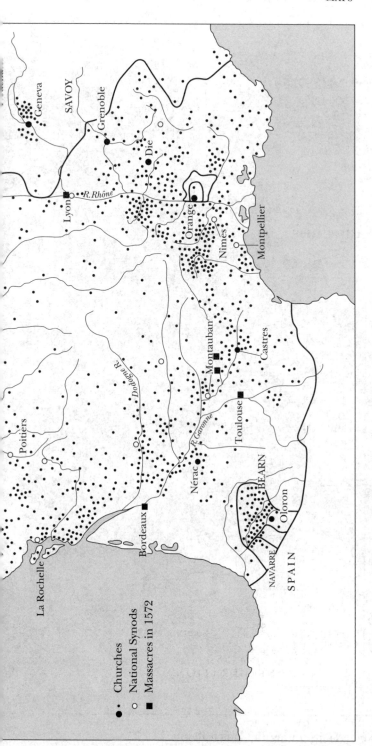

Churches •
National Synods ○ ●
Massacres in 1572 ■

7. French-speaking protestant churches in the later sixteenth century

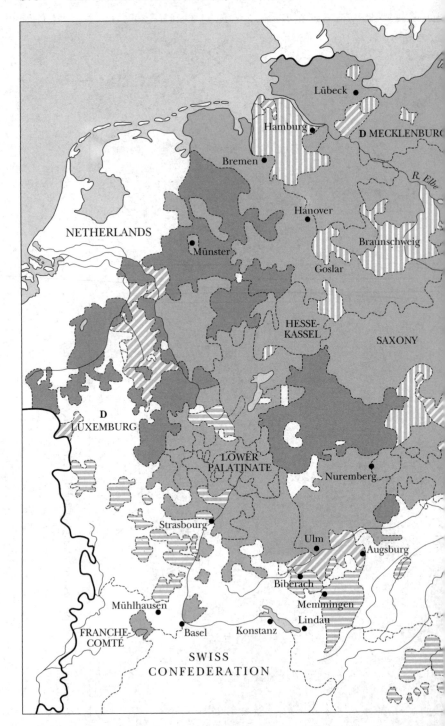

8.   The Netherlands during the Dutch Revolt

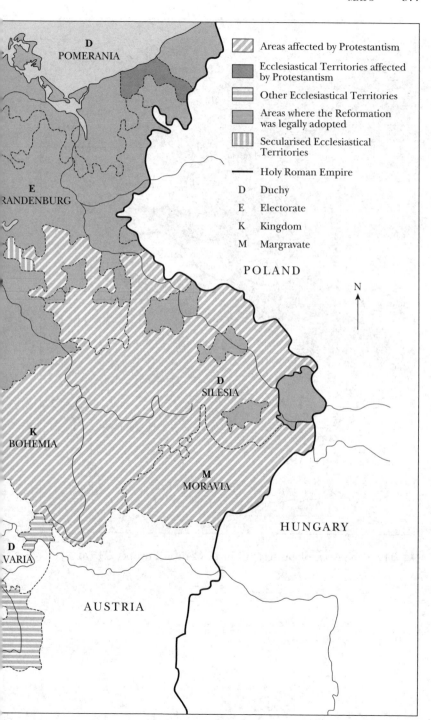

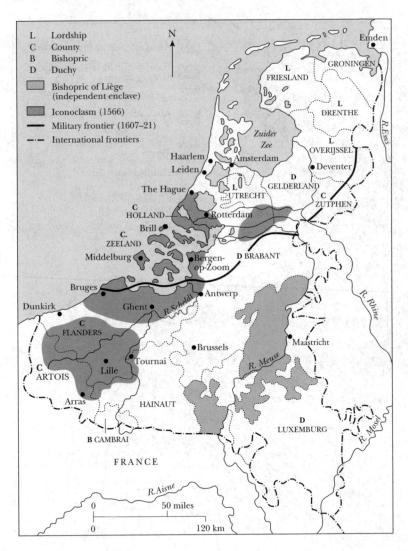

9. The expansion of protestantism in Central Europe, c.1570

Index

Numbers in **bold** direct the reader to specific definitions of particular terms. Those in *italics* refer to entries in the biographical dictionary.